AMERICAN NEWSPAPERS
IN THE 1970s

BROADCAST MANAGEMENT
Radio-Television
by Ward L. Quaal and Leo A. Martin

CLASSROOM TELEVISION
New Frontiers in ITV
by George N. Gordon

CASE STUDIES IN BROADCAST MANAGEMENT
by Howard W. Coleman

THE MOVIE BUSINESS
American Film Industry Practice
Edited by A. William Bluem and Jason E. Squire

THE CHANGING MAGAZINE
Trends in Readership and Management
by Roland E. Wolseley

FILM LIBRARY TECHNIQUES
Principles of Administration
by Helen P. Harrison

THE FILM INDUSTRIES
Practical Business/Legal Problems
in Production, Distribution and Exhibition
by Michael F. Mayer

AMERICAN NEWSPAPERS IN THE 1970s
by Ernest C. Hynds

Studies in Media Management

AMERICAN NEWSPAPERS

in the 1970s

by Ernest C. Hynds

COMMUNICATION ARTS BOOKS

HASTINGS HOUSE, PUBLISHERS

New York 10016

LIBRARY OF CONGRESS CATALOGING IN PUBLICATION DATA

Hynds, Ernest C
    American newspapers in the 1970s.

    (Communication arts books)
    Bibliography: p.
    1. American newspapers—History. 2. Journalism—
United States. I. Title.
PN4867.H9   071'.3   74-23624
ISBN 0-8038-0375-3
ISBN 0-8038-0383-4 pbk.

Published simultaneously in Canada by
Saunders of Toronto, Ltd., Don Mills, Ontario

Designed by Al Lichtenberg
Printed in the United States of America

Contents

Preface

The dual purpose of this book is: 1) to help individuals make more effective use of their newspapers by discussing what newspapers are and should be and how they operate, and 2) to help all newspapers realize more of their potential by describing what many newspapers are doing successfully in the 1970s. The study is based on the premise that good newspapers are essential if individuals are to function effectively in an increasingly complex world and if the democratic system is to prevail. Other media can complement, but not replace newspapers.

Chapter 1 outlines the roles and responsibilities of newspapers; Chapter 2 provides a brief history of their development, and Chapter 3 explores the diverse types of newspapers being published today. Chapters 4, 5, and 7 discuss the three major areas of newspaper operation: business, news and opinion, and production. Chapter 6 explores some of the major challenges faced by newspapers today in their relationships with government, and Chapter 8 summarizes some of the recognized leaders in the field.

In the brief space available, the author could not hope to acknowledge properly the many persons who have contributed something to this project. Many individual editors and others have contributed directly by providing information in response to queries; many others have contributed indirectly through their books, articles, monographs, and other studies. The author does, however, wish to thank several persons specifically. These include N. S. Hayden of Gannett Newspapers, Dean John E. Drewry, dean emeritus of the Henry W. Grady School of Journalism, University of Georgia, and Mrs. Ann Clark, a successful high school journalism teacher, who reviewed the entire manuscript; Dean Warren K. Agee, Wallace Eberhard, Charles Kopp, Rowland Kraps, and

Tom Russell of the Grady faculty; Albert Saye, alumni foundation professor of political science at the University of Georgia, and Pete Sasser of the University of South Florida, all of whom read one or more chapters; and Mrs. Florence Seagraves, Mrs. Yvonne Ivie, Mrs. Judi Hogan, Miss Jeannie Fields, Miss Barbara Antonucci, and Barry King who helped with typing, proofing, and other vital details.

In addition, the author would especially like to thank his wife Mary Ann without whose patience and assistance the project could not have been completed. Finally, he wishes to dedicate the book to his sons, Jeff and Mark, to others of their generation, and to those that will follow them. Young persons must come to appreciate and use newspapers if they are to be successful citizens in the years to come. Newspapers must strive to be worthy of their appreciation and suitable for their use.

ERNEST C. HYNDS
February, 1975

Studies in Media Management

A. WILLIAM BLUEM, General Editor, 1968–1974

AMERICAN NEWSPAPERS
IN THE 1970s

1

Roles and Responsibilities

THE UNITED STATES Department of Commerce classifies newspapers in business terms. Newspaper publishing is the nation's tenth largest industry and its fifth largest industrial employer. The United States Constitution and its interpreters see newspapers as conveyors of information and opinion vital to the operation of government and the maintenance of freedom. Their responsible operation is protected under the First Amendment. The millions who read newspapers see them in myriad roles. They read to see what is behind the latest move in government, who has a sale on lima beans, or what is playing at the local movie house. Newspapers provide information, entertainment and guidance for many; their impact reaches even those who as yet cannot or do not read them. The newspaper is at once a private enterprise struggling in a highly competitive economy and a quasi-public institution serving the needs of all citizens.

Today's newspaper is composed of newsprint and ink and is not physically durable in the sense that a table or chair is. Yet the newspaper is far more durable than these objects, for it communicates ideas and information. The newspaper is history in the making, geography brought close, science in action. It is the story of the latest political shift in Moscow, Paris or Peking. It records the newest arrival at the local hospital, the graduation of a son or daughter, the joining of families through marriage, the death of the well-known and the unknown. It takes its readers inside the Congress, the statehouse, the ball park and the concert hall. It tells of missiles, miracles and movies, of grief, pleasure and excitement. It fights the oppressor, protects the weak; exposes the criminal, defends the innocent. It stimulates, motivates, inspires, interprets, builds, preserves, excites, satisfies, and sometimes disappoints. The newspaper preserves

11

the past, chronicles the present, and helps assure the probability of a better future for those it serves. It is historian, reporter, analyst, communicator, salesman and advocate. It is all these things and more. It is the sum of all that its readers and its producers would cause it to be.

Although the newspaper now shares the communications spectrum with radio, television and cable television as well as with books, magazines and other media, it remains vital to the life and well-being of the nation and its people. Its roles and responsibilities cannot be performed adequately by other media. This chapter will 1) examine the basic functions of newspapers; 2) compare the roles of newspapers with those of other major mass media; 3) examine the concept of a free and responsible press and suggest basic newspaper responsibilities; and 4) discuss journalism reviews, press councils and other means of providing a continuous assessment of newspaper achievement.

It is easier to describe newspapers than it is to define and classify them. Generally, they can be distinguished from other publications by their appearance. Most come in either tabloid size, about 12 by 15 inches, or in standard size, about 15 by 23 inches. Most are printed on a comparatively inexpensive paper called newsprint, and most are held together by folding rather than by stapling or stitching processes used for magazines and books. Most make extensive use of headlines and pictures, and most include a large number and variety of advertisements.

Definitions are less obvious. The *New York Times* is often mentioned as an example of American newspapers, which it is. But the *New York Daily News,* the *Chicago Defender,* the *Village Voice,* and the *Hahira Goldleaf* also are examples, and they are different from the *Times* and from each other. A precise definition is elusive because the term newspaper is applied to publications issued semiweekly and weekly as well as daily, and publications that are aimed at special interests as well as at mass audiences. Some generalizations can be offered, however, in terms of the basic functions which most newspapers perform for their particular audiences.

To Inform, To Influence, To Entertain . . .

The newspaper's basic roles are to inform, influence, entertain and foster development of the nation's economy through advertising. Of these, dissemination of information is the most vital. Correct information is essential to clear thinking, and clear thinking is vital to making sound judgments. The results of opinion polls suggest that newspapers and other media must find ways to improve the communication of information. In December 1961, for example, a Gallup Poll found that 78% of Americans had not heard or read of the European Common Market. In November 1962, a similar poll found that 71% did not know of the Peace Corps. As late as 1966, only 29% of those questioned by National Opinion Research of Chicago could identify the Viet Cong. While only 3.9% incorrectly identified them as American allies, 16.5% said they did not know, and the others gave various incorrect answers. In another Gallup poll, reported in October 1970, only 53% of those questioned said they knew the name of the congressman from their district.[1] A major part of the fault for being uninformed must lie with those who make little or no effort to become informed. But part must also lie with newspapers and other media for not providing adequate information, motivating people to read it, or both.

Newspapers should consider themselves to be in the business of transferring information from sources to readers and seek better ways to gather, process and distribute information. In particular, they need to learn more about the persons with whom they are seeking to communicate and adjust their presentations accordingly. For example, it probably is easier to fill in gaps than to modify drastically the information that the reader already has stored in his human computer. Newspapers can help readers understand important issues and perhaps spur them to positive action by providing a continuous flow of accurate information about those issues over an extended period of time.[2]

Much of the information that newspapers transmit which does not deal with advertising is characterized by an emphasis on timeliness and human interest and is described as news. Broadly defined, news is any information which a receiver has not previously received; but most news stories deal with events or situations of the immediate past, the present or the future that interest large numbers of persons. What the Governor said about taxes today, not last month, is news. The nearness of an event or situation to the reader and its significance for him also help determine its news value. The local school bond issue is important because it might raise the reader's taxes or affect the education of his children. The arms limitation treaty is significant because of its far-reaching effects regardless of where it may be signed.

Sensational events such as crimes and natural disasters and unusual events of all kinds have been emphasized by many newspapers, and they still are by some who contend that reader interest in them remains high. The bank official who embezzles funds, the hurricane that takes lives and destroys homes, or the kitten whose best friend is a big dog all make news in the eyes of many editors. But many newspapers today are looking more to situations than single events to report; more editors are placing greater weight on the significant than the sensational. The rash of local robberies is news; the causes for the outbreak, perhaps involving drug addicts seeking money for their addiction, and what the police are doing about it are even more newsworthy. Good newspapers today are making an effort to show how current happenings fit into a continuing story.

Although news of crimes and disasters is at times overplayed, the amount of space allotted to such coverage is probably much less than many believe. A study sponsored by the News Research Center of the American Newspaper

---

[1] Footnotes, grouped by chapters, may be found at the end of this book beginning on page 295.

Publishers Association revealed that the average newspaper devotes only 3.9% of its space to crime news and only 2.4% to news of accidents, disasters and natural phenomena. By contrast the average newspaper devotes 12.7% of its space to state and local news, 10.2% to international news and 6.9% to U.S. government-domestic news.[3]

What is considered news will, of course, vary with the publication involved and the editor providing the definition. The appointment of a new bank president in a small town may be big news to the newspaper located there, but it may receive only a paragraph or two on an inside page of a nearby metropolitan daily. A lengthy account of some metropolitan problem in that same daily might not be included in the small-town papers nearby. Alternative publications often view news differently than do other newspapers; some may stress politics while others cover the subculture they serve. All specialized newspapers stress specialized information for their particular audiences whether they are made up of businessmen, sports enthusiasts or members of a women's liberation group.

Newspapers traditionally have sought to answer six basic questions about the stories they cover; they still do. But since radio and television frequently report the *who, what, when* and *where* of major news stories first, newspapers often concentrate on telling the *why* and *how* of these stories and explaining what they mean to the individual reader. The *who* and *what* elements may still be emphasized in the many local stories that the broadcast media cannot include or emphasize in their limited time segments.

News can be placed into categories according to geography, subject matter and perhaps other criteria. Most daily newspapers carry at least some international, national and regional news as well as state and local news. Many have special editors, and sometimes departments, to handle news of sports, business, education, family matters and other special interests. Experience indicates that people do like to read about events they witnessed or in which they participated; experience confirms the need of newspapers and other media to appeal to basic human drives such as love, recognition, new experiences and security in news stories as well as in advertising.

Information that cannot be classified as news because it lacks timeliness or some other vital ingredient is usually referred to as feature material. Such features may involve advice columns on human relations, health and other topics; human interest stories of various kinds; reviews of books, plays and other art forms; comics, and other items. Editorials, political cartoons, political columns and letters to the editor also help newspapers perform their information function; but they usually also contain opinions and are placed together on an opinion or editorial page.

Information is the staple of any good newspaper. But most hope to influence their readers as well as inform them. If read, newspapers probably exert some influence regardless of their intentions. How much influence they exert and what kind is not easy to assess. Laboratory situations to measure such influence cannot easily be created. Other types of documentation also are difficult to obtain. Still a few hypotheses, if not generalizations, can be advanced.

First, it is evident that newspapers exert influence through their total presentations and their image in the community and not through their advocacies alone. The human interest stories about the plight of the individual prisoner may evoke as much support for penal reform as the carefully documented argument of the editorial writer, perhaps more. The newspaper's coverage of an election may have far more influence on the outcome than its advocacy of a particular candidate. In 1948, for example, most newspapers opposed the election of President Harry Truman; yet they probably helped elect him by covering his whistlestop campaign so extensively and by picturing him as the underdog so consistently. The newspaper's reputation as liberal, conservative or moderate almost certainly affects the way in which its stories and editorials are perceived. It is not uncommon in some communities for persons to oppose a candidate or issue because the newspaper they disagree with expresses its support.

Second, newspapers have helped bring reforms in government and other areas by focusing public attention on existing needs and problems. They have exposed corruption in government at all levels, revealed deplorable conditions in mental health institutions, prisons and slums, and pointed out needs in health, education, transportation and other areas. Many instances can be cited where remedial action was taken after problems were pointed out by newspapers.

Third, it appears that the influence of editorial endorsements in newspapers is dependent on the amount of information that the reader has about the candidate or issue being endorsed. If the reader has little or no information, or if his information is contradictory and he has no particular bias against the newspaper, its editorial may help him reach a decision. Since undecided voters are the ones most likely influenced by editorials and since undecided voters often swing elections, the influence of endorsements may be greater than generally believed. Candidates still seem to want them. It should be noted, however, that party affiliation, the physical appearance of candidates, the economic condition of the country or community, the weather and various personal biases may influence voter decisions more than arguments or information.

Fourth, it seems likely that the greatest influence of newspapers and other media is of a long-range and cumulative nature. The effect of reading one article or editorial may be limited unless it is the reader's only source of information about the topic. But the effect generated by reading a newspaper over a long period of time may be considerable. Such reading can contribute to the reader's storehouse of information and ideas and help shape his perceptions and stereotypes. The newspaper cannot fully control what information the reader gets. He chooses what he will read. But newspapers can help those who seek information. They can help focus attention on community problems such as poor highways or inefficiency in government, and they can help keep public of-

ficials in the spotlight. Unfortunately, the influence of newspapers on government has not always been positive. At times they may have caused confusion
by omissions, condensations or inaccurate reports.

Fifth, it is possible that newspapers exert influence through a chain reaction process. Influential persons in various groups rely on the mass media, and
especially newspapers and magazines, for information. These persons receive
data from the newspapers, structure it to suit their own needs, then share it with
others.

Finally, it seems certain that newspapers exert some influence by providing an account of what takes place in society, what people think about it and
how they react to it. Present concepts of what is going on in the community and
the world are shaped to a large degree by what the mass media, including
newspapers, say is going on. President Lyndon Johnson chose not to run for
reelection in 1968, at least in part, because of public reaction to his policies in
Vietnam. The people learned of American activities, including the escalation of
the war, from reports in the media. The emotional impact of television was particularly strong in this instance. Viewers could see people dying on their television screens. But newspapers, wire services and magazines also helped to inform the American people about American involvement in Southeast Asia.
Newspapers and other media also contribute substantially to the view of this
country that is held by persons elsewhere, and newspaper accounts will be used
by historians who seek at a later date to describe this period in history.[4]

Further studies should be made to test these and other possible hypotheses
about the influence of newspapers and other media, and members of the media
should seek always to assure that their influence will be of positive value to society. Those who would document or refute the influence of newspapers can
seek evidence in many ways. They can take opinion surveys; look to the use of
newspapers by historians and other scholars in their work; review the advocacies of the newspapers and the changes, if any, that followed; examine the
readers' views as expressed in letters to the editor; compare what is purchased
with what is advertised in newspapers; examine the effects of a strike that
deprives a community of its newspapers; and compare progress in communities
with active newspapers with that of communities that do not have them.

Although most newspapers seek primarily to inform and influence their
readers, many seek also to entertain them. Radio and subsequently television
have preempted many of the entertainment responsibilities once held by both
newspapers and magazines. Their serials, variety programs and situation come-
dies provide many opportunities for individual entertainment, escape and vicarious living. But many newspapers still devote a substantial part of their non-ad-
vertising space to human interest stories, advice columns, comics, crossword
puzzles and other entertainment features. Some newspapers devote as much
space to comic strips as they devote to editorials, letters and political columnists combined. Information and entertainment should not be regarded as mutu-

ally exclusive, however. Many features admirably combine the two elements, and some influence their readers as well. A comic character may speak more aptly to some issues than a renowned columnist. But the criticism that some newspapers devote too much space to entertainment has validity in some cases. Editors normally seek to justify an entertainment emphasis by pointing to the results of readership surveys. The people get a great deal of what they say they read.

Information, influence and entertainment are roles made possible for most newspapers today because of advertising. The advertisements, which take up from 40% to 75% of the space in newspapers, pay most of the bills. Advertising is important, however, beyond its revenue-producing value. First, it provides a genuine service for readers. They depend on advertisements to find a place to live, shop for groceries and meet other personal needs. Second, advertising helps keep the free enterprise system functioning and contributes to the nation's very high standard of living. Most persons who read newspapers read at least some of the advertisements in them; some buy their newspapers primarily for that purpose.

The newspaper can be defined in a general way, then, as an unbound publication issued at regular intervals which seeks to inform, influence and entertain its readers, and foster the nation's economic development through advertising. Some will stretch the definition to include publications that are subsidized by schools or other groups and carry no advertising, publications aimed primarily at shoppers that contain little news and opinion, publications that specialize in opinion, and perhaps others. Some would insist, too, that a true newspaper must be free of government controls such as are exercised in some countries. It is, in fact, unlikely that readers, editors, and scholars will agree on a single, precise definition, and such agreement may not be important. What is important is that readers and editors of a particular newspaper try to determine an appropriate and useful role for that newspaper and pursue it together.

NEWSPAPERS AND OTHER MEDIA

All the mass media are concerned with information, influence, entertainment and advertising. Each has an important and different role to perform in serving the people, and each should concentrate on what it can do best. The mass media can and should complement each other. But since all deal to some extent with information and ideas and all are supported in large measure by advertising, competition also exists. This naturally leads to questions about which medium is the favored source of news and which can best serve the advertiser. The answers to some extent depend on who is providing them and on what data the observations are based.

The Television Information Office asserts that television has become the people's primary source of news and that it is the most believable news medium. It bases its assertions to a large extent on a series of surveys made by the Roper organization beginning in 1959. These studies, underwritten by the Television Information Office, indicate that by 1963 television had taken a slight lead over newspapers as the most common news source, that by 1967 it was well ahead of newspapers and that it remained so in 1973. In the 1973 response to the question, "Where do you usually get most of your news about what's going on in the world today?" 64% of the respondents chose television, 50% newspapers, 21% radio and 6% magazines. The recent Roper studies also have asserted that television has taken a substantial lead over newspapers and other media in credibility. When asked in 1973 which of the four media they would be most inclined to believe if news reports conflicted, 48% chose television, 21% newspapers, 10% magazines and 8% radio.[5]

Newspaper officials and others challenge the validity of these surveys and point to other studies which show that most persons rely first on newspapers for information and trust newspapers more than the other media. Dr. Alex Edelstein, professor and director of the School of Communications at the University of Washington, suggested that the differing conclusions are the result of different questioning techniques. Edelstein said the Roper method involves attitudinal research rather than behavior in that it requires the individual to sum up his evaluation of all media over time without regard to specific problems that are important to him. The respondent must sum up the important and the trivial, the past and the present, the total sum of his experience with all problems over time and come to an immediate judgment. Edelstein said that where different questioning techniques or approaches have been used, the results have been different. He said that when people are asked about important problems they say that newspapers are the source of most of their media information, followed by television, and that they trust newspapers the most. His research indicates that people prefer newspapers as a source of information about both local problems and world problems but that the degree of preference is greater for local problems. Edelstein questioned whether individuals judge the media very often on the basis of credibility. The significant question is not a matter of trusting the media, he said, but rather the usefulness of the source and the content of information for the individual.[6]

Studies by Audits and Surveys, Inc., for the Newspaper Advertising Bureau and W. R. Simmons & Associates also indicate a preference for newspapers. They show that while 77% of adults 18 and over read one or more daily newspapers on an average weekday, 52% of adults will not see any television news. Among persons 18 through 34 the number not seeing television news rises to 57%. After five days, 89% of all adults will have read at least one issue of a daily newspaper; yet over a two-week period more than half of the public will not see even one national newscast. The studies indicate that the average reading time is 30 to 40 minutes, that the average reader covers 45 pages a day, not including classified, that slightly more than half of all readers start at page one and scan each page, and that 93% will take some positive action connected with the newspaper. For example, 56% of the sample clipped and saved editorial material and 39% clipped one or more advertisements during the three months of the survey.[7]

A survey in 1971 by Opinion Research Corporation indicates that people look first to newspapers for information about news they are very much interested in, prefer newspapers for complicated news, and look to newspapers for information about special groups. This survey also suggests that persons with more education and higher incomes tend to rely more on newspapers than the other media.[8]

The debate over which medium does the most effective job in reaching people is waged most vigorously over advertising. Although all newspapers together were still getting about as much advertising as television, radio and magazines combined in the early 1970s, television had made inroads into the national advertising revenue of the other media, including newspapers. Television spokesmen assert that people spend more time looking at television commercials than they do in reading newspaper advertisements. Newspaper spokesmen reply that readers of newspaper advertisements select them and read them because they are interested in buying the product. They contend that the broadcasting of a commercial is no guarantee that anyone is paying attention to it or that those who are paying attention are interested in buying the product.[9]

Surveys conducted by the Opinion Research Corporation in 1966 and 1971 indicate a preference for newspapers as the number one medium to reach people with advertising. The 1966 study showed that while one of four persons looks forward to seeing a television commercial, two of three look forward to seeing a newspaper advertisement. Moreover, it indicated that the persons most interested in any advertisement's message are the ones most likely to return to print as the best source of information. The 1971 survey found that people turn to newspapers for facts by a three to one margin when they are ready to buy and that citizens trust newspaper advertising more than they trust advertising in other media.[10]

Many television commercials are clever, and many are effective in reaching potential buyers. But the overall image of television commercials is mixed. In one study television and radio commercials ranked third on a list of unprompted, top-of-mind responses to the question, "What is the most annoying thing in life?" They were not considered as annoying as "inconsiderateness" and "noises," but were rated four times as annoying as world problems and bad roads and twice as annoying as traffic problems and government.[11]

Ashton Phelps, president-publisher of the *New Orleans Times-Picayune* and *New Orleans States-Item*, questioned the effectiveness of television commercials in verse.

> Ten little Televiewers on the Nielsen line,
> One fell asleep and then there were nine.
> Nine little Televiewers ready for the bait,

One switched channels and then there were eight.
Eight little Televiewers handed down from heaven,
One got indigestion and then there were seven.
Seven little Televiewers, just the proper mix,
The show was a rerun and then there were six.
Six little Televiewers when who should arrive,
But an unexpected caller and then there were five.
Five little Televiewers, the remnants of the corps,
Network interruption and then there were four.
Four little Televiewers, still at the TV,
The telephone rang and then there were three.
Three little Televiewers, with nothing else to do,
One set blew a tube and then there were two.
Two little Televiewers still under the gun,
One went to get a beer and then there was one.
The last little Televiewer, the commercial had begun,
He went to the bathroom and then there were none.[12]

Rich's in Atlanta, the South's largest department store, sought to measure the relative performance of newspapers, television and radio as an influence on shoppers' decisions to buy specific items in a study in September 1970. The store employed a local interviewing firm to interview shoppers carrying the test items immediately after they made their purchases. A total of 2,176 interviews were made in three of Rich's seven stores focusing on the ten departments where the advertised test items were sold. The results gave newspapers a decided edge in effectiveness. The newspaper advertisements produced 71% of the advertising influence with only 38% of the total advertising budget. This study is especially noteworthy because it was conducted by the store in conjunction with researchers from both the local newspapers and broadcast media.[13]

Something for Everyone

The conflicting assertions in many of the studies cited here and the limited number of surveys conducted by totally disinterested parties leaves a mixed picture as to which medium is the most effective in presenting news and advertising. But it does appear that each medium has advantages over the others in certain areas and that each should concentrate its efforts there. Such concentration will help the media help the consumer with his many and varied interests. What are some of these advantages?

Television offers the dramatic impact of sight, sound and motion that cannot be matched by any of the other media. It is, of course, a primary entertainment medium. It presents movies, concerts, ball games, ice shows and myriad other entertainment forms. In the news field, television excels at presenting news as it happens. It carries its viewers into the convention hall, places them at the 50-yard line of the Super Bowl, and transports them to the moon. Its dramatic color motion pictures can bring the intense drama of the Olympics or the intense horror of war into the viewer's home. Television enables a president or governor to communicate directly with millions. They can see his facial expressions, hear his words and reach their own judgments as to his sincerity. Television can use film and videotape extensively in its efforts to provide background and analysis.

Radio can also present news as it happens, bring the voices of newsmakers and performers into the homes of listeners, and provide dramatic shows and other entertainment. It lacks the visual impact of television in doing these things, but may obtain more involvement in some shows from listeners who must conceive their own images to accompany the words. Radio's major advantages, however, lie in other areas. Unlike the other media, where the consumer often must look at something, radio requires little effort of its consumer. It thus becomes an ideal busy-time companion. The listener can get the latest news, hear his favorite type of music, or tune in on other shows while driving his automobile, working in his office or relaxing at the beach. For the most part, radio is also faster and more flexible in its presentation of the news than the other media. Radio reporters can get to the unexpected news event quickly and report it on the air almost as rapidly. Light, compact, but sturdy equipment enables the radio reporter to move in a hurry and communicate from the scene. A flexible programming format enables the radio station to get the news on the air with less apparent interruption of regular programming than television. Radio can also meet the specialized programming interests of consumers more readily than television. Different stations can concentrate on classical, popular, or rock music, or present talk shows on various topics. In a metropolitan area there usually are enough different types of radio stations to suit the tastes of almost everyone.

Magazines also provide through specialization services the other media cannot match. Television competition, rising production and distribution costs, and other factors have doomed the general interest consumer magazine that was so popular in the 1930s and 1940s. But any reports that the magazine industry is dying are unfounded. Specialized magazines are flourishing by providing information their consumers cannot get from other sources. There are magazines for children, teenagers, parents of children and teenagers, executives, housewives, senior citizens, educators, sportsmen and hobbyists. Almost every business and profession, sport, hobby, religion or other interest is served by one or more magazines. There are thousands of them. Some magazines also can compete and serve by providing in-depth coverage of issues, particularly those of national significance. Magazines have more time between deadlines to gather and analyze information, and they have more space than most of the media in which to present detailed analyses of national events. Magazine presentations may be more permanent in the sense that the magazines may remain in homes and offices for several months. In addition to their information and analysis roles, magazines can serve by providing entertainment through short stories, condensed books, a wide variety of information articles and other features.

There are, however, many advantages still enjoyed by newspapers. First, newspapers provide a wider variety of news and information than the other media, and they present far more details than the electronic media. A half-hour news program on television does not cover the equivalent of a full page of news and information in a newspaper. The *St. Louis Globe-Democrat* dramatically demonstrated this difference in 1962 when it published a special edition with shaded areas to show what the newspaper offered that all the radio and television stations in the area did not in a 24-hour period. Radio and television presented about half of the news covered on the front page and brief summaries of a few other stories; the newspaper provided pages and pages not touched by the broadcast media.[14] Many stations carry more news today than they did in the early 1960s, but even the one-hour shows present the equivalent of only a page or two from the newspaper. A 1971 study by researchers at the University of California at Los Angeles of three television stations and a newspaper in Bakersfield, California is suggestive. During an average weekday, the three stations presented an average of 63 news items, of which nine were repeated. The *Bakersfield Californian* had an average of 217 general news stories. The study also showed that the television coverage did not compare with the depth provided by the newspaper.[15]

Some persons feared that the ability of the broadcast media to cover news as it happens and provide early reports on other news would greatly curtail or eliminate the demand for newspapers, but their fears have not been justified. The broadcast media cannot match the detail and variety of newspaper coverage, and their live coverage and headline news appear to whet rather than dull people's appetites for newspapers. Many persons who spend hours watching a convention, inauguration or space venture still want to read about the event in the newspaper. They can hear and see the President make his State-of-the-Union address but still want to see the printed version and read an analysis of it in the newspaper. Magazines can provide detailed analysis of a few issues, mostly national in scope. Newspapers can provide extensive coverage and analysis of national, regional and local issues not available elsewhere.

A second advantage of newspapers is that they fit into the consumer's schedule more easily than the broadcast media. The reader can select what he wants to read and read it when he wants to at his own speed. He can easily cut out a story and save it to refer to later or share with someone else. He need not tune in at a particular time; he does not have to listen carefully when a newscaster presents many stories that do not interest him in hopes that one he wants to hear will sometime be aired. Nor is he dependent on the ability of the newscaster to read slowly and distinctly enough for him to take it all in at one time. He can skim the headlines quickly to find what interests him and invest all his reading time in those stories.

In the third place, newspapers, along with other print media, are particularly suited to the communication of what has been described as linear, sequential information. Human beings today must assimilate an astounding amount of information to keep pace with a rapidly changing world. They do this by continuously programming their brains, which can be compared to highly sophisticated computers. The printed word can be used far more efficiently in such programming than the spoken word. The average person can speak or hear about 150 words a minute. Even the slow to average reader can handle 250 words a minute. Many persons can read effectively at several times that speed. People can thus accumulate information much more rapidly reading newspapers than listening to one of the broadcast media.

Fourth, newspapers can present certain types of entertainment such as the crossword puzzle much more effectively than the broadcast media. Newspapers offer much entertainment as well as information through various types of columns, cartoons, reviews, human interest stories and special features on everything from astrology to stamps.

Fifth, newspapers can present certain types of advertising far more effectively. They are particularly suited to displaying the wares of local department stores, specialty houses and grocery stores. They may be even more suited to the presentation of classified advertisements for houses, automobiles, pets and myriad other items. The broadcast media cannot handle the volume; magazines are not published often enough and are not local enough to serve the same need.

Finally, it can be noted that newspapers are particularly effective in presenting information, developing issues and motivating action at the local level. They can give meaning and perspective to community life not possible through the other media. They can thus make the difference in whether communities fail or survive, struggle or prosper.

Newspapers need not fear competition from other media if they concentrate on what they can do more effectively than the others, do it well and let people know what they are doing. They must, however, positively reach out to coming generations reared on a heavy diet of television. A study reported in the late 1960s indicated that the average reader was still spending approximately as much time with his newspaper as he did 15 years earlier; but there are no guarantees that future generations, unless sought out, will read newspapers at all. For many youngsters newspapers are yesterday, television is today. They must be reached through special features for them and through special projects such as the Newspaper-in-the-Classroom program.[16]

Newspapers must also be concerned by the fact that large numbers of adults are functionally illiterate and cannot read a newspaper even if motivated to do so. A study published in 1970 suggested that half of this nation's adults may lack the literacy required to read such basic things as job applications, driving manuals and newspapers.[17] This is a serious problem, not just for

newspapers who seek subscribers, but also for the nation, which needs informed citizens to make its democratic system function efficiently. Newspapers
can help the nation as well as themselves by encouraging adult education in
reading as well as taking the newspaper story into the schools.

There is much that newspapers can do in today's complex world to continue their own economic prosperity and foster the continued growth of a free
republic. Although the development of other media requires some role adjustments by newspapers, their basic functions remain the same. They can still inform, influence, entertain and foster the development of the nation's free enterprise system through advertising. But their opportunities and responsibilities
for service go far beyond their basic functions. The life of the nation itself
depends on the continued development of a free and responsible press.

A Free and Responsible Press

The ability of newspapers and other media to perform the vital roles expected of them is determined to a great extent by the degree of freedom they
have from government or other interference. Only a free press can effectively
serve free persons and help them maintain their freedoms. The press must continue to be free to publish without government license or other undue restriction. It must be free to criticize fairly and truthfully the performance of public
officials, and it must have access to information about the activities of government at all levels. In return the press must act responsibly in exercising its
freedoms. The nation's press must be both free and responsible.

Newspapers and other media in the United States now operate under what
Fred S. Siebert, Theodore B. Peterson and Wilbur Schramm refer to as the
social responsibility theory of the press. This concept evolved in this country
and others out of an older concept known as libertarianism. The libertarian
concept had been developed in opposition to the authoritarian concept that
prevailed when the printing press was introduced in the fifteenth century. All
three concepts, and a fourth which Siebert, Peterson and Schramm call the Soviet Communist theory, are represented in one or more countries today.[18] Each
should be noted briefly to bring the present-day relationships of newspapers and
government into proper perspective.

The authoritarian concept of the press is a natural outgrowth of the authoritarian society into which modern communication was born about 1450. In such
a society the state is paramount and the individual is important only as a
member of the community serving the state. Truth is restricted and the thought
approved by the state becomes the standard for everyone. Autocratic leaders
recognized early that the press could be useful to them if controlled but dangerous if permitted to develop freely. They exercised controls through licensing,
censorship and the threat of punishment for sedition or treason. This approach
generally was maintained in Colonial America and Western Europe until the

second half of the eighteenth century and is still followed in a number of countries today.

The libertarian concept of the press evolved naturally out of opposition to an authoritarian society and its authoritarian press. Libertarian theorists argued that the people are paramount, that they delegate powers to government and can withdraw them as they see fit. Reason was advanced as the means to distinguish between truth and error, and the need for a free market place for ideas was urged. Under this theory the press must be free to present ideas of all kinds and serve as a check on government. The concept caught on in the fledgling United States and in some other countries. Party subsidies financed many of the early papers here, but by the middle of the nineteenth century advertising became the chief source of support. Some countries still practice this theory, which emphasizes free expression of ideas, easy access to the means of publication and the ultimate self-righting process of truth. But Americans and others in the twentieth century have developed modifications.

The social responsibility concept developed because of shortcomings in the operation of the libertarian theory and because of the twentieth century trend toward consolidation of newspapers and concentration of newspaper ownership. Some found the "objective reporting" of the libertarian era to be irresponsible. They urged that background material be included along with the raw facts of news stories to provide adequate perspective. Many realized that the self-righting process could not function in communities where consolidation eliminated competition unless the existing newspapers presented all sides of the various issues. The absolute freedom of the libertarian theory was tempered by a new emphasis on responsibility. The socially responsible press of today is not just to be free from the restraints of government; it also is to be free for the publication of information vital to the functioning of a democratic society. It seeks access to information as well as absence of restraint. The new emphasis is more positive. The press, like the people it serves, must be responsible as well as free.

The Soviet Communist theory of the press developed out of, rather than as a reaction to, the authoritarian concept. Under the Soviet concept the press is an instrument of government. Newspapers and other media are owned and used by the government. The authoritarian concept leaves ownership in private hands but provides for strict government controls. The Soviet concept make the media another tool of the state and the party which operates the state.

Many authors have discussed the various theories of the press and sought to define what is involved in a free and responsible press. Hundreds of newspapers and other media provide their own definitions in their day-to-day operations. There are no simple definitions. But the report of the Commission on Freedom of the Press, first published in 1947, does suggest a broad outline for action and discussion. The 13-member Commission was headed by Robert Hutchins, chancellor of the University of Chicago, and composed primarily of educators. Its report, entitled *A Free and Responsible Press,* suggests ways in which government, press and public can contribute; and it outlines five ideal demands of society for the communication of news and ideas. These include: "(1) a truthful, comprehensive, and intelligent account of the day's events in a context which gives them meaning; (2) a forum for the exchange of comment and criticism; (3) the projection of a representative picture of the constituent groups in the society; (4) the presentation and clarification of the goals and values of society; (5) full access to the day's intelligence." [19]

The commission urged government to foster the introduction of new communication techniques, help maintain media competition, protect the public interest where media are concentrated, provide an alternative remedy for libel laws, repeal certain restrictive legislation, and inform the public about its own policies and purposes. It suggested that the constitutional guarantees of a free press be extended also to radio and motion pictures.

It asked that the mass media accept the responsibilities of common carriers of information and discussion, assume responsibility for financing new, experimental activities in the field, engage in vigorous mutual criticism, and increase the competence, independence and effectiveness of their staffs. It recommended that the radio industry treat advertising as it is treated by the best newspapers.

Finally, the commission suggested that the public could help through the efforts of nonprofit institutions, the creation of academic-professional centers of advanced study, research and publication, and the establishment of a new and independent agency to appraise and report annually upon the performance of the media. It asked that nonprofit agencies help supply the variety, quantity and quality of press service needed by the people, and it urged that journalism schools exploit their resources to provide students with the broadest and most liberal training possible.[20]

Reactions to the report when it was presented in the late 1940s and since have been mixed. Many in the press were critical because the commission did not include a single newspaperman in its membership. *Editor & Publisher,* a prominent newspaper trade publication, responded to this defect by sponsoring in 1949 a panel of ten newspapermen and educators to consider plans for a joint appraisal of the self-improvement possibilities of American newspapers through studies of specific problems. The work of this group led in 1950 to a study by the American Society of Newspaper Editors, which produced this finding: "The self-improvement of American newspapers depends chiefly upon the character of American newspapermen, their recognition and acceptance of the great responsibilities imposed by freedom of the press, their faithfulness to duty in giving the people of this country a truthful account of the day's news and fair comment thereon, and their willingness to profit by the intelligent criticism of the newspaper-reading public." [21] A number of the commission's recommendations have been implemented; others are still being discussed.

Basic Responsibilities

Newspaper responsibilities vary with the size, frequency of publication and intended audience of individual publications. The responsibilities of the metropolitan daily, the country weekly and the college newspaper are not the same. Each must determine its particular functions and perform them as best it can. Nevertheless, there seem to be some common responsibilities that apply to all.

First, newspapers must lead in the search for truth. They must do more than disseminate information; it is not enough to publish body counts, quote prominent persons about controversies, and reprint faithfully the executive's message and his views of what it means. Newspapers must seek to explain the meaning of the information they provide and place it into perspective; they must seek to provoke understanding and expand knowledge. Newspapers must do more than react to events or announcements. They must seek out the truth about what is happening on campus, in the ghetto, at city hall, in the statehouse, in Washington and overseas. They must probe for information about industrialists, labor unions, youths, blacks, bureaucrats and every other interest group in society. They must help everyone see what each interest group wants and needs and how it proposes to achieve its goals. They must not wait for riots to report the causes of discontent or wait for wars to become concerned with the nation's foreign policies.

The search for truth is unending and difficult. Where controversy exists there is seldom agreement on what is truth. Most prefer their own definition to that provided by others, newspapers included. Reporters and editors must constantly guard against distorting truth through omissions, inaccuracies or improper emphases. It has been charged, for example, that blacks receive coverage only when their activities affect whites in some way, usually a negative way, and that youths who reject moral standards or run afoul of the law receive far more attention than those who do useful things within the accepted norms. Those involved in controversies frequently accuse newspapers of seeing only the other side. Editors can take some consolation in the fact that conservatives and liberals, white racists and black militants, all accuse them of such distortions. They must be doing something right. But the danger of distortion is great and continuous. Subjective decisions about where to seek news, what to include in stories and in what order, and how to display the finished accounts must constantly be made.

While newspapers must accept the impossibility of achieving complete objectivity in their reporting, they must seek it as a goal. Advocacy is for editorials, columns and other special features labeled as such. Responsible newspapers will keep the distinction clear. They will remain as fair and impartial as possible in their presentations of news, give all sides an opportunity to be heard, and correct distortions if and when they occur. They will endeavor to

provide information and perspective so that readers can make their own determinations about what is truth. But they will not under the guise of objectivity
fail to take a stand on important issues in their editorial columns. In a clearly
labeled opinion section, the responsible newspaper will say, "Here are the
facts, here is what we believe they mean, and here is what we think should be
done."

*Second, newspapers in a democratic society have a responsibility to help
make democracy work.* This responsibility involves providing information for
legislators, officials and citizens generally, and seeking out truth about government at all levels. Information is vital to the operation of a free society. Newspapers must also help motivate citizens to use the information given to them,
become informed about their governments and become positively involved in
their operation. In addition, newspapers must serve as a check, or watchdog,
on those who exert or seek to exert power and influence in government. They
can and should support candidates for public office as well as programs of
public action. But they should remain independent of individuals and parties
and when appropriate investigate and criticize any of them.

A number of newspapers have chosen not to endorse candidates in recent
presidential elections, and *Newsday,* the well-known Long Island, N.Y. daily,
announced in 1972 that it would no longer endorse any political candidates.
The paper, which had a circulation of 440,000, took the action independently
of its parent organization, the Times-Mirror Company of Los Angeles. *Newsday* included among the reasons for its decision the desire to avoid even the appearance of bias in news reports and the desire to maintain its independence to
criticize, investigate and disclose abuse of the public trust. *Editor & Publisher,*
the newspaper industry trade publication, and others disagreed with this reason-
ing. *Editor & Publisher* said, for example, that editors and publishers who go
on record with their choices of candidates are more likely to enforce objectivity
in the news columns than those who keep their politics to themselves. It is the
special province of the editorial page to help the reader wade through all the information he gets, *Editor & Publisher* said; the reader can be assured he is
getting a fair interpretation if he knows the newspaper's own point of view.[22]
While some newspapers may be reluctant to expose the frailties of candidates
they have supported, many seem willing to expose corruption or criticize what
they believe to be unwise government action whenever and wherever they see
it.

*Third, newspapers have a responsibility to help individuals and communi-
ties adjust to change and improve themselves.* Change is the super challenge of
the late twentieth century. Man's store of information is doubling every few
years. The lag between the discovery or invention of something and its practical application has been reduced to a few years. Generational changes that
used to come every 20 years now come every four or five years. Individuals

and communities find it difficult to adjust to such rapid changes. Bureaucracies often find it impossible.

Newspapers can do several things to help meet the challenge of change. First, they can provide greater exposure for different ideas and groups in society. They can provide greater coverage, including special sections, for emerging constituencies such as blacks; they can invite representatives of these groups or other persons with new ideas and approaches to write guest columns and letters. Second, newspapers can seek greater diversity in their own staffs, and use it to advantage. For example, the views of young staff members who may more easily adjust to change can be sought out. Third, newspapers can use special teams to explore issues or problems in depth. A basic continuing team might be augmented by specialists in a particular area under study, or completely new teams might be developed to meet different situations. Health, housing, employment, civil rights, taxes, pollution, traffic and transportation are among the many issues in most communities today. Fourth, newspapers can take more interest in understanding and reporting the processes of change and the complex social systems that are evolving. They must explore the causes as well as the effects of change and improve their capacity for exposing needs before they become problems. Study teams might have predicted and helped forestall the riots that hit a number of American cities in the 1960s. Finally, newspapers can place greater emphasis on positive news and encourage a positive attitude toward change. A society of increasingly divergent groups fed on a steady diet of sensationalism and violence could easily explode. A society that sees its advantages and achievements and sees hope for meeting its problems should not only survive but prosper.[23]

Newspapers have developed a number of special programs in recent years to help their individual readers. "Action Lines," consumer service bureaus and educational programs have been particularly successful. Newspapers should continue and expand these operations and develop other aids. The Action Line can be particularly helpful. Readers are invited to contact Action Lines with requests for specific information or assistance about anything. Action Line reporters try to answer the questions, provide the assistance, or put the questioners in touch with individuals or agencies that can help them. The idea was originated by William B. Steven at the *Houston Chronicle* in 1961 under the title "Watchem." The *Charlotte News* began a similar question-and-answer column a few years later titled "Quest," and the idea spread rapidly in the late 1960s.[24]

At times the information sought from newspaper Action Lines is trivial; someone wants to know who won the World Series in 1969 or where to get concert tickets. Often, however, the Action reporters are able to assist persons with real problems and needs. Someone may write seeking information about government or community services he needs; another person may ask help in getting service from a business or other institution. In addition the Action Lines probably further the cause of consumer education by printing general information that helps readers know what to do or avoid doing. They help build a feeling of rapport and trust between readers and the newspaper.[25] Occasionally, the queries may expose community problems or lead to changes in public policy. The Ohio Turnpike Commission began hiring women toll collectors after an inquiry about such jobs in the *Akron Beacon-Journal* in the late 1960s. The Turnpike Commission advised the *Beacon-Journal* that it was in the market for such employes and got more than 100 applications during the week after this information was printed. In late 1973 the Commission noted that almost half of its toll collectors are women.[26] Readership studies indicate that the Action columns are widely read.

The continued growth of reader services columns in the 1970s led to the establishment of an information organization to improve their operation through cooperation. This organization, or Action Clearinghouse, was designed to help editors who were attempting to deal with a business located in the home city of a fellow Clearinghouse member. Anne S. Baumgartner, Action Line editor at the *Miami Herald,* compiled a list of Clearinghouse members that was published in *Editor & Publisher* in late 1972 and invited those not included to contact her.[27]

A syndicated variation of the Action Line theme was introduced in 1973 by Consumer News Inc., in Washington, D.C. The Consumer News group offered a 1,200-word weekly feature of six to eight items called HELP-MATE to handle problems of a national nature. The basic idea, according to founder Arthur Rowse, is to build a multiplier effect through which each item published can provide enough information to benefit all readers in the same or similar circumstances. A review of HELP-MATE items indicated frequent reliance on trade associations, particularly the Council of Better Business Bureaus, for help in getting action involving nationally distributed products. Several newspapers with a total circulation of nearly two million were using the feature in late 1973. Usage patterns varied. Some newspapers used all the items together, usually on Sunday; some split the items into two or three columns; some integrated the items in staff-written columns.[28]

Consumer service programs also can provide significant help for persons seeking information about such topics as the relative cost and merits of health insurance or the dangers that may be inherent in the use of some children's toys. Newspapers can help assist individuals with specific questions about products or services; they can provide a continuous flow of information about prices, values and other aspects of consumer education.[29] There is always the possibility that a consumer reporter may turn up information that would appear unfavorable to an advertiser. But everyone, including manufacturers, should benefit from correcting faulty products or misleading assertions. In any case, the newspaper's first responsibility is to seek truth.

The Newspaper-in-the-Classroom program is perhaps the most far-reaching specific educational effort in which newspapers have become involved. Individual teachers have used newspapers as teaching aids for years, but an expanded effort to encourage teachers to use newspapers in this way was made in the 1960s. Many newspapers have provided copies of their product free or at a reduced price to students involved in the Newspaper-in-the-Classroom programs. The immediate goals of such programs are to help teachers teach more effectively and help students learn. Long-range goals include the development of a continuous flow of citizens who can and will use newspapers wisely in their daily lives.

Teachers can use pictures, comic strips and other features to motivate slow learners, interpretive stories and editorials to challenge exceptionally bright youngsters, and newspaper content generally to interest students in mathematics, science, English and other subjects. Programs sponsored by individual newspapers and by the American Newspaper Publishers Association in conjunction with the National Council for the Social Studies clearly have demonstrated the value of newspapers as teaching tools from the elementary grades up in a wide variety of subjects.

Students in a reading class in a Chicago inner city school scored an average achievement gain of nearly two years in a six-weeks' course that used the *Chicago Tribune* instead of packaged programs or traditional textbooks. The key to the gain, which was determined by a standardized test, was that the material used was contemporary and related to the students' experiences.[30]

Students in a Granite City, Illinois, school where a high percentage of children come from culturally deprived backgrounds achieved for the first time in 1972–73 an average of a year's growth in one school year by using the *St. Louis Globe-Democrat* to teach all subjects from kindergarten through sixth grade. Moreover, educators there said that the program provided their students with a broad knowledge of current things that did not show up in the standardized tests and encouraged them to retain information longer. They said the children did not display the loss of information in the fall after the program was first used that normally is shown after three months away from the classroom. Standard textbooks were not completely eliminated in this program, but about 85% of the teacher's instruction was based on the newspapers. Stories about labor contracts became the basis for mathematics problems; datelines became geography lessons; stories about a natural disaster or space flight became science lessons.[31]

Students in grades four through seven in the Hancock County, Georgia schools scored significant gains in newspaper reading skills and general reading ability through use of a Newspaper-in-the-Classroom program developed by Dr. Charles Berryman of the College of Education, University of Georgia. Classroom teachers there used materials prepared by Dr. Berryman for one period each day for ten weeks. Instead of a textbook, the classes used articles from the *Atlanta Constitution, Augusta Chronicle* and *Macon Telegraph,* all of which are circulated in the area. In grades five and seven gains in general reading ability appeared to have more than tripled those which might have been anticipated with regular non-newspaper instruction. In grades four and six the gains about doubled those which could have been expected with regular instruction. "We have assumed that newspapers can be useful, but only after students already have learned to read," Dr. Berryman said. "Now we have evidence that newspapers can help students learn how to read." He said also that there is reason to believe that without instruction a student will not become a capable newspaper reader, one who knows how to gain information from newspapers which is vital to him as a citizen. Even students with good general reading ability need to get specific instruction on how to read newspapers.[32]

In early 1973 approximately 400 of the nation's newspapers were known to have Newspaper-in-the-Classroom programs. They were serving hundreds of thousands of students and teachers in an estimated 35,000 schools.[33] Newspapers can also help themselves through the program by developing more appreciative audiences for the future. Many young teachers in the 1960s and early 1970s have had negative attitudes toward newspapers, and most students in the past decade have grown up with the electronic media. If the Newspaper-in-the-Classroom programs can help change the teachers' attitudes and help students see the values in newspapers, everyone will benefit; adults must be able to use newspapers effectively if they are to obtain public affairs information vital to the operation of a democratic government. The keys to the success of the programs are to reach teachers with the fact that newspapers have much information that is important to them and their students and help them explore ways in which they can use newspapers to help students learn. The American Newspaper Publishers Association and the National Council for the Social Studies sponsored a number of workshops for teachers during the 1960s at several universities, and individual newspapers have held their own shorter workshops for them.

Newspapers also are used as supplementary teaching materials in many on-campus colleges courses, and they may become principal texts for home-study courses in the future. The National Endowment for the Humanities provided a $96,000 grant to the Extension Division of the University of California in San Diego in 1972 to subsidize a two-year experiment titled "Courses by Newspaper." Under this plan course lectures are presented in participating newspapers and supplemented by additional notes, booklets and books. Faculty from cooperating educational institutions meet with students periodically for discussions and examinations. The pilot course, which involved 20 lectures on "America and the Future of Man," was begun in the fall of 1973. The original plan was to distribute the course through about a dozen newspapers, six dailies and six weeklies, but the response to early information about the program was so great that the list was expanded to approximately 250 newspapers with a circulation of more than 21 million and nearly 200 colleges. Copley News Service was also involved in the project, which planned a second course, "In Search of the American Dream," in 1974–1975.[34]

Fourth, newspapers have a responsibility to improve themselves. They should seek at all times to be accurate, truthful, fair, decent and sincere, as suggested in "The Canons of Journalism," first adopted by the American Society of Newspaper Editors at its first annual meeting in April, 1923. They should abide by a strong Code of Ethics such as the one adopted by the Society of Professional Journalists, Sigma Delta Chi, at its national convention in late 1973.[35] They should seek improvement in many specific ways, including the following: (1) conduct and encourage research; (2) improve their staffs; (3) improve their content and appearance; (4) establish definite procedures to resolve complaints; (5) correct mistakes; (6) engage in vigorous self-criticism; and (7) eschew the "freebie" game.

Newspapers should conduct and encourage research to find what readers want and need in their newspapers and to find better ways of gathering, processing and distributing news and other information. Many newspapers have been criticized justly for giving too little attention to planning and research and resisting change. Unions often have been resistant to new technology that appeared to threaten jobs, and some owners and publishers have been slow to adopt new and better ways of doing things.

Newspapers can improve their staffs by hiring the best persons available, giving them continued education and support, and rewarding them with good salaries and benefits. Newspapers should work closely with journalism schools and technical schools to help assure that prospective employes in all departments get the preparation they need for newspaper jobs. They should develop internship programs and cooperative programs to spot and recruit good prospects, provide training programs for new employes, and develop in-service programs for all employes. Appropriate supervisors should critique the efforts of those they supervise on a regular basis so that all will know what they are doing right and wrong and what they must do to improve. Newspapers should send employes to short courses and conferences in their fields of specialization and grant them leaves, and perhaps scholarships, to pursue more extensive training.

Good salaries are vital in attracting and maintaining good staffs. Many newspapers have lost good reporters, editors and other employes to public relations and other fields because their pay scales were not competitive. Many top journalism school graduates have been attracted into other fields by higher salaries when they might have preferred to work on newspapers. Most newspapers can afford to pay competitive salaries, and those that are doing so are reaping economic as well as other benefits. Staff efficiency and morale can also be encouraged by including staff members in decision-making regarding their areas of interest, providing good working conditions and support, and developing incentive programs for superior performance.

Newspapers can improve content by placing greater emphasis on news and reporting it better. Ben H. Bagdikian, the newspaper critic, reported in late 1973 that the American newspaper reader of 1970 got more intelligently selected news and better written news than he did in 1950 and that the daily newspaper in 1970 dealt with more central issues and provided a richer quality of news and analysis than its counterpart of 1950. But he also pointed out that 83% of the 59,000 pages added to the average newspaper since 1950 was advertising and that much of the remaining 17% was fluff or puffery accompanying food, real estate or clothing advertisements. Bagdikian said that the future of newspapers depends on their handling of news and suggested that consumers of the future might not be willing to take on increasingly large newspapers with increasing amounts of space devoted to advertising.[36]

In their coverage and commentary, newspapers should avoid the sensational and the superficial. They should be careful not to distort the truth, as evidently happened in reporting the celebration in Pittsburgh of the Pirates' 1971 World Series victory. Post-celebration investigations indicate that while some violence did occur, it did not approach the orgy of destruction, looting and sexual excess suggested by some accounts.[37] Newspapers should not be satisfied with superficial reporting of significant events or permit themselves to be manipulated and their readers misled by clever power seekers. They should be concerned about charges that the media place too much emphasis on bad news. Some ways in which newspapers can improve their appearance by more effective use of art, type and white space are discussed in Chapter 5.

Newspapers should establish definite procedures to resolve complaints and make themselves more accountable to their readers. A number have done so, according to a copyrighted study released in late 1973 by the American Newspaper Publishers Association. Only 23% of respondents to this study conducted by Keith P. Sanders at the University of Missouri School of Journalism under auspices of the ANPA News Research Center indicated that they have no formal system for accountability to readers. The systems used varied somewhat, including the following: accuracy forms sent to sources, 13%; standing head for corrections, 13%; ombudsman, 9%; advisory board, 9%; accuracy forms published in newspapers, 4%; press council, 3%; and "other system," 48%. Those without formal systems contended that they do not need outside help to insure the accuracy and fairness of their newspapers.[38]

Some years ago when the *Minneapolis Tribune* and the *Minneapolis Star* were under one editor, they established a Bureau of Accuracy and Fair Play to deal quickly and courteously with readers' complaints. When the staffs were separated in 1967, the *Tribune* continued this bureau and the *Star* established a Readers' Referee. All complaints received are referred to a senior editor for consideration. Corrections are published when necessary. The papers solicit comments from persons named in stories selected at random each day. These persons are asked to comment on the accuracy, fairness and adequacy of news reports.[39]

The *St. Petersburg Times* and *Evening Independent* adopted a hot line approach to handle complaints. Readers were invited to call a separate telephone number and speak directly to Del Marth, an assistant to the president, or someone else with authority to handle their complaints. In early 1971 Marth was getting about 40 calls and 10 letters a day. Readers complained about such things as small print in advertising, incorrect spelling and errors in facts in news stories, and they voiced opinions about the slant or advisibility of printing some stories. Marth and his staff handled the complaints, and he shared some of them with readers in a column called "The People's Voice." Nelson Poynter, chairman of the *Times* board, said the program was adopted because "Editor and reader need a hot line to build mutual confidence which will make the press a more effective instrument for building a more responsive government and society." [40]

Newspapers should respond to all reasonable accusations in some way. When they make mistakes, as all do at some time, they should correct them. Most do, or at least say that they do. A survey by the image committee of the Associated Press Managing Editors Association in 1970 indicates that a vast majority of newspapers are willing to correct mistakes. Some wait for readers to point them out; some take the initiative. Unfortunately, some newspapers are reluctant to publish corrections of so-called minor errors. Presumably they fear that printing a large number of corrections would hurt their public image and is not worth the risk. Some also attempt to present their corrections in a subtle manner, as, for example, placing standard headlines on them rather than labeling them in some way as corrections. Others contend, however, that publishing corrections can enhance rather than retard public confidence in newspapers.[41] The response, if any, to unreasonable criticisms will depend on the nature of the criticism, how widely it has been communicated and the believed influence of the critic. Responsible criticism can be answered in editorials, columns, private letters and personal conversations, or perhaps in all of these ways. The most effective answer to legitimate criticism is probably improved performance. Some irresponsible critics are best ignored. Others because of their prominence should be exposed to the public for what they are. In all cases, the press should strive harder to help readers see that most of the problems newspapers face are public problems as well. Free speech, for example, is a public freedom, not just a newspaper freedom. The *Miami* (Florida) *Daily News* devoted an entire editorial page, March 17, 1970, to a discussion of proposals for self-analysis of the press and a review of readers' grievances. It sought to show its readers that newspapers are trying to improve themselves and it invited them to help.[42]

Certainly, newspapers should engage in a continuous and vigorous program of self-criticism. They can assess their own achievements and engage in mutual critique programs with other newspapers as well as accept and analyze criticisms from readers and others. Many already do. Extensive self-criticism takes place among staff members at many newspapers. Some newspapers also participate in regional and national seminars such as the annual meeting of the National Conference of Editorial Writers, where editors critique each other's editorial pages. The *New York Times* instituted its "Winners and Sinners" report on what is right and wrong in the paper some time ago, and others have adopted similar programs. In September 1970, the *Washington Post* assigned assistant managing editor Richard Harwood to the post of "resident critic." He was to provide criticism of staff members and periodically share his comments on the *Post's* mistakes with readers in an opposite editorial page column. Harwood said the "critic in residence" approach can help editors get a better perspective on weaknesses such as superficiality, inconsistency, incompleteness, and the blowing up of stories to make big pictures out of small facts.[43]

Ben Bagdikian, national news editor of the *Post,* succeeded Harwood as in-house critic, or ombudsman, in 1971; and Robert C. Maynard, metropolitan and national reporter, succeeded him in 1972. Bagdikian, who reportedly resigned because of differences involving his relationship with management, discussed the role of the in-house critic in an article for *The Bulletin of the American Society of Newspaper Editors* in October, 1972. He cited the *Post* for being the first paper to put a man to work not just to correct errors but to comment publicly and critically on his own paper in his own paper, and he encouraged other newspapers to do likewise. Bagdikian said that while the *Post* job was sometimes referred to as ombudsman, it was not that in the traditional sense of an adversary representing the public with power to obtain redress of grievances. He received complaints and let the appropriate editor know of them but was an independent commentator on performance rather than an adversary with power to make changes. Bagdikian said newspapers employing in-house critics should first be clear in their own minds what their ultimate standards and values are. They should guarantee the critic space in the newspaper periodically and not expect him to be loyal to management, either in his public declarations or his newsroom relations. He suggested that the in-house critic on a large newspaper not be responsible for handling complaints because that is a full-time job in itself. Bagdikian said it was important for the in-house critic to get the newspaper's side of issues and that some system analogous to due process should be followed. If the critic and the reporter or editor cannot agree and the critic proceeds with his column, the reporter or editor should be given a right of reply, preferably on the same day in space adjacent to the critic's column. He suggested that the critic be separated from the newsroom to help assure that reporters would not seek to try their stories out on him first and in the process undercut the power and responsibilities of operating editors. Finally, Bagdikian suggested that since the critic has such potential power and may seem threatening to many persons in the organization, he might well be restricted to a one-year or two-year noncancellable and nonrenewable contract. He suggested that newspapers might draw on senior professionals from other newspapers or from journalism schools for their in-house critics.[44]

A Community Newspaper Self-Survey Kit developed at the Communications Research Center at the S.I. Newhouse School of Public Communication at Syracuse University in the early 1970s may prove helpful to many in the self-evaluation process. The kit includes a 30-question survey to obtain information about residents' attitudes toward their community, their media habits, their readership of and attitudes toward newspapers in their area, their news interests and their evaluation of the newspaper sponsoring the survey.[45] Many newspapers have, of course, already developed their own surveys to help ascertain such information.

Finally, newspapers can improve themselves by eschewing the "freebie" game. All newspaper personnel should avoid gifts, travel or other favors that might cause conflicts of interest or even suggest to the public that such conflicts might exist. Freebies have ranged from flying reporters across the country to the unveiling of some new product or service, to free tickets for ball games and other events, to small gifts from groups or individuals at Christmas time. Many have participated in the freebie game in the past; a survey of managing editors, reported in *The Quill* in August 1973, indicates that many still do. In this survey, two of three managing editors said they would accept free trips, three of four would not rule out all gifts, and 10% responded that their newspapers do accept advertisements on condition that reporters write a feature piece on the business or organization.[46] Increasing concern about credibility probably has caused many newspapers to adopt stricter rules on freebies even though they do not believe their reporting would be compromised by accepting favors. The revised Code of Ethics adopted by Sigma Delta Chi in 1973 notes that gifts, favors, free travel, special treatment or privileges can compromise the integrity of journalists and their employers and admonishes that nothing of value be accepted.[47]

Fifth, newspapers have a responsibility to remain free, independent, and solvent. Newspapers seeking to remain free and independent so they can carry out their many basic responsibilities face continuous threats both from government and from forces within the economic structure of which they are a part. Governments pose a threat to press freedom when they withhold or manage news, restrict the rights of newspapers to cover police and court news or other events, or force reporters to reveal confidential sources and thereby eliminate them. Government may pose even greater threats through the activities of regulatory bodies such as the Federal Communications Commission, Federal Trade Commission, or Securities and Exchange Commission, or through legislative efforts to tax newspapers or impose other restrictions.

The dangers to press freedom from within the economic structure of newspapers themselves are less obvious but no less serious. Press freedom is threatened by publishers whose first concern is making money. Newspapers must make a reasonable profit to remain solvent and continue their services, but too great a concern for profits can lead to censorship or policy-setting by advertisers. Critics contend that many newspapers now withhold information that might reflect adversely on advertisers, particularly those with large budgets. They also contend that much space which should be devoted to news is instead given to "free advertising," stories about products and services that are advertised. Critics also note that newspapers at times permit their concern for profit to interfere with their judgment on planning and zoning regulations and other matters vital to community life.

Newspaper freedom may also be threatened by the changing patterns of ownership within the industry. Although some of the best American newspapers enjoy monopolies in their communities, there is a danger in the fact that locally originated newspaper competition no longer exists in 95% of the nation's towns and cities. Although some of the most progressive newspapers are owned by chains or groups, there is a danger that such chains involving large numbers of newspapers could come under the control of persons whose interests do not coincide with the public interest. The rise of business conglomerates in which newspapers may be regarded as just one more business asset certainly poses a threat. The increasing trend to public ownership may also threaten press freedom if management must be primarily concerned with keeping stockholders happy, or if pressure groups can exert undue influence through purchase of stock.

Newspaper unions that can deprive a community of its newspapers for days, weeks or even months, and apathetic readers also pose threats to press freedom. The rights of labor should be protected but not at the expense of the public's right to its newspapers. Both labor and management should accept their responsibilities to keep newspapers in operation while they are working out differences of opinion over wages or other benefits. Readers should demand more of their newspapers, and they should support them in their efforts to remain independent of business or government pressures.

ASSESSMENTS

Because the newspapers of the United States are vital to the life and well-being of the nation and its people, it is essential that they be subjects of continuous assessment both by their producers and their consumers. How well are they performing their roles? How well are they living up to their responsibilities? The answers vary. Some newspapers are performing well; others are doing poorly. Because there are so many different newspapers, it is difficult to generalize with confidence. It did appear, however, as the middle 1970s began that the overall image of the press was better than it had been in the late 1960s.

George Gallup, the nationally known pollster, reported in late 1968 that never in his time had the media of communications been held in such low esteem. He said the public was fed up with excesses in the media such as sex, conflict and stimulated controversy. Roger Tatarian, vice president and editor of United Press International, said about the same time that he could not remember anything like the abuse the press was taking. Nick Williams, editor of the *Los Angeles Times,* said the press was going through a peak period of press abuse, and many others concurred. As the 1960s closed, it appeared that the press had become the nation's scapegoat for crime, racial troubles, the war in Vietnam and other problems. Vice-President Spiro Agnew, who was himself the subject of much press criticism, took up the attack on the press as the decade changed. He struck first at the broadcast media, then leveled his vitriolic blasts at newspapers such as the *New York Times* and *Washington Post.* [48]

Part of the abuse probably could be attributed to the long-standing custom of blaming the bearer of bad tidings for the nature of the message received. Many persons did not want to read bad news which related to them, and they resented the fact that newspapers and other media kept publishing it. The media would not let people forget that major problems existed, so they turned on the media as if they had created them. Some of the press criticism was the result of poor performance by some members of the press, but in a sense the press was a victim of its own achievements in interpretive and investigative reporting of public needs and problems. [49]

The image of the press looked better in late 1973 when Louis Harris, another nationally known pollster, reported on the status of public confidence in leaders of major institutions. The Harris studies indicated that public confidence in the press had dropped substantially between 1966 and 1972 but that it had risen again in 1973 to a point slightly above what it had been in 1966. [50] Harris had advised members of the American Newspaper Publishers Association in April, 1972, that the public wants the press and other institutions to focus on real problems as they exist and give them the raw material to make their own judgments. [51] The role of the press in exposing the Watergate scandals and improvements in individual newspapers probably contributed to the improved image enjoyed by the press; but much remained to be done in the 1970s before the press could achieve the public confidence it needed to perform its roles most advantageously.

Whatever the causes of press criticism, the charges must be carefully considered by the media. Newspapers must not write off all critics as irresponsible or dictatorial persons whose only goal is to destroy them. Instead, they should look at the critics and the criticisms carefully and seek understanding that will open the way to improvement in performance, correction of false images, or both. Newspapers should determine whether they are meeting their responsibilities, or if they are guilty as charged. Individual newspapers can make many of these assessments for themselves through surveys and other research. Additional assessments by media committees, journalism reviews, journalism schools and press councils might also prove helpful.

Journalism Reviews

Although many persons have expressed opinions about the press, and almost everyone has some comment to make about his hometown newspapers, there have been few organized efforts to provide a continuous assessment of newspaper performance until recent years. Various magazines have included occasional articles on press performance, the trade publications have provided some criticism and the news magazines have offered limited commentary. *Journalism Quarterly,* published by journalism educators to encourage research in journalism and mass communications, has provided scholarly insights into the field since the 1920s. But most efforts to establish critiques have come since World War II. In the late 1940s the *Nieman Reports* were started by the Nieman Foundation at Harvard University and *The Masthead* was founded by the National Conference of Editorial Writers. The Nieman Foundation was developed from a million-dollar endowment left by Lucius W. Nieman, founder of the *Milwaukee Journal*. It provides grants for practicing newsmen to spend a year at Harvard. The *Nieman Reports* offer commentary by some of these persons and by various authorities in the field. The National Conference of Editorial Writers was founded by editors and editorial writers to improve editorial writing and editorial pages. *The Masthead* offers articles that deal primarily with that aspect of newspapers.

In the 1960s the *Saturday Review,* in its monthly communications section, and the *Columbia Journalism Review* began to provide useful critiques. The communications section of *Saturday Review* was discontinued in the early 1970s when the magazine was acquired by new owners and Norman Cousins resigned as editor. It was not immediately revived after he regained control of the magazine and formed *Saturday Review/World*. But the *Columbia Journalism Review* has been expanded and improved. It was started as a quarterly in 1961, and is now published bimonthly by the Graduate School of Journalism at Columbia University. This review deals with all the media and includes many articles useful to the newspaper journalist.

Even more recently a new and often more outspoken breed of journalism review has sprung up to comment on newspapers and other mass media at the local level. About a dozen of these local reviews were in operation in the early 1970s, and others were being contemplated. Most appeared to be patterned after the *Chicago Journalism Review,* which was started in the aftermath of the 1968 Democratic convention in that city and dedicated to opposing such things as news management and assaults on the integrity of the press.

Among the others were [*MORE*]: *A Journalism Review* in New York City; the *Journalist's Newsletter* in Providence, R.I.; the *Philadelphia Journalism Review;* the *St. Louis Journalism Review; Buncombe: A Review of Baltimore*

Journalism; The Unsatisfied Man, a Review of Colorado Journalism in Denver; the Albuquerque, New Mexico, *Hard Times; Thorn: Connecticut Valley Media Review;* the *Review of Southern California Journalism;* the *San Francisco Bay Area Journalism Review;* the *Houston Journalism Review;* and the *Hawaii Journalism Review.*

[MORE] appeared to be seeking a broader national audience than most of the others, perhaps because New York City is a major media center. It appeared to be more strictly edited than some of the others, and it sought to protect its materials from republication without permission. [MORE] sponsored the A. J. Liebling Counter-Convention in early 1972 that brought many persons associated with the so-called New Journalism movement together in New York to discuss issues related to journalism. The program included such topics as democracy in the newsroom, alternative media, and racism, sexism and elitism in journalism.[52]

Most of the local journalism reviews were similar in appearance and purpose. Most were printed on inexpensive paper in tabloid format, or smaller. Most appeared dedicated to the idea that media should emphasize their roles as public institutions rather than their roles as profit-making enterprises. The editors evidently believed that the media must engage in extensive self-criticism and recognize their faults if they are to improve and render the service that the country needs of them. The reviews sought, as the *St. Louis Journalism Review* suggested in a first-issue editorial, to become to the regular newspapers, and the radio and television stations, what those media are to government and other institutions.[53] The media are expected to report and evaluate the performance of community institutions. The reviews proposed to report and evaluate the performance of the media.

During their early years most of the local reviews rendered an uneven performance. At times they appeared to make telling points with their accusations about manipulation of stories for economic, political or other reasons. At other times they appeared to dwell on minor, even personal, matters of limited consequence. Some writers seemed more concerned with the reporter's working conditions than the newspaper's performance. Occasional inaccuracies also cut into the credibility of some reviews, and the militant writing style adopted by some may have reduced rather than enhanced their influence with management.

Reports indicate that the reviews as a group were not the strong proponents of advocacy journalism or reporter-power that some believed they would be. Some review writers undoubtedly believed that newspapers and other media should be less objective in their news writing and more involved in activities they report. Some also wanted the media to include more reporters and lower echelon staff members in the determination of policy. But most reportedly seemed content to do their muckraking in the traditional manner.[54]

The future of local journalism reviews was uncertain in the early 1970s, although the *Chicago Journalism Review,* [MORE], and one or two others appeared to have achieved some stability early. Financial support was a major problem, since most either eschewed advertising by design or failed to obtain it. Revenues came primarily from circulation and from gifts either by groups or individuals. But production costs were comparatively inexpensive and much material was contributed free. Conflict of interest also posed a problem when reporters were asked to contribute information to reviews about their newspapers. In addition, the reviews faced the usual circulation, production and distribution problems faced by similar publications. The appearance and economic success of the reviews may not be so important, however, if they can motivate the media to engage in serious self-criticism that leads to improved performance.

Press Councils

Journalism reviews and other forms of in-house criticism can help bring the public's dissatisfaction with the performance of newspapers and other media to their attention. But is such criticism enough to bring needed improvements within the media and develop high public confidence in them? Does the United States need an independent agency to appraise and report annually on the performance of newspapers and other mass media? Should the media establish national grievance committees to hear complaints and encourage remedial action where needed? Would local or state appraisal agencies, grievance committees or discussion groups involving media and public prove helpful? These and similar questions were pondered by newspapers and others in the late 1960s and early 1970s as concern developed over declining public confidence in the press. There did not appear to be a consensus on what action, if any, to take, but some steps were taken to implement press councils at local, state and national levels. Most were modeled to a degree at least after the British Press Council, which relies on the force of public opinion to achieve its goals.

The British Press Council, which is one of about a dozen national councils in the world, was established in 1953 as a partial response to heavy criticism of the press in that country. Many British journalists opposed its creation, and some continued to find faults with various aspects of its operation; but favorable opinion increased dramatically after a council reorganization in 1963. An estimated 86% of British editors approved the concept in the late 1960s. As reorganized in 1963 the council included 20 members chosen by various news organizations and five representatives of the public chosen by the council. All members serve three-year terms and are eligible for reelection. The chairman is selected from among the public members. The Council must meet at least five times a year, and the chairman is authorized to call special sessions when needed. A permanent office staff is employed to handle day-to-day activities. Financial support is provided by the eight professional organizations represented.[55]

Noel S. Paul, Council secretary, suggested that of the seven purposes outlined in the council's constitution, three are given greatest emphasis. These are: (1) to adjudicate complaints against newspapers; (2) to issue declarations and work toward the maintenance of high journalistic standards; and (3) to exert influence on legislation that will be beneficial. Complaints get the most attention, and most of the complaints are directed at newspapers. Magazines also are covered by the council, but they have been subjects of far fewer complaints. In 1969, for example, only five of 61 adjudications involved magazines. Radio and television are not covered by the Council.[56]

The plan for hearing complaints seems fair to all concerned and has discouraged libel actions. Anyone may file a complaint with the council, but first must seek redress directly from the publication. The Council will not consider complaints in cases where legal proceedings have been started or threatened. The Council investigates the complaints thoroughly and reports its findings in the media. Public opinion is relied upon to correct the faults of the offending publications. There are no fines, prison sentences or other legal sanctions. But newspapers are expected to publish the findings of the Council adjudications. Only five times in 16 years have papers refused to print the results. In the late 1960s the Council was receiving about 400 complaints annually, and about three-fourths of them were being handled without adjudication. In those adjudicated the newspaper stood a better than fifty-fifty chance of getting favorable findings.[57]

In keeping with British common law tradition, the Council has not prepared a formal code of ethics, but its adjudications have served as a guide for acceptable journalistic practices in the nation. A six-year, case-by-case analysis of adjudications from 1963 was made by Professor Donald E. Brown of Arizona State University. He reported that allegations of inaccuracy and of misleading news reports far outnumbered other types of complaints. Brown reported that cases involving cries of "one-party press" and accusations of party favoritism such as have been heard in the United States at various times in the past quarter of a century have been surprisingly rare. In addition to criticizing what it believed to be questionable newspaper practices, the council also has defended press rights.[58]

Secretary Paul suggested five chief areas in which progress has been made: (1) fewer complaints are now being made of newsmen intruding into the private lives of people in the news; (2) newspapers are publishing on their own more corrections of factual errors; (3) clearer boundaries are being established between articles of fact and opinion; (4) fairer procedures are being used for selecting and cutting letters to the editor; and (5) with its procedure for adjudicating complaints, the Council has saved newspapers and members of the public time and considerable expense by averting many court actions.[59]

The British Press Council appears to be helping both public and press in that country. But many do not think a similar council would serve equally well in the United States for reasons such as these: (1) National press councils can be effective only in countries where there are relatively few daily newspapers and a concentrated population with similar interests, tastes and background. The United States has about 1,774 daily newspapers and approximately 9,000 weeklies serving divergent interests spread over a large area. (2) Press councils could become vehicles for pressure groups to stifle the editorial independence of newspapers. (3) Pressure groups might lead to the licensing of journalists. (4) Sufficient checks and balances already exist to guarantee free speech and the right of an injured party to seek redress. (5) Members of the media already are making their own assessments and making changes where appropriate. (6) If public opinion is not a sufficient check on the press now, press councils would not make it so.[60]

Press council proponents argue that press councils need not become the tools of pressure groups or government; that some within the media either are unaware of their faults or are unwilling to act unless more public pressure is brought; that press councils could provide useful guidance; and that councils could help bring press and public closer together. They contend that press councils should be explored further at the national level and expanded at local and state levels.[61]

At least three major proposals for action at the national level were discussed in the early 1970s. Houstoun Waring, editor emeritus of the *Littleton* (Colorado) *Independent*, urged in 1969 that a National Press Council be created by the Association for Education in Journalism to report annually on the state of communications in America. He suggested that such a council might issue separate reports on individual media, but that its principal force would come from a condensed annual statement that could be widely circulated. In 1969 and subsequent years Waring issued model reports of his own along the lines suggested for the national council. These included generalizations about the status of the mass media and brief comments on individual media and related areas. He expressed particular concern about the trend toward conglomerate ownership of the media.[62] AEJ members, most of whom are teachers of journalism at the college level, discussed the Waring proposal; but many seemed reluctant to establish such a body, perhaps fearing that it would deter efforts to build closer relationships between practicing journalists and journalism schools and departments.

Norman Isaacs, executive editor of the *Louisville Courier-Journal* and *Times,* sought during his term as president of the American Society of Newspaper Editors in 1969 to get that body to establish a grievance committee to hear complaints against the press. Isaacs and members of the ASNE board, after studying the British Press Council, concluded that a country as large and diverse as the United States could not easily adapt itself to the British model. But Isaacs urged that the ASNE set up its own committee to receive complaints of substance about the performance of daily newspapers. Some members of the ASNE board opposed the idea, and the board finally decided in February,

1970, to establish instead a special committee on ethics to probe the matter further. Additional studies were made, but it appeared in 1972 that the majority of ASNE members rejected the establishment by ASNE of grievance machinery, censure procedures or any other method of subjecting individual editors to group judgment concerning their professional ethics. The ASNE did at that time ask its ethics committee to carry out a thorough surveillance of ethical problems confronting newspaper editors and maintain a continuing review of public criticism of the profession. The committee was expected to encourage individual editors to discuss publicly questions of professional ethics and explore ways of disseminating information on ethical standards so that individual members of the public could better judge their newspapers.[63] The ASNE has had a code of ethics for about a half century, but it has shied away from taking any strong sanctions against members who violate it. The only means of enforcement is expulsion from the society, and members have been reluctant to do that.[64]

While the AEJ assessment and ASNE grievance proposals were being discussed, a task force created by the Twentieth Century Fund developed a third proposal, which in 1973 was implemented. The task force included nine representatives from the media and five laymen. Lucy Wilson Benson, national president of the League of Women Voters, and Judge C. Donald Peterson of the Minnesota Supreme Court served as joint chairmen. Members studied the press council idea for a year and a half before making their report and recommendations in November 1972.[65] They recommended that an independent and private national news council be established to receive, examine and report on complaints concerning the accuracy and fairness of news reporting in the United States as well as initiate studies and report on issues involving freedom of the press. Their proposal limits the council's investigations to the principal national suppliers of news, including the major wire services, the largest supplemental news services, the national weekly newsmagazines, national newspaper syndicates, national daily newspapers and the nationwide broadcasting networks. Included would be Associated Press and United Press International; large services such as the New York Times Service and Washington Post-Los Angeles Times Service; newsmagazines such as *Time, Newsweek* and *U.S. News & World Report;* the newspaper syndicates; national dailies such as *The Wall Street Journal* and *The Christian Science Monitor;* and the networks, including Public Broadcasting Service. Excluded would be the vast majority of newspapers, stations and other media.

With financial support from the Twentieth Century Fund and seven other foundations, the proposed National News Council was established in 1973. Justice Roger Traynor, former chief justice of California, was named chairman and head of the founding committee. Besides Justice Traynor, the council included eight "public" members and six media members. The public members included a former senator, a former congressman, a feminist, two black leaders and a law school dean; three of the public members and one of the media members are women; two of the public members had media associations.[66] William B. Arthur, former editor of *Look* magazine was named executive director of the council; and Ned Schnurman, former city editor of WCBS-TV News was named associate director. Arthur said the council would consider two types of complaints: (1) public complaints from any citizen or group in the United States concerning the accuracy or fairness of news disseminated by national news media and (2) media complaints from any news organization or person in a news organization concerning attempts to restrict the freedom of a national news organization to gather and disseminate news. He said the council would not concern itself with editorial comment.[67]

Council procedures for handling complaints were modeled after those established for the British Press Council and the Minnesota State Press Council. Complainants must seek to resolve grievances with the media organization involved before the council will initiate action, and complainants must waive the right to legal proceedings in court on any matter taken up in council proceedings. Action by the council is limited to the public reporting of its decisions. The council has no enforcement powers. When appropriate, the council staff will engage teams of experts to investigate complaints. One of the first studies launched by the council in late 1973 concerned the potential threat to a free press posed by increased demands for governmental regulation of access to the media. Many of the early complaints received by the council concerned editorial opinions and thus were not considered. But complaints concerning accuracy and conflict of interest were upheld by the council during its first year of operation.[68]

Media reaction to the creation of the National News Council was mixed. Some such as Herbert Brucker in Hartford, the *Denver Post, Cleveland Plain Dealer, Lincoln* (Nebraska) *Star, Des Moines Register* and *St. Louis Post-Dispatch* spoke favorably of its potential. Others including Tom Wicker of the *New York Times,* the *Los Angeles Times,* the *New York Daily News,* the *Phoenix* (Arizona) *Republic* and *The Miami Herald* expressed opposition. Some major suppliers of news indicated a willingness to cooperate; some did not. Barry Bingham, Sr., chairman of the board, *Louisville Courier-Journal,* and a member of the Twentieth Century Fund task force, expressed cautious optimism over the willingness of AP, UPI, CBS, *The Washington Post, Christian Science Monitor* and *Wall Street Journal* to work with the council, noting that their reactions to the proposal ranged from guarded acquiescence to actual endorsement.[69] It appeared that many members of the media were taking a wait-and-see attitude toward the experiment. They recognized its potential but were not sure if it would work.

Many persons both inside and outside the media also were watching with interest the progress of the nation's first state press council. The Minnesota Press Council was formed in 1971 through efforts of the Minnesota Newspaper

Association. It is composed of nine public and nine press members, and is patterned after the independent British Press Council. Like its British model, the Minnesota body will not consider grievances unless the complainants first seek redress directly from the newspapers involved and waive the right of future civil action arising out of the grievance. C. Donald Peterson, an associate justice of the state supreme court, has served as initial chairman of the council and chairman of its two principal committees, grievance and general purpose. He emphasized that the council is an extralegal body with no enforcement powers whose effectiveness will depend on the cooperation of the press and the public. Peterson said that if the council finds a newspaper is not in error, it will attempt to resolve the misunderstanding by the complainant; and if it finds the newspaper is in error, it will transmit its finding to the newspaper, the complainant, and the media for publication. He said this was as far as the council could go in imposing penalties for confirmed violations of good journalistic practice, but that he believed such adverse publicity could effectively correct any abuses.[70]

Robert C. King, editor of the *Minneapolis Star,* reported in 1973 that the council had heard only five cases in its first 30 months of operation. Three of these were decided against the newspapers, two against the complainants. There were other complaints to the council, but they were either worked out with both parties before the official hearing stage or were judged not to be of sufficient merit to continue. King said that there was not enough evidence to determine how the public felt about the council at that time but that the council had kept the confidence of the newspapers because of the stature of its members.[71] Selection of well-respected public members and press members for council membership probably should be a major concern of press associations or others seeking to create their own press councils.

Reports concerning the development of local press councils were mixed. Some councils were successful; some were not. Less than two dozen councils were started in the five years after a Mellett Fund grant revitalized the local council idea in 1967. Only about a dozen of these, including two of the six Mellett councils, were still in existence in late 1972. Still it was evident that the councils had had some positive effects. Members of the press involved in the councils were made more aware of the need for superior performance, and members of the public were made more aware of press efforts to achieve it.[72] In most instances the local councils included a cross section of local citizens and representatives of the press. Some local councils involved only newspapers and the public; some also involved the broadcast media. Some served smaller communities such as Littleton, Colorado; Bend, Oregon; Redwood City, California; and Sparta and Cairo, Illinois; others served cities such as Seattle, St. Louis and Honolulu. One reportedly helped improve communications between the black community and the media; another helped settle a feud between a city administration and the media; another was dropped because the newspaper believed the public representatives were being too kind.[73] About 80% of 234 daily newspaper executives who responded to a Stanford University survey reported in 1974 indicated that they do not think local councils are necessary. But 68% indicated that they probably or definitely would answer questions raised by such a body and 76% indicated that they probably or definitely would print council judgments, including those critical of their newspapers. The survey included newspapers of all sizes.[74]

Opinions expressed by Robert W. Chandler, publisher of the *Bend Bulletin,* should encourage other persons in the media to consider local councils. Chandler said the Bend council had resulted in a better newspaper and was worth continuing on a permanent basis. "What we have done over the past three years," Chandler said, "is to create a knowledgeable, literate, articulate group of citizens who meet regularly to put our performance under a microscope. They do not tell us how to run our newspaper. They do tell us what they think of the way we run it. They accept, and seek, complaints from readers about our performance, and tell us whether they think the readers are right. We were surprised and pleased when members of the council, after hearing a full explanation from both sides, agreed at least in part with the newspaper in most cases." [75]

Unquestionably, newspapers need the understanding and support of the public if they are to carry out their roles and responsibilities successfully. Newspapers can effectively serve individuals, communities and the nation only if they are willing to be served. Newspapers can survive rising costs and increasing competition only if the public understands its own need for newspapers and supports them. Newspapers should seek renewed public confidence through the exploration of press councils as well as the operation of their own accountability procedures. The National News Council could prove useful in improving the national suppliers of news, increasing public appreciation of them, and fostering the growth of a free and responsible press. A national group to report annually on the state of the media could prove helpful to the media and the public. A national council to serve the majority of newspapers and stations seems impracticable, but state and local councils could prove beneficial. Newspapers need public support and must earn it through responsible performance of their basic roles and responsibilities. The people need newspapers to help them adjust to change, improve themselves and their communities, and make democracy work effectively. They should demand the best of their newspapers and reward them accordingly.

2

The Development of
American Newspapers

THE ROLES and responsibilities exercised by contemporary newspapers in the United States evolved over a long period of time. Some knowledge and understanding of their development is essential to placing them into proper perspective today. Newspapers have been vital to American government and American life since Colonial days, but their approaches toward news and opinion have changed. They have changed in appearance as well as concept, and their methods of production and distribution have been greatly modified. It is important to review their history to see the roles they have played in the development of the nation, to absorb lessons from history that need not be repeated, to place into perspective the achievements and failures of past journalists, and to obtain a better understanding of American history as a whole.

Special attention should be given to the development of freedom and responsibility of the press. The right to publish without a license, the right to criticize public officials fairly, and the right of access to information about public affairs are basic to press freedom. But they have not always been considered rights, and some question their validity today.

Those desiring a better understanding of contemporary newspapers must look both to the history of the medium itself and to the history of its relationship to the nation as a whole. How have newspapers evolved as a medium of information, influence, entertainment and advertising? How have newspapers affected the development of the nation and its people? Several scholars including Frank Luther Mott and Edwin Emery have sought to answer these and other questions about the development of the press in some detail. Emery's *The Press and America: An Interpretative History of Journalism,* revised in 1972, is perhaps the most detailed single account of the history of newspapers

49

and other media in the United States. Mott's *American Journalism,* last revised in 1962, is also highly regarded. John Tebbel has written several books dealing with newspaper history, including *The Compact History of the American Newspaper,* published in 1963. Several other general histories and many histories of individual newspapers are available. Some of these books and pertinent articles are listed in the bibliography. This brief chapter will attempt to highlight basic developments as background for a more detailed look at newspapers in the 1970s.

A RICH HERITAGE

The history of newspapers in America might logically begin with the first efforts to produce them in the Colonial period. But better perspective may be obtained if newspapers, including those here, are discussed as a major development in the story of man's efforts to communicate with other men. Communication grew out of a need to communicate. As the need increased, the methods used became more sophisticated. Symbols and materials for communication were developed, and the information or news concept evolved. At first, men may have relied on gestures and crude sounds. Then they developed the use of objects such as knotted cords and notched sticks to serve as records and reminders. Later they began to record information and ideas through the use of pictures carved into stone tablets or on the walls of caves. The ancient Egyptians are particularly noted for their sacred writings, or hieroglyphics, of this kind. In time men gave phonetic, or sound, values to pictures or symbols, and a spoken alphabet evolved. The Babylonians and especially the Phoenicians pioneered in the development of writing. Need was a major incentive for the Phoenicians, who were the great traders of the Mediterranean world and required improved systems of communications. The Greeks modified the Phoenician system somewhat. The Romans, and subsequently the Anglo-Saxons, modified the modifications to produce the modern alphabet of 26 letters. These were the symbols of communication.

Meanwhile, improved materials for communication were being developed. At first the stone and clay tablets sufficed for most peoples. Then the Egyptians discovered that the papyrus plant which grew in abundance along the Nile could be used as a writing material. The Greeks and Romans used tablets with wax on them for a time, and the Romans developed the use of animal skins for writing. The skin from sheep and goats was called parchment. The skin of calves was called vellum. Both were and are expensive, but they are durable and still find uses today. The Chinese apparently developed a form of paper from cotton, rags, hemp and tree bark by the second century after Christ, and its use gradually moved westward. But it was not until the fourteenth century that paper really became common in Europe.

Reeds were used as pens, and various substances such as tree gum or sap mixed with soot and other ingredients were used for ink. Most of the information was transferred to paper, skins or tablets by hand until the fifth or sixth century when the Chinese developed a form of block printing. Under this system, images and words were carved into blocks, inked and pressed against the paper or other printing material. Block printing became common in Europe by the fifteenth century.

At the same time the concept of disseminating information, or news, was being developed. Information not unlike that distributed by county agents to farmers today was distributed in what is now Iraq hundreds of years before Christ. When Julius Caesar became consul in the first century A.D., he ordered that the activities of the Senate be published. Proclamations were published, and letters exchanged. Town criers and ballad-singers brought news to the people vocally, and handwritten sheets of information were distributed. The Chinese reportedly developed a forerunner of today's newspaper as early as the seventh or eighth century. As the need for communication increased, the symbols, materials and methods of providing it became more sophisticated.

Johann Gutenberg provided a major breakthrough about 1450 when he developed the means to cast and use movable type that could be used time and again. The Chinese probably developed a system of movable word type several centuries earlier, but the idea was not quickly transmitted to Europe. Gutenberg developed brass molds to cast individual letters, and he developed an improved ink out of lampblack and oil. He printed his communications on a press somewhat similar to the winepress of the day. The type was held in place by a wooden frame placed on a flat bed of wood. Ink and then paper were placed on the type, and a wooden platen was pressed down on them to make an impression.

The development of movable type opened the way for the development of mass media. Hundreds of copies could be reproduced in a short period of time. Information and education were no longer dependent on the hand-written efforts of a few nor as easily subject to controls. Numerous publications, including some newspapers, were produced in Europe in the sixteenth and seventeenth centuries. But the breakthrough in publication potential was not accompanied by an immediate breakthrough in press freedom. On the contrary, those in power who had sought to monopolize earlier forms of communication sought also to control the development and use of printing. Kings and princes and those who sought to oppose them realized the potential of printing and sought to use it for their own purposes. The modern struggle for press freedom was soon joined.

England, which in time provided the model for American journalism, was ruled by a series of autocratic monarchs during the early development years of modern printing. The absolutist Tudors came to power shortly after printing was introduced into England and remained in power until early in the seventeenth century. Generally, they used the new methods to further their own interests. They discouraged those who would use them for other purposes. The Tudors employed licensing, libel and sedition laws, and the creation of a printers' trust to keep a tight hand on the new printing processes. No true newspapers were developed in this hostile atmosphere, although some persons did produce printed materials which the Crown found objectionable.

Newspapers were developed in seventeenth century England, as they later were in America, to satisfy a need for improved communication. By 1603 when the last of the Tudors died and a Stuart, James I, succeeded to the throne of England, the people had had a surfeit of autocratic rule. They had accepted the dictatorial Tudor approach at first because the Tudors brought national security out of crises and subsequently national prosperity and international prestige. But after a hundred years the people felt secure; they wanted individual freedom, including free speech. The Stuart century, which ended in 1714, was thus one of great conflict and change. The Parliament gained supremacy over the Crown. The upper classes, at least, gained many individual freedoms, and the party system evolved. Out of this conflict, and in response to the needs it created, developed the English press—first newspapers, and later magazines. Although neither entirely free nor consistently responsible, the early newspapers did provide a vehicle for wider expression of opposing views as well as a medium for other news and advertising. Similar needs and conflicts later resulted in an American press.

The earliest English publications resembling newspapers were the corantos and diurnals. The corantos, or news books, were started at least in part to report on the foreign activities of the English monarch. Some were suppressed for criticizing the Crown; others that acted more circumspectly were tolerated. The diurnals, or day books, were among the first efforts to report domestic news, especially the activities of Parliament. They helped to document the continuing debates between Crown and Parliament.

Neither corantos nor diurnals could qualify as newspapers by modern definitions, but they did demonstrate the potential of the press and point the way toward later developments. The first publication generally designated as a newspaper was a controlled publication founded in 1665 by the head of the Crown's printing monopoly. It was first called the *Oxford Gazette* and later after being moved to London the *London Gazette*. It was essentially a court journal, but is significant because it was the first English newspaper and because it is the oldest continuous publication in the English language. In 1965 it celebrated its 300th anniversary. The *Gazette* and most other early English publications were published with the permission or approval of the Crown.

England got its first daily newspaper, the *Daily Courant,* and its first magazine shortly after the turn of the century. The *Courant,* published in London, was small in size, limited in coverage and circumspect in commentary, but it was a beginning. Although she did not remain in the post long, the *Courant's* first editor was a woman. England's first magazine, *The Review,* was started about the same time by Daniel Defoe, a persuasive and vivid writer better known for his story of Robinson Crusoe. At first it was difficult to distinguish between newspapers and magazines. But in time the newspapers came to place more emphasis on timeliness while the magazines were recognized as storehouses of information about various topics.

Perhaps the best known publications of the early eighteenth century were the *Tatler* and the *Spectator* of Joseph Addison and Richard Steele. Through their often humorous essays these editors helped to mould the ideas and tastes of urban England, and they developed a literary style that was widely emulated in England and in the colonies for many years. Although the publications might best be described as magazines, the style produced also served as a model for newspapers.

Other English writers also produced models for their American counterparts or provided them with arguments to use in their own battles for press freedom and representative government. John Milton provided a classic argument for a free press in his *Areopagitica,* published in 1644 but more widely distributed later. John Trenchard and Thomas Gordon in their famous Cato letters also provided materials which the colonists reproduced to substantiate their call for liberty and representative government.

The press in England remained severely restricted throughout much of the eighteenth century. Parliament enacted a tax in 1712, sometimes called the Tax on Knowledge, that hampered press growth for a century and a half. It was not until late in the century that the press got some protection against libel and greater freedom to cover the activities of Parliament. These early newspapers were certainly not free, but then neither were they models of responsibility. They have been accused with some justification of inaccuracies, sensationalism and inconsistencies between editorial ideals and advertising policies. But they did provide a source of information and a method of communication not previously available; and in so doing, they rendered a significant contribution to the development of government, business and other phases of English life. In so doing they also provided the model for newspaper developments in colonial America.

COLONIAL DEVELOPMENTS

Newspapers were developed in the American colonies, as elsewhere, to meet a need for improved communications. The first colonies were in the South, but the first newspapers were started in New England because people there had a need for them sooner. There were more people living closer together there than there were in the South, and as a whole they were more prosperous and better educated. They achieved a greater degree of self-government sooner, and they developed the business and industry that could benefit from advertising much more rapidly. In a sense the climate and terrain which dictated that New Englanders would settle closer together and engage in small farming and industry rather than settle on large plantations made the difference. The higher density of population fostered education, a demand for self-government and a need for advertising.

Newspapers were not developed sooner in the colonies because they were not needed sooner. Most persons knew already what was going on in their small communities. They got other news from the English papers that were shipped to the colonies periodically, and there was little business or commerce in the early years to support local publications.

The need for better communication was growing in the late seventeenth century when Benjamin Harris decided to start a newspaper in Boston. His failure signaled the formal beginning of a press-government struggle that has continued in America until the present day. Harris had received some acclaim for his almanacs and *New England Primer,* and his "newspaper" might have been well-received also if it had survived its first issue. Harris' *Publick Occurrences, Both Foreign and Domestick* was stopped, however, because Harris sought to publish without the approval of government and because he, at least indirectly, offended the government. The objectionable materials raised questions about the alleged savagery of the Indians, then allied with the English, and alleged immorality in the French Court.

After the suppression of Harris' paper, no one even tried to start another one for almost 15 years. Moreover, when the next newspaper, the *Boston News Letter,* was published, it was published with the permission of the government. The *News Letter* and many of the papers that followed it were published by local postmasters, and they are sometimes referred to as postmaster papers. In some respects, postmasters were in an ideal position to operate newspapers. They were usually well-informed about community affairs and they had a franking privilege. But since they were political appointees who owed primary allegiance to the government that appointed them, they were not likely to be critical or probing in their coverage. Postmaster papers did provide some local news as well as exchange items from other publications, but they could not be described as either free or responsible.

The first successful effort to publish a newspaper without authority in the colonies came in Boston in the early 1720s. The paper was called the *New England Courant,* and it was published by James Franklin, older brother of Benjamin Franklin. Although it survived government pressures fewer than six years, the *Courant* did demonstrate an important idea: the press supported by public opinion can be a powerful force in the affairs of man. For his criticism of government, Franklin was jailed for a time and ordered not to publish a newspaper in that colony. He moved on to the less restrictive atmosphere of Rhode Island to practice his trade and subsequently he published in Newport that colony's first newspaper. Even though its life was short, the *Courant* represented a major beachhead in the struggle to publish without a license.

James Franklin's younger brother, Ben, also made a substantial contribution to colonial journalism. In fact, he was perhaps the most successful, financially and otherwise, of all the colonial journalists. Franklin did everything well. He gained fame as a diplomat, a scientist and a businessman. He was at home with the rich and the poor, in the parlors of Europe and the backshops of America. But above all, he was a writer, a journalist, a printer.

Benjamin Franklin easily surpassed two business competitors to become publisher of the principal newspaper in Philadelphia. He made that newspaper, the *Pennsylvania Gazette,* into one of the colonies' best publications, carrying both news and literary comment. Franklin had a rare knack for tactful criticism that got his point across without bringing repressions on his newspaper. His success can be measured in terms of advertising, circulation, numbers of pages published, and similar figures as well as in influence. Franklin also was instrumental in the development of many other newspaper ventures, including a number of foreign language newspapers. Above all, Franklin demonstrated that a printer-journalist could serve his community and earn a good livelihood at the same time. Many printers who accepted the responsibility to comment on the affairs of the day suffered economic difficulties. Others who were more circumspect in their commentary about government and other affairs failed to serve public opinion as they should. Franklin managed to achieve both goals successfully, and in so doing he helped make journalism a profession rather than a trade.

Benjamin Harris and the Franklins led the early struggle of the press to publish without special permission of government. John Peter Zenger, a New York immigrant, led the early struggle to criticize that government on occasion. Zenger started his *New York Weekly Journal* in the early 1730s in part to provide a voice for the rising merchant class in New York. These city merchants were making an important contribution to the development of the colony but were restricted in their participation in its government by the landowner class that had established it. When neither the Governor nor the existing paper would support their cause, the merchants turned to Zenger. He championed their cause, and was soon arrested for making statements critical of the New York colonial government. A grand jury refused to indict him, but he was brought to trial for seditious libel on an ''information.''

According to precedent, Zenger's jury was to decide only if he had in fact published the alleged libel. The judge, appointed by the Crown, had the responsibility of determining whether the statement was libelous. The situation looked bleak for Zenger, especially when his defense lawyer, the noted Philadelphian Andrew Hamilton, opened his defense by admitting that Zenger had in fact published the statements in question. According to precedent, Zenger's trial was over. But Hamilton had just begun. He told the jurors that it was for them, not the judge, to decide if the remarks admitted by Zenger were libelous; and he told them that they should consider the truth of the statements in reaching their decision. Whether by the force of this argument, Hamilton's emotional appeal, the desirability to support those whom Zenger had aided, or perhaps all three, the jury voted him not guilty.

The court could have overruled the verdict of its jury, and, in accordance with precedence, sentenced Zenger. But it chose not to oppose the power of public opinion at this point, and Zenger was freed. The principles that in such cases the jury should decide both law and fact and that truth should be admitted as a defense did not immediately become part of the American system of law. It was not until after another libel case in the early nineteenth century that they came to be incorporated in the statutes of the various states. But the Zenger case did suggest a new precedent. It gave substance to the idea that the people should have the right to criticize public officials, provided they can support their charges with truthful data and fair arguments.

While the results of the Zenger case are laudable, some may question the method of achieving them. Should long-established legal precedents be changed through politically influenced court decisions rather than through an amending process? Others would counter by asking how long must the people wait for their will to become law. It is a crucial question that remains to confront Americans in the late twentieth century.

Little need be said of the press in the South during Colonial times. There were fewer persons in the South. They lived farther apart, and they lacked some of the impetus for press development that was present in New England and the Middle Colonies. There was no great audience for newspapers and not as much need to advertise products and services. The few papers that were developed generally were of high literary quality and compared favorably with those in other colonies. But the need, or lack of it, restricted the number until the late eighteenth and early nineteenth centuries.

Most of the colonial newspapers were small in format, about the size of modern typewriter paper. They had few pages. The headlines, if they can properly be called that, were about the size of the body type, which was small, and there were few illustrations. Although they were physically much smaller, the papers then somewhat resembled today's classified advertising pages. The contents usually included essays about various subjects, exchange items from other newspapers—especially English papers—advertising and some local news, mostly in the form of vital statistics. Opinion, whether that of the editor or someone else, generally was expressed in essay form. Production methods were not unlike those used by Gutenberg several centuries before, and distribution was limited.

Nevertheless, the vehicle was there for providing information, advertising and forceful comment when the occasion demanded. Many persons were informed, entertained, influenced and assisted by advertising. Moreover, by the middle of the eighteenth century, the newspapers had gained sufficient stature to pose as a safeguard against arrogant administrators. By the 1760s they were ready to play an important role in the rapidly developing revolutionary debate.

NEWSPAPERS AND THE RISE OF A NEW NATION

Through their advocacies and their reporting of opinions and events newspapers helped to create a new government in America. During the colonial period they helped present the grievances of the colonists and the replies of the English government. During the Revolution itself they helped rally Americans to the cause and helped them sustain their purpose through difficult times. During the years that followed they presented the debates concerning what forms the new government should take and served as spokesman for the parties that soon developed.

It would be misleading to suggest that propagandists using newspapers and other media created a revolution that most Americans did not want. There were fundamental economic, constitutional and philosophical differences between the mother country and her American colonies. Parental inattention at times and physical distance itself undoubtedly contributed to misunderstandings. But it does not seem unreasonable to suggest that the Revolution came when it did as a result of propaganda disseminated in newspapers, pamphlets, magazines and by word of mouth.

Three principal points of view were expounded in the colonial press and elsewhere prior to the Revolution. Those advancing them generally were referred to as Tories, Whigs and Radicals. The Tories sought to maintain the status quo. They conceded that some of the grievances presented against the English government were legitimate. But they maintained that the English government was the best anywhere in the world and urged that those with grievances present them through proper channels. The Whigs sought home rule. They were men of affluence in America who wanted to exercise influence. They did not want revolution, at least not at first. They wanted what they believed to be their rights as Englishmen. The Radicals, or Patriots as they became known when their cause at least temporarily became the national cause, wanted home rule and the opportunity to participate in that rule. They were members of the lower and middle class economic groups who wanted greater opportunities to participate in government.

Patriots such as Samuel Adams and Thomas Paine fired the flames of separation. Whigs such as John Dickinson made it respectable. Dickinson's arguments against "taxation without representation" opened the way for Adams and Paine to demand justice or separation. Paine's ability to convert academic arguments into action language is perhaps unexcelled in all history. He sounded the call for freedom in publications such as *Pennsylvania Magazine* and *Common Sense*. He reassured the followers in the *Crisis* papers. Colonial newspapers originated some of the arguments for freedom and spread others. Adams, for example, was a regular contributor to the *Boston Gazette and Country Journal*, which came to be known as a primary source of Patriot views. Dickinson expressed his views in a series of letters in the *Pennsylvania Chronicle*. Paine's views were widely disseminated by many colonial papers. Tory views also were expressed in newspapers such as James Rivington's *Gazette*. But in time the Patriot views prevailed.

Most newspapers had difficulty in covering the war, and many were hard-pressed to continue publication at all. There were no wire services to transmit news, and communication was poor. It took weeks for the news of Lexington and Concord to reach Savannah. There were few correspondents, and coverage was limited to what an editor could get on his own in his locale and from other newspapers. Supplies, most of which had been imported from England, were difficult to obtain. The British armies forced many papers to flee to another location or cease publication. Many newspapers did fail, but a number also were started in spite of the difficulties, and the total number at the end of the war was about the same as it was in the beginning, about 35.

Considering the hardships, the newspapers did a remarkable job of reporting events and unifying the Patriots. They disseminated important essays such as Paine's *Crisis* papers, they made appeals for recruits, described battles, and published the acts of the new state legislatures and the national government. Some newspapers even put out occasional handbills, or extras, to supply the news more quickly than their weekly editions could provide. As a result of their efforts the newspapers gained greatly in prestige and influence if not always in revenue and affluence.

Newspapers continued to play a vital role after the fighting ceased. They grew and developed with the nation they helped create and sustain. The first daily newspapers were started in Philadelphia in the middle 1780s, and others were begun in other major cities in subsequent years. Newspapers published the debates concerning important post-war questions just as they had published Colonial grievances and British replies in the earlier years. The overriding issue was whether the United States would be a confederation of states or a single nation of states. Finally, a compromise of many issues was achieved in the Constitution of 1787, and the press helped publicize this document and the arguments for and against its adoption. The best-known arguments for the proposed constitution were presented in the *Federalist* papers prepared by Alexander Hamilton, James Madison and John Jay. Most of these papers appeared first in the *New York Independent Journal* as proponents sought to win that state for adoption.

The Constitution as amended almost immediately by the Bill of Rights (first Ten Amendments) outlined at least in a general way the path that the new nation should follow. The continuing value of newspapers was recognized in the First Amendment, which reads in part, "Congress shall make no law . . .

abridging the freedom of speech or of the press. . . ." This guarantee has, of course, been subject to interpretation. The press has faced continual challenges from overzealous officials, and some of its members have failed to assure the responsibility that must accompany freedom. But the First Amendment has provided a cornerstone of press freedom. It has helped make it possible for newspapers and other media to serve as watchdogs over government and guardians of American democracy and individual rights.

Freedom was more evident than responsibility in many of the papers that helped foster the development of the party system in the United States in the late eighteenth and early nineteenth centuries. Most newspapers of the period were published either for commercial or party purposes. As the factions President Washington and others decried developed into parties, they started or purchased newspapers to spread their views. Alexander Hamilton was chief spokesman of the conservatives who favored a strong national government, loose construction of the Constitution, conservative fiscal policies and similar ideas. Thomas Jefferson was the leader of those who emphasized state rights, strict construction of the Constitution, more liberal fiscal policies and related views. Newspapers of both persuasions vied for attention and support, sometimes at a high level of debate, often not.

Many of the early party papers were irresponsible in their attacks on the opposition. Invective often took precedence over argument. Even President Washington was accused of debauching, deceiving and improperly influencing the nation. Unfortunately, but not unexpectedly for the times, the government overreacted to the criticism it received. Outspoken criticism of the Federalist party in power by anti-Federalist or Republican editors led to the Alien and Sedition Acts of 1798. These acts were designed, at least in part, to silence criticism of the government, the Congress and the President. The Sedition Act was not as bad as sometimes pictured, however, for it sought to punish anyone convicted of publishing "false, scandalous, and malicious writing. . . ." [1] The idea, advanced in the Zenger case, that truth should be considered as a defense in such matters was given new impetus. Not many persons were actually convicted under the act, but the threat may have been considerable. Some Republicans wanted to turn the law on the Federalists when Thomas Jefferson was elected president in 1800, but he suggested that such matters be left to the states and the Sedition Act was permitted to die.

Fortunately, the Zenger principles did not die but were incorporated into various state statutes after the trial of Harry Croswell in New York in 1804. Croswell was accused of making a malicious attack in his paper, *The Wasp,* on President Jefferson. He was tried under a New York law and convicted, perhaps deservedly so since the charges against Jefferson were highly questionable. But in arguing Croswell's appeal Alexander Hamilton presented a strong case for press freedom that greatly impressed many persons. The idea that truth should be a defense in libel and sedition cases was widely accepted. New York passed a law to assure the right to the people, and other states soon followed suit. The right of the press to criticize government, provided its criticism is fair and truthful, was more firmly embedded in the American system.

President Jefferson's views of the press, its roles and responsibilities, are particularly noteworthy. Although he became disillusioned by the irresponsibility of some papers in the early nineteenth century, he is generally regarded as one of the great champions of a free press. On one occasion he noted that "No government ought to be without censors; and where the press is free, no one ever will." [2] He regarded the press as essential to the formation of public opinion and the maintenance of freedom. Said Jefferson: "The basis of our governments being the opinion of the people, the very first object should be to keep that right; and were it left to me to decide whether we should have a government without newspapers, or newspapers without government, I should not hesitate a moment to prefer the latter. But I should mean that every man should receive those papers, and be capable of reading them." [3]

The responsible press envisioned by Jefferson did not evolve in the early decades of the nineteenth century. But a few papers such as the *National Intelligencer,* New York *Evening Post,* and *Journal of Commerce* offered some hopes for the future. The *National Intelligencer* was a quasi-party paper which provided fairly complete and objective coverage of the national government from the early 1800s to the early 1830s. It was criticized by some who preferred more partisanship in their papers. But its reports on Congress, published in 1834 as the *Annals of Congress,* provide the most nearly complete record of that body's deliberations during the early nineteenth century. The New York *Post* was started by Alexander Hamilton in 1801 to help keep Federalism alive, and under various editors was developed into one of the nation's best newspapers. The *Journal of Commerce* was a leading example of the business paper which developed with the rise of cities.

By the 1820s there were about 25 dailies and more than 400 weeklies being published in the United States. Circulations were not large, seldom more than 1,500 in the cities and a few hundred in the towns. Contents varied, but aside from partisan politics, most of the papers' space was devoted to literary miscellany, exchange items, local news about births, deaths and other vital statistics and advertising. Domestic news, including local coverage, gradually became more important, particularly after the War of 1812. But foreign news continued to get considerable play.

By the early nineteenth century some papers expressed their opinions in short paragraphs rather than the anonymous essays of the earlier years. Most papers continued the use of "annual advertisements," or advertisements that remained unchanged for many weeks. Only limited improvements were made in production techniques, and most papers continued to look much like today's classified pages. There were few headlines in the modern sense and few illustrations.

Undoubtedly, the most significant accomplishment of the press between 1760 and 1830 was its contribution to the development of a new nation. Newspapers were active before, during and after the Revolution in the creation of a new and more democratic government. Unfortunately, the freedom enjoyed by the press during these years was not always exercised in a responsible way. Fortunately, the free press was permitted to mature with the free country it helped to create and maintain.

NEWSPAPERS AND THE NEW DEMOCRACY

American newspapers experienced a revolution in purpose and production techniques in the 1830s. The causes were many and varied, yet sometimes interrelated. The industrial revolution was an underlying factor. It created new industry and new business which augmented the growth of cities and increased the demand for advertising. The rise of cities brought more people closer together and fostered the growth of education. Education increased the potential reading public and the demand for something to read. Some of the techniques which revolutionized other industries also helped revolutionize the production of newspapers. Equally important, the 1830s brought the rise of Andrew Jackson and the expansion of democracy. The need to inform increasing numbers of persons was greatly magnified.

Andrew Jackson made extensive use of the old party paper approach in his long campaign for the presidency and in his two terms in office. His *Washington Globe* has been described as the ultimate example of the party newspaper in action. It helped postmasters, surveyors, Indian agents and other office holders keep up with changes in party doctrine. It served as a guide for all who wished to know what the President was thinking and planning. It was a strong weapon to use against the opposition. Jackson relied heavily on his newspaper advisers. At times, it appeared that he had more faith in them than in his duly appointed cabinet officers.

But in the final analysis, Jacksonian democracy with its emphasis on widespread participation in government helped to inspire the development of an inexpensive press for the masses. The masses in the cities wanted news, information and advertising, and a new group of editors arose to provide them. The party papers and the business papers did not cease to exist, but the "newspaper" became the dominant element in American journalism. The presentation of news, not party doctrine or commercial information, became the primary function of most newspapers.

The new newspapers are often referred to as "penny papers" because they were sold on the streets for a penny each. Prior to this time most newspapers were sold by subscription at a cost which averaged about six cents a copy. To sell for a penny something that had sold for six cents meant, of course, that the new papers had to reach more people and attract more advertising. They did both, although in seeking readers the papers were at times sensational. Crime, violence, romance and excitement were emphasized. But this emphasis gradually declined, to be renewed periodically when circumstances seemed favorable.

Benjamin Day founded the first of the penny papers in the fall of 1833. He called it the *New York Sun,* and adopted the slogan, "It Shines for All." Day promised to place all the news before the public at a price which anyone could afford. Much of the early material in the *Sun* was trivial, but it was interesting and inexpensive and people bought it. Within six months the *Sun* had a circulation of some 8,000, nearly twice that of its nearest rival. This rapid growth was due primarily to the price and content of the paper, but the method of distribution also helped. The penny papers used the so-called "London Plan" under which papers were sold at a reduced rate to vendors who sold them for a penny each on the streets. The street sales encouraged improvements in appearance but probably also encouraged sensationalism. Day sold out in a few years, but the *Sun* was continued and helped give rise to a new kind of newspaper.

In many respects the most successful of the penny press pioneers was James Gordon Bennett, who started the *New York Herald* a year or so after Day initiated the *Sun.* Bennett said the *Herald'*s only guide would be "good sound practical common sense. . . ." It would not support parties or candidates, but seek "to record facts, on every public and proper subject, stripped of verbiage and coloring, with comments suitable, just, independent, fearless and good-tempered. . . ." [4]

Translated into practice the *Herald'*s opening profession meant doing what the *Sun* was doing, doing more of it and doing it better. Under Bennett's direction until after the Civil War, the *Herald* became the nation's leading paper in circulation, and perhaps in influence. Bennett included trivia and sensationalism. He spoke in plain language. But he also pioneered in the development of many departments and programs common to newspapers today. He helped to develop sports, society and financial departments. He ran letters and critical reviews. He developed the system of beat reporters, wherein a reporter becomes a specialist in some activity or "beat." He employed correspondents in key cities in the United States and abroad, and he pioneered in the use of the telegraph to get news transmitted more rapidly. The *Herald* included some background information in its news stories, and it ran some informative if not always profound editorials. Bennett's ego and eccentricities may have limited his influence. He once engaged in a street fight with a former employer and bragged in his paper about how he won the encounter. He wrote at great length and little modesty about his marriage. He was not especially noted as a reformer. But Bennett apparently believed that an informed world would be a better world, and he worked toward that end. His paper was spicy and sensational at times, but it did report the news.

Better known perhaps than Bennett was Horace Greeley, who founded the

New York Tribune in 1841. Greeley was a reformer, and he probably had at least some influence in local, state and national affairs. He said he started the *Tribune* to give New York an inexpensive newspaper that would be less sensational than the *Sun* and the *Herald* and to provide an outlet for Whig views in that city. The daily edition never attained the circulation of the *Herald,* but the weekly edition by the 1850s was reaching 200,000 readers throughout the East and Middle West. Some said it was read second only to the Bible in many areas. Its influence, though not easy to measure, must have been considerable.

Greeley was important because through the *Tribune* he emphasized a serious discussion of issues as opposed to the simple emotionalism espoused by some. He challenged people to face the great issues of the day, such as slavery, as no paper had done before. Some question Greeley's direct influence on events, and such causal relationships are difficult to substantiate. Yet progress could be noted in his time in causes that he championed, including internal improvements, western development, abolition, the protective tariff and the advancement of labor.

Greeley's influence on President Lincoln during the Civil War may have been overstated, however. It more likely was northern military successes and international pressures rather than Greeley's editorials that caused Lincoln to issue the Emancipation Proclamation in late 1862 to be effective in January, 1863. But Greeley did urge Lincoln to act on the slavery question in his "Prayer of Twenty Millions" editorial in August, 1862, and on other occasions. The *Tribune* editor may also have played an important role in the Republican convention that chose Lincoln as its standard-bearer. Greeley himself was nominated as a presidential candidate in 1872 by liberal Republicans and Democrats. But he was a compromise choice of various groups disturbed by the events of President Grant's first term in office and lost decisively. Regardless of his political influence, or lack of it, Greeley should be remembered as a man who contributed much to the development of journalism.

Many other journalists and newspapers also contributed to the development of a new press for the masses in antebellum days. Henry J. Raymond made a major contribution in founding the *New York Times* in 1851. The *Times* was started to provide a well-balanced, well-written coverage of the day's news, and it became famous for its thoroughness and its objectivity. The *Baltimore Sun* became famous for its coverage of the nation's capital, and the *Chicago Tribune* was a leader in the development of the Middle West. By the 1840s most of the nation's major cities had inexpensive papers designed for the masses. Many of the nation's smaller papers also placed greater emphasis on news, and some may have exerted considerable influence in their own areas.

As a result of the new emphasis on news, the development of new printing techniques, and new communications devices such as the telegraph, the press of the 1850s was a vastly improved communication medium over the press of the 1820s. But neither the press nor other American institutions was able to generate the communication and understanding necessary to avert a destructive civil war. The majority of the nation's newspapers did not preach extremism. Many newspapers in the South opposed secession until it became a fact. Most newspapers elsewhere were not strongly anti-South, at least not until the war began. But perhaps the newspapers and other media failed to do enough to help people in the various sections understand and appreciate others' points of view. Not enough was done to counteract the influence of the few extremist editors on both sides of the controversy.

The *New York Herald* provided the most extensive coverage of the war, and it probably caused President Lincoln some sleepless nights. The *Herald* was the paper read by most persons in England and other foreign countries for news about the United States, and it was rather soft in its policies toward the South. Many of the larger newspapers in the North had their own correspondents in some areas. All probably depended to some extent on the coverage provided by the Associated Press that was founded in the late 1840s.

Newspapers in the South had a much more difficult time covering the war. They had imported most of their paper, ink and other supplies, and their sources were cut off. There was also a shortage of personnel. The South did not have the manpower to supply its armies and function normally on the home front too. As time progressed, the Northern armies also became a problem. Some of the Southern papers were taken over by occupation forces; some such as the *Memphis Appeal* sought to flee the advancing armies. The *Appeal* was published in several different states during the war. The Southern papers got most of their information about distant events from a Press Association they formed at the suggestion of a Macon, Georgia, newspaperman. This association did a remarkably accurate and objective job of covering the war.

Generally speaking, the newspapers on both sides enjoyed considerable freedom to report and comment on the war. A few were suspended for publishing materials that might retard the war effort. Some were wrecked by mobs who became upset at their attitudes toward the enemy. But the freedom to comment generally was upheld. Censorship was, of course, employed, particularly by military forces in the field. It was a new experience for Americans, and some errors were made in the early months of the war. But the basic censorship procedures established by the United States during the Civil War have been followed by this country in subsequent conflicts.

Several new reporting techniques were tried out during the war, especially by Northern papers. The inverted pyramid form of news writing and the summary lead became popular as newspapers sought to get as much information transmitted by telegraph as quickly as possible. Photography was also used by Matthew Brady and others to provide pictorial coverage of events. Pictures could not be processed quickly for immediate newspaper use then as they can today. Nor could the cameras of the day stop action as cameras now can. Nevertheless photography provided a whole new dimension to war coverage.

After the war the press entered something of a transition period caused in part by national events and in part by developments within the media, including the death of several major publishers. A number of papers experimented with new techniques in reporting and production. Some consolidated earlier advances of the middle nineteenth century such as multideck headlines, the use of longer editorials and the abandonment of annual advertisements. Some of the giants got new leadership. Many papers in the cities became involved in crusades against the corruption that developed in government and business after the war. Some sought to heal the divisions that were caused by the conflict. The *New York Sun,* acquired by Charles Dana after the war, was probably the leader in laying the foundations for a new revolution or expansion of journalism in the late decades of the nineteenth century.

A Second Revolution in Newspapers

American newspapers experienced something akin to a second revolution in the latter decades of the nineteenth century. They did not alter their basic function, established in the 1830s. They continued to emphasize news. But their methods of collecting, processing and presenting it were changed substantially. Many of the changes came as a response to the rapid expansion of American business, industry, government and population. More persons needed more information, and they needed it more rapidly. Some of the inventions that made possible the mass circulation papers of the late nineteenth century actually came before the Civil War. Some came after. But it was not until the latter years of the century that all were employed together on a massive scale in cities such as New York.

Some of the key developments included the Linotype, the half-tone engraving, the stereotype, the web-fed rotary press, color printing techniques and wood pulp paper used in the mechanical department, and the typewriter and telephone used in the news and advertising departments. The Linotype, or line of type, machine greatly accelerated the amount of type that could be set in a given time. Previously, all type had been set by hand, one letter at a time. The Linotype made it possible to cast whole lines instead of setting single letters. As each letter is typed on a keyboard somewhat similar to a typewriter, a mold of that letter falls into place. When a line of molds is completed, lead is poured into them and a line of type is produced. The half-tone engraving is a system for reproducing photographs by taking a picture of a picture through a screen and reproducing it on metal. The stereotype is a curved solid metal reproduction of a whole page of type and pictures. First, an impression of a page is made in a matrix, or cardboard-like substance, which can be placed in a curved form. Hot lead is poured against the matrix and a curved metal page is reproduced. These stereotypes can then be placed on a rotary press through which a continuous web of paper is run and printed on both sides, then folded and cut into newspapers. The stereotype made use of the much faster rotary presses possible, and it also made possible multicolumn layouts by eliminating the need for rules between every column to hold the type together in printing. The use of colored inks made the papers more attractive, and the development of a comparatively inexpensive paper from wood pulp instead of cloth made it feasible to reproduce large numbers of them at a reasonable expense. The typewriter and telephone accelerated the gathering and processing of news and advertising. The typewriter also cut down on the number of mistakes caused by a printer having to read the handwritten copy of an editor or reporter.

Technological developments made the rapid expansion of newspapers in the late nineteenth century possible. Growth and development of the nation made it desirable. Innovative editors such as Joseph Pulitzer made it a reality. Pulitzer was one of a number of editors in the late nineteenth century who pulled together the new techniques in reporting and editing and the new technology to create bigger and better newspapers to serve increasing numbers of persons. Pulitzer at the *St. Louis Post-Dispatch* and especially at the *New York World* showed the nation what amounted to a new journalism. As a poor immigrant who worked his way up from the bottom to a position of affluence and influence, he also represented the traditional American success story of the late nineteenth century. Pulitzer came to the United States as a mercenary in the Union cause. At the end of the war he had little hope and less money. Fortunately, he migrated to St. Louis where he was befriended by an organization formed there to help immigrants. He read law and was admitted to practice, but became interested in newspapers and decided to be a reporter instead. He worked hard, saved his money and eventually bought the *St. Louis Dispatch* at a sheriff's sale. Later he acquired the *Post* and created the *Post-Dispatch,* which he made into a leading American newspaper. In the 1880s he acquired the *New York World* and made it the nation's largest and most successful newspaper. By 1892 the combined morning and evening editions of the *World* had a circulation of 374,000.

Pulitzer was not an original genius in the sense that some other newspapermen have been. His contribution lay in his great ability to gather and mesh many good ideas into a unified approach and then put that approach into practice. Most of the techniques of the new journalism identified with Pulitzer were not really new. But it was Pulitzer who brought these techniques and new technology together to create a more vital newspaper.

The new journalism emphasized accurate, thorough news coverage and clear, concise writing. Pulitzer also sought to develop a stronger editorial page, and he engaged in crusades against some of the nation's largest business monopolies. He made extensive use of illustrations, and he engaged in various self-promotion efforts, including a variety of stunts. When Congress refused to appropriate funds to provide a suitable pedestal for the Statue of Liberty, the *World* sponsored a fund-raising campaign to assure a proper site for the impressive French gift. When Jules Verne's *Around the World in Eighty Days* created a stir among American readers, the *World* sent its roving correspondent Elizabeth Cochran, alias Nellie Bly, on a similar trip and invited readers to guess how long it would take; a trip to Europe was offered for the best estimation. On occasion, Pulitzer defended sensationalism in some parts of his paper by saying he was building an audience for his editorial page. He is widely remembered for his emphasis on "accuracy, accuracy, accuracy" in reporting simple facts and more complex ideas and his willingness to fight for progress and reforms.[5]

One regrettable extension of the new approach suggested by Pulitzer was the yellow journalism that evolved in the 1890s. Yellow journalism is a term used to describe extreme sensationalism. It involved outright faking and dishonesty in reporting as well as an overemphasis on crime, sex and emotionalism. The practice grew out of a circulation war waged by William Randolph Hearst and his *New York Journal* against Pulitzer and his *New York World*. It spread to some other papers in New York and to papers in a number of other metropolitan areas such as Cincinnati, St. Louis, San Francisco and Denver. One study shows that about one-third of the nation's 21 largest metropolitan centers were distinctly yellow in 1900 when yellow journalism reached its zenith.[6]

The term itself evolved from the struggle between Hearst and Pulitzer over a comic strip which featured a character called the Yellow Kid. Hearst hired away the cartoonist who drew the strip for Pulitzer's *World*. Pulitzer then hired another cartoonist to draw a similar strip. Some of the other newspapers thought this struggle typified the unfortunate practices of the time, and dubbed the two offending newspapers "yellow journals" and much of their content "yellow journalism."

The Hearst-Pulitzer struggle began in the middle 1890s when Hearst purchased the *New York Journal* and challenged Pulitzer for supremacy in the field. Hearst was the son of a rich miner who had purchased the *San Francisco Examiner* to further his political career. When the father was elected to Congress, young Hearst took over the *Examiner* and modeled it after the *World* in New York. After achieving success on the coast he decided to challenge Pulitzer. Armed with almost unlimited financial resources he acquired some of the best newspaper features and employed some of the most talented people in the business to make his New York venture a success. Pulitzer resisted these inroads; and as the two battled for circulation, their papers became increasingly sensational.

Yellow journalism reached its extremes during the Spanish-American War, which it may have helped to cause, and in the months just after the war as the papers sought to maintain their high wartime circulations. It is difficult to assess the influence of the yellow journals in causing the war, but it may have been more than minor. Certainly, the press accounts of conditions in Cuba helped generate sympathy among Americans for the Cuban insurgents in their disputes with Spain. The Spanish captain-general was referred to as Valeriano "Butcher" Wyler. The publication of an intercepted letter in which a Spanish official supposedly described the American President McKinley as weak aroused public indignation, and the Hearst account of the destruction of the battleship Maine by persons still undetermined left the impression that Spain was responsible. Some newspapers exposed this journalistic jingoism, and the basic causes of conflict existed whether published or not; but it does appear that the yellow journals contributed through irresponsible reporting to an unnecessary war.

Whatever the causes, the war was ideal for coverage by American newspapers. It was small, close by, and the United States was successful from the beginning. Several hundred reporters covered the war, and Hearst himself took his yacht down for a closer look. While there his party even accepted the surrender of some Spanish troops. This coverage led to unheard of circulations during the conflict. The *Journal* total reached 1,500,000 and the *World* was not too far behind. But the circulation did not bring prosperity because of the high costs involved and the fact that the sensationalism tended to scare some advertisers away.

Moreover, the papers apparently felt compelled to engage in new extremes of sensationalism after the war in an effort to maintain their high circulations. The earlier reaction grew stronger, and it was strengthened even more when the man who shot President McKinley said he had been stirred up by something he had read in Hearst's newspaper. Even without this incident, however, yellow journalism had about run its course. Sensationalism is cyclical. Once the potential audience gets its fill, it demands something better, at least for a time. Both Pulitzer and Hearst toned down their newspapers and made substantial improvements in them in the early twentieth century.

Journalism in the late nineteenth century should not be remembered for its extremes, however, but for its many positive developments. Editors such as Joseph Medill, William Rockhill Nelson and William Allen White in the Midwest, the DeYoung brothers on the West Coast, and Henry Watterson and Henry Grady in the South used the new journalism and the new technology to boost their sections and communities and provide a variety of useful services. Theirs was a responsible journalism in sharp contrast to the extremes of the yellow journals. Henry Grady, for example, helped develop the *Atlanta Constitution* into a well-written, well-edited publication, and he championed the idea of a New South built on industry and diversification of agriculture. The overriding question in the South after the Civil War was, Where do we go from here? Grady and men like him provided some answers, even though their suggestions were not properly applied until many decades later. Grady, Nelson in Kansas City and others helped many to realize that new journalism and new technology provided newspapers with new opportunities and responsibilities for service.

NEWSPAPERS IN THE EARLY TWENTIETH CENTURY

Newspapers changed significantly in the early twentieth century as they adjusted to their own revolution and sought new ways to help the United States meet its expanding challenges. The increasing cost of new technology and other factors led to the consolidation of many newspapers, the expansion of corporate ownership and the growth of newspaper chains. The need for more and better news and feature coverage led to the expansion of wire services and syndicates. The excesses of yellow journalism led to reforms within the medium itself, and the excesses in American business and government caused newspapers to join with other media and many citizens in a nationwide movement for reforms.

Consolidation became a major trend in the newspaper field in the twentieth century but not before new records were established for the number of newspapers in publication at one time. In the years just before World War I started in Europe, there were some 2,600 dailies and 14,000 weeklies published to serve a rapidly growing United States. The war with its shortages and high costs led to the demise of more than 100 papers in about four years time, and many other factors began to take their toll. The high cost of operating modern plants with Linotype machines, high-speed presses and photoengraving equipment caused many papers to merge or cease publication. In some communities there was not enough advertising to justify several newspapers, and in other communities there was not enough difference in the papers to warrant buying all of them. Fierce competition for advertising and circulation forced some out of business. When advertisers decided that their money could be better spent in the one paper with the largest circulation, the smaller papers often fell by the wayside. Evening papers frequently survived morning papers because of an apparent preference for them on the part of women readers who pay close attention to advertising.

In some respects the trend toward fewer newspapers may have been beneficial. It is better, for example, that a community have two newspapers with adequate circulation and advertising to produce quality products than to have three or four newspapers struggling to survive and too poor to achieve quality. Unfortunately, the trend too often resulted in a community having only one newspaper, or perhaps two owned by the same person or corporation. This posed a serious threat to the free flow of information and opinion, and undoubtedly led many to call for a new emphasis on responsibility in newspapers. The old libertarian concept of the press was superseded by a social responsibility emphasis as the twentieth century progressed.

A trend toward more corporate ownerships and a rise of newspaper chains, or groups, as most prefer to be called, were also viewed as threats to the development of strong, outspoken local editorial policies. Editors whose newspapers are owned by many persons may not feel the same freedom as those who speak from a position of ownership. The editor is likely to be concerned about his investors even if they are not constantly reminding him of their dividend expectations. Editors of chain or group newspapers may be even more restricted in what they can express on certain issues, particularly those of a regional or national nature. Neither corporate nor group ownership is necessarily bad, however. Their greater economic strength can enable such papers to offer services that other papers cannot provide or wage battles that less secure organizations could not hope to win.

Multiple ownership of newspapers did not begin with the twentieth century. But it did become a major characteristic of the American system with the expansion of the Hearst and Scripps chains in the early years of the century. At the turn of the century Hearst owned newspapers in San Francisco and New York. He soon added newspapers in Chicago and Boston and from this base built one of the nation's largest newspaper chains. The Scripps chains were also started in the late nineteenth century and expanded in the twentieth. The primary group was the Scripps-McRae League, which by World War I had expanded to include an interest in more than 30 newspapers in 15 states. E. W. Scripps was the prime mover in this group which started in the Midwest. Generally speaking, the papers appealed to the masses in the cities and championed many of the causes of the poor and underpriviledged. Milton McRae dropped out of the organization about 1914. Roy Howard, who helped Scripps develop United Press, became more influential, and the name of the organization was changed to Scripps-Howard after World War I.

The most exciting newspaper development of the early twentieth century was neither consolidation nor the rise of corporate ownerships and chains, however. Instead it was the introduction of a more responsible journalism in the founding of the *Christian Science Monitor* and the rejuvenation of the *New York Times*. These two pioneered an in-depth, interpretative approach to covering the news that was to become more widespread among newspapers in the 1930s. The *Monitor* was started by the Christian Science Church in Boston in 1908 at the suggestion of Mary Baker Eddy, founder of the church. It was designed as a positive reply to the sensationalism that had plagued the nation but was not intended primarily to be a religious publication. Its object, according to its founder, was "to injure no man, but to bless all mankind." [7] To do this the *Monitor* emphasized complete, thorough, analytical coverage of national and international affairs. It was published in Boston but was, and remains, a national or international publication.

Under its founder Henry Raymond, the *New York Times* provided a more thorough and objective coverage of the news than most other newspapers in the middle nineteenth century. But after Raymond's death in 1869 the paper suffered many reverses. It did take an active part in the crusade that helped rid New York of the infamous political boss William M. Tweed. But in general the *Times* did not keep pace with the rapidly changing nation in the late nineteenth century. The new journalism of Joseph Pulitzer and others passed it by. The situation grew steadily worse until Adolph Ochs took over the operation in 1896. Ochs saw it would be folly to enter the mass circulation chase then being run by Hearst and Pulitzer. Moreover, he saw the need for a newspaper that would emphasize solid news coverage and editorial opinion. Ochs developed a Sunday news supplement, a book review section and a financial review to augment expanded daily coverage of important news. "All the News That's Fit to Print" was adopted as policy as well as slogan.

Ochs' rejuvenation plan worked, and the paper got bigger and better. Daily circulation rose from about 9,000 when he took it over to roughly 330,000 by 1921. The growth brought considerable revenue, most of which was reinvested to improve the operation and expand the staff. Under its tireless managing editor Carr V. Van Anda, the *Times* developed a staff of reporters, correspondents and editors that had few, if any, peers. The *Times* continued its conservative makeup but stressed good editing and printing as well as complete, accurate reporting. Its coverage of World War I has been praised by many.

Of the other New York newspapers, the *World* and the *Tribune* probably were the most successful in the early twentieth century. Pulitzer and editor Frank I. Cobb returned the *World* to respectability and made it a champion of liberal democratic ideals such as free speech, personal liberty, and constitutional government. It was a leader in the fight against the misuse of privilege whether by government or business. Whitelaw Reid continued to advocate conservative causes in the *Tribune* until his death in 1912. During the late nineteenth and early twentieth centuries he served in several high government capacities and was an adviser to presidents and other high officials. The *Tribune* also pioneered in the development of the Linotype machine that helped revolutionize the industry. Hearst curtailed the sensationalism in his newspaper somewhat and set about the development of a major communications empire, including newspapers, magazines, a wire service and a feature service. James Gordon Bennett, Jr., the sometimes brilliant but seldom effective son of the *Herald's* founder, continued to guide that paper on a relatively unsuccessful course until his death in 1918.

Aside from events in New York and Boston, the big story in Eastern journalism was the rise of the *Evening Bulletin* in Philadelphia. William Lippard McLean purchased the 48-year-old paper in 1895 when it had a circulation of only 6,000. He transformed it, made it typical of Philadelphia, supported various reforms, and by 1905 had guided it to a circulation of 220,000. McLean pioneered in mechanical improvements and developed many new circulation techniques. His paper's slogan has become a classic. It asserts, with an obvious effort to be honest and exact, that "In Philadelphia Nearly Everyone Reads the *Bulletin*."

The *Chicago Tribune, Kansas City Star, St. Louis Post-Dispatch* and

Denver Post continued to be major forces in the Midwest. Robert R. McCormick and Joseph Patterson assumed control of the *Tribune* about 1914 and expanded its interests and its audience. William Rockhill Nelson continued his positive approach to the development of a better Kansas City until his death in 1915. The *Post-Dispatch* continued the Pulitzer tradition in St. Louis, and the *Denver Post* championed the causes of the people in its city. A new voice also was heard in the Midwest when Gardner Cowles, Sr. moved from banking into the newspaper field in Des Moines. Unlike many other persons who sought entry into journalism from other areas, Cowles did well. He bought the *Register and Leader* in 1903, the *Evening Tribune* five years later, and embarked on a career that was to become more prominent in the decades after World War I.

The *Louisville Courier-Journal* and the *Atlanta Constitution* continued to provide progressive leadership in the South, and the *Examiner* and the *Chronicle* in San Francisco were leaders on the West Coast. Henry Watterson, whose career in Louisville spanned a half century, received a major journalism award in 1917 for editorials supporting American involvement in World War I. Henry Grady died a young man, but his work on the *Constitution* was continued by the Howell family, Joel Chandler Harris and others. The *Examiner* served as an important base paper for the rapidly developing Hearst chain, and the *Chronicle* continued its program of public service under the DeYoung interests.

Some of the larger newspapers could afford correspondents of their own in Washington and in some of the major capitals around the world. But an increasing number of newspapers came to rely on one or more of the wire services and syndicates developed in the early twentieth century for coverage of distant events and a wide variety of features. Wire services such as Associated Press, United Press and International News Service provided immediate coverage of the news. Syndicates such as King Features and United Features, and others provided a wide variety of news, features and other materials, including the increasingly popular comic strips.

The Associated Press traces its origin to a service formed by a group of New York newspapers in the late 1840s. It served a number of papers in the East. A Western Associated Press was formed in the 1860s, and the two groups were united in the 1880s. Smaller wire services also functioned during these years, but the Associated Press got exclusive contracts with leading European agencies, expanded its operations, and offered more and better services than the others could provide.

By 1900 almost everyone wanted the Associated Press service, but the member newspapers sought to keep their competitive advantage. When the courts indicated they could not do that under their existing structure, they reorganized the Associated Press as a nonprofit, cooperative news-gathering organization. Members agreed to exchange news with each other and share in the cost of operating the service. They also, in effect, agreed to maintain an exclusive membership. An Associated Press member in a community could keep any other newspaper there from becoming a member unless four-fifths of the total membership overruled its veto. This arrangement was maintained until the 1940s when it was successfully challenged in the courts. At first the Associated Press sought to prohibit its members from using competing wire services, but this practice was dropped in 1915 after the U. S. attorney general indicated it would be regarded as illegal.

The most serious challenge to Associated Press' dominance came from the E. W. Scripps organization, which, in 1907, created the United Press. This agency was actually a merger of a smaller service which Scripps had been operating for some time for his own papers in the Midwest and another small service in the East. Scripps correctly believed that there was a need for another service to assist newspapers not served by the Associated Press. United Press established connections with leading foreign papers and agencies not already tied up with Associated Press and developed its own system of correspondents at home and abroad. United Press gave considerable attention to human interest stories, interviews, and features of various kinds in addition to straight news reporting, and this approach helped sell the service.

William Randolph Hearst started a third major wire service, International News Service, in 1909 as an outgrowth of an earlier effort to serve his growing chain of newspapers. International News Service did not really challenge either of the two earlier operations for the top position in the field, but it did provide an excellent second service featuring special coverage of major news events by well-known writers.

Wire services, of course, proved to be a great asset to newspapers as they sought to cover the many events associated with World War I. American newspapers provided extensive coverage prior to United States' entry into the war, and many correspondents accompanied the American Expeditionary Forces in 1917. Peace talks and the debates over American entry into the League of Nations likewise got massive coverage after the war. Most American newspapers were probably pro-British, at least after the Lusitania was sunk by a German submarine, and virtually all rallied to the cause once the United States was committed to battle.

Newspapers played a vital role in the massive government propaganda effort headed by George Creel and his Committee on Public Information. Creel believed that dissemination of information was a basic weapon in achieving the nation's goals, and he established all possible channels to reach people with information. He won the confidence of the newspapers through his voluntary censorship code, and he earned the trust of government officials through his wise handling of information. Creel created the *Official Bulletin* in May 1917, to dispense information, and it achieved a circulation of 118,000 during the war. Only two of some 6,000 stories issued by Creel's agency were seriously challenged as to accuracy, although many were flavored with patriotism. Creel's office demonstrated the value of telling the people the facts to win their confidence and support.

Newspaper coverage of the war was hampered at times, however, by censorship, particularly military censorship. Restrictions were sometimes placed on where reporters could go in covering the war, and stories had to be routed through official censors. Censorship existed at home also, although the press was generally free to comment on the government's conduct of the war. The three principal censorship acts passed by Congress during the war were enforced largely by the Post Office Department rather than the Justice Department and their effect was felt largely by socialist and German language newspapers. The most offensive regulations adopted were dropped after the war.

On the whole, the newspapers did a good job of covering the war and the League of Nations debates that followed. They earned a less impressive score for their coverage of the Red scare occasioned by the Communist success in Russia. Some newspapers failed to insist on the rights of nondangerous radicals to express their views. Others such as the *World* in New York and the *Post-Dispatch* in St. Louis kept their perspective and set an example for others to emulate in subsequent challenges of a similar nature.

Unfortunately the nation was not able to achieve its highly publicized goal of making the world safe for democracy. It soon became apparent that the war to end all wars had not achieved its goal, and the high idealism of many turned to deep disillusionment. The Republican cry for a return to normalcy was generally welcomed, although the 1920s could hardly be called normal. The many positive achievements of the press in the first two decades of the century were followed by a return to sensationalism and the rise of the tabloids. But many of the reforms in business, government and other activities which the newspapers helped motivate in the early twentieth century served the nation and its people well in the years that followed.

BOOM, DEPRESSION AND WAR

Newspapers experienced another brief flirtation with sensationalism in the 1920s before shifting their emphasis to meet the challenges of depression, social and technical revolution, increased media competition and global conflict. Most newspapers reflected and contributed to the era sometimes called the roaring twenties. The failure of World War I to make the world safe for democracy and achieve other goals led to great disillusionment, frustration and confusion. Many persons sought to lose their disappointments in a new emphasis on living for the moment. Their disillusionment was fed by the scandals of the Harding administration and the failure of the great experiment in prohibition. Their thirst for living was whetted by the rise of Hollywood and its symbol, the glamorous and sexy movie star. The times seemed ripe for sensationalism in the press, and many newspapers became preoccupied with sex, crime and entertainment.

Although many newspapers were sensational in their selection and display of materials during the twenties, a new type of newspaper, the tabloid, was born that symbolized the era. The tabloids were characterized by a smaller format than most newspapers, big pictures and big headlines, and an emphasis on sensational stories. The tabloid was about 15 or 16 inches high instead of the usual 20 or 21 and about five columns in width instead of the usual eight. It was ideal for commuters to handle on crowded buses and trains, and its sensational format was designed for street sales. The front page usually had a large sensational picture and several large headlines. The stories accompanying these headlines, other pictures and stories were included inside. Crime and sex were the staples although some tabloids also carried more serious news and commentary.

The first and most successful of the tabloids was the *New York Illustrated Daily News* started by Joseph Medill Patterson and Robert R. McCormick, the co-publishers after 1914 of the *Chicago Tribune*. They apparently got the idea from the success of several similar papers in London in the early twentieth century, and it provided a solution for their own conflict of interests on the *Tribune*. McCormick, who was conservative in his economic ideas, remained in Chicago to run the *Tribune*. Patterson, who was more liberal in his approach, went to New York and developed a paper for the masses. The *Daily News* got off to a fast start in June 1919, then experienced some difficult months before starting its climb to become the most widely circulated newspaper in the United States. Heavy emphasis on pictures, sports and crime news, a variety of contests and gimmicks, and the greater convenience of handling on crowded subways and buses all contributed to its rise in competition with other newspapers.

The *Daily News* got tabloid competition in the middle 1920s from *The Daily Mirror,* started by William Randolph Hearst and the *Daily Graphic,* started by Bernarr Macfadden. Hearst already owned a number of newspapers, magazines and a wire service. Macfadden was already publisher of *True Story* and *Physical Culture* magazines. The *Daily Mirror* competed with the *Daily News* on a news basis and provided a continuing challenge for several decades. The *Daily Graphic* concentrated on sensational stories and did not even bother with a wire service. It got many readers but comparatively few advertisers and died in 1932. Other tabloids were started in other cities such as Chicago, Los Angeles, Washington and Denver; and a number of them like the *News* and *Mirror* continued to reach substantial audiences long after the supersensational era of the twenties and the *Daily Graphic* had passed.

Sensationalism was not confined to the tabloids in the 1920s, and it did not die with the depression. Many standard-size newspapers played up sensational stories in the 1920s. Some standard-size newspapers and many tabloids continued to emphasize such stories in the years that followed. But the problems engendered by the depression at home and various economic and political developments abroad demanded something better of newspapers, and many of them sought to provide it. The tabloid format should not be considered synonymous with sensationalism either. A number of weeklies and specialized publications devoted to other interests have adopted it because of its convenience for readers.

Newspapers achieved new significance and influence in the 1930s as they moved to meet new challenges with an increasing emphasis on interpretive reporting. The impact of the depression and the New Deal and the rise of science and technology challenged newspapers to provide understanding as well as information. Somebody had to explain what had happened to the nation, why it had happened and what was being done to correct the situation. Public confidence was essential for government to meet the crises, and understanding was essential to producing confidence. The newspapers reported, explained and analyzed what was being done and suggested other approaches. Some supported the President's recovery policies. Others opposed them. Most sought to explain them. At the same time, newspapers sought to help people deal with the changes being wrought by science and technology. The airplane in effect reduced the size of the world and made Europe's concerns America's concerns as well. Other developments greatly altered the way things were being done in business and industry. An increasingly literate population demanded that their newspapers help them meet these new challenges, and most newspapers accepted the challenge.

Some newspapers employed specialists of their own to explain government, business and other developments. Others relied, in national matters at least, on the syndicated columnists who rose to prominence in the 1930s. Walter Lippmann, among others, pioneered in the development of the modern political column. The *New York Herald Tribune* turned Lippmann loose in the early 1930s to explain, interpret and voice his opinions about the affairs of Washington and the world. David Lawrence, Mark Sullivan, Dorothy Thompson and many others joined in the effort. Some perhaps created more heat than light, but others helped to interpret the new challenges to the nation and society and helped keep tabs on government efforts to meet them. None were infallible, however. Lippmann in 1932 did not see Franklin Roosevelt as a crusader, a tribune of the people or as an enemy of entrenched privilege. Wrote Lippmann, "He is a pleasant man who, without any important qualifications for the office, would very much like to be President." [8] Lippmann's assessments were generally more astute, however, and his observations came to be highly regarded inside as well as outside the government.

Another specialist, the political cartoonist, suffered somewhat from the increasing complexities of life and the new emphasis on interpretation. It is difficult to say "but on the other hand" in a cartoon or to explain adequately a complex person or event with an easily recognized stereotype. The decline of newspaper competition also hurt the cartoonists, who can attack more easily than they can explain. The only newspaper in a community often feels a great responsibility to provide a balance of opinions on its editorial pages. Some newspapers continued to provide forceful local cartoonists, but many chose to rely on nationally syndicated cartoons, and local commentary suffered accordingly. Nevertheless, national political topics were thoroughly treated, and social commentary became more prominent.

Newspapers themselves were affected by some of the government activities they sought to report and explain. Some publishers tried unsuccessfully to have newspapers exempted from much of the New Deal legislation regulating business. The American Newspaper Publishers Association led this opposition, and was criticized by some publishers and others inside the industry as well as many outside it for being overly conservative and unrealistic. After much discussion, the newspapers were exempted from provisions that could lead to licensing and interference with freedom of expression, and they were included in regulations such as those providing for collective bargaining and wage and hour requirements. Protection under these laws was asserted for editorial employes through the formation of the American Newspaper Guild. Some editorial employes feared that unionization would endanger their standing as professionals, but others argued it was the only response to intransigent employers. Heywood Broun, liberal columnist for the *New York World-Telegram,* was one of the leaders in the formation of the Guild, which gradually organized editorial employes on newspapers in many of the nation's larger cities.

The government's right to regulate certain business operations of newspapers was established in the 1930s. But efforts by some government agencies to interfere with free expression through prior restraint or unjust taxation were rejected. The U. S. Supreme Court decided in a landmark case, *Near v. Minnesota,* in 1931 that the First Amendment guarantee of press freedom against the federal government could also be applied to state governments through the due process clause of the Fourteenth Amendment. A Minnesota law which permitted prior restraint on newspapers was held unconstitutional in that decision.[9] An effort by the state of Louisiana to tax the gross advertising income of certain newspapers in that state was held unconstitutional in 1936. Twelve of the 13 newspapers affected by the act had opposed the administration of Governor Huey Long. The court held the tax to be "a deliberate and calculated device . . . to limit the circulation of information to which the public is entitled by virtue of the constitutional guarantees." [10]

Newspapers generally were successful against the new competition posed by newsmagazines, radio and talking pictures in the 1920s and 1930s. But the economic pressures caused by this competition, the depression and other factors encouraged the trend toward concentration of newspaper ownership. The number of competitive situations was reduced, particularly in the late 1930s and during World War II. There were more than 360 mergers or suspensions

between 1937 and 1944 to reduce the total number of daily newspapers in the
United States to 1,745. Some of the nation's best-known voices were among
those stilled or muted by merger. Pulitzer's *World,* one of the leaders in the development of modern journalism, was merged with the New York *Telegram* in
1931 and became part of the Scripps-Howard chain. Some of the mergers were
successful, some not. One of the most auspicious came in 1924 when the *New
York Herald Tribune* came into being. Whitelaw Reid's successors on the *Tribune* acquired the *Herald,* which had passed from executors to Frank Munsey
after the death of James Gordon Bennett, Jr.

Newspaper chains, or groups, became increasingly prominent during the
1920s and 1930s. By the late 1920s there were about 60 chains involving some
300 newspapers which accounted for about a third of the total daily newspaper
circulation. The numbers remained about the same in the 1930s and then
climbed somewhat in the 1940s. The Hearst and Scripps-Howard chains, which
had achieved prominence earlier in the century, remained among the leaders.
Under the influence of Roy Howard the Scripps-Howard chain probably became more conservative in its outlook during these years. The *Chicago Tribune-New York Daily News* combine was a leader in circulation if not in
numbers of newspapers, and other chains which were to become more prominent after World War II were developed. John S. Knight succeeded his father
as editor and publisher of the *Akron Beacon Journal* in 1933. He purchased the
Miami Herald and *Tribune* and merged them in 1937, and he acquired the *Detroit Free Press* in 1940. John Cowles, whose family owned the *Des Moines
Register and Tribune,* acquired the *Minneapolis Star* in 1935 and the *Minneapolis Journal* in 1939. James M. Cox, who owned papers in Ohio, acquired
the *Miami News* and the *Atlanta Journal* in the 1930s. Frank E. Gannett developed a chain of 16 newspapers, mostly in New York state, in the 1930s and
early 1940s. Samuel I. Newhouse, who was to become a major national figure
after World War II, further developed his chain in the East during the 1930s
and 1940s. The quality of the chain papers varied then as today. Some used
their natural advantages to develop good newspapers with strong local editorial
policies. Others were concerned primarily with profits or expounding the viewpoints of their owners.

The *New York Times* and the *New York Herald Tribune* in that city and the
Christian Science Monitor in Boston were among the individual leaders in the
East. The *Washington Post* rose rapidly in prestige and influence after Eugene
Meyer purchased it from a receivership in 1933. The *Providence Journal* and
Bulletin and *Hartford Courant* were leaders in New England. The *Chicago
Tribune* may have lost some of its dominant impact after World War I but
remained a leader in the Midwest. The *Chicago Daily News* was a strong local
competitor. The *St. Louis Post-Dispatch* continued the independent, liberal
traditions of Joseph Pulitzer in that city, and the *St. Louis Globe-Democrat*
provided conservative, but public-spirited competition. The *Kansas City Star*

continued its strong local and regional coverage and its crusading spirit. The staff acquired stock control of the paper in 1926 and paid off a substantial mortgage by 1939. The *Milwaukee Journal* achieved national as well as regional acclaim under the leadership of Lucius W. Nieman. After his death in 1935 ownership passed to employes under a plan similar to that worked out in Kansas City. The *Louisville Courier-Journal,* which passed to the Bingham family in 1917, and the *Atlanta Constitution,* under the Howell family, continued to provide leadership in the South. The *San Francisco Chronicle* was noted for its national and foreign coverage in the 1930s and early 1940s, and the Portland *Oregonian* moved ahead in the late 1930s and 1940s under the editorship of Palmer Hoyt.

Many of these newspapers joined with other newspapers, wire services, magazines and radio to provide extensive coverage of the events involved in World War II. The disillusionment that was prevalent in much of the nation after World War I passed slowly. Many persons tended toward an isolationist position until the middle and late 1930s when it became increasingly evident that the Japanese and Germans had far-reaching intentions. Kansas editor William Allen White and columnist Joseph Alsop were among the journalists who sounded the warnings. Some American papers, including the Hearst chain and the McCormick-Patterson combine, took an isolationist position until the war began, but rallied to the cause when the United States was attacked.

Two government agencies were established to assist and monitor newspapers and other media in their coverage of the war. One was the Office of Censorship under the direction of Byron Price. It established voluntary censorship procedures similar to those used successfully in World War I. Price was a long-time Associated Press writer and editor, and he was widely respected by newsmen generally. His office developed *A Code of Wartime Practices for the American Press,* which outlined for publishers what might constitute an improper handling of the news. There was, of course, the threat of government action against newspapers or other media that violated the code, but most newsmen wanted to cooperate and believed that Price and his office were treating them fairly. Protection of information about the development of the atomic bomb and the invasion of Europe attest to the success of the overall program. Restrictions on local coverage of wartime contracts for local plants brought some complaints. But the primary violations of the code concerned reports of local men overseas that identified the location of their units and interviews with returning servicemen who inadvertently gave out classified information. One interview that escaped the censors could have revealed the fact that the United States had broken the Japanese code. Military censorship was, of course, imposed by the various services, and it was at times challenged by the press. Newsmen agreed that information which might help the enemy should be withheld, but they charged that some information was withheld to cover up military inefficiencies rather than assure military security.

While the Office of Censorship sought to prevent the flow of information that might harm the war effort, the Office of War Information sought to disseminate information that would promote understanding of the government's war policies and boost morale. Elmer Davis, who had worked with both the *New York Times* and CBS Radio, was named to head this agency. The domestic section of the Office of War Information concerned itself with war bond sales, salvage drives, fuel conservation and similar programs in addition to providing news releases and information for the press. The overseas division worked with the military in the development of psychological warfare techniques and prepared movies, books, magazines and other materials for distribution in allied, neutral and enemy countries.

Coverage of the war was extensive and generally impressive. Radio, magazines, press services and newspapers all were involved. Many correspondents, including several women, were cited for their efforts. Ernie Pyle of the Scripps-Howard Newspaper Alliance was particularly effective in reporting the human side of the war. He was killed while covering the action in the Pacific and buried among the GIs he knew and loved so well. President Harry Truman and many others joined in tributes. "The nation is quickly saddened again by the death of Ernie Pyle," the President said. "No man in this war has so well told the story of the American fighting man as American fighting men wanted it told. He deserves the gratitude of all his countrymen." [11]

Although much of Europe and many other parts of the world were devastated by the war, the defeat of the Germans and Japanese and the creation of the United Nations brought new hope to millions. Many were determined that the new international organization would not suffer the fate of the League of Nations created without the United States after World War I. Newspapers and other media joined in efforts to publicize the activities and goals of the United Nations when it was organized during the latter stages of the war and afterward. But the combined efforts of diplomats, press and citizens were doomed to at least partial failure by the unwillingness of the Russians to cooperate with the other major powers. Recovery from global conflict would have been difficult in any event. It was made more difficult by Russian efforts to protect themselves from any further attacks and to spread their communist system to other countries. Newspapers and other media that had served so ably in covering a hot war were soon called upon to report and explain a cold one. There were domestic problems also, and the newspapers were soon challenged by the rise of television to reassess their own roles. It quickly became apparent that the quarter century following World War II would be as challenging as the one which preceded it.

NEWSPAPERS AND THE NEW WORLD

Newspapers faced increasing challenges in the new world that developed in the quarter century after the close of World War II. They were beset by rising costs, increasing competition and growing pressures on their freedom to report the news. They were hard put to explain a society whose most persistent attitude was change. Continued shortages, rising production costs, strikes and the beginning of the Cold War with communism dominated the late 1940s. The hot war police action in Korea, the rise of television as a competitor for advertising and news, the continued decline of separately owned competing newspapers, the growth of chains and continued high costs were prominent themes running through the 1950s. Some technological breakthroughs in production improved the newspapers' competitive situation in the 1950s and 1960s, but rising costs and competition remained major challenges. The 1960s also brought rifts in press-government relations and efforts by the American Bar Association to curtail press coverage of crime and court news. The government challenged newspapers' assertions that they should be able to protect confidential sources, sought to stop some joint operating procedures by competing newspapers, and questioned newspaper ownership of broadcasting facilities. The newspapers criticized government handling of the war in Southeast Asia and the dissension it caused at home. Most of these differences and many of the pressures caused by competition remained as the 1970s opened. Still there was optimism about the future. The newspapers had made progress and they had helped the nation progress in the early years of what seemed to be a new world of change.

Rising production costs and the development of television as a major competitor for national advertising and news threatened the economic well-being of newspapers throughout the years from the middle 1940s to the early 1970s. Newspapers achieved steady growth in circulation and advertising revenues during these years, but the increasing costs generally kept pace and cut into profits. Total daily circulation increased from 52,000,000 in the late 1940s to 62,000,000 in the late 1960s. Advertising revenues increased dramatically, even at the national level where television made its primary inroads. National advertising revenues increased from about $260 million in the middle 1940s to more than a billion dollars by the late 1960s. Total advertising revenues for newspapers reached $5.2 billion in 1968 as compared with $3.1 billion for television. But costs spiraled, too. Newsprint costs rose from $68 a ton in the middle 1940s to $152 a ton by the late 1960s. Many newspaper salaries were more than doubled during the period. Rising postal rates had some effect on costs also, and the general inflationary trends in the nation created problems.

The economic picture varied greatly among the different newspapers. Some of the giant metropolitan dailies struggled for survival without success. It was estimated, for example, that the *Herald Tribune* lost between $15 million and $20 million during the decade that it was owned by John Hay Whitney.[12] A number of large papers suspended publication or were merged during the 1950s and 1960s. Others were sold to the growing newspaper groups that because of their size often could reduce operating costs. On the other hand, some of the medium-city papers turned a handsome profit. According to a report published in *Editor and Publisher* in 1966, the average medium-city paper enjoyed a net profit of 23% before taxes.[13]

Strikes periodically threatened the economic stability of newspapers, and at times prevented the flow of important information from various sources to the public. The collapse or merger of many newspapers was hastened by protracted strikes and the unwillingness of some unions to accept and ultimately profit from automation. Many unions struck to obtain higher wages and benefits or to prevent changes they believed would affect them adversely. The International Typographical Union led a long struggle against the ban on closed shop operations provided by the Taft-Hartley law of 1947. It lost a round or two but eventually got Supreme Court approval for something akin to a closed shop. The ITU was involved in more than half the strikes between 1946 and 1960, but photoengravers, stereotypers and other union employes also walked out at times. The American Newspaper Guild also engaged in a continuing and generally successful struggle to improve the wages of editorial employes. The Guild helped bring the top minimum salaries up to $100 a week on many newspapers by the early 1950s and up to $200 a week on many newspapers by the late 1960s. Some of the larger papers got top minimums of $250 or more by the 1970s.[14] The Guild had more than 30,000 members by the 1960s.

While strikes sometimes brought about desired increases in wages and fringe benefits, they also deprived the public of news and helped bring on the merger or suspension of some newspapers. There were extensive shutdowns in New York, Detroit, Boston, San Jose, Portland, St. Paul, Seattle, Cleveland and St. Louis in the 1960s. The *Detroit News, Detroit Free Press,* and the people of that city were the victims of the nation's longest newspaper strike to date, 267 days, between November 1967 and August 1968. Most newspapers and unions that had differences were able to work them out through arbitration. The majority of newspapers were not affected by the several hundred strikes that were called in the 1950s and 1960s. But some of the major strikes adversely affected some of the nation's major cities and newspapers and caused some to urge a ban on strikes that might disrupt a community's vital information system.

Rising production costs, stimulated by strikes and other factors, and increasing competition undoubtedly helped to encourage important technological breakthroughs in the years after World War II. Typesetting procedures were revolutionized. Teletypesetter machines, which were installed by many newspapers and the wire services in the early 1950s, boosted the production speed of Linotype machines. The Teletypesetter is a keyboard device similar to a typewriter that produces punched tape which is used to activate Linotype or other typesetting machines. Wire services began to send Teletypesetter tape along with their stories, and many newspapers installed their own tape punching machines for local copy. Unfortunately, the easy availability of the wire service tapes caused some small newspapers to omit less important local news in favor of wire news. The tapes also encouraged most newspapers to adopt the same style.

Typesetting was further revolutionized in the 1960s by the use of photocomposition devices and the adaptation of electronic computers to the process. Machines such as the Photon, Linofilm and Fotosetter produced words on film at much faster speeds than they could be produced in metal. By the late 1960s several companies had developed cathode-ray-tube filmsetting devices that could produce text materials at even faster speeds. In the meantime, computers were being used to accelerate the production of type. The *Oklahoma City Times* and the *Daily Oklahoman* in 1963 became the first newspapers to process their entire news content by computer. Other pioneers in new technology included the *Wall Street Journal, Los Angeles Times, West Palm Beach Post-Times* and the *South Bend Tribune.*

Another major breakthrough in newspaper operation was achieved by the improved and expanded use of offset printing. The process itself, which involves the use of photographic plates rather than stereotypes, is not new. But it was not until the 1950s that it was made readily adaptable to newspaper use. Since offset usually involves cold type and photography, it fits in nicely with the new photocomposition devices. Proponents say it is faster, more flexible and produces a more attractive product than the traditional letterpress process. They say it is cheaper, too, at least for the smaller newspapers. The number of offset daily and weekly papers expanded from fewer than 200 in the late 1950s to more than 5,000 by the late 1960s. That represented almost half the total number of newspapers in the country and included more than 400 dailies. The *Christian Science Monitor,* with a circulation of more than 200,000, in 1970 became the first major newspaper to switch from letterpress to offset printing. Some predicted that all but the largest metropolitan dailies probably would make the switch in the 1970s or early 1980s.

Smaller newspapers not switching to offset were aided by the development of less expensive picture-making processes in the 1940s and 1950s, and all letterpress papers hoped to gain from research developed in the 1960s to provide better printing plates. Although the most spectacular changes came in the production areas, improvements in technology also benefited other departments. Computers were adapted for use in accounting and other functions, and the mail room was increasingly automated.

Facsimile transmission of newspapers was explored by the *Philadelphia Inquirer, Miami Herald* and others in the late 1940s. Under this system newspaper pages are transmitted electronically from the newspaper sender to receiving sets in homes, stores or elsewhere. But various technical problems and the rise of television as a major electronic information medium for the home caused most newspapers to adopt a wait-and-see attitude on facsimile as a possible substitute for or adjunct to home delivery. The system was developed and used, however, by wire services for transmitting pictures and by some newspapers for transmitting proofs to auxiliary printing plants. Some foreign newspapers, including Tokyo's *Asahi Shimbun,* began experimenting with the possibilities of home delivery in the late 1960s. Some Americans, including Jerome Regunberg, sought to develop similar systems to transmit newspapers, magazines and other materials for home delivery. Both air waves and cable television lines were considered as potential means of moving the signals. Whether the human carrier system of delivering newspapers would be replaced by an electronic system remained in doubt as the 1970s opened. But some were suggesting that a system for transferring smaller amounts of information electronically might be available for general home use during the decade.

New technology helped many newspapers meet the challenge of rising production costs and increasing competition. Many of the smaller papers shifted to offset printing, and many of the new papers started in the suburbs and elsewhere also adopted the offset method. But rising costs and competition encouraged a continued trend toward single ownerships in cities and the continued growth of groups or chains. The rapidly growing organizations of Samuel I. Newhouse, John S. Knight and others came to challenge Scripps-Howard, the Tribune Company and Hearst groups for national leadership in numbers of major newspapers and circulations. Canadian Roy Thomson, who owned major media interests in Canada and England, also acquired a number of smaller dailies in the United States.

Newhouse expanded from his base in New York, New Jersey and Pennsylvania to acquire the Portland *Oregonian* in 1950, the *St. Louis Globe-Democrat,* the *Birmingham News* and the *Huntsville* (Ala.) *Times* in 1955, the *Oregon Journal* in Portland in 1961, the *New Orleans Times-Picayune* and *States & Item* in 1962, the *Cleveland Plain Dealer* in 1967. He also acquired stock in the *Denver Post.* The $50 million Cleveland sale set a new money record for newspaper transactions, but it was surpassed later in the same year when Lord Thomson paid Brush-Moore Newspapers, Inc. $72 million for 12 dailies and six weeklies, mostly located in Ohio.

Knight, who already had papers in Akron, Miami, Detroit and Chicago, sold the *Chicago Daily News* to Field Enterprises in 1959 but added the *Charlotte Observer* in 1954, the *Charlotte News* in 1959, the *Philadelphia Inquirer* and *Philadelphia Daily News* in 1969, and the *Macon* (Ga.) *Telegraph* and *News* in 1969. Knight reportedly paid $55 million to Triangle Publications, headed by Walter Annenberg, for the Philadelphia newspapers. At various times Newhouse, Knight and Thomson all were cited for leaving most local editorial decisions in the hands of local editors.

The Tribune group, which originally included the Chicago *Tribune* and the New York *Daily News,* was expanded somewhat in the post-war years, and it took over the top position in group circulation in the 1960s. The *Tribune* owners bought the Washington *Times-Herald* in 1949 after the death of Mrs.

Eleanor M. (Cissy) Patterson, then sold it to Eugene Meyer, owner of the *Washington Post* in 1954. They acquired the *Chicago American* from Hearst in 1956 and continued it as an evening paper along with the morning *Tribune*. The *American* was replaced by a new compact-size newspaper, *Chicago Today,* in 1969.

The Hearst organization, which had begun reductions in the late 1930s because of economic problems, continued to cut back in the post-war years. The operation was reorganized by Hearst's sons after he died in 1951 leaving an estate of almost $60 million. But their plans to give local editors more autonomy, tone down the group's sensational image, streamline typography and make other improvements did not solve all the economic problems. Further cutbacks in the publishing empire followed. The *Chicago American* was sold in 1956, and International News Service was merged with United Press in 1958. The *Los Angeles Examiner* was suspended in 1962 as was the *Los Angeles Evening Mirror,* owned by the Chandler family. The suspensions left the Chandlers' morning *Times* in competition with Hearst's evening *Herald-Express,* renamed *Herald-Examiner*. The *Mirror* in New York succumbed to economic problems aggravated by a strike in 1963 despite the fact that it had the second largest circulation of any newspaper in the country, 919,064 weekdays and 1,152,858 on Sundays. Hearst's Sunday supplement, the *American Weekly,* was dropped in 1963. The Scripps-Howard group maintained a fairly stable position among the group leaders in the post-war competition. In 1950 it acquired and merged the *New York Sun* with its own *World-Telegram*. In 1958 it bought and merged the Cincinnati *Times-Star* with its *Post*. But it sold its interest in the *San Francisco News-Call Bulletin* to Hearst in 1962, and it sold the *Houston Press* to the *Houston Chronicle* in 1964. The *World-Telegram* became part of the *World Journal Tribune* in 1966, but that venture, as noted elsewhere, failed in 1967. The Scripps company acquired more than half the stock of the *Cincinnati Enquirer* in 1956 but agreed under threat of government antitrust action in 1968 to sell it within 18 months.

All the many changes left the Tribune Company, Newhouse, Knight, Scripps-Howard and Hearst groups at the top of the group circulation list as the 1970s opened. Thomson and the Frank Gannett group, started in New York state, were among the leaders in numbers of papers. Many other groups were developing and together they accounted for about half the nation's dailies and almost two-thirds of its circulation.[15] Two of the nation's most successful dailies were involved in group transactions during the 1960s. Owners of the Los Angeles *Times* sought to extend their holdings in 1964 by purchasing the *San Bernardino Sun* 60 miles away, but they were forced to sell because of an unfavorable court decision. A lower court held that the purchase constituted dimunition of competition in the area, and the U.S. Supreme Court upheld the decision. The *Times* owners did begin to develop a group, however, by com-

pleting arrangements to buy the *Dallas Times Herald* and affiliated broadcasting stations in 1969 and by purchasing the controlling interest in Long Island's
Newsday in 1970. Owners of the *New York Times* exchanged 23% of their
stock with Cowles Communications, an intermedia group, for three Florida
newspapers, *Family Circle* magazine, a television station and other interests in
1970.

Only 5% of the nation's daily newspaper cities had separately owned,
competing general circulation dailies as the 1950s closed, and several changes
in the 1960s reduced competition even more. Two Portland papers came under
the same ownership in 1961. Two Los Angeles papers were suspended in 1962,
and the *New York Mirror* was dropped in 1963. Scripps-Howard sold the *Houston Press* to the *Chronicle* in 1964, and three New York papers sought to survive as one in 1966, but failed. In large measure because of a lengthy, expensive strike in 1965, the *New York Herald Tribune,* owned by John Hay
Whitney, the Hearst *Journal-American,* and the Scripps-Howard *World-
Telegram* sought to merge into one paper with morning, afternoon and Sunday
editions. The new paper was struck before it could publish a first edition, and
before a settlement was reached the *Herald Tribune* gave up. The *World Journal Tribune* finally came out in evening and Sunday editions in September
1966, but it was suspended the following May. These losses left the former
newspaper capital with only three general circulation dailies, the *Times* and the
Daily News in the morning and the *Post* in the afternoon.

Some of the gaps left by the suspension or merger of general circulation
papers in the nation's cities were filled by the rapid rise of suburban newspapers.
Their development in New York, Chicago, Los Angeles, and elsewhere accounts for the fact that the nation still had about as many daily newspapers in
1970 as it had at the end of World War II. Harry F. Guggenheim's Long Island
Newsday achieved a considerable circulation in that large New York suburb.

Efforts were begun in Congress in 1967 to help maintain competition
among general circulation newspapers in 22 United States cities. These efforts
resulted in passage of the Newspaper Preservation Act in 1970 which offered
limited exemption from antitrust prosecution to certain newspapers. The act
was designed to permit competing newspapers to join production, circulation
and advertising operations if one of them were in financial distress. News staffs
were to be kept separate. The act provided that 22 existing agreements would
be left alone but that any future agreements would be subject to approval by the
Justice Department. Some newspapers worked for passage of the act. Some opposed it on the grounds that it was class legislation and might prevent the start
of competing general circulation or suburban papers.[16]

Congress also passed legislation in 1968 to end the use by government
agencies of a 1789 federal "housekeeping" statute to withhold information
from the public. It passed a Freedom of Information act in 1966 to help open

some federal records to the public. The latter act generally shifted the burden of proof from the individual who wanted information to the agency that wanted to withhold it. But many agencies found ways to delay giving out information, and the act got only limited use by newspapers in the late 1960s.[17]

The United States Supreme Court issued several rulings in the 1960s that strengthened the right of the press to comment on public officials and other persons who became public figures. Newspapers and other media apparently were to have wide freedom to comment, provided they did not do so maliciously or show a reckless disregard for truth.

A 1970 ruling by a federal appeals court gave the press hope that it would be permitted to protect confidential sources of information. The ruling quashed a subpoena issued by a lower court against *New York Times* reporter Earl Caldwell, who had refused to provide information for a lower court and been cited for contempt. But this hope was dashed in 1972 when the U.S. Supreme Court ruled against Caldwell. A number of subpoenas were used by the U.S. Attorney General's office in the late 1960s and 1970 to seek information from reporters about various militant groups, and the press protested vigorously. In August 1970 the Attorney General issued guidelines that recognized the possible limiting effect of such subpoenas on First Amendment rights and promised that all reasonable attempts would be made to get information elsewhere. Some states had helped to resolve the question by passage of reporter confidentiality or "shield" laws, and an effort was promised by some congressmen in the early 1970s to get a national shield law adopted.

The long-smouldering controversy between the press and the legal profession over fair trial versus free press flared again in the late 1960s. After a lengthy study, the American Bar Association in 1968 recommended that law enforcement agencies and lawyers severely limit the amount of crime information given to the press prior to and apart from court trials. The report is sometimes referred to as the Reardon Report because it was prepared by a committee headed by Justice Paul C. Reardon of Massachusetts. Many newspapers and other media protested the proposed guidelines vigorously and urged officials in the various states not to adopt them. Newsmen and lawyers in many states sought to avoid a confrontation on the issue and assure the rights of all parties by working out voluntary agreements.

The most far-reaching restrictions on press freedom came, however, as might be expected in coverage of the police action in Korea in the early 1950s and the American involvement in Vietnam and adjacent countries because of the climate, the terrain and confusion over appropriate censorship procedures. In the early days of the Korean War the press had too few guidelines. This period was followed by one in which there were too many restrictions. Better balance was achieved in the latter stages of the conflict, but some newsmen and military officials were highly critical of each other. Many persons at home also were critical of the war for various reasons. Some were opposed to American involvement so far from home. Others criticized the government for not pushing the war to a more definite victory.

Government officials, including presidents, were criticized even more severely for their handling of information during the Cuban crisis of the early 1960s and the nation's involvement in Vietnam, particularly in the late 1960s. Presidents John Kennedy, Lyndon Johnson and Richard Nixon were accused of managing news to present a favorable picture. All presidents and most other persons involved with news have sought to manage it to some extent, but widespread dissatisfaction about United States' involvement in Southeast Asia helped intensify the charges. Government officials were accused of creating a credibility gap by the way in which they reported events in Vietnam. An accurate picture of the war was hard to come by because there were no clearly defined battle lines. In a guerilla war it is difficult to tell who controls what, and body counts are an inexact measurement of success.

Frustration over the war coupled with racial and other problems at home caused many Americans, particularly young Americans, to rise in protest in the late 1960s. College campuses as well as city ghettos were the scenes of riots. The 1968 Democratic convention in Chicago triggered mass protests in that city, and reporters as well as demonstrators and police were injured in the fighting that erupted. Newspapers sought to find the causes of the protests and improve communications and understanding between the various dissident groups and those in power with limited success.

The press itself became the subject of criticism, sometimes deserved, often not. Television newsmen in particular were accused of stirring up trouble by their very presence at events and demonstrations. Newspapers were criticized for biased reporting, particularly by young reporters who felt they should join the marchers as well as report the march. In late 1969 Vice President Spiro Agnew launched an attack on both broadcast media and newspapers for abusing their powers. He charged that too much power over public opinion was concentrated in the hands of the television networks and a few large Eastern newspapers such as the *Washington Post* and *New York Times*. The Vice President noted that the United States had the best press in the world, but said its members needed to engage in more self-criticism and improve their operations. The Federal Communications Commission may have agreed with the Vice President's charges concerning power concentration since it continued to discuss policies that would restrict cross-media ownership.

There was little doubt that the nation and its newspapers were facing their greatest challenges ever as the 1970s opened. The nation desperately needed newspapers and other media that could provide a wide range of information, explain ideas and events and motivate people to help make the democratic system work. The newspapers were beset by rising costs, competition and the immense difficulty of explaining a world in constant change. Their success, and perhaps the success of the American system itself, would depend on many factors such as approach, ownership, editorial courage, reporting techniques and use of new technology. The remaining chapters of this book will examine these and related factors in more detail.

3

Types of Newspapers

THERE ARE ABOUT as many types of newspapers in the United States today as there are newspapers. No two are exactly alike, even though they may be part of the same group or one of two jointly owned newspapers in the same city. Most will differ primarily because their purposes and audiences are different. Consider, for example, the internationally minded *Christian Science Monitor,* the tabloid *New York Daily News,* the suburban *Newsday,* the weekly *National Observer,* the weekly *Country Squire,* the black *Chicago Defender,* the collegiate *Michigan State News,* the business-oriented *Wall Street Journal* or the alternative *Los Angeles Free Press.* Even group-owned newspapers will have different audiences in different cities, especially if those cities are in different parts of the country, and jointly owned newspapers in the same city will have both morning and evening audiences. Newspapers will differ to some extent simply because the persons who publish them are different. Each newspaper has its own functions and its own staff to perform those functions.

Many groupings can be employed, however, to place newspapers into better perspective. They may, for example, be grouped according to purpose, such as general and specialized; according to frequency of publication, such as daily, weekly, semiweekly and biweekly; according to time of publication, such as morning and evening; according to circulation, such as large, medium and small; according to geography, such as national, regional, metropolitan, suburban and rural; according to method of production, such as letterpress and offset; according to format, such as standard and tabloid; or according to achievement, such as good, fair, poor and bad. Other groupings could be suggested, and most newspapers obviously could be placed in several of them. Categories will be employed in this chapter to suggest distinctions based primarily on purpose and audience. After a general discussion of dailies and weeklies, attention will be given to specialized newspapers for blacks, students and other special interest groups, including those who opt for alternative or underground newspapers.

Newspapers should be judged on the basis of the roles they choose to perform and how well they perform. In that sense a vital newspaper with a small audience might be considered excellent while one with a large audience and a less useful role might be considered only adequate. The small newspaper that emphasizes local events and issues may be as outstanding in its realm as the large newspaper with world outlook is in its realm. Any newspaper that does a useful task well can be considered a quality newspaper. But scholars have sought to designate those newspapers that effectively report and explain major national and international issues and events in a serious, unsensational manner as "quality" newspapers. Such newspapers can be readily distinguished from those that rely heavily on reporting events of the moment and presenting features with only popular or mass appeal. This category would transcend such factors as frequency of publication and interests served and include the weekly *National Observer* and the business-oriented *Wall Street Journal* along with the *New York Times, Christian Science Monitor, Los Angeles Times* and *Washington Post*. All have serious intent, all appeal to educated readers, all deal with national and international affairs, and all seek to influence opinion and action.

John Merrill of the University of Missouri journalism faculty is concerned with characteristics such as these when he seeks to identify an elite press in the United States and other countries. He says the elite newspapers are knowledgeable, concerned newspapers for serious people and opinion leaders in all countries. They appeal to thought and logic, not to prejudice and emotion. They are interested in ideas and issues, not in mere facts. They are primarily concerned with politics and international relations; business and economics; education, science and culture, and the humanities. Merrill says that the elite category is broad enough to include newspapers in both free and restricted societies. He uses the word "prestige" for good, influential, restricted papers in a closed society.[1] Merrill suggests that most United States newspapers fail to achieve quality because they seek to be something to everybody. He asserts that most general American dailies are "unfocused, undisciplined in basic journalistic philosophy, offering up all types of disorganized bits and snippets of entertainment, comics, puzzles, fiction, columns, and sensational or conflict-oriented news, and fair portions of undigested (and usually bland) local editorial opinion or comment."[2] Merrill includes about 20 United States newspapers in his list of 100 elite world newspapers.

Since the "quality" newspaper category is by definition limited to newspapers with strong national and international coverage, it may continue to be dominated by metropolitan dailies. Few newspapers have the resources to do all things well, and the smaller dailies are likely to concentrate in those areas where their readers indicate the greatest interest. Usually this will be local news. Some metropolitan newspapers may stress local and state news for the same reasons. All newspapers whose readers are not likely to get a good survey of national and international news from other sources have a responsibility to provide such coverage. All newspapers should place greater emphasis on ideas and issues and less on trivia. But each must determine for itself what mixture of local, state, national and international news can best serve its particular readers. Certainly, a newspaper does not need to be considered in the "quality" category of newspapers to be a newspaper of high quality.

Newspapers are most easily categorized by frequency of publication. The two broad groupings are dailies and non-dailies. Most newspapers must be published at least five days in the week to be considered dailies; college newspapers are considered dailies if they are published four days of the week. Most non-daily newspapers are published weekly, but some are published semiweekly, triweekly, biweekly, monthly or at other intervals. Many persons, however, including newspaper associations, tend to use the classifications daily and weekly for purposes of division. Both types are, of course, subject to further division by geography, intended audience and other descriptions.

Dailies often are subdivided into categories such as metropolitan, suburban and small-city to determine roles and responsibilities. Some division is essential to understand what is happening in the field and make assessments. For example, there are approximately the same number of dailies being published today (1,774) as there were at the end of World War II (1,750). But the papers are not necessarily the same. The number of metropolitan newspapers has declined and the number of suburban newspapers has increased as the people have moved from the cities to the suburbs.

Contrary to some reports, however, the metropolitan newspapers are not "on the skids." Rising costs, labor problems and other factors have caused the merger or suspension of many large newspapers, including some of high reputation such as the *New York Herald Tribune*. Most have problems. But many are doing well, and the overall picture is not as bad as it is sometimes painted. Professor Kenneth R. Byerly pointed out, for example, that metropolitan dailies gained circulation between 1950 and 1968 in 15 of 24 major population centers. The decline in New York City, where the number of metropolitan dailies fell from eight to three, accounted for 90.6% of the total metropolitan daily circulation loss of 2.5 million. Metropolitan dailies in Boston, Chicago, Pittsburgh and Philadelphia also had substantial losses, but they were offset by gains in other cities such as Washington, Dallas and Houston.[3]

What must metropolitan dailies do to survive and prosper? What are their proper roles and responsibilities as compared with those of other dailies and weeklies? The metropolitan dailies must assume primary responsibility for providing information and perspective about central city, state, national and international issues and events. They are the only ones that have the resources to provide this information in depth and detail. They may wish to provide separate editions for some communities nearby in which news of those communities is substituted for city news, or they may wish to provide additional sections with news of these communities for these communities. But the major thrust must be in coverage that other newspapers cannot provide. Metropolitan newspapers must tackle state, national and international questions; they must help resolve the crises that threaten to destroy all cities. They must go beyond the spot news to the heart of urban issues such as housing, unemployment, taxes and transportation. Some of the better-known metropolitan dailies are discussed in Chapter 8.

Even that special breed of metropolitan newspaper, the tabloid, may have to make some adjustments to prosper. As conceived in the 1920s the tabloid was a sensational publication in a format about half that of the standard newspaper. It was concerned mostly with spot news, particularly about crime and well-known persons, and it relied heavily on large headlines and large pictures to attract a street-sale audience. Many tabloids still rely on those basic techniques, but some include more solid materials; and a number have sought to tone down the old tabloid image. When the Tribune Company replaced the *American* with *Chicago Today* in 1969 it emphasized that its new publication was a "compact" newspaper not a "tabloid." Some newspapers which are not particularly sensational also have adopted the tabloid or compact size because it is relatively easy to handle.

The *New York Daily News,* owned by the Tribune Company of Chicago, has been the most successful of the tabloids. Its circulation far exceeds that of any other United States daily, and it has received new stimulus from a home delivery program initiated in late 1966. This program was begun in Nassau and Suffolk counties on Long Island and later developed in Queens, Brooklyn, upper areas of Manhattan, the Bronx, Staten Island and Hudson County, New Jersey. By late 1971 home delivery accounted for more than 10% of the *News'* circulation of 2,130,000 daily. Jack Underwood, the circulation director, said the future of the program was bright and challenging and offered the best possible opportunity for continued and solid growth in the changing New York metropolitan area. The *News* obviously expects to grow since it broke ground on a new $29 million plant at the southwestern tip of Long Island City in late 1970. The formal groundbreaking came about a year and a half after the newspaper marked its fiftieth anniversary in June 1969. One aspect of the anniversary celebration was the private printing of a 428-page hard-cover book which tells about the newspaper's first 50 years. The book ends with chapters that illustrate both the human interest and the in-depth aspects of the newspaper's reporting efforts. One tells how the *News* cut through official red tape to help an American G.I. adopt an orphaned Chinese girl whose life he saved in 1945. The other chapter recalls a 1958 exposé on conditions in Batista's Cuba that won Pulitzer Prizes for two *News* reporters. The *News* is a mass appeal newspaper as contrasted with some of the "quality" category newspapers noted earlier, but it is not without substance. Moreover, its home delivery program suggests that it may become more substantial in the future.[4]

Chicago Today was introduced after several years of study and planning as a new kind of "compact" newspaper. Publisher Lloyd Wendt defined the "compact" as "an exciting, convenient, easy-to-read newspaper smaller in page size than standard, greater in editorial content than most standard evening newspapers; a crisp attractive superbly-written and edited newspaper with superior graphic arts and advertising facilities." It evidently was aimed at the youthful, affluent market which economists predicted would expand greatly in the Chicago area during the 1970s. The emphasis on good graphics was immediately evident and resulted in two major awards in 1970. *Chicago Today* won the Edmund C. Arnold award for the nation's best design among metropolitan dailies and the Inland Daily Press Association award for typography. The newspaper also was one of the first to create a separate department to deal with consumer affairs when it established a Consumers Bureau in March, 1970. *Chicago Today* introduced some good features such as "Focus," which provided an indepth report on some current topic, and "Sound Off," which gave reporters a chance to disagree in print, and it offered an "Action Line" in addition to its Consumers Bureau. But at times it was short on hard news and long on sensation and trivia.[5]

Both *Chicago Today* and its afternoon competitor, Marshall Field's *Daily News,* were said to be having financial difficulties in the early 1970s while the *Tribune* and Field's morning *Sun-Times* were doing well. The Tribune Company decided to eliminate *Chicago Today's* Saturday and Sunday editions, effective January 1, 1973, and it subsequently announced the paper's demise, effective September 13, 1974. Stanton R. Cook, chairman of the Tribune Company, said the decision was a difficult one. *"Today* has always had quality journalism," he said. "Unfortunately, its revenues did not match its journalistic excellence." He said the *Tribune* would be operated on a 24-hour basis to fill the gap.[6]

Perhaps the 1970s will determine if the compact, or tabloid, newspaper has the proper mixture to attract and inform large numbers of Americans. As the decade opened there were about 50 being published in the United States, including the *News* and *Post* in New York, *Sun-Times* and *Chicago Today* in Chicago, *Newsday* on Long Island, the *Rocky Mountain News* in Denver and the *News* in Philadelphia. There is continued evidence to indicate that this type newspaper can serve a metropolitan audience not normally reached by the traditional, standard-size newspapers.

GROWTH IN THE SUBURBS

Suburban newspapers usually are not as well-known outside their immediate environs as their metropolitan brothers, but they have provided the industry's big growth story in the past two decades. Professor Byerly noted in the study cited earlier that the combined circulation of suburban newspapers in the metropolitan areas he studied jumped 52.2% between 1950 and 1968. Their gain of almost 3.3 million to a total of more than 9.5 million more than offset the almost 2.5 million loss of the metropolitan dailies in the same areas during the same period. The largest gains in suburban and other community newspapers were in New York, 921,911; Los Angeles, 550,495; San Francisco, 362,218; Philadelphia, 352,177; Boston, 180,323; Cleveland, 148,570; Detroit, 127,022; and Chicago, 111,103. Suburban and other community newspapers accounted for about one-third of the total number of newspapers read in the 21 metropolitan centers Byerly studied. The suburban ratio was 31.3% in 1968 as compared with 21.1% in 1950. In some of the large cities such as San Francisco, 54.7%, and Cincinnati, 48%, it was considerably more.[7]

The prospects for future suburban newspaper growth also appear excellent if recent population trends continue and the newspapers perform as they should. During the 1960s the United States' population grew about 14%, but the growth in the suburbs was two and one-half times that rate. If this trend continues, nearly half of the nation's people will be in the suburbs in the 1980s as compared with about a fourth in the central cities. The American Newspaper Publishers Association suggests that by 1980 there will be from 12 to 22 million potential new readers for newspapers, most of them in the suburbs.[8] The suburban newspapers can best serve these persons by providing local coverage and advertising. They can tackle local issues in depth and provide information about local individuals and organizations. Since some of their readers may not subscribe to a metropolitan daily, the suburban newspapers must also offer some coverage of central city, state, national and international affairs. The proper mixture between local and other types of news will depend on the availability of a good metropolitan newspaper in the area and how many of the suburban newspaper's readers actually read it.

Many suburban newspapers have been criticized in the past as being little more than community bulletin boards, and excellence was not widespread among them in the early 1970s. But some were producing quality coverage of social and political issues in their areas, and others were being challenged to improve. The Sun Papers of Omaha, for example, earned the Sigma Delta Chi public service award for their efforts in 1972. Suburban residents generally are active in school, church, civic and political organizations and want their newspapers to report on issues as well as activities that concern them. As the newspapers increase their readership and improve the quality of their coverage, they also expand their influence. Contenders for public office and supporters of bond issues and other proposals seek their editorial endorsement as well as their coverage.

Where suburban newspapers can attract and hold readers with a reasonably good editorial product, they should have no difficulty in obtaining advertising support. Community newspapers that people read provide an ideal vehicle for community stores to use in reaching their primary buying market. Many downtown dailies are now offering zoned editions so community advertisers can buy only a part of their circulation, and these editions can be helpful to the stores and their customers as well as to the downtown dailies. But suburban newspapers can provide far more attention to community news and thus have an advantage.

Suburban newspapers also have attracted more attention from national advertisers in recent years. Encouraging this interest has been U.S. Suburban Press, Inc., a privately owned sales representative for a national network of suburban newspaper packages. Two years after its formation in 1971, this group was representing more than 800 newspapers with a combined circulation of more than 10.5 million in 40 major metropolitan markets. On its agenda for discussion in the early 1970s were proposals for developing a national television supplement and obtaining more national advertising inserts for suburban newspapers.[9]

Newsday is perhaps the best-known and certainly is one of the most successful of the suburban daily newspapers. It was started in September, 1940 by Harry F. Guggenheim and his wife, Alicia Patterson, who served for many years as its editor and publisher. Their idea was to establish a community newspaper for the people of Long Island, and they succeeded admirably. *Newsday* and the area it serves have grown together. Circulation rose from 11,000 in 1940 to 450,000 in 1970. The newspaper survived some early financial challenges by winning the confidence of its readers, and it prospered by providing community leadership. It won numerous awards during its first three decades, including a Pulitzer Prize in 1954 for public service. *Newsday* adopted the tabloid format because its owners believed the smaller newspaper was easier to handle and provided better opportunity for displaying news, advertising and pictures. It developed an image as a serious, liberal, internationalist-minded newspaper that would fight to improve its community and the lives of those living in it.[10]

Mrs. Guggenheim died in July, 1963, and Mr. Guggenheim assumed the duties of publisher. He continued to own the controlling interest in the newspaper until May, 1970, when he sold his 51% to the Times Mirror Company of Los Angeles. Heirs of Mrs. Guggenheim exchanged the remaining 49% for Times Mirror stock later in the year. Mr. Guggenheim died in January 1971, at the age of 80.[11]

Some persons thought *Newsday* might shift its emphasis to the metropolitan market after it was purchased by the Los Angeles firm. But the new owners indicated their desire was to build a complete newspaper serving its own community of Nassau and Suffolk counties on Long Island. They indicated they would enlarge the newspaper's presentation of state, national and world news but remain fully attentive to local coverage. They assured readers that *Newsday* would continue to be an independent Long Island newspaper. Richard Attwood resigned as editor-in-chief of Cowles Communications, Inc., to become president and publisher of *Newsday* in 1970. *Newsday* added a Sunday edition in April 1972 which involved about 215 full-time employes and $1.3 million in capital spending. By late 1973 the Sunday edition appeared to be on solid ground with a circulation of 350,000 and advertising running ahead of original projections.[12]

Newsday got suburban competition in November 1966, when Cowles Communications, Inc., started the *Suffolk Sun*. It seemed a propitious time since three metropolitan newspapers had just decided to merge and the Long Island population had been growing rapidly. But the high hopes were not realized and the *Sun* ceased publication in October 1969, after losses of more than $6 million. Inability to retain delivery boys was cited as a factor in the newspaper's failure to develop circulation. Some suggested, however, that the newspaper's real problem was a failure to understand and become an integral part of the community it sought to serve. "The people who work for the paper come from somewhere else," was a complaint voiced frequently. "They never lived here—they don't know us or this county." The transitory nature of the county may also have been a factor. Many new persons were moving into the suburbs from New York. "Suffolk has not jelled," one Cowles official was quoted as saying. "The county is still diffused. It is still a county of isolated communities and they don't want to be unified. It just might be that the county was not ripe for a county-wide newspaper." Whatever the reasons for failure, many of the 73,000 subscribers probably missed the *Sun*. One teen-age girl expressed it this way: "Reading a newspaper can be a horrible chore to a 17-year-old girl (me). But I was always eager to read this particular paper because, although all the depressing news was there, happiness, humor and a sincere joyful respect for the human conditions were also there." [13]

The *Sun* deserves more than a footnote in newspaper history because its experience should provide lessons. For one thing, it demonstrates that success is not assured for all suburban newspapers just because some have done exceedingly well. Many factors, including money, community interest, advertising potential and existing competition must be considered carefully. The *Sun* might have succeeded in time; its advertising revenues were growing more rapidly in comparison than its circulation. But the owners believed that their stockholders should not be asked to accept more losses until the corner could be turned. The owners may also have misread the readiness of the community for their product and underestimated the competition of *Newsday*, which already served Suffolk County as well as Nassau County where it was published. Those contemplating newspaper ventures in the suburbs would do well to review the story.[14]

Persons interested in starting suburban newspapers also should review the struggle waged between January 1966, and June 1970, in the northwest suburbs

of Chicago. The principals involved were Paddock Publications, Inc., publishers of weeklies in that area since the turn of the century, and Field Enterprises, publisher of the metropolitan Chicago *Sun-Times* and Chicago *Daily
News*. The rapid growth of the area and perhaps other factors encouraged Field
Enterprises to create Day Publications, Inc., and begin several daily newspapers in competition with the 17 Paddock weeklies. *Arlington Heights Day* was
started in January, 1966; *Prospect* (Mount Prospect and Prospect Heights) *Day*
three months later; *Des Plaines Day* in August, 1968; and *Northwest Day* in
June, 1969. Paddock responded by increasing the publication of a number of
his weeklies to triweekly and eventually making about half of them dailies.
Residents could get a Paddock newspaper in the morning and a Day newspaper
in the afternoon in addition to one or more of the metropolitan Chicago newspapers. For a time local coverage in the Northwest Chicago suburbs was extensive and intense. One local mayor was quoted as saying, ''The people's right to
know is so well executed that I feel like I am living in a fish bowl on Main
Street.'' The people benefited greatly from the competition, but the publishers
had problems. Losses reportedly were incurred by both sides. Finally, in June
1970, Paddock purchased the four Field Enterprises suburban dailies and
Field's southwest suburban weeklies group, and the heated competition was
ended. Three of the Day newspapers were merged with their Paddock counterparts and the *Northwest Day* dropped.[15]

Although both publishers reportedly lost money in the 54-month struggle,
both probably learned from it. The people of Northwest Chicago were the principal beneficiaries, however. In June 1970, when the changes were completed,
there were 11 suburban dailies and several triweeklies being published in areas
once served by weeklies. In addition, the metropolitan newspapers were encouraged to improve their packages to compete more effectively with the
stronger suburban competition. Stuart R. Paddock, Jr., president of Paddock
Publications, was quoted as saying that the competition had provided ''local
media with the challenge and incentive to adjust to new conditions, to change
old concepts and practices, and to look to the future with broader insights and
new perspectives.'' [16] The struggle also may have demonstrated the complementary as well as the competitive relationships between suburban and metropolitan newspapers. Other publishers in the greater Chicago area and elsewhere
can learn from the experience.

Developments in Los Angeles and San Francisco can also provide insight
into the growth of suburban newspapers. By the late 1960s the rapidly growing
Los Angeles metropolitan area, including Los Angeles and Orange counties,
had more than 100 newspapers. Among them were two metropolitan dailies,
the *Los Angeles Times* and the *Los Angeles Herald-Examiner*, 24 suburban
dailies and numerous weeklies. This area seems ideal for suburban newspaper
growth because its population is growing so rapidly and creating numerous
suburban communities of some size. Orange County, with 1.2 million resi-

dents, was the fastest growing county in the nation in the late 1960s. It had doubled its population three times in two decades and was expected to double it again in the next decade. The *Times* responded to this opportunity in 1968 by creating an Orange County edition published in a new Orange County plant and integrated with the regular edition of the newspaper published in downtown Los Angeles. The idea was to give Orange County residents about 100 pages a week of Orange County information in addition to the regular coverage of the *Times*. The edition might be considered more an indirect than direct competitor of the community newspapers, however, since it emphasized county-wide interests.[17]

The San Francisco Bay Area also had developed more than 100 newspapers by the end of the 1960s. There were five metropolitan dailies, including the *Chronicle* and *Examiner* in San Francisco, the *Mercury* and the *News* in San Jose, and the *Tribune* in Oakland, 23 suburban dailies and a number of weeklies. These newspapers were analyzed in some detail in a 1971 report of the Institute of Governmental Studies, University of California, Berkeley, by William L. Rivers and David M. Rubin of the Department of Communication, Stanford University. Rivers and Rubin concluded that journalism in the Bay Area was mediocre, although they had compliments for some newspapers. They suggested that the Bay Area newspapers could improve markedly by raising the pay scales for reporters and editors dramatically and by disentangling themselves from local establishments.[18]

Suburban newspaper groups have been developed in a number of metropolitan areas during recent years. Fairly typical is ComCorp Inc., which purchased its first newspaper in Cleveland in 1965. By late 1972, the group had bought 10 other newspapers in a move to encircle the downtown Cleveland area. David Skylar, ComCorp president, said the organization could attract many more large advertisers by offering coverage throughout Cleveland's suburbs. Harte-Hanks Newspapers, Inc., a Texas-based firm, acquired three publishing groups involving 19 newspapers around San Diego in the early 1970s, and The Minneapolis Star & Tribune Co. in 1972 had 20 newspapers ringing Denver.[19] Other organizations made similar moves in an effort to attract advertisers and enjoy the other benefits of group ownership.

Many publishers of suburban newspapers have sought to work together through organizations such as Suburban Newspapers of America, formed from three other organizations in 1971 with a nucleus of about 50 publishers. By 1973 the SNA was representing some 225 publishers who collectively owned nearly 1,000 newspapers with an aggregate circulation of more than 10 million. Kenneth R. Ketcham, executive director, said that SNA was represented in every major market and many of the smaller ones and was in touch with about 1,200 additional publishers identified as suburban. SNA membership included free circulation and voluntary-paid circulation as well as paid circulation newspaper members. Ketcham said the notion that free circulation newspapers are of subpar quality when compared with paid-for newspapers was slowly changing and that ultimately such newspapers would be recognized as not being detrimental to professional journalism.[20]

One important outgrowth of the Suburban Newspapers of America organization was the creation in August 1971, of the Suburban Newspaper Research Center in Chicago. The center was to develop programs of special interest to suburban markets and suburban newspapers; it began its efforts with a study to construct a recognized and acceptable national profile of member suburban newspapers, measure their community impact, examine the life style of their readers and measure their advertising effectiveness. The results of this study, conducted by H.D. Ostberg & Associates, New York were heralded in 1973 as proof of the strong position that suburban newspapers have in the national marketplace. A suburban newspaper was defined as one covering areas described as suburban by census data and having 65% or more of its editorial content devoted to local news. The suburban reader was described as someone who is stable and settled and who has high needs and purchasing interests. Suburban readers are involved in community activities, such as PTA, church organizations and political clubs. The average suburban reader buys 50% more items than the national average, and two thirds of the suburban readers do their buying in suburban stores.[21]

Small-city dailies close to expanding metropolitan areas often have adopted formats similar to those employed successfully by the suburban newspapers. They emphasize coverage of local news and local issues which neither the metropolitan newspapers nor the other media can cover so intensively. Except for major stories, they confine their national and international coverage to summaries or roundups. The exact news mixture of these small-city dailies like that of the suburban dailies will, of course, depend to a great extent on the availability of a good metropolitan daily and whether their readers also subscribe to it. Those persons who have a good metropolitan daily and a good suburban or small-city daily in their area, and read them, should be reasonably well informed on issues that are important to them.

WEEKLIES AND OTHER NON-DAILIES

Weeklies and other non-dailies serve a variety of special interest groups and residents of cities, suburbs and small towns throughout the nation. In the early 1970s there were approximately 9,000 non-daily newspapers being published in the United States and an increasing number of "shoppers," which have some characteristics of newspapers and at times are published by newspapers. Weeklies still outnumbered all other units of the news-reporting mass media combined.

Predictions by some that the weekly newspaper industry is dying seem unfounded. Some weeklies have ceased publication because the small towns in which they were located lost business and population and could not support them, but others have prospered. New technology including the widespread adoption of offset printing has helped many weeklies. Central printing plants have reduced the production problems of some, and the growth of groups or chains has given economic stability to others. Many new weeklies have been started to serve the expanding population of the suburbs. Weeklies can provide a specialized service for a particular group of persons not readily available elsewhere. They can serve a geographical community such as a small town or suburb of a large city, or they can serve an interest group such as an ethnic community or members of a religious denomination. They can effectively complement what other media do for these persons.

John Cameron Sim, who in 1969 published an extensive study of non-daily newspapers titled *The Grass Roots Press: America's Community Newspapers*, was optimistic about their future. Sim chose to speculate rather than predict what the next half century would bring in physical format and methods of production and distribution. But he did predict that "essential functions will remain much the same because human nature and human wants will remain the same. There is no doubt that the news consumer of the future *will be able* (italics his) to get his news and opinion in exotic electronic forms, but it is doubtful that the demand for this will be widespread." [22]

Most of the weeklies are based on geographical communities, either small towns or city suburbs. These publications generally are not well known outside their own geographical areas, but they often perform vital roles within them. Like their daily counterparts in larger geographic areas they have basic responsibilities to inform, influence, entertain and contribute to economic growth and individual well-being through advertising. Ideally, they provide a forum for local citizens to exchange views. They may also provide their readers with a sense of identity and belonging.

Small-town and suburban weeklies vary greatly in quality. Some are unattractive, poorly written, unresponsive to local needs and largely filled with trivia. Too many still fail to provide editorial leadership concerning local issues. Sim's study indicated that fewer than half of all weeklies in the nation run editorial comment of any kind. Many of those which do run something rely on syndicated materials, exchanges or comments suggested by various public relations agencies.[23] Some editors say they do not write editorials because they lack time or skills or because they believe too few persons read them; but this argument may be more of a rationalization than a reason. On the other hand, many weeklies have improved their appearance, especially through the use of offset printing; some are well written, and some concentrate on providing coverage of issues and events that no other medium can provide. Many do a respectable job of covering routine news; some provide in-depth reporting and incisive editorials on important issues.

Sim and others have questioned the reported reliance that national political leaders place on small-town newspapers for gauging public opinion. Sim said the contention that the community editor has the closest rapport with and truest understanding of grass roots opinion is not borne out by scientific polling or the results of national elections. Ben H. Bagdikian, the noted newspaper critic, said the idea of the community newspaper as the grass-roots opinion maker is a myth. He particularly criticized the newspapers that run as their own editorials propaganda supplied to them by various special-interest sources. Bagdikian charged that almost any private citizen or special group could buy into the editorial columns of smaller newspapers with relative ease and low cost.[24]

The outlook for small-town newspapers could improve greatly in the next few years if efforts to revitalize the nation's small towns are successful. New technology, joint printing arrangements and other developments could help produce vital local newspapers if other signs of life can be infused into apparently dying communities. Free subscriptions on a mass-distribution basis may be part of the answer. Certainly, the small-town newspapers should encourage efforts by Congress and by state legislators to reverse population trends and encourage growth in rural America.

In the meantime, the big growth area for weekly newspapers as well as daily newspapers is in the suburbs where increasing numbers of persons are making their homes and opening shopping centers and other businesses. Some suburbs are sufficiently developed to need daily coverage. Many others can be served well at this time by weeklies, semiweeklies or triweeklies. Growth has been promoted by the development of new technology, especially offset printing, and the expansion of newspaper groups such as Paddock Publications in Chicago. These suburban weeklies provide the community news that the metropolitan dailies and other media cannot.

Suburban weeklies have obvious advantages over their small-town counterparts. They are located where the people are and where the greatest advertising potential is. But they also face competition from the zoned editions of metropolitan dailies and especially from the shoppers, or give-away papers consisting largely of advertising. Some of the metropolitan newspapers seek to provide special sections with news of particular communities. This is offered along with the regular package of state, national and international news and other features. The shoppers seek to provide advertisers with blanket coverage in a particular area. They may or may not have any substantial amount of news or features, but their primary concern is advertising. If the advertisers believe they are getting sufficient exposure from the shoppers, they may be reluctant to advertise in the weekly newspapers.

Weeklies can best compete with the metropolitan newspapers by providing more and better local coverage, particularly of important local issues. The larger newspapers usually do not have the time and staff to get as fully involved in issues at the community level as the community newspapers do. The *Country Squire,* published in a wealthy suburb of Kansas City, was cited in an article in the *Grassroots Editor* in 1968 for its coverage of racial news. The newspaper devoted an entire issue on April 18 to "our attitude and the Negro." Business-men, housewives, school administrators, ministers, high school students and other residents of suburban Johnson County spoke candidly of their attitudes. Editor Tom Leathers was quoted as saying, "this free expression represents an important step for this community. When people feel able to freely express their own views and their attitudes, the answer to many problems will come more easily." [25] The weeklies often compete with the shoppers by starting shoppers of their own. They have the printing facilities, and they often can improve the shoppers by providing news and feature material to accompany the advertising.

While most non-dailies fall into the small-city and suburban classifica-tions, there are other groupings. Some weeklies, for example, are published for geographic areas within the city rather than in the suburbs. Many weeklies are published for ethnic groups or special interests. A few general interest weeklies also were reaching national audiences in the early 1970s. The most significant was the *National Observer,* started in 1962 by Dow Jones & Company, Inc., publisher of the *Wall Street Journal.* The *National Observer* was designed to present information about world-wide events and cultural developments in an attractive newspaper format. It has had a strong cultural and educational flavor and has included many in-depth reports designed to help readers with basic problems such as health, jobs and education. Although it is published only weekly and has a comparatively small audience for a national publication, the *National Observer* is regarded by many as a quality newspaper. It is discussed in more detail in Chapter 8.

The *National Enquirer,* a tabloid published by Generoso (Gene) Pope, Jr., with headquarters in New Jersey, achieved considerable success in the 1960s with a somewhat different formula. It appealed to a broader audience with a wide variety of stories. One issue, for example, carried a story about new cars, several stories about an accident involving prominent Americans, stories about the neglect of mentally disturbed children, the cost and frustration involved in building the John F. Kennedy Memorial in Washington, the "hysteria" of women over actor Tom Jones, and a success story about how to make a million dollars. The *Enquirer* was started in 1926 by the Hearst Corporation as a Sun-day afternoon newspaper, and it passed through several owners before being purchased by Pope in 1952. At that time it had a circulation of about 17,000. Pope used a fairly sensational formula during the 1950s and early 1960s to build the circulation to about one million, but he began to sense a change in public attitudes about 1966. He toned the paper down somewhat and it lost circulation for a time; but it was soon over the million mark. The *Enquirer* is now distributed at supermarkets and convenience stores, and the product is aimed at those who shop there. The *Enquirer* got competition in 1974 when Australian Rupert Murdoch launched a weekly tabloid called the *National Star*.

Murdoch achieved financial success in his native country and England with a somewhat sensational formula involving cheesecake, splashy layouts, and promotions, and it appeared that the *Star* would be cast from a similar mold.[26]

All this considered, the future of the weekly or community newspaper is not as bleak as some have pictured it. The future of small-town newspapers will, of course, depend to some extent on the revitalization of rural America. But the prospects for growth in the suburbs look promising, and the need for special interest newspapers likely will continue. Some of the suburban areas will require dailies; others can be served adequately by weeklies. The prospects for special interest newspapers likewise are encouraging and should be considered further.

BLACK NEWSPAPERS

Black newspapers were started in the United States during the nineteenth century to oppose the exploitation of black persons and to secure for them equal rights and opportunities. They have continued, at least in part, because blacks have continued to feel a need for such publications. Many blacks say that the white press has been discriminatory in its coverage as well as in its editorial policies. They charge that most newspapers have run stories about blacks only when those blacks have affected the white community in some way. Blacks who were accused of crimes were publicized; those who succeeded in business, contributed to arts and letters, or did other useful things were not. As a result of the human rights movement of the 1960s and 1970s many white newspapers have increased their coverage of blacks, their needs and their achievements. But many persons believe that black newspapers still are needed to cover the everyday affairs of the black community and support causes of interest to its citizens just as other specialized newspapers are needed to serve other specialized groups.

What exactly is a black newspaper, and why is it called "black" rather than Negro, colored or some other term? Basically, a black newspaper is one owned and operated by blacks, intended primarily for a black audience, and concerned with blacks' struggle for equality and justice in a society dominated by whites. Some consider newspapers owned by whites but intended for blacks as black newspapers; others would insist that for a newspaper to be considered black the majority of the stockholders and employes must be black.

The term "black" is used here because an increasing number of blacks seem to prefer it and because most of the scholarly works done in the field recently have used it. "Negro" is still used by many, including the National Newspaper Publishers Association, composed of Negro or black publications. "Afro-American" is preferred by others and is used in the title of a number of black newspapers. Roland E. Wolseley in *The Black Press, U.S.A.;* Martin Dann, editor, in *The Black Press (1827–1900)*; and Henry La Brie III in *The*

Black Press in America: A Guide all have used the term "black." Wolseley noted a lack of uniformity and explains that his choice is based on the fact that many persons actively concerned with the welfare of this group use "black." [27]

An estimated 3,000 black newspapers have been published in the United States since the first one, *Freedom's Journal,* was started in 1827. But they received scant attention in the standard histories until at least the 1940s when Gunnar Myrdal made his classic report on the American racial situation. In *An American Dilemma* Myrdal referred to the Negro press as the greatest single power in the Negro race. At that time there were about 150 Negro newspapers with an estimated circulation of 1.6 million. The *Pittsburgh Courier,* with a circulation of 257,000; the *Chicago Defender,* 202,000; and the *Baltimore Afro-American,* 137,000 were the most influential. All were national in approach and reached a national audience. [28]

Whether the black newspapers of the early 1970s had the influence ascribed to such publications by Myrdal in the middle 1940s is doubtful. There were more black papers; some estimates ran as high as 250 to 300. They reached more than twice as many persons; total circulation was estimated at 4 million. But their competition also had increased. White newspapers were giving more attention to the black community. Radio and television were providing news coverage as well as entertainment, and a number of black magazines had been developed. Several newspapers representing organizations such as the Nation of Islam and several local newspapers with national editions probably exerted considerable national influence, and many black newspapers exerted influence at the local level. Although they had considerably less circulation, the *Courier, Defender* and *Afro-American* all had national as well as local editions. [29]

Muhammad Speaks, the Islam weekly published in Chicago, had by far the largest circulation of any black newspaper in the early 1970s. According to a report compiled by Henry LaBrie and published in 1973, it had a circulation in excess of 600,000. LaBrie's study, [30] supported by *Editor & Publisher* and by the Institute for Communication Studies at the University of Iowa, indicated that there were 208 black newspapers being published, including four dailies, five biweeklies, and 10 monthlies or bimonthlies. Their total circulation in early 1973 was more than 4 million. Only 22 of the black newspapers were members of the Audit Bureau of Circulation at that time; they had a verified circulation of 517,392. The largest black newspapers audited by ABC were the *Amsterdam News* in New York, 82,000; the *Los Angeles Sentinel,* 49,000; *Philadelphia Tribune,* 38,500; *Chicago Daily Defender,* 35,000; and *Baltimore Afro-American,* 34,000.

LaBrie's study indicated that two states, California and Texas, had more than a fifth of the black newspapers. California had 25 newspapers with a reported circulation of more than 800,000, and Texas had 20 newspapers with a reported circulation of more than 250,000. Other states with substantial numbers included Florida, 14; Illinois, 13; New York, 11; and Alabama and North Carolina, 9 each. More than four-fifths of the papers were being printed by the offset process. Figures compiled from 195 of the papers showed that the black press employed 2,324 persons, of whom 234, or 10%, are white. No whites were employed on 116 of the papers.

Several of the better-known black newspapers were members of the half-dozen black newspaper groups, or chains, that existed in the early 1970s. The largest was the John Sengstacke group, which included the *Chicago Daily Defender* and the *Pittsburgh Courier,* renamed *New Courier.* Sengstacke is the nephew of Robert S. Abbott, who is sometimes called the father of the modern Negro press. Abbott started the *Defender* in 1905 and in subsequent years led many struggles to obtain fairer treatment for blacks. When he died in 1940, he left two-thirds interest in the newspaper to Sengstacke, who helped it obtain a secure footing again after depression problems. Sengstacke converted the *Defender* into a daily in 1956 and developed a newspaper group of nine units. The acquisition in 1966 of the Courier papers, including Couriers in Ohio, Georgia, Florida and Philadelphia as well as Pittsburgh, was a major one. The group also had newspapers in Detroit, Shreveport, and Memphis as the 1970s opened. Circulation for all units was in excess of 200,000.[31]

The Afro-American newspapers, with a total circulation of more than 130,000, formed the second largest group. Included were Afro-American editions for Baltimore, Washington, Richmond, New Jersey and the nation at large, all published in Baltimore. John H. Murphy, Sr., was one of several persons who helped develop the *Afro-American* about the turn of the century, and his descendants have continued to operate it. The *Afro-American in* 1969 became the first black publication to win the annual achievement award of the American Society of Journalism School Administrators. The award was made "In recognition of the distinguished record of a newspaper which has served a predominantly black community and which has actively engaged in community service." All five editions of the paper were cited.

Other black newspaper groups included the Post Newspapers in Oakland, Berkeley, San Francisco and Richmond; the New Leader group in Louisiana, and the World, or Scott, group in Atlanta, Birmingham and Memphis.[32] The *Atlanta World* is the oldest of the Scott papers and was one of only four black dailies being published in the early 1970s. It was started by Alexander Scott in 1928 and converted into a daily in 1932. Its generally conservative political outlook may have been a factor in the formation of other more liberal black newspapers in the Atlanta area in the 1960s. Georgia got a second black daily in 1970 when Ophelia DeVore Mitchell started *The Columbus Times.*[33]

Some individual black newspapers and newspaper groups appeared to be doing well financially in the early 1970s, but the black press generally was facing economic problems. Black newspapers needed more advertising revenues to

attract and hold competent staff members and purchase the equipment necessary to produce a competitive product. They had been successful in getting advertising from many black businesses and from small white businesses operating in black neighborhoods, but they had made limited progress in attracting
the large white advertisers they needed. Moreover, an increasing reliance on
white advertisers threatened to create a credibility gap between the newspapers
and some of their constituents. Some critics argued that the black press could
not attack the roots of institutional racism as long as it depended on white advertising for survival. It appeared that the newspapers were caught between a
vocal segment of blacks that regarded them as too conservative, outdated, and
irrelevant, and the rising costs of production and news gathering which forced
them to look for white advertisers.[34] Somehow the newspapers had to satisfy
their critics that they could accept white advertising and be relevant, build their
circulation to attract advertisers, and not scare those advertisers away by appearing too militant.

Black newspapers also had to answer a variety of other criticisms, some of
which were the result of inadequate financing. Various papers were accused of
providing inadequate news coverage, distorting their coverage through use of
opinions and through omissions, sensationalism in both news and advertising,
careless editing, poor makeup and poor printing. It was charged that many
black newspapers filled their front pages with crime and violence and their inside pages with publicity handouts and trivia. It was said that much of their advertising appealed to superstition or was preoccupied with sex.[35]

Individual newspapers, newspaper groups, the National Newspaper Publishers Association and others were seeking answers to these challenges in the
1970s. The publishers' association took on added significance in the late 1960s
and 1970s as younger executives from smaller newspapers became more active
in its operations. Two men associated with this influx were elected to serve as
the group's top officers in 1971. Garth Reeves, publisher of the *Miami Times,*
was named president, and Dr. Carleton Goodlett, physician and publisher of
the *San Francisco Reporter,* was named vice-president.[36] Dr. Goodlett was
named president in 1973.

The outlook for black newspapers appeared uncertain as the middle 1970s
began. Continuing inflation, the threat of newsprint shortages and an energy
crisis cast additional shadows over an already cloudy economic picture. However, it appeared that black newspapers could serve definite needs in society.
First, they could provide coverage of black persons and activities not available
anywhere else. Conventional newspapers did not have the space to report on all
births, deaths, marriages, business developments, church news, school news
and myriad other events. Second, they could provide information and comment
on general stories from a black vantage point. Other media could and would
cover these events, but the black newspapers could give them a different perspective. Finally, they could provide the vehicle for getting advertisers that

wanted to reach black audiences together with those audiences. Black newspapers could do for black communities somewhat the same thing that suburban
newspapers and small city newspapers were doing for their communities. As
long as black communities exist, there would seem to be a need for black newspapers.

College Newspapers

College newspapers form a divergent, sometimes controversial, but none-
theless significant segment of the United States press. Like black and other specialized newspapers they serve a need that is not met by general newspapers,
dailies or nondailies. An estimated 1,800 college newspapers were being published in the early 1970s with a total circulation of about 6 million. Approximately 80 of the newspapers were published at least four times a week and
were classified as dailies. Their circulations ranged from a few hundred to
50,000 or more. Their staffs varied in size from a handful to more than a
hundred, and, at times, they included full-time professionals as well as
hundreds of contributors. Upwards of 20,000 students worked for them in some
capacity. Costs ranged from a few dollars to as much as $5,000 a week, and in-
come varied from a few hundred dollars to more than half a million a year in
advertising revenues. Readership generally was higher for college newspapers
than it was for newspapers of general circulation. One survey showed that 96%
of the students read at least part of the campus newspaper. Influence is not easy
to measure, but many of the causes championed by college newspapers have
succeeded.[37]

The roles and responsibilities of college newspapers vary somewhat from
campus to campus and often are regarded differently by students, administrators and other constituent groups. Student editors may see the newspapers as
their own journals of opinion and expression. Other students and often faculty
may see them as publicity vehicles for campus organizations. Journalism faculty may see them as training opportunities for future professionals. Administrators may see them as a means of communicating official information to
students and faculty, and those outside the campus community may see them as
a means of keeping up with student views and activities. The good student
newspaper may do all of these things, and others, to a degree. Their challenge
is to develop a mixture that will best serve the needs and interests of their particular audiences.

Student newspapers should seek to inform, influence and entertain their
readers just as other newspapers do. They should offer a wide range of information and provide a forum for the discussion of topics important to the
campus community. These topics may include national issues such as elections,
Congressional programs and environmental reforms as well as local issues. The
newspapers should seek to help their readers individually and collectively, and

they should perform a watch-dog function both for student organizations and the institution as a whole. They should provide a representative picture of the constituent groups on campus and, whenever possible, foster understanding and promote cooperation among students, faculty, administrators, alumni and the public generally. In some communities where the campus newspaper is also the principal town publication, they must also give attention to off-campus needs and activities.

How well the student newspapers perform these tasks will be determined to a considerable degree by the way in which they are organized and administered. The traditional method of relating campus newspapers to their school administrations has been to appoint a faculty or staff member as adviser. The roles of advisers have varied greatly; often their jobs have been difficult to define and more difficult to perform. Some advisers have read all copy for the newspapers; others have read stories only when asked to offer an opinion on some specific question. Some advisers have had authority to change or eliminate stories before publication; others have had authority only to express an opinion about stories before publication and offer a critique later. Too often the advisers have been caught between administrators who looked upon the student newspaper as a public relations arm of the college and editors who were determined to exercise their concept of free expression. Recent court decisions restricting the right of advisers and administrators to review or censor stories before publication [38] could clarify the adviser's role in tax-supported schools at least, but they may or may not make it easier. If advisers are expected by administrators to accomplish controls through their personal influence that they cannot exercise under law, their jobs will be difficult if not impossible.

Other and perhaps better methods of student newspaper operation include the use of publication boards that employ and dismiss editors but do not supervise their day-to-day performance, the employment of full-time professional journalists to supervise operations, and the creation of independent corporations to operate the newspapers. The publications board approach can work reasonably well if board members have a good understanding of the roles and responsibilities of colleges newspapers and exercise good judgment in the selection of staff members. Boards like advisers can no longer exercise the censorship powers over newspaper copy that some sought to exercise in the past; but they can exercise a form of censorship in their selection of personnel for the newspaper. Boards probably should include a cross-section of students, faculty, university or college staff members and professional journalists to operate effectively. Procedures for selecting newspaper staff members and conducting other business should be spelled out carefully and adhered to strictly. Some student newspapers may operate under the supervision of a publications board and also have an adviser to advise them on the day-to-day operations.

Some large student newspapers such as the *Michigan State News* have found it helpful to employ full-time journalism professionals in key positions such as publisher, business manager, advertising director and editorial director. The idea is to have trained professionals supervising the operation on a continuing basis. Students still make decisions, write editorials, report news, sell advertising and perform other basic tasks but under professional supervision. Michigan State took this step in 1961 after university funds had been cut and the newspaper's subsidy of $45,000 a year had been eliminated. Louis J. Berman, owner of a weekly newspaper in Whitehall, Michigan, was employed as general manager of the *State News*. Under his direction in the 1960s, the newspaper not only paid off a $32,000 debt but achieved a $200,000 balance. In 1970 the *State News* was the largest college daily in the world and the fifth largest daily in the state of Michigan. It had a circulation of 50,000 and averaged 14 pages daily, six days a week, including a Sunday edition. The newspaper had advertising revenues in excess of a half million dollars a year and was financially independent except for a $1.00 a term fee charged each full-time student. Berman was in charge of the newspaper's financial affairs, but he did not run its editorial policy. An advisory board, including four faculty members and four students, selected the editor-in-chief and advertising manager.[39] The use of professionals as supervisers will not necessarily eliminate conflicts between student editors and college administrators, as the University of Florida *Alligator* found out in the early 1970s; but such persons can provide more continuity and guidance than an adviser who is only that.

At times the conflicts between student journalists and college administrators can be resolved or avoided by the creation of independent corporations to operate the campus newspapers. The *Daily Californian* at the University of California at Berkeley, the University of Kentucky *Kernel,* the University of Florida *Alligator,* and several others have taken this step in recent years. The University of Michigan *Daily* and a number of the Ivy League college newspapers have been independent operations for many years. Independent college newspapers do not receive funds from student fees, and they do not get direct subsidies from their colleges. Some listed as independent have got indirect subsidies in the form of rent-free office space on campus. Like other independent newspapers the independent college newspapers must look to advertising and circulation for financial support.

In view of recent court decisions affirming the rights of college newspapers to freedom of expression, the independent corporations approach may help college administrators more than college editors.[40] The corporations, of course, assume the responsibilities once incumbent upon the administrators. Editors of independent newspapers need not resort to legal action against administrators to assure their freedoms, but they also must assume new responsibilities. The student body and ultimately the institution could suffer from the arrangement, however, unless the newspaper can obtain sufficient revenue from advertising to provide free distribution to all students. Newspapers that charge for subscriptions reportedly reach only a third to a half of the student body. Reliance on advertising for most of their support can also bring student newspapers into more direct competition with commercial newspapers and other media in the community. Such media may not feel kindly toward the college newspapers or the college administrators that encouraged the independent arrangement.

It seemed unlikely in the early 1970s that any simple or ideal solutions for the problems of the collegiate press would be forthcoming in the immediate future. But studies of what had been done at various institutions using various approaches did offer guidelines that individual institutions could consider in seeking to work out their own operations. Major studies were accomplished by the Special Commission on the Student Press appointed by the University of California in 1969 and by a committee of the American Association of State Colleges and Universities commissioned in 1972. The California commission, which was headed by Norman E. Isaacs, a long-time Louisville newspaperman, reviewed campus journalism in California and other states before making its report in 1970. This report challenged the widely held view that student publications necessarily constitute a form of official publication for which university administrations bear an inherent responsibility; it urged all concerned to recognize that these publications are not official organs of the schools where they are published.

The commission noted that fiscal and editorial independence contribute greatly to the development of good campus newspapers. At the same time, it insisted that the principal newspaper on campus has an obligation to report accurately and fairly on all important campus matters, to distinguish between opinion and news, to report all sides of controversies, to correct mistakes with reasonable prominence and to afford ample opportunity for answers to editorial opinions. The commission agreed that campus newspapers should publish important administration announcements but suggested that the administration provide a newsletter or other means to circulate official statements, interpretations and news. It cited a need for journalism seminars at institutions where journalism instruction is not available and a need for advisers who can provide practical advice when such counsel is solicited by publications boards, editors or staff members. The commission did not see the sporadic use of obscenity as a major issue, but did make several observations about it. For instance, it suggested that the older generation was not likely to get anywhere with protests about obscenity in campus publications as long as it patronized obscenity in books, motion pictures and other areas. Finally, the commission cited a need for patience and understanding on the part of students, administrators and others in working out common problems.[41]

A committee of the American Association of State Colleges and Universities that included college and university presidents, journalism professors, metropolitan editors and student editors also made an intensive study of the college press. Its work was financed by the John and Mary R. Markle Foundation; its report was prepared by Julius Duscha, director of the Washington Journalism

Center, and Thomas C. Fischer, consultant in higher education and former assistant dean of the Georgetown University Law Center. This committee concluded that the independent student newspaper is the best answer to the problems of the student press, but warned that it was not easy to turn a subsidized
newspaper into an independent, financially solvent publication. The committee
said the independent newspaper enables students to operate in the best traditions of the free press, encourages more responsible journalism and clearly sep-
arates the views of the students from those of the administration. The committee suggested that on campuses where independent newspapers are not feasible
that student editors should seek to establish a corporation similar to that for an
independent newspaper. This corporation would then contract with the institution for a direct subsidy or with the student government board for a portion of
student activity fees. The committee said that independent newspapers should
remain a part of the university community and lead in bringing its diverse elements together in a cohesive force. But it also recommended that where campus
newspapers do go independent that colleges or universities should consider
publishing a house organ to serve as a link of communication for faculty, staff
and interested students. Soon after the Duscha and Fischer report was published, its case for independent college newspapers was challenged by Dr. Louis
E. Ingelhart, chairman of an ad hoc committee of the National Council of
College Publications Advisers to examine the legal status of college newspapers. His report argues for freedom but not independence of college newspapers, asserts the validity of the faculty adviser's role, and argues for continued
financial support of college newspapers by the institutions they serve.[42]

It was important that college newspapers achieve and maintain editorial
and financial independence in the 1970s if they were to continue the trend
toward investigative reporting that many had developed in the years after World
War II. Many college newspapers have reflected, and perhaps led, an increased
student awareness of social, political and other human problems in society.
Melvin Mencher, an associate professor of journalism at Columbia University,
suggested in a May 1971 article in *The Quill* that in some states college newspapers had taken the lead in reporting four important areas: civil rights, foreign
affairs, politics and education. College newspapers exposed discrimination in
fraternal social systems, athletics and other areas on campus; they explored discrimination and poverty in the communities near them; they criticized American involvement in Southeast Asia and questioned the role of American higher
education in conducting research for the military. Student newspapers exposed
what they believed to be failures in the nation's system of higher education;
they attacked the concept of *in loco parentis* which permitted colleges to act in
place of parents, and they raised questions about teaching methods and campus
administrative structure.[43]

Some college newspapers became involved in the radicalism that swept
some campuses and threatened others in the late 1960s. For a time many

college journalists viewed objective journalism with contempt, and some turned to the alternative rather than the straight press for inspiration. But as the mood on campus changed in the early 1970s, the approach of many college newspapers was modified. They did not lose interest in reporting issues of concern to the campus and community and return to the campus trivia that dominated many college newspapers before World War II. But many apparently abandoned or rejected a shift to personalized journalism. Douglas E. Kneeland, roving reporter for the *New York Times,* indicated in a March 1972, article in *The Quill* that this trend was evident in a survey of a dozen newspapers from coast to coast taken by the *Times.* There was almost unanimous agreement among the editors surveyed on the need for straight reporting rather than personalized journalism and on the importance of keeping editorial opinion separated from news columns.[44]

The *Daily Californian,* which became an independent corporation and accountable for what it printed, was among the college newspapers that underwent substantial change in the early 1970s. Its editor-in-chief noted that establishing credibility was a life or death matter. "It simply comes down to the fact that if we present the material in a traditional way, as far as we can, more people are going to believe it," she said. The newspaper's associate city editor added, "It is basically more effective to try and present the facts as objectively as possible. If we report the facts accurately, and we have a cogent editorial policy giving our opinion on them, that is the strongest presentation." The editor-in-chief of the Purdue *Exponent* reported that his newspaper had abandoned advocacy journalism because it was ineffective and involved half-truths and because a really complete story will be indicting. He did suggest that activists in the newsrooms could help keep the newspapers on the right path.[45]

All things considered, the prospects for college newspapers looked good as the middle 1970s began. Differences of opinion with administrators, student councils that control student activity funds, and others were expected to continue; but court decisions helped to assure editorial freedom, and guidelines such as those suggested in the California and AASCU studies should help resolve differences. The need for more investigative newspapers seemed great and the market potential for supporting them seemed good. Students had more money to spend in the 1970s than ever before, and advertisers were eager to reach them. Campus newspapers had a higher readership than many general circulation newspapers and usually had fewer distribution problems. Lowering the voting age to 18 also opened up new possibilities for political reporting and advertising. New technology was evolving that could improve the appearance of the newspapers and reduce their production costs. It appeared that college newspapers which could solve their financial problems and work out reasonable relationships with their administrators could serve many useful purposes on campus and in their broader communities.

OTHER SPECIAL INTERESTS

Black newspapers and college newspapers were only two of many types of newspapers that were serving special interest groups in the early 1970s. Ethnic newspapers, business newspapers, military newspapers, shoppers, and other specialized publications also were meeting a variety of needs not met by the general circulation newspapers. At times the influence of these special interest publications in their fields was considerable. Often they provided advertising appeals. A few of them will be discussed briefly, beginning with the ethnic press.

The ethnic press was reported in 1970 to be alive, well, and in some areas experiencing growth symptoms. About 330 foreign language newspapers disappeared between 1940 and 1960 and another 300 dropped out in the 1960s. But these losses were described as fewer than those of the general circulation English-language publications by Read Lewis of the American Council for Nationalities Service. Ethnic newspapers have been defined as those published in a foreign language or in English but addressing themselves to a national group. Using this definition there were about 440 such newspapers in 38 languages, excluding English, in 1970. Precise circulation figures were not available but it was estimated that the total was more than two million.

Spyridon Granitsas discussed the status and prospects of the ethnic press in a series of articles in *Editor & Publisher* during late 1970 and 1971. He reported a general agreement among observers that the ethnic press, at least in some areas, would not only reverse the trend toward decline but gain some ground. Granitsas noted that advertising volume was up, that both conservative and liberal candidates had advertised in ethnic newspapers in recent elections, and that 36 new ethnic newspapers in English had been started in 1969 and 1970. He also suggested that the ethnics might be helped by the increasing acceptance of a "pluralistic" America and by the fact that they provide a cheaper means of reaching ethnics with advertising than other media. Changing patterns of immigration since passage of a 1965 immigration law abolishing the old national origins quota system may also promote the growth of an ethnic press.[46]

Chicano Newspapers

The development of a Mexican-American, or Chicano, human rights movement in the middle 1960s promoted the development of about 50 bilingual newspapers to serve Americans of Mexican descent. These newspapers were different, however, from the Spanish language press that already was in operation in a number of cities; the Chicano newspapers were more radical and some would include them as part of the underground or alternative press movement. The term Chicano is a Mexican slang expression used by Mexican-Americans to refer to themselves. It has no literal English translation, and its origins are obscure. The Chicano movement started about the time of the California grapeworkers strike in 1964. Grapeworkers under the leadership of Cesar Chavez walked out of the fields of Delano, California, to begin their strike. They formed a union, the United Farm Workers Organizing Committee, and a union newspaper, *El Malcriado,* which in Spanish means a precocious, ill-bred child. Other newspapers soon followed to serve Chicanos in the cities as well as in rural areas. A number of these newspapers were located in California, some in New Mexico, Arizona, Texas and Colorado, and a few in other parts of the country, including the Midwest and Florida. Some of the newspapers formed the Chicano Press Association to foster the exchange of information and improve the news media in Spanish-speaking communities.

Most of the Chicano newspapers have been very much involved in their communities and the movement to help Mexican-Americans. They have tended to ignore traditional objectivity in their writing and emphasize politics rather than straight news. Their rapid development probably has been in response to the failure of many general circulation newspapers to report fully on events and needs in Mexican-American communities. Chicanos believe that often the major media either have ignored or misrepresented them. They believe that newspapers such as theirs are needed to keep their people informed and work for their interests. Few have carried advertising and most have lost money. But the use of offset printing has helped to keep costs down, and donations from those who sympathize with the movement have helped to provide funds. Chicano editors reportedly are more concerned with making their human rights movement a success than with making money. The failure to seek objectivity could cause them problems. If their readers do not also read other publications, they may lack the perspective necessary to achieve lasting progress. The rapid growth of Chicano newspapers indicates the size of the vacuum they have sought to fill.[47]

Business Newspapers

Many other specialized newspapers have filled information gaps left by the general circulation newspapers. Several prestigeous national newspapers and several hundred regional newspapers now serve the business community. Best-known perhaps is *The Wall Street Journal,* which is discussed along with other leading dailies in Chapter 8. It includes a good summary of national and international news along with its business reports.[48]

Business news was provided at local and regional levels in the early 1970s by an estimated 400 regional business newspapers, including about 40 dailies. These publications concentrated on basic local data such as new incorporations, contract awards, mortgages, conveyances, new appointments, and local over-the-counter stock listings. National publications such as *The Wall Street Journal* can only touch on much of this material. Regional publications such as *Cervi's Journal* in Denver, the *Long Island Commercial Review* and the *Los Angeles Daily Journal & Independent Review* can report it in depth and detail.

Most of the regional business newspapers have been started in the past quarter of a century to meet expanding information needs of business.[49]

Military Newspapers

A specialized press also has been developed to meet the needs of military personnel at home and abroad. Many of these newspapers have been fairly bland in the past, but their image may be changing. One observer noted in September 1971, that if the Army newspapers were not in the midst of a revolution of change, they at least were in the process of reformation. He said that platitudes and official language were giving way to action and plain talk. The rise of underground, or alternative, newspapers on military bases may have had something to do with the change. But at least part of the shift in policies regarding newspapers was probably part of a larger shift in policies evoked by the volunteer army concept and other changes in military regulations.

Major General Winant Sidle, the Army Chief of Information, provided guidelines for the military newspapers to use in their efforts to improve communications among military personnel. Sensationalism was to be avoided. American principles and the American system of government were not to be attacked or ideologies hostile or contrary to the interest of the United States advocated. Key personalities were not to be lampooned and, in general, the standards of good journalism were not to be compromised. Discussion of relevant and controversial issues was to be monitored but encouraged.

Staffs were quick to respond to the new guidelines. Problems in areas such as race relations and drug usage were probed. Frank exchanges of ideas about controversial questions were included on editorial pages, and in-depth reports tended to replace routine coverage. One newspaper invited and got reaction to the publication of the Pentagon Papers. Another newspaper explored charges that there was discrimination in the Army, and another looked into charges about prices at the post commissary. Ombudsman and "Action Line" approaches were adopted in some instances. Many of the newspapers were made more attractive, and some evidence was offered to suggest that the new freedom to report also improved writing and general coverage.[50]

Military newspapers in Southeast Asia were perhaps less free to gather and comment on the news than those in the continental United States. It was alleged in the early 1970s that the GIs in Vietnam often knew less about what was going on in the war there than the people back home. Even the Pacific edition of *Stars and Stripes,* famous soldier newspaper, reportedly was subject to heavy pressures regarding its reporting of the war. *Stars and Stripes* was started in World War I by Americans in Paris but disbanded after the war. It was revived in London in 1942 and continued after World War II in both European and Pacific editions because many American troops remained abroad. For a time after World War II the paper reportedly was given over largely to propaganda, but in recent years it has been removed from the immediate jurisdic-

tion of the Army's public relations operation and has engaged in various crusades. The paper has exposed drug abuse among the troops, discrimination
against black soldiers and reports of Army dependents living in slum housing
abroad. The Pacific edition has been less restricted than other service newspapers in Southeast Asia in covering the war there, but it became subject to increasing pressures in the late 1960s and early 1970s. Although the overall prospects for soldier journalism looked brighter in the 1970s than earlier, the future
status of these newspapers remained very much in doubt. The appropriate roles
for such newspapers quite properly were subjects for discussion.[51]

Free Papers

Shopping guides and free circulation newspapers also have filled information gaps left by general circulation newspapers, and they could produce one of
the biggest stories in the newspaper industry in the 1970s. George Brandsberg,
who has made the most intensive study of them, suggests in his book *The Free
Papers* that they should be considered a major mass medium in hometown
America. He points out that their aggregate national circulation of 30 million in
the late 1960s was equal to that of the paid circulation weeklies and equal to
about half the circulation of the nation's dailies. Brandsberg defines shopping
guides as papers that consist mostly of advertising which are delivered free to
every household in a designated circulation area. Most are published weekly
and distributed by carrier boys, third class mail or both. They also are known
as shoppers and pennysavers in some communities. He defines free circulation
papers as community newspapers that are provided free to at least half of those
who receive them. Most are located in suburbs or specific subdivisions of metropolitan areas. Most, like the shoppers, are published weekly. Some of these
newspapers have only free circulation; others have partial paid circulation.
Some employ a voluntary pay system in which the carriers ask for fees or donations of those who receive the papers but do not stop delivering them to those
who do not contribute.[52]

Brandsberg identified 1,070 free papers in his study, and he estimated that
some 2,000 were being published in 1968, about half of them shoppers. Most
were located in the West Coast states, the Midwest, the North Atlantic States
and New England. California, with 231 papers; New York, 133; and Illinois,
86 had the largest numbers, but almost every state had at least one. Circulations
varied greatly. More than half of the papers had fewer than 10,000 circulation,
but some were quite large. The *Detroit Shopping News,* with nearly 700,000
circulation twice a week, was the largest in 1968.[53]

Free papers appear to have some advantages over the traditional paid
circulation papers. Brandsberg noted that they were in competitively superior
positions in some communities because of their total circulation, lower capitali-
zation, small staffs, weekly publication and offset printing. He noted, however,
that paid circulation papers have a number of advantages besides the revenue

that is derived from subscriptions. These include the prestige of being a traditional newspaper, the benefits of low second class postal rates, legal advertising, more national advertising, larger staffs, more capital and sometimes better printing facilities. It appears that there are good and bad free circulation papers just as there are good and bad paid circulation newspapers. Brandsberg said he could find no evidence to suggest the publishers of free circulation papers are less ethical or less responsible than those of paid circulation newspapers.[54]

The values of free circulation newspapers and shoppers were still being debated in the early 1970s. Some conventional newspapers that started shoppers of their own reported that most persons tended to ignore them; others were more enthusiastic about their potential. Most of the newspapers in a study reported by the Inland Daily Press Association in 1973 indicated that they were making money with their shoppers. Newspapers under 10,000 circulation were obtaining 7% to 8% of their total advertising revenue from their shopper operations; those over 20,000 circulation were getting only 2% to 3%. About seven of 43 dailies participating in the study appeared to be losing money on their shopper operations.[55] As noted earlier in this chapter, a number of free circulation papers are working with paid circulation newspapers in the Suburban Newspaper Publishers Association. More research is needed to determine where these specialized papers fit into the communications spectrum. In the meantime, the response to them by both advertisers and readers indicates that some are meeting needs.

Prison Newspapers

The list of special interest publications is indeed long and varied. Not only are there free papers, but there also are newspapers for persons who are not free. Russell N. Baird did an extensive study of the penal press which was published by the Northwestern University press in Evanston in 1967. Baird received responses from more than 90% of the state and federal correctional institutions in 50 states and collected data on 222 general inmate publications and 113 special interest publications. About half were newspapers and half were magazines. More than half of the correctional institutions had an inmate publication, and more than three-fourths of those with populations of 1,000 or more had them. Total circulation was estimated at close to 260,000, including about 80,000 sent to persons outside the institutions. Baird found the range and quality of publications extreme. One of the best was the *Menard Times,* a monthly tabloid published by the Menard Branch of the Illinois State Penitentiary. It was selected as the best prison newspaper in the country in a national contest sponsored by Southern Illinois University.

Baird noted that prison officials, sociologists and psychologists were not in agreement on the value of the penal press. But he suggested that these publications can provide information to inmates and prison personnel, provide information about prison life to persons outside, serve as a learning experience and morale booster for inmates, and provide an outlet for creative self-expression and an aid toward rehabilitation. In the early 1970s a number of prison newspapers were cited for writing about the need for prison reforms and how they might be accomplished. They offered a point of view that should be useful to those on the outside seeking to improve the nation's prison systems.[56] Certainly the penal press supports the contention that there is a newspaper for virtually every interest group of any size in the country. The alternative, or underground press, discussed in the next section, provides further evidence of newspaper diversity.

ALTERNATIVE NEWSPAPERS

An alternative or underground press was developed in the United States in the late 1950s and 1960s to express and reflect the views of some Americans, especially young Americans, who felt alienated from the mainstream of national life. This other press developed in part because those disenchanted with the system or Establishment found little opportunity to express their views and feelings in existing media. They were rejected in part because their views were considered ultraliberal or radical, in part because of their methods of expressing them, and in part because of the lifestyles that many chose to follow. Some within the Establishment tended to regard all dissidents as political radicals who used illicit drugs, played loud rock music and engaged in free sex. The long hair and hippie dress adopted by many accentuated their differences from the mainstream and made their views less acceptable to the majority. Important points which the alienated needed to make about American life almost were lost in a massive credibility gap.

Robert J. Glessing, author of the first comprehensive book about the underground press of the 1960s, suggested that it grew out of the social and political indifference of the Eisenhower years, youthful involvement in the Southern civil rights movement, the drug culture of the early 1960s, moral resentment of the war in Vietnam, and bitterness toward a government incapable of solving racial and poverty problems in the world's wealthiest nation. He suggested that the term "underground press" probably stemmed from the fact that many of the anti-Establishment newspapers started in the 1960s reflected a drug culture, some members of which used illegal drugs.[57] Although there were many types of underground newspapers to serve various groups, most could be placed into one of two broad categories; either they were politically oriented and opposed to much in the existing political system, or they were culturally oriented and interested in music, art, drugs, sex or all of these. Some reflected both categories.

The recent underground press movement probably began in 1955 when Norman Mailer, Don Wolfe, John Wilcock, Ed Fancher and others started *The Village Voice*. The *Voice* provided liberally slanted political and cultural news of Greenwich Village in New York, and it was the first to report news without restriction on language; but it was less of an advocate and less profane than many which followed. By the middle 1970s the *Voice* had a circulation of almost 150,000 and seemed to reflect the liberal politics of New York's Upper West Side more than the radical politics of the East Village. The *Voice* and Clay Felker's *New York* Magazine were joined in a corporate merger in June 1974. The *Voice* parent company's debt was absorbed by *New York*'s publishing company and the paper's principal owners received cash and stock in New York Magazine Co. Their holdings amounted to about 34% of the outstanding shares. Felker said he had no plans for intermingling the *Voice* with *New York*, which is aimed at a more affluent, establishment-oriented audience.[58]

Leader in the major wave of underground newspapers that broke in the middle 1960s was the Los Angeles *Free Press;* it was founded in 1964 by Art Kunkin, a 37-year-old critic of the American dream. The *Free Press,* or *Freep* as it came to be called by its hip readers, soon gained a reputation as being against the Great Society as presented by President Lyndon Johnson and for rock music, persons who used drugs and classified mating-game sex advertisements. It sought to serve a subculture not reached by traditional journalists in Southern California, and it evidently succeeded in reaching them and others. Within six years the *Free Press* had expanded from a four-page circulation giveaway to a 48-page weekly with 95,000 paid circulation. Editor Kunkin reportedly saw it as an organization to provide communication, reflect the political and cultural left, and provide a conscience for the movement. The newspaper took an active political role at times, and it reported news of local events not published in other media. Unfortunately, its warnings were not heeded when it provided a sociological report on conditions in Watts before the 1965 riots tore the area apart. This type of coverage helped to explain its diversified audience and substantial circulation. While the *Free Press* did not abandon its interest in sex, it did seek to change its image from that of a radical sex-rag so that more persons would read its editorial content. Chris Van Ness, who moved up from managing editor to editor in 1974, emphasized that the paper's primary concern was people. At that time the paper had comprehensive coverage of the arts, columns by writers such as Jack Anderson, Ralph Nader, and Nicholas Von Hoffman, and many other excellent features.[59]

Many other alternative or underground newspapers were started in the late 1960s, including the *East Village Other,* which challenged the *Village Voice* in New York; the *Berkeley Barb,* which reflected the subculture at the University of California and its neighboring community; the *San Francisco Oracle,* which not only reflected the psychedelic lifestyle in part of that city but also set standards of graphic excellence for other alternative newspapers; the *Washington Free Press,* which dealt with federal government activities and came to emphasize radical politics; and the *Great Speckled Bird,* which served the subculture that located in Atlanta in the late 1960s. Perhaps the most successful of the alternative publications, however, was the *Rolling Stone,* which many classify as a magazine although it appears in a tabloid format on newsprint. The *Stone* was largely concerned with the rock music scene in the years after it was founded by Jann Wenner in 1967. It was particularly successful in reporting on the youth culture and "youth revolution" of the late 1960s. In the 1970s it has expanded its interests to include more on politics, lifestyle and general culture.[60]

Donna Lloyd Ellis, in a penetrating article on "The Underground Press in America: 1955–1970," suggested that many of the several hundred underground newspapers that were developed shared three common characteristics: their interest was primarily local; they were loosely tied to an underground community that shared cultural forms and leisure activities, such as rock music, outside the Establishment; and they were concerned in some way with the "Revolution" or "Movement." Ellis said the exact nature of this movement was unclear and was interpreted differently from newspaper to newspaper, but appeared to be in opposition to the American system.[61]

While some of the alternative papers were devoted primarily to the music scene, the military or some other special interest, many were concerned with refuting or correcting what they believed to be false impressions given by the Establishment press. Often the alternative papers would have reports on confrontation politics, alleged harrassment by police, reports on rock music, information about the drug situation and astrological data. Many ran calendars of events such as rock festivals and concerts that would be of special interest to their readers, and some ran advice columns and interviews with persons such as Buckminster Fuller and Herbert Marcuse.

Some alternative newspapers used reports, features and other materials from the Underground Press Syndicate, founded in 1966, and the Liberation News Service, founded in 1967. UPS was organized somewhat along the lines of the Associated Press cooperative service, but Glessing noted that it was not a news service but rather a combination of a library, clearing house, publishing company and advertising representative for the underground press. In late 1972 UPS reportedly had 450 subscribing newspapers, including 250 syndicate members who had reprint rights to each other's copy. LNS was organized more along the lines of United Press International service. It provided members with packets twice a week that contained news stories, essays, poetry, photography and underground comics. It swung more toward revolutionary politics after an internal dispute in the late 1960s. In late 1972 LNS reportedly was sending 10 to 18 stories twice a week to some 500 newspapers and 300 other subscribers who paid from $200 to $500 a year for service. A late-summer packet that year included stories about drug addiction among Vietnam veterans, a major soft drink corporation, interviews with the Paris Peace delegation and male chauvinism in Gay Liberation.[62]

Most of the alternative newspapers carried some advertising. Some of it, particularly the classified advertisements in some newspapers, was judged to be obscene by some critics. But some of the advertising was aimed at new products and services such as boutiques, organic foods and water beds. The music industry placed a great deal of advertising in the alternative newspapers, presumably with good success. The rates were comparatively cheap, the audience was selective and the pass-along readership was high. Many alternative newspapers would not accept advertising for products or companies that would not be compatible with their editorial viewpoints. Some rejected advertising offered by a company engaged in making equipment for the military; some rejected advertising for products such as cigarettes, alcohol or insecticides which they regarded as harmful.

One of the major criticisms of alternative newspapers concerned their use of profanities and alleged obscenities. Defenders argued that such usage presented a more accurate picture of the way people really spoke, that they were not bothersome to the newspapers' regular readers and that, in any case, obscenity was in the eye of the beholder. Critics contended that such usage was designed for a shock value that would increase sales or irritate people and that it was unnecessary to show realism. The alternative papers also were criticized frequently for their lack of objectivity in reporting issues and events, their inaccuracies and their exaggerations. Some may have been guilty on all counts, and most made no pretense at objectivity. Their goal was to correct the alleged distortions in the reports of the Establishment media.

Despite their failures in some areas, the alternative newspapers probably had considerable influence on their readers. They appeared to have some effect, direct or indirect, on hair and clothing styles, music, education, attitudes toward sex and morality, and attitudes toward foreign and domestic political issues. They raised important questions for everyone about United States' involvement in Southeast Asia, the nation's commitment to human rights at home, and the use or misuse of the environment. Ironically some attacked the democratic, capitalistic system that made it possible for them to publish. Some championed bad causes and suggested bad approaches to achieving good ends. But some also provoked policy makers and citizens generally to reconsider some of their positions and their reasons for holding them. Glessing suggested that their greatest opportunity for influence was to provoke the conventional newspapers to take a fresh look at important issues.[63]

It appeared that the alternative press reached high marks in numbers, readership and influence about the turn of the decade. Exact figures are hard to come by because the turnover, especially among smaller papers, was high, and most of the circulations were not audited. Glessing in his *Underground Press in America,* published in 1970, listed more than 450 papers. Various estimates indicate that several hundred were still being published in the early 1970s, but by April 1973 many of the better known papers were gone and others were said to be in serious trouble. During the late 1960s and early 1970s the total circulation almost certainly was several million, and pass-along readership was high. The highest figures cited showed a circulation of 5 million and a total readership of 20 million.[64]

Significant changes in the alternative press movement appeared to be taking place in the early 1970s. Young persons still expressed dissatisfaction with the Establishment, but many seemed content to work for change within the established system. Some of the better-known alternative papers in cities such as New York and San Francisco ceased publication, but others were started in smaller cities. As the war ground down and other changes took place, some of the papers concentrated their attention on housing problems, welfare needs, pollution and other community needs.[65]

Donna Ellis suggested in 1971 that the underground press had lost much of its original vitality and motivation. She suggested that it was in a state of flux, that it had passed through a heyday in its sixth year, perhaps due to its place in a transient pop culture. Ellis said the original undergrounds had passed away or had been modified to meet new situations, that the movement was looking for new forms and new readers. Douglas Kneeland, roving correspondent for the *New York Times,* suggested in an article primarily on college newspapers in March 1972, that the underground press was fading. His sources indicated to him that it was a phenomenon of a time that had passed, that change had to be effected through the established press.[66]

As the middle 1970s began it appeared that the alternative or underground press which had flourished during the previous decade was facing extinction. A few of the papers that it had spawned had grown strong and likely would be continued, but often they had assumed characteristics if not viewpoints of the established press. Many of the better-known papers had died or were in financial difficulties. Others were seeking to adjust to new times and changing needs. Whether the movement of the 1960s would be revived or perhaps replaced by a new movement was not clear. There will always be causes to champion, and there likely will be new sub-cultures to develop. If the general and specialized papers of the conventional press do not meet these needs, an underground or alternative press likely will.

4

The Newspaper as a Business Institution

TODAY'S NEWSPAPER OWNER is constantly challenged by his publication's dual roles as quasi-public institution with special privileges and responsibilities and free enterprise business operation with a need to pay expenses and show a profit. The newspaper must serve the needs of the public for facts and opinion in an unselfish way if it is to justify its special status under the First Amendment; yet it must succeed as a business enterprise in the information field if it is to exist and serve the public in any way. How is the economic health of newspapers today? What are the prospects for the future? Are newspaper monopolies good or bad? Should the public be concerned about cross-media ownerships and the development of conglomerates including newspapers? Should newspapers be publicly owned? How do government regulations affect the business operation of newspapers? How are newspapers' business functions organized and operated? This chapter will consider these and other questions related to newspapers' business functions and give attention to recent developments in advertising, circulation, personnel and promotion.

Despite increasing competition, rising costs and other problems in the quarter century since World War II, the economic health of the newspaper industry has remained good. The newspaper business in the early 1970's continued to rank tenth among all United States industries in the value of goods shipped and fifth among them in terms of employment. Jon G. Udell, director, Bureau of Business Research and Service, University of Wisconsin, reported in late 1970 that newspapers had exhibited strength and vitality in the postwar period. His study of *Economic Trends in the Daily Newspaper Business, 1946 to 1970* indicated that they had adjusted successfully to a rapidly changing society, the introduction of a new communications medium, and a change in read-

124

ing habits. During the period of the study newspaper growth generally equalled and in some ways exceeded the growth of the economy. Expenditures on newspaper advertising grew faster than the Gross National Product, newsprint consumption increased about as rapidly as the Real Gross National Product, circulation advanced about as fast as population between the ages of 21 and 65, and newspaper employment expanded more rapidly than that in manufacturing or total United States employment. Udell predicted substantial growth in the future based on continued expansion in advertising and circulation.[1]

The United States Department of Commerce also forecast that newspapers would do well in the 1970s. As the decade began, the department predicted that the newspaper industry would grow at an average of 4% a year during the period from 1970 to 1975 and grow slightly faster during the period from 1975 to 1980 to provide an overall growth rate of 5% a year for the decade. It predicted that the value of receipts would approach $8.5 billion in 1975 and $11.4 billion in 1980, and that circulation would increase by as much as 18% in the decade if it continued to grow in direct proportion to the growth of the reading age segment of the population. As the decade began the daily newspaper circulation was about 62 million, and the circulation for all newspapers was more than 140 million. The Commerce Department further predicted that the expenditures for capital investment would continue at a high rate, exceeding the $2 billion investment during the 1960s. It said, too, that newspaper production would come to involve totally integrated work systems, and that the trend toward multiple printing plants and the establishment of satellite editions and plants in the metropolitan areas would become commonplace.[2]

Circulation did not increase dramatically in the first few years of the decade; daily circulation was 63.1 million in 1974. But other economic indicators, including expansion, profits and advertising revenues, looked favorable. For example, 731 dailies participating in a survey conducted by the American Newspaper Publishers Association reported spending $233.6 million in 1972 for expansion and modernization. That figure represented an all-time high for surveys conducted by the association, and, of course, did not include all newspapers.[3]

Although some competing newspapers in large cities might be cited as exceptions, the overall profit picture for newspapers in the early 1970s was good. Reports indicated that most newspapers had earned substantial profits in the first years of the decade and could look forward to rising profits in the years ahead. Precise figures for the newspaper industry as a whole are difficult to obtain because most of the companies are privately owned and many do not choose to report their earnings to the public. Figures are available for publicly owned newspaper companies, however, and analysts indicate that there is not a significant difference between the profits of privately owned dailies and publicly traded dailies that are well managed. Ben Bagdikian, national correspondent for *Columbia Journalism Review,* reported in that publication in early

1973 that the average pretax profit of publicly traded newspapers for the last five years for which figures were complete was 15.6% of sales.[4] Lee Dirks, president of Dirks Brothers Division, Delafield Childs Inc., noted newspaper analysts, reported in early 1973 that the earnings of the 13 publicly owned newspaper companies climbed an average of 22% in 1972 over 1971 as compared with a rise of 16% for U.S. industry as a whole.[5]

Figures compiled by Newspaper Analysis Service for *Editor & Publisher,* the newspaper industry trade publication, also suggest that profits were substantial in the early 1970s. This service annually presents figures for a theoretical newspaper of some 250,000 circulation based on the aggregate performance of "average" newspapers. This theoretical newspaper showed a pretax profit of more than 23% in 1970, 1971 and 1972.[6]

While all newspapers may not have enjoyed the good profits reported for publicly owned newspapers in the early 1970s, most were expected to do well in the middle years of the decade. A comprehensive analysis of the newspaper industry reported in late 1973 predicted that newspaper profits would likely rise considerably over the next three to five years, primarily because of the introduction of new production technology and consequent labor savings. The study, entitled *Papers and Profits: A Special Report on the Newspaper Business,* examined every aspect of the field, including government regulation, the newsprint situation, labor and management problems and the strategies of 16 major newspaper companies. It was written by Benjamin M. Compaine, journalist, management consultant and professor of business administration.[7]

Optimism about the newspaper industry was expressed by business analysts and supported by continued advertising growth and other data. In late 1972 Edward Dunleavy, industry analyst for Merrill Lynch, Pierce, Fenner & Smith, stock brokers, told advertisers not to be misled into believing that the newspaper industry was suffering from severe competition and wracked with labor problems, rising costs and less affluent markets. Dunleavy indicated that while such a picture might be accurate in some major metropolitan markets, it definitely was not accurate for the industry as a whole. He presented a table of compounded annual growth rates of advertising expenditures by medium which showed an upward trend for newspapers in recent years. Newspapers' share of the market reached a low in 1963 and has been climbing since.[8] In late 1973 a group of men and women who earn their living studying and analyzing printing and publishing companies for large banks and other institutions with money to invest expressed a bullish attitude about newspaper stocks after touring newspaper plants and talking with corporate and local management. They noted that automation was revolutionizing the newspaper industry and achieving considerable savings in production and manpower costs; they said that newspaper company stocks in general were undervalued and might offer immediate value for investors.[9]

Advertising revenues, which provide the major source of income for dailies, continued to rise, and newspapers maintained their 30% share of the total advertising market in the early 1970s. Newspapers continued to get about 70% of all local advertising among the major media, and their total advertising continued to be almost as much as television, radio and magazines combined. The most dramatic growth occurred in preprinted inserts as advertisers sought to avoid the impact of higher postal rates upon direct mail. Careful planning is needed in this field to avoid a ''clutter'' similar to that which 15-second commercials have caused on television.[10]

The *Papers and Profits* study cited earlier reported that newspapers had stabilized their share of the national ad dollar and predicted that revenues would grow from the $7 billion level of 1972 to a minimum of $9 billion in 1978. The study suggested that the strongest growth would come in local and classified advertising, and noted that the use of preprinted stuffers could add significantly to revenues, provided the papers establish the right price structure for them.[11]

This bright outlook is, of course, subject to possible clouds. Rising costs, newsprint shortages, distribution problems, and competition from other media and other activities demand that newspapers apply proper management techniques and take full advantage of new technology. The need for and cost of newsprint provided a major challenge in the early 1970s. Newsprint consumption increased by 37% between 1962 and 1972, and newsprint prices increased from about $135 a ton in the early 1960s to $170 a ton in the early 1970s. Strikes in Canada, bad weather that hampered wood operations in both the United States and Canada, and increased needs helped to produce newsprint shortages and higher prices. By early 1975 the price of standard 30-pound newsprint in some areas was expected to be more than $250 a ton. Some newspapers reduced news holes, some cut web widths on newsprint rolls, and some rationed advertising to conserve newsprint. The supply and demand balance was expected to be tight for a time, but expansions of newsprint plant capacities and more efficient use of paper were expected to help.[12]

Although the newsprint shortages were attributed to labor problems rather than to any reduction in wood production, some experiments were under way in the 1970s to find substitute pulp for paper production. Some turned to the recycling of newsprint to provide materials; others looked for other substances from which paper could be produced efficiently and economically. Dr. Gordon B. Killinger of the agronomy department at the University of Florida suggested that kenaf (pronounced kuh-naf) might provide an answer for possible wood pulp shortages in the future. Kenaf is a hibiscus plant which looks somewhat like marijuana to the untrained eye. Kenaf requires much less processing and chemical treatment than does pulpwood to be turned into paper, but it has drawbacks. Its seedlings are extremely water sensitive and must be planted in raised beds; a kenaf crop must be rotated with other crops such as cotton or corn; and the plant is susceptible to root knot nematodes and the parasitic pink bollworm. Killinger said, however, that the cost of producing kenaf could be fully competitive with that of producing conventional timber pulp sources, perhaps cheaper. It can be grown and harvested annually, whereas pine trees usually require at least 15 years before they are mature enough for harvesting.[13]

Newspaper distribution problems increased with the expansion of medium-rise and high-rise apartments whose tenants were difficult to reach, the increasing reluctance of carriers to service ghettos and inner-city areas, traffic congestion and rising costs. One major group official reported that distribution costs rather than production costs might be the newspapers' major problem of tomorrow. Some newspapers sought to make routes more attractive by emphasizing paid-in-advance subscriptions; some sought to provide more revenue to pay carriers and meet other needs by increasing the cost of their newspapers.[14]

The major challenge of the 1970s and beyond may, however, be competition with other media and other activities, particularly if the Principle of Relative Constancy, suggested by Charles E. Scripps and propounded by Maxwell E. McCombs, continues in effect. This theory, which McCombs says has been applicable for the past 40 years at least, holds that the mass media will get a relatively constant share of the money invested in the nation and that the amount will fluctuate with the ebb and flow of the economy, not with competition and technological changes within the media. Moreover, it suggests that new media do not change the amount of the economy available to finance mass communication but require a redivision of a relatively fixed amount. Television, for example, did not add to the amount of money available for mass media; it took money away from motion pictures, national magazines and to a lesser extent radio and newspapers. New breakthroughs such as cable television will not add additional dollars, but require a redivision of those available for existing media including television. McCombs suggests further that as more and more goods and services become available, a scarcity of time may serve as an ultimate constraint on the development of mass media. Not only will there be a limitation of money for the media, but a limitation of time that individuals can devote to them and other activities. McCombs contends that in the decades immediately ahead time and money will jointly constrain the growth of the mass media in the marketplace.[15]

On the basis of past newspaper performance and available data, it does appear, however, that newspapers will be able to hold their share of the market if they fully analyze their potential, determine what informational needs they can satisfy better than the other media and concentrate their energies there. They could probably help themselves by making information on their physical assets, return on invested capital and related data more readily available to the public. The newspapers' secrecy about corporate information that might help provide a clearer view of the national economy and their place in it seems ironic in view of their insistence on disclosure of information by others whose affairs affect the public. Since there are so many newspaper corporations, it seems unlikely that publication of figures about the industry as a whole would reveal anything damaging to individual firms. Moreover, the availability of full data on all newspapers, not just those that have gone public, could foster the development of independent analyses that could help newspapers achieve greater efficiency and adjust more readily to changing technology.

TRENDS IN OWNERSHIP

There is no general agreement on the best means of achieving the financial security essential to producing the kinds of newspapers that the American people need. Some believe that independent ownership and competition are vital to producing good newspapers. Others point out that some outstanding newspapers enjoy monopoly status in their communities, are parts of groups, or both. Regardless of who is "right," locally originated newspaper competition has declined drastically in this century, joint operating agreements between competing newspapers have been sanctioned, group ownership has expanded rapidly, and cross-media and conglomerate ownerships have evolved.

Fewer than 4% of the nation's cities had competing newspapers in the early 1970s. More than half of the nation's daily newspapers, which together account for almost two-thirds of the daily circulation, were owned by groups. The 10 largest groups had annual revenues in the early 1970s estimated at \$2.2 billion, approximately one-fourth of the industry total. Cross-media owners controlled more than a third of the daily newspapers, a fourth of the television stations, and almost a tenth of the AM and FM radio stations. The combined holdings of groups, cross-media owners, conglomerates and firms related to the mass media encompassed almost three-fifths of the daily newspapers, slightly more than three-fourths of the television stations, and slightly more than one-fourth of the AM and FM radio station.[16] Many newspaper owners have sought to diversify their investments by making purchases in other areas of the mass media or in other activities. Some in other fields have bought newspapers as additional investments.

Newspaper monopolies do not appear to be inherently good or bad, although there may be a potential danger to the free flow of information inherent in them. It is argued, for example, that newspapers which do not face competition can present the news in a better balanced format; they need not sensationalize for the sake of selling papers. Their reporters, freed from the pressure of having to beat a rival newspaper to press with a story, can take more time and do a better job. Newspapers without competition may be better insulated from financial pressures, and they may be in a better position to take an unpopular stand on some matter of principle. There is also evidence to indicate that some newspapers accept the greater responsibility that comes with being the only voice in town and act accordingly.[17]

Monopolies are opposed for many reasons. Foremost, it is argued that monopoly holders could seek to exercise a form of information control in their communities. This danger is offset by the presence of other local media, perhaps including weekly newspapers, and the possibility of publishing information on a particular subject in some specialized form. A newspaper could not exercise the same sort of monopoly in a community that a public utility could. But monopoly newspapers could hinder the free flow of information. Secondly, monopolies are opposed because of the possibility that they will not take strong stands on important issues. This may be true, but it is also true that newspapers in competition for economic survival may be even less willing to risk offending anyone by taking a controversial stand. In the third place, monopolies are opposed because the lack of competition rather than encouraging reporters to do better may dull their energy and initiative. Fourthly, monopolies are objectionable to many because a company with a monopoly is likely to set advertising rates at a higher level than one which has competition. Finally, monopolies are objectionable to some simply because they are monopolies; the potential for evil is there even if never exercised.

Whatever the arguments for or against newspaper monopolies, it seems likely that many of them will be continued in the foreseeable future. Some government regulations may be used to monitor their activities, but it is likely that monopoly newspaper performance will depend largely on who holds the monopoly and on the public's reaction, if any, to what the owners do.

Local newspaper competition of a sort has been kept alive in more than 20 American cities by passage of the Newspaper Preservation Act of 1970. This act grants limited exemption from antitrust laws for joint operating agreements between two newspapers. The act permits two newspapers, at least one of which is failing, to enter into a joint operating agreement that combines all commercial operations but retains separate and competing news and editorial departments. The act overturns a United States Supreme Court ruling in a case involving a joint agreement between the *Citizen* and *Star* newspapers in Tucson, Arizona. The court in that case, decided in 1969, held that the price fixing, profit pooling and market allocation features of the Tucson newspapers' agreement violated antitrust laws.[18]

The joint operating agreement issue, which sharply divided the newspaper industry itself, was joined in the late 1960s when the Justice Department instituted its suit against the arrangement in Tucson. The newspapers affected, and there were at the time 22 such agreements involving 44 newspapers, decided to seek relief through Congressional action. Senator Carl Hayden of Arizona first introduced legislation in 1967 designed to protect the Tucson newspapers, and others with similar arrangements, from the Justice Department, which had indicated that if it won its case in Tucson would proceed against other agreements elsewhere. Newspapers in Nashville, Salt Lake City, Miami, Pittsburgh, San Francisco and other cities with joint operating agreements urged support for the legislation, first called the Failing Newspaper Act but later the Newspaper Preservation Act. The American Newspaper Publishers Association and a number of Congressmen from the areas affected supported the argument that the act was needed to correct inequities in existing antitrust laws. Proponents pointed out that under existing laws it was possible for two newspapers, one of which was failing, to merge their entire operations and become one company but not possible for them to combine commercial operations and retain separate news and editorial departments. They said the purpose of their bill was to preserve independent and competing editorial voices and help stem the historic trend toward newspaper monopolies.

Representatives of the American Newspaper Guild and other labor organizations, a number of independent newspapers, including the *New York Times,* and many small dailies and weeklies, joined the Justice Department in opposing the legislation. The opponents argued that while the number of metropolitan dailies was declining, their places generally were being taken by prospering suburban dailies and weeklies that could be hurt unfairly by the legislation. They said the proposed act was an invitation to the newspapers involved in the joint agreement to stop competing with each other and that it gave them an unfair competitive advantage against any existing or potential competitors in the area.

Those seeking to uphold joint working agreements won a major victory in getting the Newspaper Preservation Act adopted, but the opposition did score some points. While it sanctions all agreements existing at the time of its adoption, the act requires that any future arrangements be submitted to the Attorney General for approval. His office is to determine if one of the two newspapers involved in such a proposed agreement is in fact a failing newspaper, and approve only those arrangements that would effectuate the policy and purpose of the act. Moreover, to counteract the arguments that legalizing existing agreements would permit predatory use of price fixing and other provisions to stifle competition, the act includes a section which provides that if the exemptions granted the joint arrangement are used to drive out or prevent the establishment of a competing newspaper the parties to the arrangement can be prosecuted under antitrust laws.[19]

Within a few days after the act was signed into law by President Nixon, its constitutionality was challenged. The Bay Guardian Company, which operates a semimonthly magazine in San Francisco, brought suit against the publishers of the *San Francisco Examiner* and the *Chronicle* in the U.S. District Court in Northern California. The Bay Guardian Company charged that the preservation act threatened its existence by sanctioning the creation of a monopoly position in the San Francisco area that produced substantial profits. The agreement, signed in 1965, eliminated a third newspaper, the *News-Call Bulletin;* allotted the afternoon and morning markets to the *Examiner* and *Chronicle,* respectively; created a jointly owned subsidiary to print the papers; and provided that profits on all operations be pooled and shared on a 50-50 basis; it maintained independent editorial staffs except for a joint Sunday newspaper. In a ruling on the case, Judge Oliver J. Carter upheld the constitutionality of the act but raised questions about its application to the San Francisco situation in view of the elimination of the *News-Call Bulletin*. He said the act does not violate either the First or Fifth amendments, does not preempt but merely modifies in part the operation of state antitrust laws, and can constitutionally be applied to conduct occurring both before and after passage. But he also said it was a matter of evidence to be determined at trial whether the conduct of the defendants while entering their joint operating agreement bars them from protection of the act. The Bay Guardian Company was expected to include in its arguments at the trial the contention that the Newspaper Preservation Act does not apply in the San Francisco situation because the *News-Call Bulletin* was eliminated.[20] The U.S. Supreme Court may ultimately be asked to resolve the issue.

A final chapter in the trend toward newspaper consolidation at the local level may be forestalled by the continuance of joint operating agreements and by the success of some competitors in a few large cities. But other monopolistic trends such as group ownership appeared to be gaining momentum as the middle 1970s approached. Dr. Raymond B. Nixon, author of many articles on newspaper ownership trends, reported in July 1971, that 883 of the nation's 1,748 newspapers belonged to one of 155 newspaper groups. Together the group-owned newspapers accounted for 63% of the total weekday circulation and 65% of the Sunday circulation. Both the number of groups and the number of newspapers owned by groups doubled in the quarter of a century after World War II. The average size of the groups also rose between 1945 and 1971 from 4.8 newspapers per group to 5.7 newspapers per group, the highest average on record.[21]

The Tribune Company, which included the *Chicago Tribune, Chicago Today,* the *New York Daily News* and others, was the leader in total circulation. It was followed by Newhouse Newspapers (*Syracuse Herald-Journal, New Orleans Times-Picayune* and *States-Item, St. Louis Globe-Democrat,* Portland *Oregonian, Cleveland Plain-Dealer,* et al.); Knight Newspapers (*Akron Beacon-Journal, Miami Herald, Macon Telegraph* and *News, Charlotte News* and *Observer, Philadelphia Inquirer, Detroit Free Press,* et al.); Scripps-Howard Newspapers (*Cleveland Press, Columbus Citizen-Journal, Pittsburgh Press, Memphis Commercial Appeal,* et al.); and Hearst Newspapers (*Los Angeles Herald-Examiner, San Francisco Examiner, Baltimore News-American,* et al.).

Next in order came the Times Mirror Company (*Los Angeles Times,* Long Island *Newsday, Dallas Times Herald,* et al.); Gannett Newspapers (*Rochester Times-Union, San Bernardino Sun,* et al.); Ridder Publications (*San Jose Mercury, St. Paul Pioneer-Press, Seattle Times,* et al.); Dow Jones (including four regional editions of *The Wall Street Journal* and Ottaway Newspapers in Connecticut, New York, and Massachusetts); Ochs Estate (*New York Times, Chattanooga Times,* et al.); Cowles Newspapers (autonomous units in *Des Moines*

Register and *Tribune,* and *Minneapolis Star* and *Tribune,* et al.); James M. Cox Newspapers (*Dayton News, Atlanta Journal* and *Constitution, Miami News,* et al.); Thomson and Thomson-Brush-Moore Newspapers (*Dalton Citizen-News, Canton Repository,* et al.); and Central Newspapers (*Indianapolis Star, Phoenix Arizona Republic* and *Gazette,* et al.).[22]

Although the average number of newspapers per group in 1971 was only 5.7, 19 groups each had a total of 10 dailies or more. Thomson Newspapers, including Thomson-Brush-Moore, and Gannett Newspapers, with Federated Publications, led the way with 43 and 44 dailies, respectively. The Scripps League Newspapers (with newspapers in Arizona, California, Idaho, Montana, New Mexico, Oregon, Texas, Utah, Washington, Wisconsin and Wyoming) had 31 dailies; and Donrey Media (Arkansas, California, Hawaii, Missouri, Nevada, Oklahoma and Texas), Newhouse Newspapers, Freedom Newspapers (California, Florida, Nebraska, New Mexico, Ohio and Texas), and Worrell Newspapers (Alabama, Iowa, Kentucky, Mississippi, North Carolina, Tennessee and Virginia) all had more than 20. Five of the Worrell papers were owned jointly with Walls Investment Company.

In order after that came Scripps-Howard Newspapers, Ridder Publications, Lee Newspapers (Iowa, Wisconsin, Montana, and Oregon), Harte-Hanks Newspapers (Texas), Stauffer Publications (Kansas, Missouri, Nebraska, Oklahoma), Copley Newspapers (*San Diego Union* and *Evening Tribune* and others in California, Illinois), Dow Jones, Knight Newspapers, Speidel Newspapers, Inc. (Nevada, California, Iowa, Colorado, South Dakota, Ohio, Nebraska), Cox Newspapers, Ingersoll Newspapers (New Jersey, Pennsylvania, Rhode Island, Massachusetts, Connecticut and New Hampshire), and Palmer Newspapers (Arkansas, Texas).[23]

The trend toward group ownership continued between early 1971 and early 1974. The total number of group dailies increased 11.2% to 977 or 54.9% of the total of 1,774; the number of groups increased from 157 to 165, and the average number of dailies in each group increased from 5.6 to 5.9. The Gannett group with 56 newspapers, Thomson with 47, and Scripps League with 36 continued to lead in numbers of papers owned by groups. The Tribune Company continued to lead in group circulation in early 1974; but the elimination of *Chicago Today* and the merger of Knight Newspapers Inc. and Ridder Publications Inc. in September opened the way for a new leader, Knight-Ridder Newspapers, Inc., at year's end. The trend toward group ownership was expected to continue, although perhaps not at the same rapid rate. Ben Bagdikian, national correspondent for *Columbia Journalism Review,* reported in early 1973 that newspaper groups had been buying independent newspapers at the rate of 62 a year since 1968. He said that at that rate the last independent would disappear in 1984, an appropriate year for the demise.[24]

The continued expansion of groups has resulted from a number of causes. First, newspapers have been good investments; most have earned good returns for their owners in recent years. Second, as the process of local consolidation has been completed, and few opportunities for such consolidation remained after the late 1950s, newspapers have had to look farther afield to invest surplus earnings. Third, tax laws and rulings have encouraged newspapers to invest their earnings in related enterprises. Finally, some group owners may be seeking an expansion of their ideas and philosophies as well as an expansion of their wealth. Antitrust rulings have encouraged newspapers to spread their interests over a larger geographical area. For example, the *Los Angeles Times* was forced to sell its morning-evening-Sunday combination in nearby San Bernardino on the grounds that such ownership gave it too great dominance of the regional market, but the *Times* was not prevented from acquiring the more distant *Times Herald* in Dallas and *Newsday* on Long Island, New York.[25]

Some persons regard the development of groups as a logical step in efforts to help serve information needs and meet competition more effectively. Others see in them a distinct and growing danger to the American system. Whether concentration in groups is good or evil depends to a considerable degree on who the group owner is and how he operates. Some group-owned newspapers are among the nation's best; some newspapers belonging to groups are at best mediocre.

Those who defend newspaper groups argue that their greater financial resources enable them to do many useful things that smaller, individual operations cannot do. They can provide the capital necessary to develop new technology that will enable newspapers to serve better and compete more effectively. They can provide training programs and career opportunities that many individual operations cannot match. They have the resources to engage in investigative efforts and public service programs and produce a quality product; they have the resources to resist more easily pressures that might be brought by a local group.

John C. Quinn, vice-president/news for the Gannett Company, Inc., told the annual assembly of the International Press Institute in Munich in 1972 that press concentration and monopoly are not threats to editorial independence. He said that competence and integrity are the real benchmarks of responsible and responsive newspapers. Quinn said that "concentrated ownership can provide great resources; only independent local judgment can use these resources to produce a responsible and responsive local newspaper. The exercise of these group resources and that local judgment measures editorial independence and excellence. That measure cannot be inflated by competition nor can it be diluted by monopoly." [26]

Those who oppose press concentrations point out that the increased resources of groups can be used for evil as well as good. They contend that some group owners are primarily concerned with making money, not serving people. Such owners may avoid local issues that might be controversial and hurt business; such owners might be content to fill up the newspaper with national features and wire service materials and slight local coverage with its higher costs and greater risks. The critics also point out that with the exception of one base newspaper in each group all group owners are absentee owners who may know or care little about the local community; some group owners also may seek to control the flow of information by not reporting some things and providing only their version of others. Finally, it is argued that group owners can use their greater resources to discourage if not eliminate local competition; this can lead to higher advertising rates and more expense for everyone.

The debate over press concentration grows more intense when cross-media ownerships and conglomerates are considered along with local consolidation of newspapers and the development of newspaper chains or groups. Newspapers were among the first to invest in radio, and many of the best early stations were affiliated with newspapers. Many newspapers have expressed a similar interest in television, cable television and related technology, and cross-media owners now control about a fourth of the television stations and a tenth of the AM and FM radio stations.[27]

Many persons, including former Republican Vice-President Spiro Agnew and former Democratic standard-bearer and Vice President Hubert Humphrey, have raised questions about concentration of control over the mass media. The President's Commission on Violence in 1969 urged that the development of competing news media be encouraged, and the Newspaper Preservation Act of 1970 spoke of the need for separate and independent voices in local communities. The potential danger should a limited number of persons gain extensive control over the media is obvious. But how serious is the threat at either national or local levels today? Some argue that any national threat is remote; the present groups are not that large, and the Federal Communications Commission would block any additional mergers involving broadcasting interests. Others note that the 10 largest groups do control about a third of the total daily circulation even though many of the newspapers involved have competition. The danger of monopoly at the local level would appear more imminent, although the numbers of communities involved are small and monopoly ownership is not necessarily good or bad. According to FCC figures, reported in 1970, there were 11 cities where the only newspaper and the only television station were under the same control. There were 256 daily newspapers that had common ownership with radio-TV licensees in the same city and 68 communities in which there was one commercial radio station owned by the only daily newspaper. Of the 666 commercial television stations reporting data as of November 1, 1969, there were 160 with newspaper affiliations.[28]

Research findings reported by the National Association of Broadcasters in 1971 indicate, however, that newspaper ownership of broadcast stations does not bar the free flow of news and that joint ownership of newspaper and television stations does not significantly affect advertising rates. The NAB said that research conducted by the Ohio University Research Center showed there is wider diversity in news content and attitude between newspapers and allied radio and television stations than between the same newspapers and non-affiliated broadcast outlets. Only one substantial difference between the newspaper-allied and non-newspaper-allied stations showed up in the study: newspaper-allied broadcast stations write more of the stories they present. On the basis of this difference the service provided by newspaper-allied stations appeared to be better recommended.[29]

Research conducted by Resource Management Corporation of 546 television stations and 357 daily newspapers found no evidence that joint media ownership leads to significantly differential price effects in either the national TV advertising or the national newspaper advertising markets. This study rejected contrary findings of earlier studies, which it said erred in not including station audience size and newspaper circulation in their analyses.[30]

Those concerned about the potential dangers of cross-media ownership have sought action by the Federal Communications Commission to discourage it. The Commission considered the matter at some length in the early 1940s. At that time it voted unanimously not to adopt general rules against newspaper-broadcast cross ownership, although it said it believed in the principle of diversified control of the media. The Commission again took up the question in 1968 after the Justice Department urged that a rule be adopted to divorce the ownership of daily newspapers and television stations within the same city. In 1970 the Commission offered for discussion a proposal that owners of daily newspapers and either television stations or radio stations in the same city sell either the station or the newspaper within five years. It also proposed that newspaper ownership of cable TV facilities in their cities of publication be prohibited.[31]

Strong opposition to the Commission's proposal was voiced by both newspapers and broadcasters. They said its adoption would violate the First Amendment, go beyond the Commission's authority under the Federal Communications Act, constitute an invidious discrimination in violation of the due process clause of the Fifth Amendment, and clearly would be contrary to the public interest. The American Newspaper Publishers Association asserted in 1971 that the immediate effect of the proposal, if adopted, would be the forced sale over a period of five years of 476 television and radio stations in 155 communities with an aggregate market value of $1.9 billion.[32]

By late 1974 the Commission had compiled 24 thick volumes of written testimony and heard oral arguments on the proposal, but had not made a decision. Meanwhile, the Congress took up the question. The House passed a bill in May 1974 concerning license renewals that would have barred the Commission from denying renewals because of cross-ownership between newspapers and broadcasters in the same city, but in September a Senate committee rejected this proposal. The outcome remained in doubt in both the Commission and the Congress.[33]

Cross-media owners concerned about the issue may have received some encouragement from the recommendations of the Cabinet Committee on Cable Communications reported in early 1974. This committee included Clay T. Whitehead, chairman, and Robert H. Finch, Herbert Klein, Peter G. Peterson, Eliot L. Richardson and George Romney. It recommended to President Nixon that cable television be given the same freedom from control as print media and that owners of other media be permitted to own cable television in the same community or others. Under the proposal cable television would become a common carrier system and all potential users would lease channels on a non-discriminatory, first come, first-served basis.[34]

Newspapers can be expected to battle vigorously to maintain interests in cable television for several reasons. First, cable television, like radio and television, should be a good investment; it has great potential for development. Second, cable television could become a major means of transmitting news, if not newspapers themselves, in the future. Newspapers want assurance that if electronic transmission provides the hometown newspaper of the future they will have the right to own the equipment necessary for its production and delivery. A Newspaper Committee for Cablevision was formed in 1969 to free cablevision from undue restrictions and to prevent class discrimination against newspapers or others from owning cablevision in their home markets.[35]

Another major struggle also was developing in the 1970s over the ownership of newspapers and other mass media by conglomerates, or diversified corporations that have far-ranging interests. As noted earlier, about three-fifths of the nation's newspapers and three-fourths of its television stations already are involved in groups, cross-media ownership, conglomerates and firms related to the mass media. Many believe the government should discourage media involvement in conglomerates. They see such involvement as a distinct threat to the free flow of information vital to the public. Suppose, for example, a newspaper member of the conglomerate developed a story about consumer action or research that would hurt the stock value of another member of the conglomerate. Would it be free to print the story? Or suppose legislation were being considered that would vitally affect a member of the conglomerate. Could the newspaper make an objective study of the situation and take the stand it believed best for the public? Or suppose members of the conglomerate depended on the good publicity, or free advertising, that a newspaper could provide. Would the newspaper become a purveyor of free advertising at the expense of news? Could it keep perspective about any matters in which fellow members of the conglomerate were involved? Critics say conglomerate membership places too many pressures on the media and should be prohibited. Morton Mintz, a *Washington Post* reporter, and Jerry S. Cohen, former chief counsel of the Senate Antitrust and Monopoly Subcommittee, in their book *America, Inc.* assert that the strong trend toward concentration of ownership of communications media is a menace to democratic government and a danger to the market place of ideas. ''A democratic society must have a free exchange of ideas, dissent and diversity,'' they assert. ''It may survive a concentration of manufacturing assets in a few conglomerate corporations but it cannot withstand a similar concentration of communications media.'' [36]

The free flow of information could face an even more subtle threat from ownership if the movement toward public ownership started in the late 1960s continues to expand. In 1969, the first year in which *Editor & Publisher* made tabulations, 16 publicly owned newspaper companies controlled 129 daily newspapers (6.5% of the total) with 9.3 million (14.5% of the total) circulation. By 1973 there were 19 companies controlling 247 daily newspapers (13.9% of the total) with a total circulation of more than 15 million (24.1% of the total) and 128 Sunday papers (21% of the total) with a circulation of 13.5 million (27% of the total). Large groups such as Knight Newspapers, Gannett, Thomson Newspapers (U.S.), Dow Jones, Ridder Newspapers, and the Los Angeles Times-Mirror Company, the New York Times Company, and the Washington Post Company were included on this list.[37]

Some problems are encountered in going public. There are considerable expenses involved; the company may have to reveal some of its financial secrets; if its stock offering is large, it must meet the requirements of the Securities & Exchange Commission; and it may have to be concerned about an increasing number of unhappy stockholders. But in the minds of an increasing number of owners, the benefits outweigh the problems. Companies can get additional capital in this way for pressing needs or expansion programs. They can raise values before proposing mergers through stock swaps, and they can avoid some major tax problems. High inheritance taxes can take a large bite out of family held or closely owned properties.[38] The potential economic values of public ownership are considerable. Its ultimate impact on newspapers remains uncertain. It could cause reader-owners to be more responsive to the needs of newspapers; or it could produce additional pressures to make money and avoid controversy that might interfere with making money.

In summary, it appears that some fairly definite patterns of newspaper ownership have evolved over the years. Because of the large amounts of operating capital required, most daily newspapers today are corporations. Individual ownership and partnership approaches are no longer practicable for most dailies. Some newspapers are employe-owned, and an increasing number have been opened to public ownership. More than half of the nation's dailies are now members of groups, more than a third are involved in cross-media ownerships, and almost three-fifths are involved in groups, cross-media ownerships or conglomerates. Efforts to discourage the expansion of cross-media ownerships and conglomerate ownerships involving newspapers may be more successful than those seeking to discourage the growth of groups or public ownership. Some concentration may be acceptable to assure the economic well-being of the media, but an over-concentration must be avoided as a threat to the free flow of information. Newspapers must succeed in their role as public servant as well as in their role as free business enterprise.

BUSINESS DEPARTMENT TRENDS

The organization and operation of newspapers will vary somewhat with their size and historical development. Titles and responsibilities related to those titles will not be the same. But certain basic functions are common to all whether they are performed by one person who also has another job or by a large staff distributed over several sub-departments. At the top of the organizational chart is the owner, or owners. Next in line comes the publisher, or general manager, who is responsible for the day-to-day operation of the newspaper. The publisher may be the owner if the newspaper is small, but in most instances he is appointed to oversee the operation. Various organizational patterns may be followed, but there usually are three main functions: business, production, and news and opinion. The business function will include basic office activities, advertising, circulation, personnel, and promotion. This section of Chapter 4 will survey briefly what is done in these various areas and examine some of the trends and problems related to them in the 1970s.

The business department of a newspaper has responsibilities similar to those in other business departments. It is concerned with the revenues that come into the business and the payments that go out. The business department is engaged in bookkeeping and accounting; it purchases supplies and materials; it pays for services received and bills others for services provided, and it handles the payroll. Perhaps the most significant development in this department in recent years is the adaptation of computers to perform many of these functions. The business department will work closely with top management in establishing cost and profit centers and instituting management and systems techniques to achieve the most efficient and economic operation possible.

Advertising

Advertising is a basic function of any newspaper in a free enterprise system. Not only does it provide about three-fourths of the revenue to operate the newspaper, but it also provides a valuable service for readers who want to buy something, sell something, hire someone, or find a job. Simply stated, the function of advertising is to persuade people to buy products or services. Basically there are two ways to get people to do something: one is coercion or force; the other is persuasion. Advertising is sometimes forceful and is sometimes considered a force, but it does not force anyone to do anything; it can only persuade. Advertising can be divided into various categories, such as local or retail, national, classified, and legal. Local advertising is composed of display advertisements for local stores or business firms and is generally prepared by them or by the newspaper staff. National advertising includes display advertisements for national companies, such as automobile manufacturers, and is usually prepared by them or by advertising agencies and obtained by the newspapers through national advertising representatives. These representatives seek to get advertising from national concerns for various local newspapers. Classified advertising includes notices for jobs, houses for sale or rent, and various other short listings grouped by categories. Legal advertising includes those public notices which laws require governments and others to publish. They may include such things as grand jury presentments, notice of legislation to be introduced, or notice of incorporation of a new firm.

Over the years some have sought to blame advertising for the economic ills and perhaps other problems of society. But the positives generated by advertising clearly outweigh the negatives. Moreover, the ills of advertising can be corrected far short of killing the patient. What does advertising do for people? First, it is a primary factor in the mass production, mass distribution system. Larger numbers of persons can obtain products and services and enjoy a high standard of living because of mass production; mass production is possible because large numbers of persons hear about products and buy them. Advertising is the stimulant that sets these marketing forces in motion and keeps them moving. It helps to make it possible for businesses to sell, produce and prosper; it helps create jobs for people, and it helps make possible the nation's high living standards. Some authorities on advertising challenge this view, however. They admit that advertising can increase the sales of some items at particular times and thereby influence the flow of cash in the economy, but they contend that advertising does not have a significant effect on the overall amount of money spent for goods and services.

Advertising is also cited for encouraging the development and production of better products and contributing to the spread of information and education. The competition stimulated by advertising encourages companies to come up with something better, cheaper or more attractive, or, hopefully, all three. Advertising itself provides information, and the revenue it produces makes possible all the services of newspapers and other media. In a real sense, advertising makes the free press possible. Moreover, it does all of these things with an investment of only 2% to 3% of the Gross National Product.[39]

What are some of the criticisms of advertising, and how valid are they? First, it is accused of influencing people to buy things they do not need. This may be partially true, but who is to say what people need? Do they need washing machines, electric stoves, air conditioners, automobiles, television sets or radios? Advertising may encourage people to want more things than they can afford to buy at a particular time, but it does not force them to buy anything. Its stimulation of the mass production system makes it possible for most persons to acquire items they otherwise would have to forego. Second, advertising has been accused of being dishonest. Some ads have been guilty on this count; the advertising industry is seeking reforms, and the government has adopted regulations to protect consumers. Third, advertisements have been accused of being offensive. Advertisements that some persons find objectionable undoubtedly do get printed or broadcast. But newspapers often reject advertisements they find objectionable. For example, a number of newspapers have quit carrying advertisements for X-rated movies, and many screen their entertainment ads closely. At times whether an advertisement is objectionable is a matter of personal taste. Some probably would object to any deodorant ad; but most of these advertisements are less offensive than a ride on a crowded bus used to be. Finally, advertisers are accused of having an undue influence on other newspaper operations. It is argued that they can get unfavorable stories suppressed or changed and that they can get much free advertising in the form of news stories about their products. Some instances in which newspapers have withheld information at the request of advertisers probably can be documented, and many business stories are little more than free advertising. But it seems unlikely that advertisers have the influence attributed to them by some because they need the media as much as the media need them.

Many newspapers have joined with other media, advertisers and consumer groups in efforts to correct the admitted faults of advertising. They hope to achieve through self-regulation what some believe can be accomplished only through government action. One of the major developments was the creation in 1971 of a National Advertising Review Board. This board was formed by the major advertising trade associations in cooperation with the Council of Better Business Bureaus. The board was established to hear and investigate complaints about advertising. If the board finds the advertiser is guilty, it hopes to get him to mend his ways. If this effort fails, the board plans to release its findings to appropriate government agencies and the press.[40] While hopeful that the board will have beneficial effects, the Federal Trade Commission and various consumer groups can be expected to pursue their own efforts to get wrongs righted. A survey taken by Grey Advertising Inc., in January, 1972, indicated that the majority (94%) of those in the marketing-advertising community favored a form of consumer protection and that two-thirds believed more needed to be done in that area. The respondents were about equally split on the question of whether existing regulation of advertising is adequate. The majority (82%) favored closer business-government cooperation and self-regulation (87%). The majority (92%) indicated that the most effective method of protection is to educate consumers. A survey reported by the American Newspaper Publishers Association in early 1974 of 488 daily newspapers in the United States and Canada indicated that complaints about advertising and advertised products were not a major problem. Most attributed the absence of complaints to advertising screening and editing processes they employed. Eighty per cent of those responding to the survey indicated that they had received complaints about business opportunity advertising. The next highest complaint categories involved mail order (47%) and home improvement (25%) advertisements.[41]

Newspapers can exercise considerable control over their advertising. The United States Supreme Court in 1971 upheld the right of a newspaper to refuse advertising with or without explaining its reasons for doing so. The Court held that a newspaper is not a common carrier and does not have to sell its space to everyone who requests it. The individual publisher has the authority to determine what he believes to be in the public interest and publish or not publish advertisements accordingly.[42]

Efforts to improve advertising through self-regulation, consumer pressure and government regulation have provided one of the major continuing developments in the field during recent years. Others have included the struggle against those who would tax advertising, the use of cold type in advertising, the expanded use of color in advertising, and the continuing competition among media for advertising revenue. In early 1971 eight states and two municipalities had a gross receipts tax on advertising and a dozen states were considering other forms of taxation on advertising, including a sales tax. Advertising was included under gross receipts tax laws in Alaska, Arizona, Hawaii, Indiana, New Mexico, Oklahoma, Washington and West Virginia, and the cities of St. Louis and Pittsburgh.[43] Newspapers opposed taxation as a threat to their very existence. The American Newspaper Publishers Association produced and distributed 20,000 copies of a booklet titled "7 reasons why you can't afford a sales tax on advertising." The booklet asserted that such a tax would be 1) a drag on the selling effort, 2) a brake on the state's economic growth, 3) discrimination against local merchants, 4) a burden on local commerce, 5) a penalty on a needed service, 6) double taxation, when customers pay twice, and 7) a blow to information media.[44]

Many newspapers that have not switched to offset presses have turned to cold type production of advertisements in search of more flexibility and other advantages. Most reportedly were satisfied with the change, although some problems were reported. Some complained that the large capital investment had not produced greater speed in their composing rooms, had not resulted in greater efficiency, or better reproduction, and in some cases had increased advertising deadlines.[45] Efforts to develop this potential are continuing.

One additional problem created by the growing use of the photo-offset process is the potential for "ad piracy." During the late 1960s and early 1970s two newspapers brought suit to protect local advertising copy created in their plants from being lifted bodily and reproduced in shoppers. Both newspapers lost their cases, but the results did give indication of what newspapers can do to protect themselves against such piracy. According to a discussion in the General Bulletin of the American Newspaper Publishers Association, newspapers can protect themselves from shopper piracy by "(a) obtaining copyright and (b) inserting a proper assignment clause in rate cards and advertising contracts which establishes the fact that the newspaper owns title to all advertising produced by it and that no reproduction can be made without prior written consent of the newspaper.'' [46]

Color advertising became a way of life for all major media during the years from the late 1950s until the early 1970s. By 1972 more than 1,000 newspapers representing more than 80% of the daily circulation were offering full color advertising. Almost 1,500 dailies representing more than 90% of the circulation were offering one color and black. The use of preprinted color was also growing. By 1972 Hi-Fi was available in more than 1,550 newspapers and SpectaColor in more than 400. Color usage, in part because of the switchover to offset, increased six-fold in the two decades before 1971 while black-and-white advertising was increasing about 50%. Studies indicate that both Run-of-Paper color and Preprinted color (Hi-Fi and SpectaColor) in both national and retail advertising are bargains. Demonstrated increases in effects due to the use of color are considerably greater than the increases in costs. [47]

The number of newspapers publishing two million lines of color advertising a year almost doubled in 1972 over 1971, rising from 32 to 61, and the number publishing a million lines of color advertising almost tripled, rising from 62 to 178. The *Miami Herald* published more than 6.5 million lines of color advertising in 1971 and 1972 to lead in linage both years. Others with large amounts in 1972 included *The Salt Lake City Tribune, Phoenix Republic, St. Petersburg Times* and *Ft. Lauderdale News*. The top 25 color users published 82 million lines in 1970, 87 million in 1971, and more than 97 million lines in 1972. [48]

Many newspapers eliminated sex designations from their help-wanted advertisements in the early 1970s to avoid charges of discrimination. There was much confusion for a time as to whether classification of advertisements by sex violated human rights legislation. Some argued that using ''male'' and ''female'' in the advertisements was discriminatory; others argued that the practice was a service for potential employees as well as for employers who ran the advertisements. Some contended that newspapers were subject to laws and ordinances forbidding the practice; others argued that they were not. Two United States district courts ruled that newspapers were not employment agencies and not subject to the jurisdiction of the Equal Employment Opportunity Commission and its attempts to regulate advertisements. But state courts in Connecticut and Pennsylvania held that state and local laws did cover newspaper classified practices. Finally, in 1973, the United States Supreme Court, in a five-to-four decision, upheld the constitutionality of a Pittsburgh ordinance forbidding newspapers to publish sex-designated advertisements. The Pittsburgh ordinance banned discrimination in employment on the basis of race, color, religion, ancestry, national origin, place of birth or sex. Complainants said the *Pittsburgh Press* violated the ordinance by permitting employers to place wanted advertising under ''male'' and ''female'' headings, and the newspaper was ordered to discontinue the practice. The *Press* contended that the order contravened its rights of freedom of the press. The majority of the court held that "truly commercial advertising" was not protected by the First Amendment, that a distinction can be drawn between commercial and other speech. The dissenters argued that the majority decision set a dangerous precedent for prior restraint on the press.[49]

As indicated earlier in this chapter, the prospects for increases in newspaper advertising in the latter 1970s look good. The Bureau of Advertising (now Newspaper Advertising Bureau) of the American Newspaper Publishers Association forecast in early 1972 that newspaper advertising revenue would range between $10.3 billion and $12.6 billion a year by 1980. Leo Bogart, executive vice-president and general manager of the Bureau, said the total would be comprised of between $3.7 and $4.6 billion classified billings, between $5.2 and $6.2 billion retail billings, and between $1.5 and $1.8 billion national billings.[50] The use of color, cold type and split runs, which enable a neighborhood advertiser to advertise only in the papers distributed in his area at a lower rate, may also grow; efforts to improve advertising and make it more useful for consumers certainly will be continued.

Circulation

The circulation department is responsible for bringing the producers and consumers of newspapers together. It is expected to produce up to a fourth of the newspaper's revenue, and how well it performs its basic functions will help determine how much revenue can be obtained from advertising. If the newspaper does not reach enough potential buyers, the advertisers will seek other outlets for their messages. The circulation department sells the newspaper, delivers it and collects for the service provided. Sales depend on the quality of the product produced by editorial and other departments, how well it is packaged, and the sales and service abilities of circulation personnel. The rise or fall in sales is an indication of how well the other departments are performing their tasks, and circulation personnel who are close to the consumers often can provide suggestions about what the readers want.

Newspapers are distributed in several ways. Many are sold and delivered directly to homes and offices by carriers who may work on a straight salary but more likely lease a route or have some other contractual arrangement with the newspaper. Carriers usually buy their newspapers at a reduced rate from the publisher then sell them at the established daily, weekly or monthly prices to the consumers. Some persons prefer to pay the newspaper directly, in which case the carrier's account is credited for the amount received. Some newspapers, particularly in metropolitan areas, are sold singly at newsstands or by vendors, and many are sold in cities of all sizes in newspaper boxes. Street vendors once were a principal factor in newspaper sales, but the rise of radio and television and the decline of extras has drastically reduced their numbers. Finally, some newspapers, particularly in rural areas, are distributed and paid for by mail. The number processed in this manner may be greatly reduced by projected increases in mail rates. Buses, trains, and even airplanes have been used to get newspapers more quickly to customers in outlying areas. Most publishers rely on trucks for getting newspapers to carriers, newsstands and boxes in the local community and in nearby cities. Truck routes and billing procedures have largely been computerized in recent years to get newspapers out more rapidly and more efficiently.

The Little Merchant System, under which independent carriers, often youngsters, have provided home delivery of newspapers, is still an important part of the total circulation operation. But some newspaper executives have raised questions in recent years about its continued viability, and many have taken steps to improve its operation. Critics of the system, which has delivered 90% of the nation's daily newspapers over the years, say it may be partly to blame for sluggish circulation growth in recent years. They question whether the carriers who deliver the product are qualified to sell it and keep it sold in today's competitive era; they point out that carrier turnover has exceeded 100% a year in many places and ask how adequate training programs can be developed under such circumstances. Some suggest that newspapers might be better off economically to accept the added expense of taking on carriers as employees rather than continuing the independent contractor operation. They argue that adequate training could then be provided and programs developed to reach people with the newspaper message and build and maintain higher circulation.[51]

Defenders of the Little Merchant System argue that it is still viable and should not be blamed if circulation is not rising fast enough. They point out that the system has helped newspapers, young persons and business generally over the years. The system has provided a means of introducing millions of youngsters to the business world; many successful persons today were newspaper carriers yesterday. Moreover, defenders say, the system can still serve effectively if newspapers provide adequate training, motivation and support for the carriers.[52]

Increasing newspaper involvement in carrier activities could, of course, add to the controversy over the legal relationship between newspapers and carriers. More than 20 newspapers have been involved in National Labor Relations Board decisions since 1948 dealing with whether their dealership programs actually involved independent contractors or amounted to a form of employe relationship. Some carriers have sought to be regarded as employes and entitled to employe benefits. Some have preferred the freedom that comes with being independent operators. Newspapers that wish to maintain an independent relationship have been advised against using leasing contracts, paid-in-advance solicitation, and other actions that might be regarded as employe supervision and control. They have been advised to let the carrier have proprietary interest in the delivery of newspapers with no restrictions.[53]

Some newspapers have turned to prepayment plans, however, in an effort to attract and hold carriers and build circulation. Carriers do not like to fool with collections, especially when they may have to make several trips to collect for a week or two. Subscribers do not like to be bothered at times and often do not have the correct change for their bills. Prepayment plans, perhaps employing bank credit cards, can be more convenient for all concerned. The *Richmond* (Va.) *Times-Dispatch* and *News Leader* reported an overwhelming response to a prepayment plan promotion involving the use of credit cards and direct billing in late 1973. They had expected to get 40,000 carrier-served subscribers to switch during the program's first year but got 50,000 during the fall promotion alone.[54]

Prepayment plans also have been suggested as a partial solution to the escalating problem of attracting and holding circulation in low-income neighborhoods. Mailing out bills reportedly has helped in some communities; using adult carriers and including more information about community residents also have helped; and hiring blacks to supervise and conduct circulation activities in black neighborhoods has helped in those neighborhoods. Aside from market possibilities, newspapers want to increase circulation in these areas because the overall community needs to reach these people with information and these people need the information. Present circulation problems in some low-income neighborhoods have been attributed to difficulty in collecting carrier accounts because of family instability and the high mobility of residents as well as low incomes.[55]

Among the other problems facing circulation managers in the early 1970s were rising costs, including rising postal rates, increased leisure time, increased apartment living, and the struggle over new technology, including cable television. The United States Postal Service, created by the Postal Reorganization Act of 1970, has projected increases in mail rates for newspapers and magazines that could cause severe economic problems for some and eliminate an important service for many Americans. After hearing protests the Postal Service indicated that it would reduce the increases somewhat, but an average increase of 25% a year for the next five years was indicated in 1973. By contrast the average previous increase since World War II had been less than 7% a year. These increases might not greatly affect metropolitan newspapers because they make limited use of the mails for delivery, but they might well destroy many magazines and place some daily newspapers beyond the reach of persons in rural America.[56]

Newspaper spokesmen argued that the Postal Service proposals would violate the concept of a national communications system envisioned by the founders of the post office system. They pointed out that such a system cannot be entirely maintained by postal revenues, that its cost must be apportioned between mail users and taxpayers generally. They noted, too, that if the Postal Service eliminates this circulation as its rates allegedly would do it would have to look elsewhere for the revenue it now derives from delivering newspapers and magazines.[57]

Congress was urged to preserve the public service aspect of the mails in making information available to the people at low cost, and legislation to that end was drafted. One proposal which called for Congressional endorsement of low second class postal rates as a service to the public was defeated in the House in the summer of 1973, reportedly because publishing groups did not agree on the specific proposal. But talk that fall of additional postal rate increases brought new efforts to obtain controls. One proposal that drew much support asked that the phasing-in period for new rates be ten years instead of five.[58]

Increased leisure time could help newspaper circulation in the sense that subscribers would have more time they could devote to reading. But there is a strong possibility that additional time, such as might be provided by a four-day work week, could lead people into a variety of other activities, such as trips to the mountains or beaches, that would reduce reading time. Newspapers must be concerned also about sustaining a youth delivery system seven days a week if the youths' families are working only four days and taking periodic if not regular three-day vacations.

Increased apartment living could present special problems for circulation managers because it frequently is difficult to solicit inside apartment complexes. Newspapers must develop such a demand for their product that apartment dwellers will insist that management do whatever is necessary to assure its availability.

The struggle over cable television could have a long-range effect on circulation; some believe that newspapers ultimately will be delivered electronically. Already, new technology has improved circulation procedures. In many plants computers have taken over the routing of newspapers, billing procedures and other chores and improved efficiency. New equipment has been developed for bundling and routing newspapers, and satellite plant operations could make it possible to tailor newspapers for communities and get them to consumers more rapidly.

Circulation managers and editors should work closely together in meeting problems, producing a better product and telling people about it. Editors can let circulation managers know when stories or features are being run that might be publicized to boost circulation in a particular area. They can let the circulation department know quickly of major news breaks that may increase the demand for newspapers, and advise them early of book serializations and other features that could affect circulation. Conversely, circulation managers can let editors know about possible news stories or features in various areas served. They are in close touch with the readers and can communicate with editors about what is going on and what readers say they want.

Newspapers must continue to improve their product and their methods of selling and distributing it if they are to realize their potential readership in the 1970s and beyond. Circulation growth slowed in the 1960s and early 1970s after making rapid strides in the late 1940 and 1950s. Daily circulation rose from about 48.4 million at the end of World War II to almost 54 million in 1952; it jumped to more than 59.8 million in 1962 but rose only to about 62.5 million in 1972. In that year the 337 morning newspapers had a circulation of 26,078,386 and the 1,441 evening papers had a circulation of 36,431,856. Total circulation for 603 Sunday papers was 49,338,765.[59] Circulation growth continued in the 1970s but not at the pace hoped for; daily circulation reached 63.1 million in 1974. If the newspapers can keep pace with their potential, they should have well over 70 million readers in the 1980s. Whatever the figure, it will be verified for advertisers by the Audit Bureau of Circulation, an agency formed in 1913 to standardize statements of circulation, verify data, and disseminate it to advertisers and other interested parties.

The price of many newspapers could rise in the decade also, but such increases are not expected to deter circulation growth. Dr. George Gallup, the nationally known researcher, advised publishers in 1971 that they could raise their prices from 10 to 15 cents a copy without fear of losing much circulation. His research indicated that nine of ten subscribers would continue to buy a newspaper at 15 cents a copy and that half of them would be willing to pay 20 cents. The greatest resistance to the 15-cent price was reported to be in the largest cities while acceptance ran heavily with the age and economic groups most important in the advertisers' viewpoint. Publishers apparently heeded Gallup's suggestion, for the number of 15-cent newspapers increased from 200 in early 1971 to 350 by the end of 1972. Almost all of the dailies had raised their prices to at least 10 cents for daily editions by that time. In late 1973, Allen H. Neuharth, president of Gannett Company, Inc., said that the economics of the newspaper business dictated a 25-cent daily, perhaps in five years. By early 1974 Gallup's research indicated that 70% of the newspaper readers would continue to get a daily newspaper if the price went to 20 cents.[60]

Electronic home communication systems and other competition could cause circulation problems for newspapers in the future. But the high cost of such technology and the continued interest in the newspaper package suggested an optimistic forecast for the 1970s. Newspaper-in-the-Classroom programs and other projects are being encouraged to help assure that rising generations know about the values of newspapers and acquire the habit of reading them. The Newspaper-in-the-Classroom programs serve the double function of helping teachers teach their subjects more effectively and helping youngsters learn about newspapers.

Personnel

The success of a newspaper or any other business enterprise ultimately depends on the people involved in its operation. It is important that personnel

be selected carefully, trained well, rewarded adequately and otherwise motivated to perform their tasks to the best of their abilities. As employment has
increased dramatically in recent years, increasing numbers of newspapers have
employed specialists and created personnel departments to help assure that they
obtain and retain the best persons possible and get the maximum possible performance from them. The future of newspapers is very much dependent on
providing good career opportunities, competitive salaries and continuing training programs. Trends in these and other areas will be considered briefly.

Newspapers' growth and development during the past quarter century is
reflected in rising employment figures. The daily newspaper business is the nation's fifth largest employer. Newspaper employment has risen in every year
except 1958 since the close of World War II, and it has risen much faster than
employment in other industries. Between 1947 and 1970 newspaper employment increased from 248,500 to 373,200, a gain of 50.2%. During this same
period all manufacturing employment grew 27.3% and total United States employment grew 37.5%.[61]

Employment growth figures should help dispel the fear that increasing automation of newspapers throws large numbers of persons out of work. Many
jobs of course have been eliminated, but many new ones have been created and
retraining programs have made it possible to keep persons already employed as
well as employ new ones. Most newspapers have sought to achieve reductions
through attrition.[62] The expanded use of new technology is essential if newspapers are to compete with other media and continue to provide jobs for those in
the field and information services for all.

Job opportunities fluctuate with the economy and depend to some extent
on the size and location of the newspapers concerned. When the economy is in
trouble newspapers, like other businesses, will hire fewer persons. When the
economy is doing well newspapers, like other businesses, can be expected to
expand their operations. Jobs are usually more available on smaller dailies and
weeklies than on metropolitan dailies where the prestige and pay at least appear
to be greater. Smaller papers may offer more opportunity for beginning employes to assume responsibility, and variations in the cost of living have a lot to
do with who enjoys the most real income.

Specific job needs also fluctuate, although good reporters and writers appear to be in continuing demand. A report by Thomas E. Engleman, executive
director of the Newspaper Fund, Inc., in November 1972, indicated that copy-
editors were in great demand and that specialists in photojournalism and
graphics would become more important to newspapers as competition from new
media increases.[63] An increased interest in journalism careers occasioned by
the success of the Watergate exposés threatened to glut the job market, especially in the cities, in the middle 1970s.

Salaries vary greatly with the size and location of the publication and the
experience and ability of the employe. One study reported in *Journalism Quar-*

terly in 1969 indicated that salaries for reporters, advertising salesmen and newspaper workers generally had not increased nearly as much between 1954 and 1966 as had salaries for production workers in other industries. Salaries of reporters and display advertising salesmen were up 44% and salaries for all newspaper workers were up 43% during the period as compared with a rise of 60% in the salaries for all industries' production workers. The study indicated that the increases in salaries were considerably lower than the increases in newspaper revenue and in community affluence as measured by retail sales.[64] This suggests that many newspapers could increase their salaries substantially and some apparently are doing so. Newspaper salaries were increased an average of 5.7% a year between 1964 and 1970, and the average starting salary for reporters in 1971 was $140 a week.[65] American Newspaper Guild locals reported that salaries were up an average of 9.5% a year during the fiscal year ending in March 1972. The average reporter starting minimum was up 10.4% to $139.35 a week, and the average reporter top minimum was up 9.8% to $226.86. The Guild's report included a list of 24 newspapers with contracts providing for $300 a week top minimums. Thirteen of them were already paying $275 or more by April 1972. The *Washington Post* was scheduled to reach $400 in August, 1973.[66]

Employment opportunities for women and minority groups appeared to be improving as the 1970s began, although the actual numbers employed were not large. Joann Lublin, who in July 1971, became the first woman reporter in the San Francisco bureau of *The Wall Street Journal,* did her master's thesis at Stanford earlier that year on sex discrimination. She concluded that ''some but not extensive discrimination because of sex still exists on American newspapers. . . .'' She said that between one-third and one-half of the newspaperwomen surveyed perceived sex bias in hiring, job status and promotability—and to a lesser extent, in salary. She said that numerous jobs and beats in the newsroom were still linked to traditional sex roles and that opportunities for women to advance into news management jobs were still restricted. Men generally are assigned to beats such as police, crime, sports, business, labor and real estate, while women are assigned to cover women's news, education and medicine. Nevertheless, Lublin concluded that she believes women and racial minorities will be getting first crack at more and more jobs in the near future. In late 1974 Helen K. Copley, chairman and chief executive officer of Copley Newspapers, said there were about 26,000 women in the nation's newsrooms as compared with 17,000 five years before. She said they fill every conceivable newsroom task from straight reporting to supervisory roles.[67]

Responses to a survey by the Women's Rights in Journalism Committee of the American Society of Newspaper Editors indicated that the area of best opportunity for women was on newspapers with circulations of less than 25,000. Most of the women executives who responded indicated that they got less pay than men holding similar or equal positions. They did, however, rate journalism as somewhat better than other occupations so far as discrimination was concerned, and most expressed optimism that the progress made on small papers would lead to similar progress on larger ones.[68]

Blacks held even fewer jobs than women on nonblack newspapers as the middle 1970s arrived. A report of the Committee on Minority Employment of the American Society of Newspaper Editors in early 1974 indicated that the total professional newsroom employment of minority individuals was about one percent, up about one-fourth of one percent over the previous year.[69] These figures may change dramatically in the 1970s as a result of efforts by the American Newspaper Publishers Foundation, individual newspapers and other groups to provide scholarships and encourage blacks to consider careers in journalism. Some increases were indicated in the early 1970s. But many blacks still appeared to have a negative image of white media, and others were uncertain about becoming involved with them at a time when many blacks were stressing a black cultural nationalism. Black reporters often found themselves in something of a dilemma; on the one hand, they had obligations to their brothers and sisters in the black community; on the other they had obligations to their white employers. To help deal with the dilemma the first National Conference of Black News Media was held in 1970 at Lincoln University. Out of this conference came the National Association of Black Media Workers with several regional chapters.[70]

The job outlook for trained, capable black newsmen who could also cope with the challenges involved appeared excellent. There appeared to be more jobs than persons ready to fill them.[71] The *Washington Post* has been a leader in hiring blacks, and in 1972 approximately 9.3% of its 396 newsroom employes were black. Some of these persons were critical of the paper, however. They said it had not hired enough blacks and that none were in news policy-making positions.[72]

Most newspaper employes, whites as well as blacks, probably would agree that newspaper salaries should be improved. But studies indicate that money is not what attracted most persons into the business. Although many reasons have been cited, the ones noted most often involve self-fulfillment, desire to write, or the fact that the field is interesting and challenging.[73] Some reporters and junior editors, particularly in recent years, have expressed a desire for greater participation in policy decisions and a greater freedom to express their opinions in their stories. Some have found an adequate outlet for this expression through signed columns and analyses; the most militant have moved on to alternative newspapers. Most executives indicate they are interested in what their employes think but do not plan to put editorial decisions on a staff referendum basis.[74]

Aside from improved salaries and benefits, the greatest personnel need of most newspapers today is continuing education. Journalism schools are doing an increasingly good job of preparing their graduates for newspaper work. Internship programs that permit college students to work on a newspaper for a quarter or two before graduation are particularly helpful. But too often the newspapers do not have adequate inservice training programs or released-time programs to continue their employes' educations. Most employes could benefit from attending short courses and seminars every year or two, and some employes should be encouraged to obtain advanced degrees in fields of reporting specialization such as science or business. Some very good seminars such as the American Press Institute exist, but more are needed and more employes need to attend them.

Unions and Strikes

Over the years newspaper unions have both benefited and damaged the welfare of newspaper employes. Production departments have been unionized since before the Civil War; editorial employes formed the American Newspaper Guild in the 1930s. Unions have forced some recalcitrant employers to raise salaries and provide benefits, and pressure from these organizations probably improves the bargaining power of employes today. But at times unions have been shortsighted, and their resistance to automation in their lengthy strikes has helped cause the demise of good newspapers. Employes, employers and the public all suffer from prolonged strikes which curtail or eliminate the newspapers' services. Labor problems and strikes contributed to the demise of several New York newspapers, including the highly regarded *Herald Tribune,* during the 1960s. Lengthy strikes in Detroit and other cities caused many problems for persons and organizations dependent on their services.

Almost everyone in the community is affected by a newspaper strike. Retail firms, theaters and other businesses cannot conduct their usual advertising campaigns, and their revenue drops appreciably. Citizens generally miss out on bargains and fail to learn information they need to know. Persons looking for houses or apartments cannot find them because there are no want ads. School programs that use newspapers must be curtailed, and everyone who depends on the newspapers for information is adversely affected. Even funerals may be poorly attended because persons outside the family fail to learn about the death in time. Government, with the possible exception of the Sanitation Department which has fewer old newspapers to pick up, suffers. Information cannot be communicated; investigations may be delayed. The losses suffered by local businesses mean tax losses for government; some important programs may go unfinanced. Other media can expand their news and advertising programs, but not nearly enough to meet the public's needs. The problems caused everyone by newspaper strikes make it clear that people need newspapers.

What can be done to curtail or eliminate strikes without giving either labor or management an unfair advantage over the other? Some have argued that newspapers and other mass media are so vital to the national welfare that strikes should be barred by government. Presumably any such regulation would be accompanied by some provision for compulsory arbitration. Such arbitration is often regarded as an answer by those not directly involved, but it is not necessarily welcomed by newspaper unions or management. Others favor changes in laws that would place additional restrictions on the right of unions to strike; they contend that the laws now are overbalanced in favor of the unions. Many believe that the problem can at least be alleviated by providing a single bargaining arrangement for all unions at a newspaper; a federation of unions could bargain for all, and all contracts could be renegotiated at the same time. Finally, it is argued that the institution of profit-sharing or other employe-sharing programs could go a long way in discouraging strikes. All employes would have a greater stake in keeping the newspaper in operation. One or more of these approaches, or others, must be used to resolve labor-management problems and eliminate strikes in the future. Neither the people directly involved at the newspaper nor the public generally can afford them.[75]

Promotion.

Many small newspapers may not have a promotion department as such, but all newspapers are involved in promotion or public relations efforts. Promotion has been defined as "anything that serves to advance the interests of a newspaper within its community." [76] This would include the beneficial effects of an editorial, news analysis or feature story as well as a campaign to celebrate an anniversary, promote a special edition or provide a public service. Promotion departments are growing in numbers and size as newspapers come to realize the importance of selling their product and becoming more deeply involved in community affairs.

The overall goals or objectives of the newspaper promotion department have been outlined as follows: "(1) to increase advertising; (2) to build circulation; (3) to increase reader interest in the paper; (4) to build respect and good will for the paper; (5) to improve community life; (6) to show the newspaper as a 'human' institution and (7) to increase the net profit of the newspaper." [77] Those are laudable goals which require effort and cooperation of all staff members and which can be advanced more rapidly through the concentrated efforts of those assigned to develop promotion or public relations. A former president of the International Newspaper Promotion Association suggested several guidelines for newspapers to follow in achieving goals. Vince Spezzano, public service director for Gannett Company, Inc., said that newspapers need to develop and retain an intimacy with readers through audience profiles and readership studies. He pointed out that the average American moves every five years and suggested that too many newspapers have lost touch with their readers. Spezzano also asserted that public service programs must be meaningful and must accomplish something. He cited the Newspaper-in-the-Classroom program as an effort that not only reaps immediate tangible benefits but can have tremendous long-range effects.[78] Newspaper promotions may involve some specific effort to sell the newspaper and its services, or they may involve such things as sponsoring concerts, basketball leagues, soap box derbies, spelling contests and other special events.

Virginia Butts, director of public relations for Field Enterprises, warns in her public relations handbook, however, that newspapers, like other businesses, must always be honest with their readers. "All . . . efforts to create an impression of a strong, honest, aggressive newspaper can be seriously impaired . . . if in times of crisis or a situation unfavorable to the paper or one of its executives, the public relations department tries to cover up. If the truth cannot be told to inquiring media, no story should be given. Almost inevitably it is far better to tell the story of the circulation drop, the realignment of key personnel, the accident, the fire, than to try to withhold it." [79] A few newspapers have public relations departments separate from their promotion departments, but most combine these functions in one operation. All newspapers must be concerned with improving their promotion and public relations efforts regardless of their organization. All operations on the newspaper and the public can benefit from such efforts. Irvin S. Taubkin, who retired in 1971 after 35 years in promotion work for the *New York Times,* said that for many years more newspaper promotion was bad than good, but that over the years it has improved tremendously. He noted that more newspapers today are involved in positive promotion efforts and that the quality of their work is improving.[80]

Those seeking help in improving their promotion efforts can examine the winning entries in the annual Newspaper Promotion Awards Competition sponsored by *Editor & Publisher,* and study the latest revision of the International Newspaper Promotion Association's promotion handbook called *Promoting the Total Newspaper*. The fourth revision of the handbook, prepared in 1973, was completely updated by a panel of 16 authors, each a specialist in some area of newspaper journalism.[81]

5

News and Opinion

THE NEWS/EDITORIAL DEPARTMENT carries out the functions which produce the title "newspaper" and which justify the newspaper's special privileges under the First Amendment. Actually, two operations are involved, news and editorial. The news department is charged with reporting the news fully, fairly and accurately. The editorial, or opinion, department is charged with commenting on the news and the newsmakers to bring about desired changes in society. The two are often considered together as one of three basic divisions of the newspaper: business, news/editorial and production. One person, perhaps called an editor-in-chief, may have supervision over both and be on an organizational level with a business manager and production superintendent. Or the heads of each may report directly to the publisher, who is or speaks for the owner.

Whatever the organizational arrangements, most newspapers today seek to keep the functions separate. News, reported as objectively as possible, is supposed to go on the news pages. Opinions, supported by facts which may also be part of the news reports, are supposed to go on the editorial or opinion pages or otherwise be identified as the views of the newspaper or writer. Although challenged in some quarters today such as the alternative newspapers, the separation of news and opinion has become a fundamental principle of most American newspapers. Many believe that their credibility, which has been challenged along with that of most other American institutions in recent years, depends on it.

News and opinion have not always been separated in American newspapers. The division came about as a result of the increasing irresponsibility of early editors; it was encouraged by the development of wire services in the latter half of the nineteenth century and by decreasing competition among local newspapers and the rising complexity of life in the twentieth century. As indicated in the chapter on the development of the American press, colonial editors frequently advocated causes in their news columns; there were no editorial columns or pages identified as such. The advocacy became even more pronounced during the evolution of the party system that followed the revolution and adoption of a national constitution. The party papers of the late eighteenth and early nineteenth centuries were so filled with activist propaganda and scurrilous reporting that the period has been referred to as a dark age of American journalism.

Some efforts to separate news and opinion were made during these years, but it was not until the "news paper," started in the 1830s, came to replace the party paper in the middle of the century that much substantial progress was made. Civil War reporting on both sides has been cited as more factual than partisan. The expansion of the wire services, which required objectivity to serve many clients of differing views, and the development of more responsible newspapers such as the *New York Sun* and *New York World* encouraged the separation of news and opinion. Wire services may have affected American newspaper reporting as much through their insistence on objectivity as in their development of summary leads and inverted pyramids to get the most important facts first in their stories.

Separation of news and opinion was encouraged in the early twentieth century by the demise of many newspapers and the rise of newspaper consolidations. Advocacy in the news columns can be more readily defended in communities where readers can select from several newspapers and decide for themselves what is truth. The only newspaper in town has a greater responsibility to be impartial and to separate its opinions from its reporting. Unfortunately, the separation was carried to unacceptable extremes on some newspapers in the early decades of the twentieth century. Their news columns were so careful to be objective that they were incomprehensible or misleading. The editorials' subjectivity was not always supported by demonstrable facts. An ill-defined objectivity allowed public figures to distort the truth as long as they were quoted accurately. The newspapers too often failed to provide the perspective required for readers to understand what was going on and act intelligently.

The need for explanation and background information in news reporting was intensified in the 1920s and 1930s by spectacular technological developments, the depression and the rise of big government. Newspapers joined with news magazines, radio commentators and others in an effort to meet this need through interpretive reporting. Newspapers sought to place the news they reported in their news columns into its proper setting, to give it perspective so that readers could more readily understand it. Efforts to provide such perspective may range from an identifying word to one or more paragraphs, to one or more related stories. This emphasis on interpretive reporting has been continued by most good newspapers to the present. Wire services and syndicates also have provided more interpretive reporting as well as by-lined opinion analyses.

Many newspapers and other media also have expanded their emphasis on research and investigation in an effort to explain government and society and point out matters that need correction. This effort, commonly called investigative reporting, got a boost in the early 1970s from the development of the Fund for Investigative Journalism. This fund was started in 1968 as an auxiliary of the Stern Fund but later became a separate organization. Its recent financing has come from contributions both by foundations and individuals. Between September 1971 and September 1973, more than 60 investigative projects were financed. Some did not result in exposés but some uncovered questionable activities related to political campaign irregularities, government corruption and other matters. Perhaps the best known expose was the one on the My Lai massacre by Seymour M. Hersh, who won a Pulitzer Prize.[1]

The use of interpretation in stories has, of course, opened the way for a new intrusion of opinion into news stories. But good editors insist that distinctions can be drawn between facts, interpretation of those facts, and opinion about them. Lester Markel of the *New York Times* has suggested, for example, that to announce the appointment of a new cabinet officer is fact; to tell why the President made the appointment is interpretation, and to comment on whether he was right or wrong in doing so is opinion. Others would disagree, at least in part. They would contend that to tell "why" the President made the appointment is to inject the reporter's opinion, unless the "why" is generally accepted, in which case it becomes fact. Markel believes his point is borne out weekly in the *Times'* Review of the Week section. He sees interpretation as "the deeper sense of the news. It places a particular event in the larger flow of events. It is the color, the atmosphere, the human elements that give meaning to a fact. It is, in short, setting, sequence, and above all, signficance." [2] One way to distinguish between interpretation and opinion is to consider the reporter's approach to his work. Herbert Brucker of the *Hartford Courant* poses this question for use in making such an analysis: "Is he digging up the truth in the dispassionate spirit of the scientist, collecting all the relevant facts he can get—on both sides—or is he openly and subtly arguing a case, plugging a point of view?" [3] Ideally, the reader should not be able to tell from a news story about a controversy which side the reporter favors. Reporters should continuously ask themselves whether they are seeking to inform their readers or advocate causes.

Complete objectivity, as most probably would agree, is an unattainable goal. Many subjective decisions are made concerning a newspaper story from the time of its origin to its publication. Subjective decisions are made in determining what events will be covered, what stories will be assigned to which reporters, and what stories from wire services, syndicates, or other sources will be used. The reporter makes subjective decisions about the sources he will probe, the facts obtained that he will use, the order in which he writes his story and the language he uses in writing it. He will be influenced also by his own experience, his stereotypes, his way of viewing the world. Subjective decisions will be made by the editors who check the story, assign it a headline size, position it in the newspaper, and write the headline that precedes it. Newspapers must be concerned about this subjectivity and the further subjectivity of those who receive the end product. A subscriber will make subjective decisions about what to read and how much, and he, too, will be influenced by his preconceived ideas about the subject, the newspaper and perhaps the reporter who wrote the story.

Most editors today are agreed, however, that the acknowledged inability to achieve complete objectivity is not an acceptable reason for abandoning the effort. They contend that the credibility of newspapers depends on their efforts to reach this unattainable standard or goal. They do not reject advocacy of causes, but insist that such advocacy be limited to the opinion columns of the newspaper which are clearly labeled as such. Members of the American Society of Newspaper Editors voted decisively in favor of the principle of objectivity after a debate on the topic at their 1971 convention.[4] Most editors, except those involved with alternative publications, probably agree, even though performance may at times be disappointing. A study of more than 20 top circulation newspapers reported by a professor at Northwestern University in 1970 indicated the presence of opinion in both interpretive and spot news stories. The difference between the use of opinion in the two categories reportedly was more in degree than in kind.[5]

More opinions may have got into news stories in the late 1960s than in preceding years because many young reporters, and some older ones, urged such advocacy as a means of righting things in society they believed to be wrong. This advocacy may also have been a factor in the crisis in credibility described by various commentators and discussed in Chapter 1. More about the causes of the credibility gap between the citizenry and American institutions may be known after the completion of a five-year study begun at the University of Indiana in 1972. It is financed by a $500,000 grant from the Poynter Fund established by Nelson P. Poynter, chairman of the board of the *St. Petersburg Times* and president of the *Congressional Quarterly*.[6] A failure to distinguish between news and opinion could be a factor insofar as the mass media including newspapers are concerned.

Although some might argue that the *New York Times* and other newspapers have not lived up to the model, many editors probably would subscribe to a statement made by A. M. Rosenthal, managing editor of the *Times,* to his staff in 1969. ''The duty of every reporter and editor is to strive for as much objectivity as humanly possible,'' Rosenthal wrote. ''The turmoil in the country is so widespread, voices and passion are at such a pitch that a newspaper that keeps cool and fair makes a positive, fundamental contribution without which the country would be infinitely poorer." [7]

New Journalism

Objectivity, summary leads, inverted pyramids and other characteristics of mid-twentieth century American journalism have been challenged from one or more directions in recent years. Many of the challenges in the 1960s were developed by persons unhappy with the orientation of the media in society, the ways in which the media were performing their work, or both. Everette Dennis in *The Magic Writing Machine* suggests that the various approaches which in recent years have been termed "new journalism" can be grouped in five categories: advocacy, alternative journalism, underground journalism, precision journalism, and the new nonfiction. [8] None of the approaches are really new, but each has provided an alternative method of approaching present tasks. All have had some effect on the journalistic mainstream, sometimes negative, sometimes positive. Each should be judged on its own merits.

Advocacy journalism is based on the premise that the journalist has both a right and an obligation to become involved in the events that he reports. The advocate, or activist, says that since objectivity in reporting cannot be obtained, it should not be attempted. The reporter should instead tell the truth of the event or situation as he sees it. Advocacy is, of course, not new in American journalism. It was the staple of many colonial and early United States newspapers. Nor is advocacy frowned upon by those in the mainstream today. Most newspapers encourage advocacy in their editorials, columns and other articles clearly identified as having a point of view. The point of divergence between the modern advocates and the mainstream is in the use of advocacy in the news columns. Most editors believe that advocacy in the news columns would bring an end to believability and credibility. It would not produce new light but a return to the dark ages of journalism.

Alternative journalism is a form of muckraking or investigative reporting that began in small publications outside the establishment press and seeks to make the larger press responsive. In a sense it is a return to the personal journalism and muckraking of the early twentieth century. That emphasis began in *McClure's* and a few other magazines and spread to other media. The idea is to examine the system and call attention to any defects.

Underground journalism today involves several hundred publications started in the 1960s to serve the counterculture that developed in the decade. These publications, discussed in Chapter 3 as a special type of newspaper, have had different emphases and have covered various interests, including protests against the establishment, rock music, drugs and sex. Such publications are not a new phenomenon, however. Other groups not accepted by the mainstream have had their own publications in the past.

Precision journalism is an effort to apply scientific method to reporting the news. The precision journalist, like the social scientist, collects extensive data through the use of questionnaires and interviews and analyzes it with the help of computers. The idea is not new. *Literary Digest* and others popularized the approach a half century ago, and many newspapers today carry reports of professional pollsters such as George Gallup. But not many newspapers have applied the techniques to their own local situations, perhaps because of the expense and time involved. The potential of such reporting for predicting and analyzing urban and other problems and how people feel about them seems great.

The *new nonfiction,* or *reportage,* involves the application of fiction techniques to reporting news and events. Much emphasis is placed on the characters involved and the scenes in which they perform. The idea of using literary techniques in journalistic writing is certainly not new. Narrative, dialogue, description and other techniques employed regularly by the fiction writer also have been used by the journalist, particularly in writing feature stories. But a new emphasis has been provided in the 1960s and early 1970s by nationally recognized writers such as Tom Wolfe, Norman Mailer, Truman Capote, Gay Talese, Jimmy Breslin and Willie Morris. Reportage seeks to provide a more complete picture of persons and events. It involves what Wolfe has described as ''saturation reporting.'' The saturation reporter is not content with using the interview for information or limited to a consideration of who, what, where, when, why and how. He is concerned with whole scenes and stretches of dialogue and gives attention to minute facts and details. The saturation reporter may have to spend days, weeks or even months with those about whom he is writing.[9] The reporter often seeks to reveal what the story subjects are thinking and feeling as well as how they look and what they are saying.

Each of the reportage journalists has his own style and approach and should be judged on his own. But several techniques have been identified with the movement. One is the assumption of a point of view in reporting. The scene may be recreated from the point of view of the subject, the author and other persons involved. Gay Talese has used an interior monologue based on what the character is thinking rather than saying to present that point of view. The writer ad-libs a stream of consciousness based on what the subject has told him he was thinking of at the time. Writing from a point of view also dictates another characteristic of reportage, a rambling if not jumbled story organization. Still another reportage device is extended dialogue, which involves the actual lines of a conversation between two persons. Some new journalists also make use of composite characters to depict what they believe to be a representative picture of a group. The idea is to avoid the gaps between the ordinary and the interesting in most individuals' lives and to avoid missing details and dimensions that may be lacking in a single member of a group but apply generally to the group.[10]

Like other forms of "new" journalism, the new nonfiction has been controversial. Some charge that the writers become too involved in the story and may, in fact, appear more important than the central characters. Others criticize the lack of organization, and some question the validity of composite characters. Dwight MacDonald calls the new journalism a parajournalism that exploits the factual authority of journalism and the atmospheric license of fiction. He says the new journalism specializes in details that cannot be checked.[11]

New nonfiction could be harmful to the credibility of journalism if practiced by incompetent persons. The real danger may be from those who are attracted by the style and flair of the movement but who are unwilling to spend the days, weeks and months necessary to making it work. On the other hand, the approach, if handled by competent writers, could provide an additional dimension for journalism. The literary approach, the time required for research, and the space necessary for presentation suggest that the new nonfiction may continue to be more prevalent in magazines than in newspapers. It has made its major inroads in *New York, Harper's, Esquire* and others. But newspapers should not overlook its possibilities as a complementary story form, or the reporting lessons to be learned from an emphasis on saturation reporting. In some respects it is not so different from the interpretive reporting that now complements spot news reporting on many newspapers.

Some aspects of new journalism will be included along with the more traditional forms in reporting the news of the late 1970s. Some new approaches may even be included as newspapers seek the most effective ways to communicate information. The traditional news story approach with its summary lead and inverted pyramid organization probably will be continued with some variations, especially for spot news stories. The interpretive news story with its emphasis on objectivity and fairness will continue to be a staple. The precision approach of some new journalists will provide a useful variation for interpretation and background accounts. The new muckraking of the alternative journalists likely will find its way into the mainstream, perhaps under the heading of investigative reporting. Advocacy journalism may be expanded also, but will remain clearly labeled what it is. The saturation techniques of the new nonfiction likely will be incorporated into some forms of interpretive reporting. More specialists will be employed and teams of reporters likely will be used in covering broad challenges such as urban affairs, health, housing or racial problems. In addition to telling the who, what, where, when, why and how of things, newspapers will increasingly attempt to tell what the story means to the reader, individually and collectively. What Alex S. Edelstein and William E. Ames have described as humanistic reporting may be more widely adopted. This type of reporting is concerned with the impact of the news on the individual. It is individualized and personalized in an effort to enable the reader to see common threads of experience between his life and that of another. Edelstein and Ames suggested that if the reader can identify with another person's experience, he will feel less isolated as a human being. The reader will develop a greater understanding of others and become more able to cope with events. The humanistically inclined reporter, for example, instead of leading his story with something about the Planning Commission recommending a new classification for the zoning ordinance might suggest that it soon will be possible for a poor family to slowly buy an apartment with enough room to seem like a home.[12]

Hopefully, the reporters, whatever their format, will also develop the clarity, punch and precision of a James Jackson Kilpatrick, columnist for the Washington Star Syndicate. A spot news story, an interpretive series or a new journalist's essay is dependent on the writer's use of language as well as his use of research. Yet the approach and the language are but means to achieve the goal of communicating ideas and information. Communication is what old journalism, new journalism and the newer journalisms of the future must be all about.

Sources of News

Newspapers obtain much of their news through the efforts of their own reporters, the wire services and the newspaper syndicates. Some information is provided by public relations representatives of various firms and organizations, and some is provided by individuals who have something they would like to share with others. News previously reported is also recorded for reference as needed in the newspaper's library or morgue.

Most newspapers get most of their local and area news through the work of their own reporting staffs. Traditionally, these staffs have included beat reporters, who cover the same offices such as City Hall on a continuing basis, and general assignment reporters, who cover whatever news happens to break on a particular day that is not covered by a beat reporter. Some newspapers now are developing special reporting teams to investigate particular problems such as health, education and welfare needs. Many newspapers have part-time correspondents in nearby communities who provide information about their communities, and the larger newspapers have full-time correspondents to cover the state capital, Washington or other producers of news they believe need staff attention. Some newspapers also have special contributors who write articles and columns about matters in which they have some special knowledge.

Most newspapers rely on the wire services and syndicates for much of their nonlocal news. The two major wire services today are the Associated Press, which was started before the Civil War, and United Press International, which was formed by the merger of United Press and International News Service in 1958. These two were originated early in this century from earlier efforts on a smaller scale by E. W. Scripps and William Randolph Hearst, respectively. Both the Associated Press and United Press International are newsgathering agencies that supply information for both newspapers and broadcast stations on a worldwide basis. They are commonly called wire services because their offices or bureaus literally are linked to their clients by wires and cables over which news and pictures flow. Large newspapers may subscribe to the reports of both services and one or more of the smaller wire services such as the New York Times Service, the Los Angeles Times-Washington Post News Service, and others. Smaller newspapers may subscribe to one of the two major services and one of the smaller ones, or they may supplement their major service with one of the many syndicate services that rely more on the mails than leased wires to communicate their news. The smaller newspapers are likely to get a distillation of the several reports prepared by the major wire services whereas the larger newspapers may want full reports on national, regional, sports and business information.

The major wire services are organized into regional bureaus which gather and disseminate news and pictures for the media. News of state or regional interest gathered by the bureau might be distributed only in the area whereas news of major importance would be sent throughout the nation and overseas. The wire services have their own reporting staffs and supplement them with correspondents at various newspapers or stations. Since Associated Press is now a cooperative, each paper or station is asked to make its stories available to other members. Together Associated Press and United Press International provide much of the information that Americans receive about national and international news and a substantial amount that many in smaller communities get about state news.

Some persons have expressed concern about the extent to which the wire services along with the broadcasting networks dominate the daily flow of news. A book-length study was initiated in the early 1970s to determine the extent to which Associated Press, United Press International and other services compete with one another in news coverage, the effect of internal and external pressures on their news content, and the quality of their output. The study was to be conducted by Arthur E. Rowse, director of Consumer News, a Washington-based newsletter, as a project of the Twentieth Century Fund.[13] It would appear that the wire services have a lot to say about what is covered, how it is covered and written, and how much about any particular story is provided for clients. But clients and member newspapers can complain about the service and make requests. It is also argued that the wire services appeal to a low common denominator in selecting news because they have so many different clients to please and that they encourage a sameness about American newspapers in both style and coverage.

Both major wire services have placed increased emphasis on interpretive reporting in recent years. The Associated Press has stepped up its investigative reporting and added specialists in areas such as science, religion and urban affairs. United Press International has been developing a two-tiered service, one for basic coverage of spot news and one for analysis and interpretation.[14] Associated Press formed a "New Establishment" team of young reporters, an AP Mod Squad, in 1970 to seek out and report news of special interest to the 50 million persons in the nation between 18 and 34. These young reporters sought to tell contemporary America about itself and provide a bridge between the two sides of the generation gap. The new team was as concerned with how young adults spend their money, raise their children and buy homes as it was with the phenomena of long hair, drugs, protest and rock music. United Press International reporters were exploring similar interests.[15]

Both Associated Press and United Press International also have pioneered in the development of new technology, including video screens for composing and editing stories. These developments are discussed in more detail in Chapter 7, but it can be noted here that within a short time editors should be able to order only the stories they want from the wire services after seeing abstracts and have these stories fed directly into the newspaper's computers for storage until they are called out for editing and makeup.

News services developed by the *New York Times, Washington Post, Los Angeles Times* and other large newspapers have provided a supplement to those of Associated Press and United Press International. They can help alleviate the danger of news domination by the two major services and perhaps free the reporters of other newspapers to engage in investigative reporting of their own. The use of several such services can provide newspapers and their readers with greater variety and perspective. Several of the major services have combined their efforts in recent years to save on leased wire costs and give their clients more from which to choose.[16]

Newspaper syndicates of various sizes have provided their clients more variety in news coverage in addition to a host of features including comic strips, cartoons, and feature stories and columns about most anything. The syndicates perform services for newspapers somewhat similar to those of the wire services; they bring them a wide range of materials the newspapers could not easily or economically obtain for themselves. But they are different in several respects. First, they deal less with spot news or other timely information; they use the mails for distribution rather than leased wires. Second, their scope is much broader; more than 40 different categories of features were listed in the "Syndicate Directory," which is published annually by *Editor & Publisher* magazine.

Newspapers can get a substantial part of their total content, including cartoons, columns and even editorials from the syndicates. They can get features on food, fashion and other topics for their women's pages. They can get reviews and features on the arts and literature for their culture pages, and they can get features on business, sports, youth, movies, religion, science and just about any other topic for use in special sections or alone. Whether the use of these features is helpful or harmful to the newspaper's efforts to serve its readers and community depends on how they are used. Syndicates make it possible for readers of newspapers throughout the country to see columns by noted commentators such as James J. Kilpatrick and Jack Anderson, see cartoons by Herbert Block and Bill Mauldin, get advice on living from Ann Landers, Abby Van Buren and others. Some interesting, thought-provoking materials are made available, and this can be good. But if newspapers use syndicated materials to the exclusion of locally produced news stories, features and editorials, then their use can be deleterious. A proper balance must be maintained.

Newspaper syndication can be traced to the Colonial period, but widespread use of syndicated materials probably did not come until the time of the Civil War. There was considerable growth in the field around the turn of the century and in the early twentieth century. S. S. McClure was one of the pioneers of the syndicated features movement in the 1880s. E. W. Scripps and William Randolph Hearst, who started United Press and International News Service, respectively, to challenge Associated Press in the wire service field, also started syndicates. The Scripps-Howard interests founded Newspaper Enterprise Association and United Features Syndicate, and Hearst initiated King Features Syndicate early in the century. These syndicates contributed to the rise of the comics and cartoons, the development of the gossip columnists in the 1920s and the political columnists in the 1930s.

There were more than 350 newspaper syndicates in operation in the United States in the early 1970s. Some were small, but others had 150 or more features to offer. The three pioneers mentioned above, North American Newspaper Alliance, Publishers-Hall Syndicate, the Chicago Tribune-New York Daily News Syndicate, and General Features Corporation, affiliated with the Los Angeles Times Syndicate, were among the major ones in the early 1970s. A complete list of syndicates and features available may be found in the most recent issue of the "Syndicate Directory." A former syndicate executive estimated that the odds against getting one's work accepted for syndication may be as high as 10,000 to 1, but the rewards are also great for those who succeed. Many artists and writers were earning between $25,000 and $50,000 a year in the early 1970s, and some of the most successful syndicators earned far more than that. A typical financial arrangement guarantees the contributor a fixed sum plus an even share of proceeds over a specified amount.[17]

Like most others in the newspaper business, the syndicates have had to contend with newsprint shortages. A number of syndicates in late 1973 asked contributors to "write tight" and several asked for specific cuts in length. The size of some comics also was reduced to save valuable paper.[18]

Wire services and syndicates provide newspapers with a great deal of useful material to complement their own staff output at an inexpensive price. Public relations organizations for businesses, industries, educational institutions and other groups are happy to provide favorable information about their activities free. While much of this material must be rejected because it is biased or because it properly belongs in the advertising columns, some can be useful in developing stories. Newspapers rely on public relations offices for much of the routine news about business, government and other activities. Some newspapers may fail to give proper perspective to some situation by using material from a public relations office instead of digging on its own; some just as mistakenly reject virtually everything produced by a public relations operation as being publicity and not news. Good newspapers judge individual stories on their news value and do their own digging where the subject indicates. They take the same approach toward stories or suggestions provided by individuals who have something they want to get in the newspaper. Readers can provide a great deal of useful routine information and oftentimes suggest topics for further research and development by staff members.

Finally, newspapers can make use of libraries, including their own, in compiling background information and other data for their stories. The operation of newspaper libraries varied considerably as the 1970s opened. Many newspapers still relied on standing files to house old clippings and other materials. A number were switching to microfilm to save space and guard against the deterioration of paper materials, and some were using new electromechanical filing systems to save space and reduce the time and effort required to get information. *Newsday* installed an automated system as early as 1967 which included Lektriever machines manufactured by the Remington Office Systems Division of the Sperry Rand Corporation. Under this system the file trays are brought to the information retriever at a predetermined standing or sitting height on a conveyor belt. The system is not only more convenient but utilizes air above file cabinet level that might otherwise be wasted.[19] The *St. Petersburg Times* and *Evening Independent* installed Lektriever machines in their new library in 1969 and also provided a giant compressed air tube system between the news rooms and the library that can carry 9″ x 12″ photo files in addition to other materials. This library also has a reading room and two research rooms where those working on special projects can use microclip and microfilm equipment.[20] Looking to the future, a few libraries are probing the development of sophisticated information retrieval systems using computers for quick retrieval of information. Widespread usage of such systems may be some time off for most newspapers, but the *New York Times* installed such a system in the early 1970s.[21] Newspaper libraries already provide a valuable source of information for staff members and others. They may render even greater service in the future as they are improved and as even more emphasis is placed on background and interpretive reporting.

THE BIG STORIES

Newspapers must employ their best resources and techniques to report adequately the many challenging stories of the late twentieth century. Probably the most difficult domestic story of the era has been the rapidly developing human rights movement. This was primarily a struggle by and for black Americans in the 1960s; it has encompassed them, women of all races, and smaller groups in the 1970s. Although various individuals and groups had acted before then, the major push for black rights began in the early 1960s with the massive non-violent campaigns of Dr. Martin Luther King and others. Newspapers devoted hundreds of columns of space to covering the sit-ins, marches, demonstrations and riots that evolved in the 1960s as part of the struggle. At first much of the coverage centered on the violence that erupted; in time many newspapers began to report more in depth on needs in housing, jobs, education and other areas that helped create the problems. For a time, some newspapers eschewed coverage, particularly of events in their own areas; perhaps they hoped issues not reported or discussed would go away. But as it became obvious that these issues must be faced and resolved, more newspapers accepted the challenge to report fully and help find solutions.

Studies of newspaper performance in covering the rights movement in the early and middle 1960s often were critical. Newspapers were accused of being unfair and biased, of giving undue emphasis to violence and conflict, of not reporting in depth on the issues, of token employment themselves, of creating black leaders and other alleged shortcomings. The National Advisory Commission on Civil Disorders asserted, for example, that the communications industry had failed to communicate to the majority of its audience, which is white, a sense of the degradation, misery and hopelessness of living in the ghetto. The Commission said the media had failed to communicate to whites a feeling for the difficulties and frustrations of being a Negro in the United States.

Various study groups including the Commission urged that newspapers recruit more black employes, improve and expand their coverage of black communities, probe areas of discontent and offer solutions, distinguish between real and phony black leaders, and take other positive steps. In general the response has been good. In fact, some newspapers pointed out that they had been doing some of these things before any study groups asked them to. Many sought to employ more blacks and improve and expand their coverage of black Americans generally. More improvements involving employment, routine coverage of black communities and individuals, and in-depth coverage of issues are, of course, needed.[22]

The human rights struggle has continued to be a major topic of coverage in the 1970s as blacks, women and others have sought a redress of grievances. The information explosion, the space race, increasing urban problems, changing cultural patterns, especially among young persons, and other challenges of the 1960s also have commanded continuing attention in the 1970s. But the domestic news has been dominated by the Watergate scandal, the resignations of the vice-president and the president, the development of an energy crisis of undetermined proportions, and growing inflation. The Watergate story began in the late summer and early fall of 1972 when conspirators arrested for breaking into Democratic headquarters in the Watergate building in Washington were linked to members of the Committee for Reelection of the President. The Democrats sought to make a campaign issue out of the Watergate break-in, but the American people re-elected President Nixon by a substantial majority in November. Additional information on Watergate was reported during the trials of the alleged conspirators in January 1973, but it was not until the Senate Select Committee on Presidential Campaign Activities began its hearings in May of that year that persons close to the President himself were tied to the conspiracy. As the Senate committee's investigations proceeded, it became apparent that nearly a dozen interlocking scandals were involved. The President's use of executive privilege to withhold or delay providing information that might have resolved some of the questions raised was widely criticized.

Many Americans were incensed when the President ordered the firing of Archibald Cox, the government's special prosecutor of the Watergate affair. Cox had sought to subpoena several White House tapes which Senate committee witnesses indicated could help clear up the case. He was fired after refusing to accept a presidential compromise which proposed that summaries of the tapes, verified by Senator John C. Stennis, be provided. Attorney General Elliot L. Richardson, who was confirmed at the time Cox had been appointed, resigned rather than fire Cox on orders from the White House, and Deputy Attorney General William D. Ruckelshaus was also fired for refusing to do so. Solicitor General Robert H. Bork finally carried out the order to dismiss Cox.

The Cox dismissal following the insistence on executive privilege and the testimony of Senate committee witnesses that implicated persons high in the administration severely shook the people's confidence in their chief executive. Some persons defended the principle of executive privilege as essential to the national welfare, and the President did subsequently release a number of tapes on order of the U.S. District Court. But the cries for impeachment which reached a crescendo after the Cox dismissal in October 1973, continued into 1974. The fact that the White House denied the existence of two of the tapes being sought and the fact that one tape turned over had an 18-minute gap in it added to the confusion. Judge John J. Sirica upheld the President's claim to executive privilege on nearly all of two tapes and part of another which had been subpoenaed, but several other recordings were turned over to a Watergate grand jury for consideration.

The revelation of Spiro Agnew's personal problems and his subsequent resignation as vice-president also shook the people's confidence in the President who had twice selected him for that office. In October 1973, under an arrangement worked out with the attorney general, Agnew pleaded no contest to a single count of tax evasion, was fined $10,000 and placed on three years' probation. He immediately resigned. The vice-president's decision not to remain in office and fight the charges against him undoubtedly left some questions about him unanswered in the minds of some but probably saved the nation from an uncomfortable legal trial involving its second-ranked executive. Acting under the 25th amendment to the U.S. Constitution, President Nixon nominated Rep. Gerald Ford of Michigan, Republican minority leader in the House, to succeed Agnew as vice-president. After extensive hearings, the Senate approved Ford's nomination 92 to 3 on November 27; the House followed suit by a vote of 387 to 35 on December 6, and Ford was sworn in on that day.

President Nixon's Watergate problems continued to mount in 1974. Leon Jaworski, who was appointed special prosecutor to replace Cox in November 1973, pressed the investigation with vigor and sought additional tapes. In March a Watergate grand jury indicted seven Nixon aides or reelection officials for conspiring to obstruct justice. Subsequently, several Nixon aides pleaded guilty or were convicted of crimes. In late July the Supreme Court by an 8–0 vote rejected President Nixon's claims for executive privilege and ruled that he must turn over tapes subpoenaed by Jaworski. Several days later, after two months of hearings, the House Judiciary Committee voted 27–11 to recommend the impeachment of the President for obstruction of justice. Subsequently, two other articles of impeachment also were approved. On August 5 the President admitted that he had known of the involvement of White House officials and members of the Committee to Re-elect the President in the Watergate break-in six days after the event took place, and Republicans who had supported him in the Judiciary Committee hearings indicated that they would change their votes on the House floor. Faced with impeachment and the likelihood of conviction, Mr. Nixon resigned and Mr. Ford was sworn in as the nation's 38th president. It was uncertain at first whether further legal action would be pressed against Mr. Nixon; then on September 8 President Ford granted the former president full, free, and absolute pardon for all offenses against the United States which he had committed or may have committed or taken part in from January 20, 1969 through August 9, 1974.[23]

Aside from human rights and politics, the major domestic news maker in the early 1970s was the ecology. Food and fuel shortages in 1973 helped focus attention on the need to use the planet's human, land, water and other resources more intelligently. It was obvious to most that the people had been wasteful with their natural resources and that government had failed to provide adequate long-range planning and control. But remedies were not so obvious. Some possible answers to fuel shortages posed potential threats to the environment. The media were challenged to overcome the various special interests involved and help suggest solutions that would be in the public interest. The challenge was made more difficult by the fact that some companies which pollute also advertise.

Ecological problems are not limited by national boundaries, and efforts to solve them could produce some of the major international as well as domestic stories in the late 1970s and beyond. The energy crisis that struck the United States in 1973 was in part the result of the Mid-East war between Israel and the Arab states and the accompanying Arab restrictions on oil supplies. Other industrial nations such as Japan and those of Western Europe were hit even harder by the Arab action. A settlement to the Israeli-Arab difficulties that had existed for years seemed necessary to resolving many of the world's energy problems.

The new war in the Middle East, and its attendant oil problems, succeeded the war in Vietnam as the major international story for American newspapers. The American involvement in Southeast Asia had dominated the overseas headlines since the number of Americans there was accelerated in the middle 1960s. The war in Vietnam was always difficult to cover because the troops and the fighting were scattered over a large area. At one time in the late 1960s there were more than 500,000 Americans operating in a territory that covered more than 66,000 square miles. The number of accredited correspondents in Vietnam reached almost 500 by the latter part of 1969. The three major television networks had staffs of about 30 persons, the Associated Press had eight correspondents and six photographers, and United Press International had eight writers and four photographers. Many large U.S. newspapers, including the *New York Times,* the *New York Daily News,* the *Los Angeles Times,* the *Chicago Daily News* and the *Washington Post,* maintained smaller bureaus of their own. The press accused the military of delaying reports of unfavorable news, "foot dragging" in response to queries, and slowness in arranging sufficient transportation into battle areas. The military accused the press of sensationalizing the war, manufacturing some stories and exaggerating others. Military press officers also said too many queries were barbed with questions about marijuana usage among American troops, venereal disease rates, and tactical judgment errors by U.S. commanders.[24]

Peter Arnett, a Pulitzer Prize winning Associated Press reporter who spent eight years in Vietnam, told a Sigma Delta Chi journalism convention in late 1970 that an aggressive, cantankerous and unlovely press corps had enabled the world to see the war in Vietnam for what it was. He said the press corps sought to tell the American public what the war was costing in terms of human life and national effort and let it decide for itself. He suggested that if the public was continually confused over Vietnam it was not a failure of the press but of the government.[25]

Looking back, it is evident that the press had both successes and failures in its efforts to report the major domestic and international stories of the past decade. Hopefully, it can learn from its own mistakes and obtain sufficient public support from its successes to deal effectively with the challenges of the future. Newspapers seem especially well suited to providing the information about human rights, political functions, environmental questions, international affairs and other matters that people need to function effectively.

DEPARTMENTS AND SECTIONS—SPORTS

Because of the diversity and enormity of information to be gathered and processed, most newspapers divide their total news operation into several departments and their product into several sections. Organizational patterns and designations vary with the size and historical development of the newspaper. Most will have a department, perhaps called news department, to handle city, area, state, national and international news. This department may be headed by a news editor, who may be assisted by a city editor, state editor, wire editor or other editors as needed. Most of the major news and all of the news not assigned to particular departments is processed here. Most newspapers will have at least two other designated departments, one for sports and another for women's news. Some will also have separate departments to handle news of business, the arts and perhaps other special interests. News produced in these departments is usually grouped in special sections of the paper, such as the sports section or the women's section. Newspapers may also have special pages or sections on youth, education, religion or other topics that justify special treatment but may not provide enough information to warrant separate departments.

Sports news has been covered on a fairly regular basis by newspapers since the development of the Penny Press in the 1830s. The larger newspapers developed separate sports departments in the latter decades of the nineteenth century, and these departments were producing several columns of sports news daily by the 1890s. The larger papers also developed specialists to cover sports such as baseball, horse racing and prizefighting, which were attracting widespread attention.[26] Sports pages and subsequently sports sections were developed in the twentieth century, and the various sports were given prominence in keeping with their popularity. Newspapers often positioned their sports sections so they could be pulled out of the newspaper and read separately; some printed them on colored paper so they could be quickly spotted. Baseball, football and basketball were perhaps the three most widely covered sports in the early 1970s, but golf, tennis, ice hockey, soccer, auto racing, swimming, track and field, and other sports also attracted considerable coverage. In addition, increasing attention was given to hunting and fishing, bowling and other sports that draw far more participants than spectators. The rise of professional sports in many cities reduced the amount of space allocated to college and high school sports in the metropolitan newspapers there, but some of this coverage was picked up by suburban newspapers.

Many sports departments, especially at larger newspapers, have placed increasing emphasis on interpretive reporting in recent years. This is in part due to the rise of broadcasting, especially television, which now provides the scores and often play-by-play accounts of specific sporting events long before they can be covered by newspapers. Newspapers are now looking more to the *how* and *why* of events covered by the broadcast media and to interpretive stories about trends involving teams or sports. The rise of sports as a big business also has encouraged some newspapers to delve into the economics of sports and the effect that sports can have on local, state and even national economies.

Even in smaller communities newspapers have become aware of a need for more interpretation and analysis in their sports coverage. But many newspapers still carry straight news stories about events that the broadcast media do not have time to cover. Small newspapers can provide a community service and build reader interest by providing information, including scores, from church and recreation department leagues and information about various minor sports in the community.

Although improvements have been made on many newspapers in recent years, sports writing is still not as good as it should be. The number of clichés has been reduced, but jargon is still overused in many stories. Some reporters still express too much of an idolizing theme in writing about sports heroes, and some become too subjective in encouraging support for local teams. Critical commentary is sometimes limited because the reporters live so close to those about whom they are writing. It is difficult to socialize repeatedly with a team and then report its faults as well as its achievements in an objective manner.[27] Rotating assignments may help relieve this problem, but there are no easy solutions. Some newspapers such as the *Atlanta Journal* in its "Perspective" column, written by various members of the sports staff, have in recent years provided more critical analysis in features clearly labeled as such. Others should consider this approach. All sports sections should, of course, guard against replacing an overly laudatory approach toward their subjects with one that is overly critical.

Better reporting and analysis by sports reporters are needed because sports departments do have a considerable influence on sports and the millions of persons interested in them. The *New York Times, Los Angeles Times, Washington Post, Newsday* and a few others have been cited for their thoughtful reports.[28] Sports departments can help cities obtain professional sports franchises that can bring millions of dollars into the local economy. They can help determine whether coaches or other key officials are employed and retained.They can influence the ambitions of children and the recreation habits of adults and children. Despite the impact of television coverage, it appears that newspaper sports departments can continue to enjoy high readership and exert influence if they adjust to changing needs and observe the basic principles of good writing and reporting.

WOMEN'S PAGES

Most daily newspapers in the early 1970s had a women's department that each day produced one or more pages of news intended primarily but not solely for women readers. A study made for the Bureau of Advertising (now Newspaper Advertising Bureau) by Audits and Surveys, Inc. reported in 1973 that 90% of women readers and 80% of men readers look at the women's pages.[29] The origins of these pages can be traced at least to the 1830s when James Gordon Bennett and others enlivened their Penny Papers with news of Society with a capital "S." Newspapers and magazines both ran increasing amounts of information about fashions, food and other women's interests along with society news in the latter half of the century, and by the 1890s this pattern was taking hold. The rise of department store advertising directed mostly at women, who did much of the purchasing, stimulated the expansion of both news and features aimed at women around the turn of the century.[30] By the middle of the twentieth century some newspapers were devoting whole sections to women's news or society news, and the women's department had developed along with the sports department as primary emphases on many newspapers. Many of the women's departments have de-emphasized society news in the 1960s and 1970s and expanded their concepts of what women want in their sections of the newspaper. In some instances the women's section as such has been replaced by a family news or feature section; in many newspapers the women's section format has been retained but the content altered.

The reasons for changes in women's pages vary somewhat from newspaper to newspaper; but it appears that many of the changes are in response to criticisms by readers. Women's pages have been charged with printing too much trivial information, serving a too limited audience and providing a great deal of free advertising disguised as news and features. It was argued that the interests of career women and the interests of all women in public affairs were slighted, that high society got too much space and minorities were ignored, and that the interests of advertising set the format and tone for the pages.

One of the most noticeable changes on most large newspapers and many smaller ones has been the de-emphasis of so-called society news such as engagement and wedding announcements, parties, and club news. Many newspapers now restrict the amount of space allotted to these items, and some have begun to sell space for wedding and engagement notices much as they sell space for classified advertising. The *Washington Post,* for example, began a new bridal desk policy in 1972 under which free standard announcements of approximately two column inches are given to all who wish them and fees are charged for additional space and pictures. The paper reported that during the first five months of 1973 it ran 47,108 lines of free announcements and charged for 17,609 lines at the same rate as the lowest classified ads. The "Weddings and Engagements" page has been run on Wednesdays in the Style Section, successor to the women's section of the *Post*. Readers now know what to expect and when, and the paper is deriving revenue from the operation.[31] This type of policy should help newspapers serve more persons who want such information published, save space for other types of news, or both. Smaller newspapers may continue to allot a higher percentage of their space to society news, and few newspapers are likely to eliminate it entirely. Most persons enjoy reading pleasant things about themselves and their friends and many enjoy reading almost anything about famous persons.

While de-emphasizing society many women's sections have expanded their coverage of public affairs and increased their use of interpretive and investigative stories. Articles on abortion, alcoholism, consumer needs, crime, hunger and human rights, especially women's rights, have appeared in increasing numbers. Some women's pages have given considerable attention to the proposed Equal Rights Amendment and efforts to use existing laws against discrimination to obtain better jobs and higher pay. Many have tried to explain how various public issues affect women as individuals and as members of family units. The *New York Times*, for example, did not eliminate its coverage of brides, especially on Sunday, but the emphasis in its "Family, Foods, Fashions, Furnishings" section did change considerably after Charlotte Curtis became Family/Style editor in 1965. She seemed more interested in sociology than social chit-chat and pointed out that the overturning of the family could be as significant as the overturning of a president. Jean Taylor, women's editor of the *Los Angeles Times*, did not drop fashion and society news either but did seek to develop coverage that would reflect the contemporary California lifestyle in the newspaper's "View" section.[32]

Smaller newspapers also developed interesting new approaches. In 1971 the *Holyoke* (Massachusetts) *Transcript* began running a special page every two weeks called "Tomorrow's Woman" to supplement coverage in its daily women's page. It developed two regular columns, "Witch Watch" and "Dear Eve" to explore feminist ideas, and it ran irregular columns by professors at colleges in the area on topics such as women and education, religion, welfare, and the economy. The section also did investigative stories on such topics as the roles filled by women in the police department, policies of local firms regarding pregnancy leaves, involvement of women in the decision-making process at local churches, and women on welfare.[33]

In addition to de-emphasizing society coverage and expanding their interest in public affairs, many women's sections have improved their layouts in recent years; some have expanded their coverage of blacks and other minority groups, and some have begun to provide more perspective for their coverage of foods and fashions. But the need for more improvements in coverage of fashions and foods seemed great in the early 1970s. A seminar on "Women's Pages in the 70s" at the University of Kentucky in 1972 concluded on the note that promotion no longer has a place in women's pages and that changes are needed in the handling of food, fashions, home furnishings and club stories that too often have been publicity billed as news.[34] The Newspapers Food Editors and Writers Association, formed in 1973, and a number of newspapers sought ways to improve food pages and help consumers in the middle 1970s.

More changes may be in store for many women's pages in the future. Mrs. Colleen Dishon, editor and president of Features and News, Chicago, predicted in 1971 that the women's department of tomorrow will have an investigative reporter or team to check such things as whether a little girl who died in a fire at a party died because the permanent-press dress she had on was not flame-proof; a nutrition expert who cares more about getting hungry children fed than about recipes for chocolate cake; a writer who knows as much or more about the operation of day-care centers as she does about private schools; a home editor who can analyze the mayor's plans for low-income housing and what effect it might have on children; a black woman who can talk to her sisters where they are; a graphics expert who can lay out material so that readers will feel it as well as see it; young women, and men, who can report what they see without being overwhelmed by guidelines of the past; and above all a women's editor who is so secure in her professionalism that she is aiming for Pulitzer Prizes.[35]

Women's news editors have been warned, however, not to abandon conventional interests that remain important to their readers. Mrs. Dorothy Jurney, woman's editor of the *Detroit Free Press,* suggested in July 1972, that some of the sections that have replaced the traditional women's sections are not women's sections in any sense of the word. They are, she said, feature sections and they have lost a great deal in change. Mrs. Jurney indicated that women's pages should reflect the fact that women have a life-style that is different from that of men, that they are still generally responsible for family, food and interpersonal relations. She suggested that the women readers related most to stories benefiting them in some way.[36] Mrs. June Anderson Almquist, women's editor of the *Seattle Times,* said in 1973 that some women's sections, in their eagerness for change, have lost their identities. She said some have become at best feature sections, and in some cases, hodgepodge sections. Mrs. Almquist also cautioned women's editors against becoming so involved in writing about social issues and attention grabbers that their sections become nothing but sorrow and strife. She said that these social issues should be covered, but that women's pages should also cover fashion, food and homemaking.[37]

Mrs. Gloria Biggs, who developed the family news section of Gannett's *Today* in Cocoa, Florida, before being named editor and publisher of the group's *Melbourne* (Florida) *Times,* said she believes women's pages should have four elements. These she identified as information of immediate interest to women; appearance including fashion, beauty and home furnishings; people; and emotion, which she said was perhaps the least important. Mrs. Biggs said that modern women's pages should not only cover newsworthy events but also create their own news by delving into important issues. She cited as an example a series that Gannett News Service did in May 1970, on "Woman, the Polluter," in which it was explained how women could help minimize pollution problems.[38]

A study of six highly regarded women's sections reported in 1970 indicated that personality pieces, syndicated advice columns, and fashion news were among the most used features. By-lined commentary, entertainment, literature, food and women's liberation ranked next in order of use, according to the study made by Mrs. Flo Smith, a student at the University of Southwestern Louisiana. Mrs. Smith reported that a poll of 20 women's news editors revealed the following women's sections as leaders: *Miami Herald, Los Angeles Times, Atlanta Constitution, Washington Post, Arizona Republic* and *New York Times.*[39]

Newspapers must, of course, conduct surveys periodically to determine if what they are running is what their readers want to read. A study conducted by a graduate student at the University of Wisconsin in 1967 indicates that editors may need to make these reassessments often. Joan McGee compared the reading interests of Wisconsin homemakers with the editors' judgments of their interests. The editors correctly estimated interests in 13 of 25 topics and either overestimated or underestimated interests in the others. They overestimated interest in outdoor cooking, early marriages, clothes-making, home decorating and community recreation and underestimated interest in music, civil defense, family nutrition, home food production, home landscaping, older women's clothing and teenage charge accounts.[40] Some generalizations probably can be made about what readers want on the women's pages as well as in other sections of the newspapers, but audiences vary widely and newspapers need to make their own studies.

Women's pages that adjust to the needs and interests of their readers probably can have a great deal of influence on their communities. In their handling of clothing and fashion stories, they can influence what people wear and perhaps what they have to pay for it. In their handling of issues they can encourage positive attitudes and develop support for useful legislation. They can foster progress in areas such as integration by the manner in which they cover news of the black community. In their reporting and commentary, they can encourage improvements in the life-style of women, whether they choose to be homemakers, pursue careers, or both.

Women's news coverage may take diverse formats in the future. Some newspapers may prefer to incorporate their women's pages into larger sections with reviews, feature stories and other items; some may seek to develop more of a family page image; some may hold to the more traditional format. But the need for some type of women's coverage appears to be a continuing one. The principal conclusion noted in a report on the "Women's Pages in the 70s" seminar mentioned earlier was that women's pages are needed, are here to stay and for the most part are getting better.[41] The most successful sections in the future may well be those that find a mix which their particular readers like between the new emphasis on issues and the improved coverage of traditional topics such as foods, fashions and homemaking.

BUSINESS NEWS

United States newspapers were providing the public with information about business long before Calvin Coolidge, the nation's thirtieth president, said that the business of America is business. Many of the republic's early newspapers not devoted primarily to partisan politics were devoted to mercantile matters; a number of these were among the circulation leaders of the early nineteenth century. Special interest newspapers have continued to report on the business world, and the general interest newspapers, which developed in the middle of the nineteenth century, also have devoted space to the subject.

Unfortunately, the amount of space devoted by most newspapers to business reporting seldom has been adequate, and the quality of the coverage too often has been poor. Despite its pervading influence on American life, business gets far less coverage on most newspapers than does politics, sports or women's news. Moreover, the space provided often is devoted to "mere surfaces and facades, an unstructured flow of executive promotion announcements, earnings reports, speeches and press conferences." [42] The *Wall Street Journal*, which is predominantly a business newspaper, and the *New York Times* evidently provide the best coverage, and the quality of the *Times'* effort has been challenged. Freelance writer Chris Welles asked readers of *Columbia Journalism Review* to compare, on an average day, "the overwhelming preponderance of stories on the financial pages of the *New York Times* that merely regurgitate handouts and spot news events against the investigative effort and thoughtful analysis in other parts of the paper." Welles said, too, that the financial section of the *Times* is probably better than that of any other newspaper of general circulation in the country; beyond the *Times*, he said is a "bleak wasteland." [43]

Other writers are more charitable in their assessments, but most are quick to point out deficiencies in business coverage and reporting on most newspapers. Jerome K. Full, director-information services, Eastern Airlines, noted, for example, that "most media do the requisite job in covering the security markets, the swings in our economy. Newspapers record the promotions, corporate mergers, the plant openings, the commercial births and deaths. But the news media do not, generally, concern themselves with the public substance of a corporation. They will not offend the most craven or vicious enterprise nor encourage, for fear of committing the heresy of commercialism, the most socially responsive." Full said that excellent stories on business affairs appear in the *Wall Street Journal, Fortune, Business Week*, the *New York Times*, the wire services and other publications. What is excellent, he said, "are the analyses, the surveys, the interpretations, the handling of financial data. What is not excellent is that which is missing; the hard-nosed assessment of individual company performances in relation to customers, employees and the public.'' [44]

The deficiencies of business coverage probably can be attributed to several factors, including the nature of the newspaper industry itself. Most newspapers in a free enterprise system are dependent on advertising for existence. This fact leads many publishers to assume that what is good for their advertisers must also be good for them. Some are eager to advocate land use planning, pollution controls or other community programs only if they do not interfere with the plans or operations of an important advertiser. Carrying this thinking a step further, some publishers may assume that anything which appears good for business at the time is good for them and the community at large. Too often the newspapers, which effectively serve as watchdogs on government, leave to others the documentation or refutation of charges concerning price fixing, antitrust violations, questionable sales practices including misleading advertising and other unethical if not illegal practices concerning business. Many newspapers not only overlook the sins of business, they also devote many of their precious column inches of news space to advertising disguised as news. Real estate and travel pages have been especially suspect in this regard.

Another major cause of deficient business coverage is public indifference. Persons who own stocks may check daily to see how their holdings have done, and most have some interest in reports about inflation and deflation as they may affect the price of food, clothing or housing. But many readers do not find the business pages stimulating. Some newspapers such as the *Philadelphia Inquirer* are trying to open up their business pages to a more general audience. William Lyon, the *Inquirer*'s business editor, reported in early 1973 that his paper in addition to its regular coverage of stock market tables, promotions and earnings has incorporated into the business page consumer affairs, retailing and wholesaling, home furnishings, real estate, transportation, and regular personality features. Lyon said he sees a move toward larger business news holes and broader-based information as a national trend, and innovations similar to those at the *Inquirer* were reported at the *Detroit Free Press, Miami Herald* and Long Island's *Newsday*. [45] More investigative reporting, especially in areas of consumer interest, probably would spark reader interest, but such investigations can be difficult. For one thing, fewer persons in the business community seem as willing to leak information as those in government; many of the investigative stories relating to business also have related to government where leaks are more common. Investigative reporting is also hampered by the pro-advertiser attitudes of publishers noted above. Even good newspapers reportedly have killed stories that might have offended advertisers. [46] Investigative reporting of business matters remains scarce on most newspapers; consumer affairs coverage has increased, but the potential for development offered by such reporting has only been scratched.

Business coverage may also be hampered to some extent by a shortage of well-informed, aggressive reporters in the field. Some good persons may avoid the business jobs because of the restrictions on their activities suggested above. Others may find more remunerative work on specialized publications or in public relations work for business firms. On the other hand, some may plod along in the work because of the largesse offered by the firms whose activities they cover. Business reporters and their newspapers must guard against possible conflicts of interest. Stanley Sporkin, deputy director of enforcement of the Security and Exchange Commission, urged in 1972 that each daily newspaper should have specific guidelines to help prevent any conflict of interest in reporting news of business. A survey in 1967 indicated that few newspapers had such guidelines; a followup survey several years later indicated that more had guidelines but most did not believe a problem existed. In May 1974 the Society of American Business Writers adopted a seven-point code of ethics that includes an admonition to avoid any practice which might compromise or appear to compromise objectivity or fairness. The writer is not to let any personal investments influence what he writes.[47] Some business writers evidently lack the business understanding themselves to provide any sort of perspective for their readers; some excellent reporters are handling business news, but more are needed.

Correcting the deficiencies in business coverage will not be easy. Newspapers must take the initiative by reporting in-depth on how business functions; they must describe the bad as well as the good in business operations and they must make it interesting. Readers must demand more investigative reporting of business activities; they must insist that newspapers help safeguard the rights of consumers. They must be willing to read and react. If the public becomes sufficiently aroused, the newspapers need not fear retaliation by advertisers. Newspapers, businessmen and citizens generally can benefit from better financial pages.

The Arts

The coverage of the arts by United States newspapers remained uneven in the early 1970s. A few papers such as the *New York Times* provided extensive information and commentary on both popular and fine arts. Some newspapers largely ignored the subject; others were content to fill the space devoted to it with publicity releases and commentary of questionable quality. Only a few hundred newspapers reported having weekly book columns or pages during the 1960s, and other fine arts probably got much less attention. Television and motion pictures got attention because newspaper readers wanted to know about new shows and individual performers, but the quality of coverage was not uniformly high. A survey of arts page editors reported in 1972 indicated that their newspapers devoted considerably more attention to athletics than to the arts.[48]

Various reasons have been offered to explain why newspapers have tended to neglect the arts. Two stand out. First, many editors see the publication of reviews and other information about the arts as free advertising. They argue that publishers and others promoting the arts should buy space to advertise their products. Some editors may provide more space to report motion picture news than report news about books and other arts because the movie houses advertise. Second, some editors contend that extensive coverage of the arts is not justified by reader interest. Space in the newspaper is often severely limited, and it must be used to provide the information that readers want and need.

Books among the fine arts, and television and motion pictures among the popular arts, probably get the most attention because they have the highest reader interest. Some newspapers also cover music, drama, painting and other fine arts; some also give attention to radio, recordings and photography among the popular arts. Many newspapers have an arts page or pages on the weekends; a few may have arts sections. Daily coverage in most instances is limited to reports on rapidly changing mediums such as television and motion pictures.

Coverage of the arts may take one of several forms. Some newspapers concentrate on reporting about the arts. They provide information about the book or other topic but eschew critical analysis. Others seek to appraise or analyze the work in terms of accepted standards, personal impressions or both. Most of the top critics have worked in New York and a few other eastern cities where the theater, music and other arts have themselves been centered. But the development of theaters, orchestras and other arts in other cities has led to the development of more extensive arts coverage in those cities. Most of the arts reporters and critics probably have exerted a positive influence by informing people about new books, dramas or other productions. A few, such as the New York drama critics, have been able to exert a negative influence on plays which they thought to be less than adequate.

Many criticisms have been made of United States newspapers concerning their coverage and criticism of the arts. First, it is argued that many newspapers do not provide enough coverage or criticism. They may run a few book reviews once a week and report on new movies and television shows but do not do much else. Second, it is argued that the critics or arts reporters are little more than promoters. They only rehash information on book jackets or rewrite handouts from motion picture companies and networks. Third, it is argued that the reporters and critics are not qualitifed to do their job. They have too little knowledge of literature, theater and other topics being covered.

While such criticisms would be unjust if directed at the *New York Times,* the *National Observer* and some other newspapers, one or more of them may well apply to many United States newspapers. Most newspapers need to spend considerably more time developing their arts coverage. It may not be financially feasible for most newspapers to employ critics to discuss each of the arts, although those in metropolitan areas and university communities may be able to get competent commentary for a reasonable price. But it would seem feasible for most to provide more adequate reporting of new books and other developments. Reporters, periodic contributors such as college professors or other specialists, wire services and syndicates can provide a variety of news stories, features, commentary and illustrations for arts pages or sections.

Newspapers must also work with those in the arts and with the schools in developing a greater appreciation of all the arts. Newspapers can work with teachers in developing regular arts features that can be used in the classrooms as curriculum supplements. Newspapers should not wait for reader interest in the arts to develop before they provide more adequate coverage. They should help develop the interest as a means of expanding readership and public service.

RELIGION

Religious beliefs always have been important in the lives of many Americans, and news of religion has been reported in American newspapers since the Colonial period. One of the major stories of that era dealt with the missionary efforts of the Reverend George Whitefield, who visited America on seven occasions during a period of 30 years. Whitefield's sermons from Maine to Georgia "aroused the fires of controversy, to which the newspapers often contributed fuel." [49] A number of religious newspapers were developed in the early nineteenth century which reported denominational matters and religious miscellany as well as some secular news. By the time of the Civil War most denominations had their own papers, and some of the major dailies were devoting attention to the subject. The religious papers showed a marked tendency after the war to desert the general news field and become denominational reporters and journals of opinion; the general newspapers continued to show interest in religion.

Newspaper coverage of religion has fluctuated in the twentieth century with reader interest and concern; it also has varied in quality from newspaper to newspaper. Many newspapers have improved their coverage in the past decade or so. Some are doing in-depth reports on controversies within the church and efforts of the churches to help human beings meet their daily problems as well as reporting on ground-breaking ceremonies and listing sermon topics in the Saturday edition. It does not appear, however, that the coverage of religion in most newspapers is commensurate with the people's interest in religion. George Cornell, Associated Press religion writer, reported in 1973 that on a single Sunday 84 million persons attended church, far more than attended a weekend's professional sporting events. He noted that people are spending $8 billion a year in religious enterprises, far more than the amount collected at professional sporting events. Yet the amount of space devoted to news of religion is only a fraction of that assigned to sports. Cornell said that surveys indicate news of religion is near the top in news interest and commands space in people's concerns whether they attend church or not.[51]

Louis Cassels, religion editor of United Press International, suggested several broad categories of religious news that need attention. Cassels said that it is the duty of community newspapers to report the controversies that have developed in churches over doctrinal questions, church involvement in social and political issues, and other matters as fairly, dispassionately and fearlessly as it presumably does other controversies. He said the institutional activities such as revivals, pastoral changes, bake sales and bazaars should be reported because they involve a good many persons in the community. Most significantly, perhaps, he said the newspapers should report on man's never-ending quest for a confident faith to live by. People want to know if God exists, if the Resurrection actually happened, if there is life after death. Because they seek to provide answers to these and other basic questions, religions will always be important to people and, therefore, to newspapers.[52]

Better reporting of religion can help the churches, the newspapers that provide it and the people who read the newspapers. Competent reporters can be obtained in two ways. Trained writers with a special interest in religion can be encouraged to develop their knowledge through self-study, seminars and perhaps even seminary courses. Or persons with a theological training background can be taught to write. The religion beat can be expected to draw talented persons if the coverage is expanded along the lines suggested by Cassels. The work of staff reporters can, of course, be supplemented by materials from the wire services, syndicates and special contributors. The potential for improved coverage of religion has only been scratched by improvements in recent years. This is an area that could be greatly developed to the benefit of all concerned.

OTHER SPECIAL INTERESTS

Special attention is given by many newspapers to other special interests such as youth and education, and virtually all newspapers provide news coverage as well as advertising space for obituaries. Newspapers must seek to win youth to their readership for several reasons. Today's children are strongly oriented toward television and radio; newspapers must help them discover the value in reading their product. Advertisers are especially interested in the 18–34 age market, largest among the age classifications, and the teen market; newspapers must reach these youths to get their share of this advertising. Good government depends on the actions of a well-informed citizenry; only newspapers can provide the information these young persons need to exercise citizenship responsibilities fully.

Studies indicate that many teenagers and young persons do read newspapers, particularly if the newspapers have information directed at them. But studies also indicate that many young persons have unfavorable attitudes toward newspapers. Some evidently believe that newspapers are biased and slanted and represent an establishment they do not trust. Others may simply not identify with them as readily as they do with television and radio.

Many newspapers are seeking to reach the youth through surveys to determine their interests and needs, through special features and stories, through special pages and sections, through special programs such as the Newspaper-in-the-Classroom Program and other efforts. Reader involvement may be a key factor in reaching young persons. Teenage sections should include articles, reviews and other contributions by young readers; young persons should help with the planning if not the actual development of the sections. Sections aimed at younger children should have special participation features such as games and pictures and maps that can be colored or completed. Youths should be encouraged to visit the newspaper and see how it functions and meet staff members; they and other readers would like to know more about how stories and pictures are obtained and how newspapers reach decisions on editorial subjects. Spot announcements on radio and television and free one-week or one-month subscriptions might be used to attract young readers to the features being made available. Many newspapers are taking specific steps to reach young readers in an effort to serve them and to help assure that newspapers will have large audiences in the future.

One of the most successful efforts in recent years to reach preteen children has been the MINI PAGE developed by Betty Debnam in Raleigh, North Carolina. Miss Debnam is a writer, artist and former first-grade teacher who comes from a family of newspaper publishers. Her weekly page provides news, features, art work and other information especially for children. It helps to make them more aware of the world around them and more aware of newspapers; moreover, it's fun. The MINI PAGE, syndicated by MSC Features, was appearing in approximately 175 newspapers with a combined circulation of almost 10 million persons in late 1973.[53] Newspapers can, of course, use features by staff members and area children to complement what is prepared by the syndicate feature or develop their own sections.

More newspapers also need to give more attention to education at all levels. Few activities touch more readers today than education. Millions either are enrolled in schools or other educational programs or have children who are. Adult education has become increasingly important in a rapidly changing world; new skills must be acquired for continued employment and new insights must be obtained to cope with change and function effectively in society. Most persons are involved in some type of educational experience, informally if not formally; most also are helping to pay through their taxes for public education programs. Newspapers need to help provide educational opportunities, encourage interest in and concern for education, and report on developments in education, especially those related to public school programs.

Although newspapers have provided educational features and reported on

educational activities for many years, it probably was not until the late 1940s
and early 1950s that education reporting received major emphasis. Many newspapers increased their coverage as a result of the space race, the information
explosion, the integration of the public schools and other developments. A
major study reported in *Journalism Quarterly* in 1967 suggested, however, that
the proportion of educational assignments had not increased in relation to all
editorial assignments. The number of educational assignments had more than
doubled between 1950 and 1963, but so had the space devoted to listing all editorial assignments. This study concluded that the "celebrated 'Boom on the
School Beat' appears to have been limited to metropolitan dailies, and to have
been more a sign of recognition than a rise in the proportion of all special editorial employes holding school news assignments on American daily papers." [54]

More education writers and better salaries for education writers were cited
as top priority needs for improved media coverage of education in a national
survey of education writers in the early 1970s. Respondents included persons
who write for the media and persons who process education news for schools,
colleges and educational agencies. This study, which asked respondents to rank
a list of proposed improvements or list their own, also reported a need for seminars to help education writers, college courses to prepare specialists in education reporting, research on problems of education reporting, and college
courses to educate school administrators in communications. Responses to this
survey also indicate that a communications gap may exist between education
writers and educators. Respondents indicated that while their primary news
concerns are interest to readers and accuracy, they believe educators are primarily concerned about the usefulness of the material published to the source. [55]

If educators are concerned about getting more "good news" of education
into the media as education writers believe, the concern is probably under-
standable. The media, including newspapers, have given much attention in
recent years to campus protests and demonstrations, the furor over busing to
achieve integration, and disciplinary problems in schools but only limited attention to special education programs, improvements in teaching and curriculums,
and other positive developments. What is needed is more interpretive, in-depth
reporting of all aspects of the educational system. In view of the public interest
in education and the public expense for education, increased newspaper space
for education reporting and the money required to develop it properly should be
more than justified.

Many newspapers could also improve their coverage and handling of obituaries. Coverage may be ineffective at times because the newspapers lack
space to cover all deaths or cover them adequately, lack writers who have the
proper attitude and ability for the job, or fail to realize the importance of such
coverage. Too often editors regard obituaries as necessary but comparatively
unimportant assignments and give them to young reporters who regard them
more as an ordeal than an opportunity for expression. At other times editors ask

their obituary writers for eulogies that more appropriately might be recast as editorials. More newspapers should take the approach of the *New York Times* which does considerable advance preparation for the obituaries of prominent persons and devotes extensive space and appropriate prominence to the deceased. Alden Whitman was assigned the task of obituary editor of the *Times* in the middle 1960s. His job has been to interview prominent persons and prepare biographical essays on them for use with appropriate leads at the time of death.[56] Such interviews can provide a feeling and perhaps information also that would not be available in the usual biographical sources and histories. Most newspapers may be justified in relying on the wire services for obituaries of prominent world figures, but all should develop their own biographical essays on local, state and perhaps some national personalities.

Depending on their resources and their community's interests, newspapers may also provide special stories, pages or sections on agriculture, tourism, news of servicemen or nearby military bases, and other topics. Anniversaries, holidays, or events and important issues such as racial relations and environment may also be the subject of expanded coverage.

THE COMICS

The comics section is one of the most popular features in most United States newspapers today, perhaps because people like humor and the primary purpose of the comics is to entertain. Comic strips at times may refer to news events or personalities, and they often express opinions; but they usually employ humor and satire to make their observations. Surveys confirm their popularity. On the basis of readership of the average page in a section, the comics rank higher than the main news section for men and women, higher among women than the women's section and equal to the sports section among men readers.[57] Adults, teenagers and children all read them. Metro Sunday Newspapers reported in 1971 that 60% of the Sunday comics readers are adults 18 years old and over, 15% are teenagers (12–17), and 25% are in the 2–11 age group. The comics had an estimated 140 million readers in 1974.[58]

Such a diverse group obviously has varied motivations for reading and achieves varying satisfactions. Some may be seeking vicarious adventure and excitement; some may be seeking a way of escape from personal problems; others may be motivated by a sense of nostalgia. Many are simply looking for a laugh. A motivation study conducted by Social Research, Inc. for Metro Comics suggested a variety of special functions which are performed by the comics, including the following: Comics are a widespread social requirement; they can instruct; they make physical realities familiar; they give moral instruction; they teach solutions to individual problems; they help people learn larger social environments, and they mirror social reality.[59]

Comics may, of course, be used as propaganda vehicles for the ideas of their creators, but on the whole they probably serve to bring people together. As Arthur Berger suggests in his discussion of "Comics and Culture," the comics "are a distinctively American idiom and are one of the few things that we all have in common, one of the few things in our society which cut across class barriers (for the most part), regional differences, ethnic distinctions— whatever you will—to give us a communality of experience and of reference points." [60]

Some form of the comics probably can be traced to ancient times, but the traditional newspaper comics got started in the middle 1890s. Richard F. Outcault's "Hogan's Alley" was one of the most successful. It depicted life in the tenements, and included a character called the Yellow Kid. William Randolph Hearst provided an eight-page color comics section in his *New York Journal* in 1896; Sidney Smith pioneered the continuing story idea in "Andy Gump" in 1917; and United Features helped push the action story with its presentation of "Tarzan" in 1929.[61] The number of syndicated comics reached a peak of some 500 during pre-television days; 204 cartoons and panels and 225 strips were syndicated in 1974. Most of the casualties have been adventure serials such as "Terry and the Pirates" and "Smiling Jack," [62] which were discontinued in 1973 after long and successful careers. The discontinued comics will, of course, live on in the minds of comics readers. Information about them and other favorites can be found in the Museum of Cartoon Art, opened in 1974 at Greenwich, Conn.

The most successful comics today appear to be the self-contained, gag-a-day strips such as "Peanuts," "Blondie" and "Beetle Bailey." Charles Schulz uses an assortment of children, a remarkable dog named Snoopy and a bird in "Peanuts" to reflect on life and those who live it; most can see themselves in there somewhere. Chic Young has dealt amusingly with the middle class American family in "Blondie," and Mort Walker has poked fun at the military in "Beetle Bailey." A recent edition to the gag-a-day genre is Garry Trudeau's "Doonesbury," started in the *Yale Daily News* in 1969 and subsequently picked up by many papers. "Doonesbury" has ridiculed every point on the political spectrum, but gently. Some papers refused to print some strips, however, because of the satires on President Nixon.[63] Walt Kelly in "Pogo" and Al Capp in "Lil Abner" have successfully employed political satire over the years.

Optimism about the current state of the comics was suggested in a survey of syndicates, cartoonists and editors reported by Robert Lubeck, *Detroit News,* and chairman of Newspaper Comics Council, in 1972. Lubeck reported that 69% believed the quality of comics in the past few years had improved, 26% believed there had been no change, and 5% thought quality had deteriorated. Respondents indicated they thought "Andy Capp" (29%), "The Wizard of Id" (26%), and "Doonesbury" (21%) were the best new comics introduced in the previous ten years.[64]

One of the keys to the continued success of many comics may be their continued relevance. They demonstrate relevance by using up-to-date material, by being honest, and by showing an understanding of people and their basic character traits. Many cartoonists try to mirror life, although the life they reflect may in many instances be middle class life in the suburbs. The racial integration of the comics has been slow, in part perhaps because of reader acceptance and in part because the white cartoonists felt reluctant to create characters whose feelings they could not hope to understand fully. Some major strips such as "Peanuts" and "Beetle Bailey" now have black characters; a few such as "Quincy," "Wee Pals," and "Friday Foster" feature blacks. There were perhaps a tenth as many taboos in comics in the early 1970s as there were ten years before, but artists still had to be wary of the way they handled racial relations, dress (or lack of it), religion, divorce, death and other subjects.[65]

While it is difficult to predict specifically what may happen to comics in the future, it appears likely that the continued story will continue to give way to the gag-a-strip approach. Satire should remain as a strong element in many strips. Cartoonists may be given more freedom to comment in their drawings. Newsprint shortages could curb the number and size of comics.

SUNDAY MAGAZINES

Many of the nation's leading newspapers distribute independently produced magazine supplements, usually in tabloid format, with their Sunday editions. Several hundred distribute one of the two major national supplements, *Parade* and *Family Weekly;* many others, including some with comparatively small circulations, produce and distribute their own supplements. The Sunday magazine idea was developed in the latter third of the nineteenth century and expanded on a national level after the development of national advertising around the turn of the century. At least four of the nationally distributed magazines have achieved prominence. These include *American Weekly,* which grew out of the *Sunday American Magazine* started by William Randolph Hearst in the *New York Journal* in the 1890s; *This Week,* started by United Newspapers Magazine Corp. in 1935; *Parade,* started by Marshall Field III in 1941; and *Family Weekly,* started in 1953 and acquired by Downe Communications Inc. in 1966. The *New York Times Magazine,* developed by Adolph Ochs after he acquired the *Times* in 1896, has a national emphasis and is perhaps the best known of the locally edited magazines.

The rising impact of television on national advertising, the decline in newspaper competition, and other factors probably contributed to the demise of *American Weekly* and *This Week* in the 1960s. *American Weekly,* which had been an exclusive in Hearst newspapers until the 1930s, was withdrawn from newspapers outside the Hearst organization in 1962 and dropped entirely in 1963. *This Week,* which reached a circulation high of 14.6 million but sold only 538 pages of advertising in 1963 was dropped in 1969.[66] Of the big four,

Parade and *Family Weekly* not only survived but reported strong advertising sales in the early 1970s.

An optimistic report on Sunday supplements was issued in August 1973, by N. W. Ayer & Son, Inc. This report indicated that supplements generally had regained some ground lost to television and for all practical purposes were back on their feet. It noted that the total ad pages reported for the major supplement field had increased 5% for the period 1968–1972. Among the major supplements listed in the report were *Family Weekly,* with a circulation of more than 9 million; *Parade* with more than 17 million; the Sunday Group, with a combined circulation of more than 23 million; and *Tuesday* and *Tuesday At Home,* each with a circulation of more than 2 million. The Sunday Group is considered as a syndicated supplement but is actually a hybrid in that it sells national advertising in independent supplements on a group basis. The two major classifications of supplements are (1) syndicated supplements, which are sold to newspapers that want to carry them and sold to advertisers in groups on either a regional or national basis and (2) independent supplements, which are owned and published by the papers in which they appear and are available on an individual market basis. The *New York Times Magazine* with a circulation of more than 1.5 million and the *Los Angeles Times Home Magazine* with a circulation of almost 1.2 million are among the major independent supplements not included in the Sunday network. Of the 590 Sunday newspapers in the United States in 1972, approximately 375 carried one of the syndicated supplements and approximately 110 had independent supplements.[67]

Parade was founded in July 1941, by Marshall Field III as *Parade—The Weekly Picture Newspaper.* It did not carry paid advertising but did get some revenue from its newsstand price of 5 cents. Silliman Evans, owner of the *Nashville Tennessean,* saw the potential of distributing *Parade* with his Sunday newspaper; and other newspapers, including the *Washington Post,* soon followed. Field included the magazine as a worthwhile addition when he started the *Chicago Sun* later in 1941. *Parade* was not economically successful until after advertising was added in the early 1950s and other developments completed, but it made a newsy adjunct for the newspapers that carried it. Under the direction of Arthur H. "Red" Motley and Jess Gorkin, who joined the magazine in the middle 1940s, it moved steadily ahead in spite of television and other challenges. Marshall Field III died in 1956, and Marshall Field IV sold *Parade* for approximately $10 million to John Hay Whitney in 1958 to help finance the purchase of the *Chicago Daily News.* But Motley and Gorkin remained and continued their emphasis on news. By the early 1970s the magazine supplement was being distributed in approximately 100 newspapers with a combined circulation of more than 17 million homes. Motley was chairman of the board and Gorkin had completed 25 years as editor.[68]

Aggressive, innovative leadership probably has been the key to *Parade's* success. The magazine tries to stay on top of the news and provide its papers with stories they cannot get themselves. Lloyd Shearer, west coast editor, has been responsible for two of the magazine's most popular features, "Personality Parade" and "Intelligence Report," and for various special features. "Personality Parade" provides readers an opportunity to ask questions of famous personalities; it is presented in a question and answer format. "Intelligence Report" is a synopsis of interesting facts about almost anything. Jack Anderson, the syndicated columnist, has provided another important feature for the magazine as its Washington bureau chief. Most of the articles and features are tightly written; at times the presentations may be somewhat sensational. Gorkin contends, however, that *Parade* has changed the Sunday magazine field from an entertainment device and filler to a vehicle for serious and meaningful news. He and his staff are proud of the roles they played in encouraging the installation of the hotline telephone between the United States and Russia and encouraging the joint space effort between these two nations.[69]

Family Weekly, which had some economic problems in the early 1960s after a successful start, has been doing well since its acquisition by Downe Communications, Inc. in 1966. By early 1974 the supplement was being distributed by more than 300 newspapers which had a combined circulation of 10.5 million. Morton Frank, who became publisher after Downe acquired the magazine, has guided its growth. *Family Weekly* has in recent years appealed to broad family interests in contrast to *Parade's* emphasis on politics and government.[70] It has a question-answer feature, "Ask Them Yourself," which gives readers a chance to pose questions for well-known persons, and it deals with news topics. But it also has features such as "Family Weekly Cookbook" and the "Sewing Corner." The supplement also includes a "People Quiz," which provides questions and answers about some person-related topic such as whether a person is influenced by his fears. *Family Weekly*'s economic situation was good enough in the late 1960s and early 1970s to share its profits with subscribing newspapers on a pro-rata circulation basis spelled out in contracts with the newspapers.[71]

An important addition to the natonal supplement field in the middle 1960s was *Tuesday,* published by Tuesday Publications, Inc. in Chicago. W. Leonard Evans Jr. was publisher and editor of the supplement, which was edited by blacks and circulated in conventional newspapers. By the early 1970s the supplement had a circulation of 2.4 million; it was estimated that about 20% of the readers were white.[72] Besides features and news, the supplement included departments for teenagers, women and shoppers generally.

The purpose of the independent magazines varies somewhat with their circulation, location and other factors; but a survey reported in 1972 indicates that many of them publish personality profiles, historical articles, arts and entertainment features, and news events and analysis.[73] The *Journal-Constitution Magazine* in Atlanta, for example, has run numerous profiles of famous persons, especially Georgians, and many stories on local and state history. In addition it has run in-depth articles on such issues as drugs and prisons, and human interest features on almost anything from magic to snake roundups. The magazine did a particularly interesting series built on the rivers of the state.

Processing the News

Millions of words of copy may flow into a large daily newspaper on a given day from staff members, correspondents, wire services, syndicates and others. Several hundred pictures may be readily available from similar sources. Yet depending on the amount of advertising sold, newsprint supplies and other factors, the newspaper can use only a fraction of these stories and pictures. Many difficult decisions must be made about what news stories, features and pictures to use and how to display them. Should a particular story go on page one, page ten, or not be used at all? How much of the story should be used? What size headline should it have? What should the headline say? Should pictures or other art work be used with the story? Can several stories logically be grouped together? Similar decisions must be made about pictures. Should a particular picture be used? If so, where? How large should it be? If it is available in color, is the extra cost of reproducing it in color justified by the value of the picture?

The selection, processing and display of information are as important to the production of a good newspaper as the coverage and writing of the news. Information must be presented in a fair and balanced manner; it must be carefully edited to eliminate errors and foster understanding, and it must be presented in a format that encourages people to read. The titles of persons responsible for these functions vary from paper to paper, depending on the size of the operation and other factors. On a metropolitan newspaper, the selection responsibilities might be divided among an assistant managing editor, who would be responsible for page one and the jump page, where stories from page one are continued; a news editor who would be responsible for inside news pages; and sports, women's and other departmental editors, who would be responsible for selecting materials used in their departments. The key editors likely would be assisted by a wire editor, city editor, picture editor and perhaps others. A managing editor, who would be responsible for all news operations except the editorial pages, would provide supervision and guidance where needed. The functions would be the same on smaller papers where the sports or women's staff may consist of only two or three persons. On many newspapers the copy is edited and headlines are prepared by specialists variously known as copy readers and copy editors. These specialists check for errors in facts, grammar and spelling, divergence from the newspaper's style, libel, poor taste, important omissions and possible imbalance or bias in reporting; they trim stories when necessary to improve them or to meet space requirements; and they write headlines, hopefully accurate ones that will captivate readers and demand attention for their stories. Copy editors cannot be expected to transform poorly written copy into fine prose; some stories need to be rewritten. But often they can make poorly written stories acceptable or provide the final polish that makes a well-written story an excellent one.

The copy editor's success likely will depend on his ability to see the stories he edits from the vantage points of both the reporters who write them and the readers. He must understand what good reporting is and what the reporter is trying to do; yet he must also be able to view the work as might a reader who is unfamiliar with the subject. A broad education, good memory, great inquisitiveness, lively imagination, some cynicism and skepticism, and a great ability to think clearly and make sound judgments all are important to the job.

Some reporters look down on the copy editor's work as too restrictive and unexciting. Neither the motion picture industry nor television has made films about the glamorous copy editor. But it is a challenging and rewarding task that is essential to producing a good newspaper. Copy editors today are usually paid well, and their experience on the desk often gives them a substantial edge over reporters in obtaining executive positions on the newspaper.

Many newspapers have sought to raise the pay and prestige of copy editors in the 1970s to offset the critical shortage of them in the late 1960s. This shortage, which affected both large and small newspapers, evidently had various causes. An expanding industry needed more good copy editors than were available or could be obtained under traditional on-the-job training procedures. Wire service technology which provided tapes to activate type-setting machines discouraged creative editing by many newspapers and reduced the prestige of the copy editor's job. Pay in many instances did not keep pace with ultimate responsibilities. The reporter's life was made increasingly attractive with the development of new specializations in science, education and other areas and with greater emphasis being placed on interpretive and investigative reporting.

Aside from higher pay, steps taken to meet the shortage have included the employment of more women on the desk, the assignment of young persons just out of college to desk work without any apprenticeship as reporters, the use of part-time persons, especially high school and college teachers of journalism and English, and the development of in-plant training programs to improve the skills of current employes who are paid overtime for attending the training sessions.[74] Critiques and seminars by professional organizations and journalism schools and departments also have been used to teach and upgrade skills, and The Newspaper Fund has experimented with an editing internship for college students.

Paul Swensson, executive director of The Newspaper Fund, said in the late 1960s that newspaper journalism was due for a revolution in the art of editing. He suggested this revolution would include replacing the old-fashioned slot man and the conventional rim with editing desks in which reporter, photographer and editor could function as a team, assigning to copy editors responsibility and authority for preparing and executing assignments, providing copy editors with the basic job of getting people to read the news, and establishing continuing education programs for news and copy editors.[75] Under the traditional system, a copy chief or slotman sits inside a horseshoe-shaped desk and parcels out copy to copy editors sitting around the outside of the desk or rim. If all the newspaper's copy passes through this one control point, it is referred to as a universal copy desk. Larger papers frequently employ separate copy desks for sports, women's news and perhaps other departments.

Many changes in editing procedures have taken place in newspapers across the country in recent years, and more changes are certain as the use of new technology expands. Some newspapers have abandoned the old horse-shoe for H-shaped desk arrangements or others that provide more work space and get editors who need to be close to each other closer together. Many newspapers are adjusting their editing procedures to accommodate the use of optical scanners, video display terminals and other equipment. Some feared that the use of scanners would discourage creative editing because corrections must be typed on the copy to be picked up by the scanning device. A typical procedure is for copy editors to make corrections in a blue pencil which the scanner will not read. These corrections are then typed in or the story is retyped by someone on the desk, the reporter or a typist. The use of video display terminals should encourage high quality editing of both locally produced and wire copy.

IMPROVING THE PACKAGE

Many newspapers have discovered in recent years that the manner in which they display their contents can be vital to their success in a visually oriented world. Most still cling to basic design patterns developed in the nineteenth century, but many are making modifications intended to attract and hold readers and make it easier for them to use the product. Newspapers are coming to accept the possibility that the manner in which information is presented may be as important to communication as the content itself, that the consumer's decision to read may be determined by the mood of the moment as well as by the need to obtain information. The somewhat disorganized, bulletin board appearance that seemed to suffice in the past may not be sufficiently competitive in an era where viewers are accustomed to organized design in almost everything.

Phillip Ritzenberg, design editor of the *New York News,* suggested in 1971 that principal changes in the past generation have included a move toward more readable text types, airier layout and cleaner graphic devices. He said their adoption probably can be traced to the efforts of Edmund Arnold, professor of graphic arts at Syracuse University and former editor of *Linotype News.*[76] Arnold has worked directly with a number of newspapers and indirectly assisted others through his books and his column, "Talking Typographically," in *Editor & Publisher,* the newspaper trade publication. Arnold suggested in one of his columns in 1972 that the "optimum format" is the big thing in newspaper design right now. This format derives its name from the optimum line length of body type for easy reading and comprehension. For conventional news body typefaces this optimum, determined by mathematical formula, is about 15 picas (two and one-half inches). The six-column page, or the five-column page with some type faces, provides this optimum and has been coming into greater usage in the early 1970s especially on front pages, editorial pages and other pages where advertising is not involved. A study commissioned by the American Newspaper Publishers Association's Research Center reported in 1974 that readers preferred modern format newspapers with six-column pages and horizontal emphasis in headlines and story display to those with eight-column pages and traditional vertical make-up. Generally speaking, both men and women, young and old, preferred the modern format.[77]

Some newspapers also are placing greater emphasis on the left-hand side of page one. The *Minneapolis Tribune,* which was redesigned in 1971, chose to keep the traditional eight-column format on page one, but it abandoned the long-standing practice of placing the lead story on the top right-hand side of the page. *Tribune* officials, who moved the dominant news to the left, pointed out that it is natural to read from left to right. The emphasis on the right may have developed out of the practice of assembling the right-hand columns last and placing the latest news in the last column available for it. Significantly the *Tribune's* new design is based on engineering needs as well as readability principles; it combines graphics engineering compatible with computer-assisted production. All body type can be set by computer in one operation for each piece of copy; hand-leading of lines is eliminated.[78]

Although many of the nation's newspapers had not abandoned their eight-column formats on page one or shifted the lead story to the left side of the page, a large number by the early 1970s had made less drastic modifications to improve appearance, satisfy technological changes, or both. Newspapers such as the *Kansas City Star* and the *Baltimore Sun* that had long maintained conservative formats began to use larger headlines and fewer decks to display their stories more attractively. A number of newspapers experimented with stories above the flag on page one and at times reduced the traditional full-page width of the flag. Some such as the *Philadelphia Inquirer* and the *Atlanta Constitution* opened new opportunities for expression to their cartoonists by enabling them to draw long vertical cartoons or other odd shapes in addition to the more traditional sizes. Even the traditionally gray *New York Times* has taken steps to improve its appearance. The basic news pages have been enlivened by greater use of photography, an attractive op. ed. page has been developed, and special sections such as *The Week in Review* have received extensive graphic improvement. In time the *Times* may be recognized as a leader in graphics as well as coverage.

Portland's *Oregon Journal,* which wanted to improve yet look different from its sister paper, the *Oregonian,* which had gone to the six-column format, adopted what Edmund Arnold refers to as the W-format on page one. This format has six traditional width columns plus a wide, or "W" column which is one and one-half columns wide. The space saved is used to provide alleys or white strips between columns and open up the page. The *Journal's* page one "W" matter was placed in a page-long box, usually in color, that included the weather, bulletins, a humorous story, teasers for inside features, and the index.[79]

Inside pages with advertising as well as front pages, and other open pages are also getting increasing attention on many newspapers. Variations are being developed in both vertical and horizontal makeup patterns.

Some newspapers have sought to brighten their pages in recent years through expanded use of color for news and feature pictures as well as advertisements. Technological progress has made the use of color more financially feasible for many, including both large and small newspapers. The *Miami Herald,* the *St. Petersburg Times* and the *Fort Lauderdale News,* all in Florida have been among the leaders in color advertising lineage in the early 1970s. Others have been the *Salt Lake City Tribune* and *Salt Lake City Deseret News* in Utah, the *Phoenix Republic* and the *Phoenix Gazette* in Arizona, the *New Orleans Times-Picayune, Dallas Times Herald* and *Dallas News,* the *Omaha World-Herald* and the *Houston Chronicle.* The *Miami Herald* used more than 8.2 million lines in 1973.[80] Color advertising, of course, makes possible more extensive use of color in news and features.

What has happened in recent years may be the forerunner of a much greater revolution in approach toward content and appearance in the late 1970s. William C. Sexton, editor of World Book Encyclopedia Science Service, Inc., suggested in the late 1960s that a convergence of progressive trends in marketing, behavioral research, design and editorial philosophy might bring great changes in newspapers' personalities, including appearance, content and attitude in the 1970s. Changes indicated as possible by him included a new concept of makeup that would emphasize type's ability to communicate feeling as well as fact and a greater emphasis on high-impact roundups, trend stories and personality pieces as opposed to day-to-day routine coverage. Sexton suggested that newspapers must first determine their intended identity, keeping in mind their heritage and development, then establish design, content and attitude plans to carry out the basic identity. Among specific changes he predicted is the addition of an art director in the newsroom to help with layouts, picture selection, story planning and other matters.[81]

Frank Ariss, a British design consultant who helped redesign the *Minneapolis Tribune* and *San Francisco Examiner,* said in 1974 that many of America's big newspapers are put together in a manner that is 50 years behind the times. He said on a scale of 100 he would rank American newspapers between one and five. Ariss recommended that newspapers have fewer headline styles and that they be the same throughout all sections, which should be departmentalized. He said he favored photo-journalism on the right side of the leading pages with short captions and recommended that newspapers replace the 15th century type they are using. Ariss said he opposed the use of italic type and suggested that Helvetica is the best type for today. It's larger than the old type, he said, but takes no more space. Ariss recommended that weather, sports, and other features have the same position each day so readers would not have to search for them, and he said that if jumps are needed they should go from the first page to the back page of a section.[82]

Phillip Ritzenberg, design editor of the *New York News,* suggests that newspapers can be journalistic without being strident, contemporary without being humorless or colorless in design, modular without being boring and predictable, and easy to assemble in a demanding production environment without precluding a few visual surprises each day. He says editors today should be confronting the problems of compartmentalizing their editorial content and curing the bulletin board syndrome; confronting their advertising colleagues with the need of selling space in even modules for better display of both editorial and advertising matter; exploring the use of illustrations and graphics that will inform, amuse and stimulate, not plug holes in type, and wondering whether, and how, a medium designed for the nineteenth century can continue to be a force in the twentieth century.[83]

Daniel E. Kelly, senior vice-president and creative director of Foote, Cone & Belding advertising agency, and his art directors, conducted an experiment in early 1971 that pointed up how similar newspapers are in appearance and how they might be changed. Kelly invited each of his art directors to pretend that he had just inherited one of the nation's newspapers. He was to examine the appearance of this paper in terms of his own graphic background and suggest changes for page one, keeping in mind that he would not want to do anything that would destroy a profitable enterprise. As might be expected, most of the proposed front pages reflected magazine design. Some designers, in their efforts to produce attractive formats, substantially reduced the quantity of page one copy, which might not suit many editors; some showed a lack of concern for news values. But as Kelly pointed out, the purpose of the experiment was not to suggest that the newspapers implement what had been done, but to suggest that the newspapers can be more exciting, more inviting to read, and more relevant to people's life-styles in this decade.[84]

DEVELOPMENTS IN PHOTOGRAPHY

One of the best ways to improve both the appearance and content of newspapers is to improve their use of photographs. Effective pictures can pull readers into the newspaper and help it compete with television and other activities for the consumer's time. Good pictures can communicate information and draw readers to the word stories that contain more information. Expanded use of cold type and offset production procedures greatly enhance the potential for effective use of photography on many newspapers. Improvements also are being made in traditional operations to produce clearer and more effective pictures. Yet most of the nation's newspapers were not realizing their photographic potential in the early 1970s. Many were still running an excess of self-serving pictures, especially in relation to matters such as real estate and travel; many were still using trivial pictures that lacked both news and human interest values; some still relied too much on sensational pictures of human suffering to gain attention without saying much; some were expressing bias, perhaps unintentionally in reporting controversy; some were failing to crop pictures effectively. But perhaps most distressing, many were not using photojournalism to supplement and complement their verbal reporting; numerous opportunities for reaching people through pictures were being overlooked. Newspapers' failure to realize their potential can perhaps be attributed in part to the word orientation of key personnel. Most newspapers did not have picture editors, and some of the picture editors employed had limited authority to control assignments and select pictures. Some editors were doing exciting things with pictures, but many seemed to regard them primarily as a means of separating headlines over the really important content or as a means of keeping advertisers, civic clubs and others happy.

Pictorial excellence of newspapers in the past has been attributed to the individual creativity and technical skill of photographers rather than to the newspaper's organizational structure. But it seems likely that if very many newspapers are consistently to make effective use of pictures in the future they will need persons with visual perception in places of authority. Such persons need to help make assignments and help determine what is done with the pictures that result from them.[85] On many newspapers better rapport must be developed between departmental editors and photographers. News personnel must have or develop a better feel for pictures and photographers must have or develop greater news sense.

Newspapers seeking pictorial excellence should, in addition to providing adequate personnel, provide adequate space in their products and use it effectively. Many self-serving or trivial pictures can be deemphasized or turned into good feature shots. Instead of picturing the man who donates money to a hospital for equipment handing a check to an official, some persons, perhaps including the donor, could be pictured using the equipment or helping someone else use it. Instead of using several columns to picture individuals receiving awards from employers or civic clubs, one-column mug shots of the honorees might be grouped together. The *Denver Post* has done something along these lines, which it referred to as its "Hall of Fame."

Newspapers taking pictures of controversies such as demonstrations or riots should be careful to assure that the essence of the confrontation is captured. A picture of black students carrying rifles, shotguns and bullets taken at Cornell University in April 1969, suggested to many that these students were ready to shoot it out if they did not win their confrontation with administrators and police. But later it was reported that these students were carrying weapons out of fear after a cross had been burned in front of a black women's dormitory and radio reports had indicated that carloads of armed whites were headed toward the campus.[86] Some instances have been reported where photographers knowingly reported only a part of a story in pictures or even encouraged individuals to, in effect, perform for the camera. Pictures not set in a proper frame of reference can lie, and all coverage of controversy must be handled with great care and concern for truth. Editors as well as photographers must be careful, lest they crop out something that is needed for true perspective or run a seemingly action-packed or emotional picture that harms someone unjustly.

Newspapers must be concerned about pictures of automobile accidents, fires or other incidents that could invade an individual's privacy or be in poor taste. Curtis D. MacDougall, professor of journalism emeritus at Northwestern, in his *News Pictures Fit to Print . . . or are they?* [87] contends, however, that some pictures that might be objectionable to some should be printed if the printing serves the public interest. The challenge for editors is to determine if, for example, seeing pictures of persons die in war, fires or accidents is likely to prevent the recurrence of such tragedies. Did the pictures of the slayings at My Lai or other incidents in Vietnam have a positive effect on United States policies there? Privacy laws, of course, provide some guidance for editors, and more restrictive laws and judicial interpretations could in the near future provide greater restrictions against invasion of individual privacy by photographs as well as words.[88]

Interesting subjects are the key to good pictures, but effective cropping, good captions and selective use of color can enhance the creativeness of assignment editors and photographers. Pictures should tell stories, depict action, create moods. People should be emphasized because readers are interested in people. Babies and children, along with animals, have long been favorite subjects of feature pictures. Pictures of women in bathing suits or other provocative attire also have been favorites and still are used in many newspapers. Some newspapers have curtailed the use of cheesecake pictures, however, because of objections that they are degrading to women or because they want to use pictures they believe to be more newsworthy. All persons can be interesting subjects for pictures if they are doing interesting things; most can be uninteresting if they are not. Persons can be used as a point of comparison when photographing objects whose size might not be easily discernible, and various props can be used to convey ideas. Conventional captions should be written for persons who have not read an accompanying story, but they should not duplicate the information there; identifications such as left-to-right should be avoided when feasible. The use of display type with conventional cutlines reportedly can increase their readership by as much as 25%.[89] Some editors oppose any retouching of pictures; others believe that some retouching may be useful, provided it does not distort truth. The Associated Press noted, for example, that it may retouch a picture of firemen rescuing persons in revealing night clothes. Some newspapers routinely improve the facial features in women's photographs on society pages. Others eliminate distractions that might mar a picture's integrity such as a youngster mugging in an accident picture, or retouch to eliminate mechanical flaws.[90]

Series of pictures and picture pages also can contribute to pictorial coverage, provided the individual pictures are logically tied together in some way. To run a page of pictures just to fill space may detract from individual pictures on the page and other pictures used elsewhere in the newspaper. As is true of news stories, features and editorials, pictures should be used for some definite, useful purpose. Judiciously used along with other art work in carefully planned layouts, they can contribute greatly to the development of better newspapers.

EDITORIALS AND EDITORIAL PAGES

The editorial section, which normally consists of from one to two pages, depending on the size of the publication, is vital to the development of a good newspaper. Someone has suggested that the news section is the heart of the newspaper and the editorial section is its soul; that is a reasonable analogy. The editorial page sets the tone of the newspaper and expresses its character on a continuing basis. Basically, the editorial section performs two functions. First, it provides a continuous expression of the newspaper's opinions on important issues. Second, it provides a forum for the expression of opinion by others on these issues. The newspaper's own opinions are expressed in institutional editorials, run most often at the left-hand side of the main editorial page under the masthead or under some heading such as "In Our Opinion." These editorials, whether written by an editorial writer, the editor or someone in an even higher management position, represent the institution itself and its owners rather than any one individual. Institutional views may also be suggested in editorial cartoons or columns, which are signed, but these editorial page features also are used at times to express the views of others. Cartoons, columns, letters to the editor and other special features are used to present a variety of viewpoints and satisfy the newspaper's vital role as a forum for expression on vital issues. Newspapers may refer to their editorial pages as battle pages, for it is here that the views of editors, cartoonists, columnists and letter writers compete for the attention and support of readers. Unlike the news pages, where writers are expected to be as objective as possible, the editorial pages are designed to provide a clash of opinions.

Dynamic, effective editorial pages result from good editorial policies, carried out by good editors, who write good editorials, augment them with good features and display the total product in a pleasing manner. Good editorial page policy must, of course, be part of a total effort to achieve excellence throughout the newspaper. Strong editorial stands on issues are vital, but they are not enough. Those issues must also be covered thoroughly and fairly in the news columns. Editors must write about things that are important to their readers; for most newspapers, this means an emphasis on local issues. They must not make up their minds too quickly or be afraid to admit mistakes, but they must consider the facts and take stands. They cannot be all things to all persons. Editors must not throttle ideas by denying them space, and they must seek out reasons for silence on matters that perhaps should be issues but are not. What is not being done by government or others may be as significant as what is being done wrong or ineffectively. Editors must investigate fully, think deeply, organize carefully, and write clearly themselves and encourage such actions in the columns, letters and other materials that they present for readers. At all times, good policy demands that the public good be placed ahead of private gain. The newspaper's true character is always present in its editorial page.

Editorial staffs vary in number, depending on the size and resources of the individual newspapers. On weeklies and some small dailies, one person may write all the editorials and also perform other tasks such as those of the reporter or copy editor. Some large dailies may have four or more persons who do nothing but research and write editorials. A study sponsored by the National Conference of Editorial Writers in 1971, following up a similar study made ten years before, suggests a "Profile of the Editorial Writer." [91] Findings from the study indicate that most editorial writers are men. Only 2.4% of the total responding in 1971 are women, about the same percentage as in the earlier study. The median age for editorial writers was 48.4 years, only slightly younger than the median of 50 reported in the previous study. Only 4.7% of the respondents were under 30, while 45.3% were more than 51. Of those responding, 82.8% held baccalaureate degrees, about 10% more than a decade before; 20.5% held master's degrees; an additional 19.6% had done some graduate work, and half had participated in special fellowship programs at colleges and universities.

The median salary for editorial writers participating in the NCEW study was $16,751. The estimate was up from $12,300 in 1962, but the Consumer Price Index shows that the gain was only $606 above the decade's cost of living increases. A majority, 83.7%, indicated they believed their salaries compared well with those of other newspaper staff members. The majority also indicated they were "very satisfied" (62.27%) or "satisfied" (29.7%) in newspaper work, and most (63.95%) indicated they expected to continue in editorial writing; 22.5%, mostly younger writers, indicated that they expected to move into management. About a third of the total had part-time jobs such as teaching, lecturing, consulting or free-lance writing.

Approximately two-thirds of the respondents indicated that their employers discouraged public participation in politics by editorial writers. Most (78.4%) agreed that the editorial writer should avoid membership in partisan political organizations to preserve impartial judgment on public issues. However, 42% said they had engaged in some form of political activity beyond voting in the 1970 Congressional elections. Approximately half the editorial writers classified themselves as Independents while 30.5% said they are Democrats and 17.1% said they are Republicans.

Good editorial writers make use of both inherited and acquired talents. Inherited potential for thinking and writing are important, but these must be developed through education and hard work. Experience as reporters is helpful in preparing editorial writers for their work, for they must first dig out the facts before commenting on them. Good editorial writers must be able to think analytically; they must be able to see the whole picture, organize logically, and write forcefully and clearly. They must be able to view emotional and controversial matters in a dispassionate manner and arrive at judgments on the basis of the public good. They must be able to withstand criticism and persist when they know they are right, yet be honest and courageous enough to admit when they are wrong. They must be team players, for many decisions are the result of group decisions and few by-lines are placed on editorials. A sense of humor helps the editorial writer in his work, and occasional humor is likely to help his editorials also.

An editorial may be defined as an expression of institutional opinion or reaction to an issue of public significance. Editorials inform their readers and motivate them to think; often they seek to persuade their readers toward the institution's point of view. At one time many newspapers seemed content in their editorials to provide information and analysis and leave the decision making to the readers; some still take that approach. Others contend that with the rise of interpretive reporting the analysis function is well-performed by the news department; the true editorial must express an institutional reaction and often should recommend a course of action. Editorial writers are supposed to recognize problems, analyze them and suggest solutions. The subjects may range from urging support for the United Way campaign to urging impeachment of some prominent public official.

As noted in an earlier chapter, it is difficult to separate the influence of editorials and editorial pages from that of the newspaper as a whole and difficult to assess the newspaper's influence in any case. Newspapers may be one of many factors that cause people to think and act as they do. Editorials are much more likely to confirm basic views that readers hold than to change them. Editorial pages read over a long period of time may contribute to the reader's views on many subjects whether he is acutely conscious of it or not. Editorials on issues about which the reader has little other information may affect his viewpoint on that issue. Editorials may stimulate action by public officials simply by calling public attention to problems and needs. In many instances, if editorials cause people to think about the issues discussed, they will have succeeded. Newspapers should continue to seek ways in which they can influence positive public action on important issues.

Cartoons

Newspapers often seek to influence public thinking through the use of cartoons. Since cartoons are signed, they do not have the same institutional impact as editorials, but newspapers normally run cartoons that support their basic points of view. The larger newspapers employ their own cartoonists, who can deal with local, state and national affairs as conditions warrant. Most newspapers rely on syndicates which deal primarily with national issues. They can still provide a liberal or conservative impact, however, on national affairs through their selection of syndicated cartoons.

At the turn of the century many newspapers employed their own cartoonists. But the decline of newspaper competition at the local level, the increasing complexity of issues, and the expansion of other visual means of communication caused many newspapers to turn toward syndicates. The cartoonist is perhaps most effective in dealing with clear-cut issues, for the cartoon tends to be an offensive weapon. There is always the danger of oversimplification. Still the cartoon is probably the most-read feature on editorial pages, and its potential for calling attention to problems or graphically emphasizing points is great.

The assessments that readers make of cartoonists may depend to a considerable degree on whether they agree with them politically and philosophically. Still, a number have been recognized for outstanding work. Among those cited in recent years have been Herbert Block (Herblock) of the *Washington Post,* Paul Conrad and Frank Interlandi of the *Los Angeles Times,* Bill Mauldin of the Chicago Sun Times, Pat Oliphant of the *Denver Post,* John Fischetti of the *Chicago Daily News,* Bill Sanders of the *Kansas City Star,* Charles Werner of the *Indianapolis Star,* Dick Yardley of the *Baltimore Sun,* Cliff Baldowski of the *Atlanta Constitution,* Ross Lewis of the *Milwaukee Journal,* Tom Little of the *Nashville Tennesseean,* Joe Parrish of the *Chicago Tribune,* C. D. Batchelor of the *New York Daily News,* Don Hesse of the *St. Louis Globe-Democrat,* Tom Engelhardt of the *St. Louis Post-Dispatch,* Hugh Haynie of the *Louisville Courier-Journal,* Lou Grant of the *Oakland Tribune,* Jim Ivey of the *San Francisco Examiner,* Frank Miller of the *Des Moines Register,* Scott Long of the *Minneapolis Tribune,* and Dan Dowling and Vaughn Shoemaker of the old *New York Herald Tribune.*

Herblock has suggested that the cartoonist generally serves as critic; he tries to point out things that could be done better or differently. He sees the cartoonist as an unofficial check in the nation's checks and balances system.[92] Conrad has said his function is to illustrate problems, express concern about them and call for change.[93] Like the editorial writer, the cartoonist can be considered successful if he causes people to think about important issues. It is unfortunate that so many newspapers believe they must rely on syndicated cartoonists and thereby omit cartoon commentary on local issues. Some newspapers have overcome this deficiency in part by the use of part-time cartoonists and by using issue-related photographs in place of cartoons.

Columns

Another popular feature used by most newspapers to encourage readers to think as well as provide them with information is the personal column. Most newspapers carry columns about politics and government on their editorial pages or opposite-editorial pages. Many carry syndicated columnists to cover national and international affairs; some have one or more local columnists to cover local and state affairs. In theory newspapers use political columns in their editorial sections and other types of columns in other sections where they are appropriate. In practice, many papers may use business columns, humorous columns, advice columns and even gossip columns in the editorial section. Small papers may do this as a means of grouping columnists in a limited amount of space. Many papers regardless of size may use some of these allied columns to draw readers to their editorial pages.

Political columnists, many of whom are based in Washington, can provide both information and insights for newspapers and their readers. They can be a strong drawing card for the editorial section, and they often provide ideas for editorials and local angle columns. Some newspapers fill their editorial section with columnists that agree with their own philosophies, but most attempt to provide a balanced menu of liberals, conservatives and investigative or in-depth reporters. If the reader samples opposite points of view on important issues as presented by columnists he should be motivated to think and react more intelligently.

Walter Lippmann is generally considered to be the first of the true political columnists. Correspondents had been reporting on Washington events since the early nineteenth century, but it was not until the early 1930s that the *New York Herald Tribune* invited Lippmann to both report and express his opinions about political affairs. It proved an excellent choice. Lippmann, former editor of the *New York World,* continued to analyze the world scene with remarkable depth and perception for several decades through his column, "Today and Tomorrow." Public officials including presidents joined with other newspaper readers in considering Lippmann's opinions and recommendations.

Although readers, including newspaper editors, continue to disagree about who are the most effective columnists, occasional surveys may be suggestive. One such survey in the early 1970s sought the opinions of members of the National Conference of Editorial Writers. Their responses indicated that James Reston, Tom Wicker, Joseph Kraft and Marquis Childs were highly regarded as liberal spokesmen; James J. Kilpatrick and William F. Buckley, Jr. were leaders among the conservative spokesmen; and the team of Rowland Evans-Robert Novak and columnist Jack Anderson were among the leaders in the "best reporter" category. Many other excellent columnists were mentioned, however, and those conducting the survey cautioned that rankings must be accepted with caution because of the nature of the questionnaire.[94]

Although newspapers cannot always get the columnists they want from the syndicates because other newspapers in the area have them, most can get several representative viewpoints for a reasonable price. Some large newspapers may rely more heavily on their own columnists for editorial page comment; some small dailies may use wire service analyses rather than syndicated columnists on their editorial pages. Some newspapers also have turned to specialists in various fields for columns. The *New York Times* when it redeveloped its editorial section in the early 1970s began using such specialists in addition to its own columnists. The writers vary greatly as the *Times* seeks out top persons in various areas to comment. Smaller newspapers, especially those in college and university communities, can also make good use of specialists as columnists. The *Athens* (Georgia) *Banner-Herald,* for example, has run guest columns for some years by specialists in political science, law, sociology, education and other areas at the University of Georgia.

Letters

Letters-to-the-editor columns also help newspapers encourage thinking and provide a forum for debate on public issues. There are some dangers, of course, in opening the newspaper to letters. Propagandists often flood newspapers with letters as well as stories favoring their points of view; individuals with nothing to say sometimes want to say it to a wider audience. But the benefits of a good letters column are many. Of great importance, it helps build rapport between the newspaper and its readers. The letters columns generally are well read and draw attention to the editorial pages. Readers feel represented in the letters column; even readers who never write letters themselves can see that the newspaper cares about what its readers think. The letters column also provides for dissemination of views that otherwise might be overlooked. Readers concerned about some aspects of government or community life can call public attention to these problems in the newspaper. In addition, the letters column provides readers with an opportunity to disagree with the newspaper's editorials in print. Good newspapers always assure ample space for readers to disagree with them.

Most metropolitan newspapers receive far more letters than they can print in the limited space available on editorial pages. Such newspapers are likely to print between 7 and 15% of those received and may limit them to 300 words or less. Smaller newspapers that receive comparatively few letters may publish all that are not libelous or profane.[95] Studies indicate that most letter writers are well-informed persons with strong community interest.

Features, Typography, Criticism

In addition to institutional editorials, cartoons, columns and letters-to-the-editor, some newspapers use exchange editorials from other newspapers on their editorial pages. These exchanges may be used to show that others agree with the newspaper's point of view, provide a differing opinion to that held by the newspaper, or point out how some other community has been meeting its problems. Many papers that use exchanges look for humorous editorials to help offset the sometimes weighty material on the page. Some newspapers, especially smaller ones, may use interpretive news stories, spot news or other features to fill out their pages. While most newspapers do not run advertising on the editorial page itself, many that have opposite editorial (or op. ed.) pages, do use some advertising there.

Most newspapers have improved the appearance as well as the content of their editorial sections in recent years. At one time editorial pages were likely to have small headlines, large masses of uninterrupted type and few pictures. But some today are among the most attractive pages in their newspapers; most have been brightened by larger headlines, more pictures and other illustrations, the elimination of column rules, increased use of horizontal makeup and greater use of white space generally. Since editorial pages normally do not have advertising, they have been among the first to convert to the six-column and five-column formats that are supposed to aid both readability and appearance.

Critics have argued in recent years that many newspaper editorial sections are not close to realizing their potential for service. Criticisms vary somewhat from paper to paper but often include the idea that newspapers too often are too close to the business community; they do not see it as objectively as they do other sectors such as government. Some contend that advertisers have a direct effect on editorial policies; others say that newspapers, which often are big businesses themselves, are establishment oriented when they should be consumer oriented. Editors also have been criticized for ignoring local problems while speaking out on distant matters of less impact, throttling opposing ideas, and failing to exert real leadership in local matters where their impact could be great. They are at times accused of rushing into print with opinions not thoroughly researched or carefully written, of giving simplistic answers for complex problems, or of writing editorials that merely restate news stories. Some are accused of printing only one side in their editorials, cartoons and columns; others are chastised for unattractive layouts and duller content.

While many of these and other criticisms cannot be applied fairly to many of the nation's newspapers and generalizations must always be made cautiously, it does appear that many newspapers are not realizing the full potential of their editorial sections. Most could provide more effective leadership in their coverage and discussion of vital local issues. Many could improve their writing, and some could substantially improve their appearance. Guest columns by experts, pro and con presentations of issues, opinion polls, locally oriented cartoons or pictures, and expanded art work are all possibilities for development. A representative letters section and a balanced presentation of columnists also are important. But the key to editorial page excellence is using thoroughly researched, well-written editorials that take people-oriented stands on important issues.

6

Right To Know—
Right To Publish

THROUGH THE FORESIGHT of those who drafted the nation's constitution, wise decisions by judges through the years, and a continued willingness of many editors and publishers to fight for press and public rights, American newspapers in the early 1970s exercised a considerable freedom to publish news and commentary. The right to publish without a license and the right to comment on public activities in a fair and reasonable manner seemed generally well-established. But other rights, including the right of access to information about government, were less secure, and the press was subject to continual criticism and harassment from various sources. Officials at all levels of government sought to block public access to information through delaying tactics and other strategies, and officials at both national and state levels in singular instances succeeded temporarily in exercising prior restraints on the press. Officials also used subpoenas in an effort to force reporters to reveal sources of confidential information, and some reporters were forced to serve jail sentences for not divulging these confidences.

The adversary relationship that always exists between the President and the press seemed especially intense during the Nixon administration. There were reports of FBI checks and wiretaps on phones of reporters who were considered "unfriendly"; there were reports that the Internal Revenue Service had been asked to audit the income taxes of reporters whose stories, whether factual or not, had been deemed to be unfavorable.[1]

The press had considerable freedom to serve the public, yet it was under constant attack or threat of attack. Areas of special concern for reporters and editors seeking to keep the people informed included the following: relationships between the President and the press, and Washington coverage generally; efforts to exercise prior restraints on the press; access to information; the protection of news sources; public access to the media; coverage of the judicial process; and questions of libel and invasion of privacy. Each will be reviewed briefly in this chapter.

THE PRESIDENT AND THE PRESS

The adversary relationship between the President and the press has existed since the early days of the republic, and properly so. Presidents, like other persons, wish to present themselves and their administrations to the public in the most favorable light possible. The press, in its role of public watchdog, must check closely on all activities of the administration and report the favorable as well as the unfavorable, regardless of how reporters and editors may feel about the President and his staff personally. Presidents Dwight Eisenhower and John Kennedy were not the first to engage in what has been termed "news management." Presidents Lyndon Johnson and Richard Nixon were not the first to experience "credibility" gaps with their constituents. Most presidents have sought to manage the news, and many have had credibility problems. But the extent of news management in recent administrations and the events which prompted it have perhaps produced deeper fissures between government and those it serves than in the past. The public's confidence in their leaders has been severely tested at times. The press, as bearer of bad tidings, has often been criticized both by the administration that produced the unpleasant news and the people who have been recipients of it.

A major credibility problem developed toward the end of the Eisenhower administration over the government's handling of the U-2 reconnaissance plane incident. At first, the government asserted that a weather plane on a routine mission had got off course and been shot down. The press accepted this report and printed it. Later it was revealed that the United States had been conducting reconnaissance missions over the Soviet Union for several years. Then came the Cuban missile crisis of 1962. Americans no doubt preferred temporary secrecy about the crisis to a nuclear war, but many were shocked when an assistant secretary of defense suggested later that the government has a right to lie, if necessary, to save itself. He did say that officials did not have the right to lie politically or to protect themselves; but how is the citizen to know whether the government is lying to save the nation or lying to save an administration? The "credibility gap" that developed out of such incidents grew wider as a result of the secrecy which shrouded American activities in Southeast Asia during the 1960s. Reporters on the scene could not confirm the optimistic reports flowing from government sources. Distrust of the government reports increased as the war dragged on and on without the hoped-for successes. The people were confused as to what was going on there and why Americans were involved in it. The press was frustrated in its efforts to help them by government efforts to manage the flow of information about the war.

Many persons hoped that the Republican administration elected in 1968 would bring an end to the war in Vietnam and close the growing credibility gap between the government and its constituents. But the hoped-for changes did not come; the war dragged on, and the people became more frustrated. Many newspapers supported President Nixon's election and continued to support him throughout his first administration. But some newspapers had opposed him since his early days in Congress, and others joined with them in questioning his policies in Southeast Asia. The adversary relationship between the administration and other segments of the media became more intense in late 1969 after Vice-President Spiro Agnew lashed out at critics of the President. Agnew struck first at network television commentators, then turned his attention to newspapers, including the *Washington Post* and *New York Times*. The administration charged segments of the press with being unfair and biased. Many in the press countered that the administration was seeking to control and restrict information to which the public was entitled and seeking to intimidate and discredit the media. Major disputes developed over the government's handling of war news; its efforts to prevent the publication of the Pentagon Papers, which contained information about the war; the government's use of subpoenas in an effort to force reporters to reveal confidential sources; the President's neglect of news conferences, and the vice-president's verbal assaults on the media.

Eugene V. Risher, White House correspondent for United Press International, suggested in 1971 that Mr. Nixon felt the adversary relationship with the press more deeply than most of his predecessors. Risher said the President "feels—and this is reflected in the attitudes of other top level White House aides—that the press is either incapable or unwilling to accurately reflect his motives and his personality. This is a basic distrust of the press over and beyond the normal adversary relationship. It has engendered in many newsmen a mutual feeling of distrust, a feeling that they are being manipulated and not getting an accurate view." [2]

Newspapers questioned Mr. Agnew's accusing the media of being pro-liberal and anti-administration, when in fact most newspapers tended to be conservative and Republican. Many also disagreed with his attacks on liberal Eastern newspapers, which often are regarded as being among the nation's best. The vice-president said his purpose in criticizing the media was to encourage the profession to look critically at itself.

The feud between the administration and the press appeared to subside during the 1972 election campaign. The administration evidently felt it would be well not to stir up the press when it seemed intent on finding faults in Democratic candidate George McGovern. Most newspapers evidently believed that Republican President Nixon was a better choice for the White House than his liberal opponent. There were some exceptions, however, including the *Washington Post,* which began its explosive series on the Watergate scandal late in the campaign. Information reported by the *Post* and others linked the conspirators who broke into Democratic headquarters in the Watergate building to members of the Committee for Reelection of the President. Members of the administration denied any knowledge of or involvement in the incident, and Democratic efforts to make Watergate a campaign issue failed. Ronald Ziegler, White House press secretary, accused the *Post* and its reporters of shabby journalism and efforts at character assassination. President Nixon, supported by far more newspapers than his opponent, was reelected in November by an overwhelming majority of the voters.

Public confidence in the President remained high in early 1973 as American troops and prisoners of war came home from Vietnam. The press joined in welcoming these developments. But as the Watergate story was unfolded confidence in the administration began to wane. President Nixon sought to reassure the people of his personal innocence and his determination to get to the bottom of the whole mess in a nationwide broadcast in late April. He praised the American system that had brought the facts to light and that would bring the guilty to justice. The system in this case, he explained, included "a determined grand jury, honest prosecutors, a courageous judge—John Sirica—and a vigorous free press." After the address the President made a further appeal to members of the media in the White House press office. "Ladies and gentlemen of the press," he said, "we have had our differences in the past and I hope you give me hell every time you think I'm wrong. I hope I'm worthy of your trust." Subsequently, Secretary Ziegler apologized to the *Post* for his remarks in October, and Vice-President Agnew reported that the administration would like to begin talks with the media aimed at reducing the hostility between them. He described the relationship between the media and the White House as a hostile "deep feeling that runs beyond the normal adversary relationship," and suggested that they "put aside visceral reaction and engage in a productive and intelligent discussion of their differences." [3]

These statements gave the appearance of a thaw in relationships between the administration and the press, but the continuing Watergate story and other developments made any significant melting unlikely. Testimony before the Senate Select Committee on Presidential Campaign Activities implicated persons close to the President in the Watergate affair and raised serious questions about the President's judgment in relying on these persons and his possible knowledge of their activities. His use of executive privilege to withhold or delay information that might have helped to clear up the whole incident further damaged his credibility with many newsmen and Americans generally. His dismissal of a Watergate prosecutor who insisted on getting tapes the President believed were covered by executive privilege prompted calls for impeachment. The appointment of a new prosecutor and the release of some of the tapes sought did not satisfy the critics, especially when it was discovered that parts of a presumably important conversation had been erased. Some found it difficult to believe that the tape could have been erased accidentally as asserted.

If there was a lull in the feud between administration and media, it appeared to be ending in late 1973. In a late October news conference the President accused the television network news programs of "outrageous, vicious, distorted reporting." He said the public's confidence in the nation was shaken because "people are pounded night after night with that kind of frantic, hysterical reporting." By this time Vice-President Agnew had resigned, but other administration spokesmen picked up the attack on the broadcast media. The National News Council sought to investigate the charges but was not immediately successful in getting lists of specific charges from the administration. It reported in late January 1974 that it would renew its investigation if the White House supplied a list of specific instances of objectional reports.[4]

As the Watergate story gradually was unfolded in 1974 newspapers that traditionally had supported the Republican party and strongly endorsed Mr. Nixon became increasingly critical of his actions and called for his resignation or impeachment. The *Chicago Tribune* was among those calling for such action after the tape revelations of the spring; the *Wall Street Journal* was among those calling for resignation after the President's disclosures in early August of his involvement in the Watergate cover-up. After Mr. Nixon left the government, the press like the nation, appeared divided over what, if any, legal action should be pursued against him. The alleged crimes could not be ignored, yet removal from office was a strong form of punishment in itself.

Most members of the press welcomed President Ford's accession to the nation's highest office and applauded his administration's declared intention to be open and candid with the press. The press appeared enthusiastic about the President's appointment of Jerald F. terHorst, Washington bureau chief of the *Detroit News,* as White House press secretary. But the honeymoon was brief. Within a few weeks terHorst resigned under circumstances that raised questions about President Ford's future relationships with the press. Some speculated that terHorst quit because White House advisers gave him misleading information about the Nixon pardon. He said he resigned solely because he disapproved of the pardon. Ron Nessen, White House correspondent for NBC television news, subsequently was named press secretary. Nessen, who was assigned to the White House when Ford was named president, previously had been assigned to cover Ford as vice-president. While the terHorst resignation undoubtedly damaged the credibility of the new administration with the press, the appointment of Nessen and the fact that the President held two press conferences during his early weeks in office gave rise to continued hopes that relationships between President and press would be better during the Ford administration than they had been during the previous one.[5]

It was not possible in early 1974 to assess adequately the intense adversary relationship between the Nixon administration and the press. It seemed evident that there was a mutual distrust and dislike between the President and substantial segments of the press, including persons who covered the White House.

This distrust may have been a factor in the President's limited use of press conferences and extensive use of network television to speak directly to the public. Repeated verbal assaults on the press, use of subpoenas against reporters, use of the fairness doctrine in an apparent effort to impose self-censorship on television news programs, efforts to make the Federal Criminal code more restrictive on the press, and the limited accessibility of the President in press conferences gave some credence to charges that the administration was seeking to intimidate the media. Differences of opinion among newsmen about the fairness of presidential coverage lent some credence to charges that media coverage was at times unfair.[6] Those charging unfairness said it showed up in pictures, headlines, and the emphasis and space given stories. They said it was evident in exchanges between the President and some reporters at press conferences. Defenders of the press argued that while instances of unfair treatment might be cited, the overall coverage of the administration had been fair.

Continuing studies of the fairness issue by members of the press and others are needed. One such study of the Watergate coverage was done for the *Los Angeles Times* by Edward Jay Epstein, author, political scientist and frequent critic of the press. Epstein studied the coverage of the *Washington Post, Washington Star-News, Los Angeles Times, New York Times, Miami Herald,* and *Time* and *Newsweek* from the time of the Watergate break-in in June of 1972 through the first phase of the Senate committee hearings the next year. He concluded that "on almost any reasonable criteria the press showed a consistent—and unexpected—degree of fairness."[7] Some questions have been raised about the Watergate coverage by persons within as well as outside the media, and some errors have been cited.[8] But most seem to agree that the exercise as a whole was, as the President himself suggested, an example of the vigorous free press at work.

Louis Harris, the national pollster, found in the summer of 1973 that most Americans, 59% to 12%, believed that the Watergate exposé was an example of the free press at its best. The majority, 56% to 18%, said if it had not been for the press exposés the Watergate scandals would not have been uncovered. Those surveyed, 46% to 40%, said they did not believe the press and television had given more attention to Watergate than it deserved, and most, 61% to 17%, rejected the proposition that the press was just "out to get" President Nixon on Watergate. The majority indicated they believed their local newspapers and the television networks had been "very fair" in their coverage. It appears, however, that many persons did tire of reading and hearing about Watergate as the months dragged on. A Gallup poll conducted in late June 1974 indicated that 53% of the American people believed the mass media were providing too much coverage of Watergate. This was compared with a 44% response to the same question in a Gallup poll one year earlier.[9]

Most persons probably would agree that the President retains advantages in his adversary relationship with the press. He has the capacity to make news;

he controls the flow of a great deal of government information; he is in a position to reward friends and punish enemies. But some believe that this condition is not inevitable, and that to tip the balance too far in the direction of the press would weaken the nation's capacity for effective democratic government. Daniel P. Moynihan, an adviser to the past three presidents, said in the early 1970s that several circumstances existed that could together reverse the balance of power and cause problems. These included the muckraking traditions of the press that tear things down without necessarily offering alternatives, the separation of the working journalist from the masses, the dependency of Washington reporters on more or less clandestine information from bureaucracies that may be antagonistic to Presidential interests, the concept of objectivity, and the absence of a professional tradition of self-correction.[10] Newsmen might challenge one or more of Moynihan's contentions, but they should also accept the challenges to improve that are inherent in his presentation.

Many improvements in press coverage of the national government seemed desirable in the early 1970s. Some of them depended on action by newspapers and other media; some depended also on action by the administration and other government officials. The government needed to provide better access to information and eschew actions that restrain the press from doing its work fairly and effectively.

Among the suggestions for improving Washington coverage are proposals to redefine the roles of White House correspondents, restructure the system of holding presidential press conferences, and expand the coverage of agencies and activities that now receive only limited attention. In the early 1970s about 40 reporters were regularly assigned to the White House beat and a few others worked there on a semi-regular basis. They have what appears to be the most glamorous job in the world, covering the President of the United States. But in fact they spend much of their time attending briefings and processing handouts concerning routine White House business. When they travel "with" the President they are seldom really close to him and often must rely on a pool reporter to tell them what is going on; they usually stay in hotels some distance from the President and his aides. Whether at home or on the road they rarely even see the President much less get to talk with him. Some say the nature of the job is such that White House press reporters often are an extension of the President's propaganda mill. They point out that the Watergate story not only did not originate with the White House press corps but was not much advanced by them. Presidential coverage probably could be improved if newspapers left the routine coverage to the wire services and assigned their reporters to do more analytical and enterprise stories.[11]

Presidential coverage almost certainly could be improved if a better system for conducting press conferences were developed. At present the President can disseminate information to the people through radio and television speeches, press releases, daily press briefings by his press secretary, and by holding press conferences. The people have access to him only through the press conferences, which may be held infrequently and which may not provide for an adequate exchange. Many suggestions for improving press conferences have been made, including the following: (1) They should be held on a regular basis announced in advance. This would not preclude the President from calling unscheduled conferences when the news dictated, but would assure access to the top at regular intervals. (2) Some press conferences should be televised to provide citizens an opportunity to see them, but some should not be televised because the cameras encourage a show-like atmosphere. (3) Some press conferences or parts of conferences should be restricted to specific topics announced in advance. The additional time allotted would enable a deeper probing of important issues, and the media could bring in their specialists to help conduct the questioning. (4) Some efforts should be made by the press corps to screen questions in advance and assure that important, relevant ones of national import are asked during the limited time available; localized questions could be raised through other channels. (5) Questioners should be given an opportunity for at least one follow-up question. (6) Some press conferences should be limited to a small number of questioners selected by the press corps, who could also suggest questions. (7) Some conferences might be held in places other than Washington to give a wider segment of the press an opportunity to participate.[12]

The White House is, of course, not the only area where Washington coverage could be improved. Much more attention needs to be given to developments in other areas of the executive branch of government and to the legislative and judicial branches. The seven regulatory agencies that so vitally affect much of American life have not been given nearly enough attention. These are the Civil Aeronautics Board, Federal Communications Commission, Federal Maritime Commission, Federal Power Commission, Federal Trade Commission, Interstate Commerce Commission and the Securities and Exchange Commission. These other areas do not have the glamor of the White House beat or the Congressional beat, but they do have a far-reaching effect on the lives of American consumers and should get great attention from everyone.[13]

PRIOR RESTRAINTS

As the 1970s opened it appeared that the right of the press to publish information without prior restraint was generally well established. In a landmark case, *Near v. Minnesota*,[14] in 1931, the Supreme Court struck down a Minnesota statute that would have permitted prior restraint on publication. The court pointed out that a publisher could be held responsible for what he printed, that an individual could seek public and private redress against him under the libel laws, but that he should not be restrained from publishing. Chief Justice Hughes, who wrote the majority opinion, said that protection against prior restraint was not absolutely unlimited but that the limitation had been recognized only in exceptional cases. He indicated that providing information of value to an enemy in wartime, obscenity and incitement to violence could constitute exceptions but that censure of public officers and charges of official misconduct would not. Justice Hughes noted that liberty of the press historically considered and as taken up in the constitution has meant principally, although not exclusively, immunity from previous restraints or censorship. Except for the unusual situations suggested by Justice Hughes, prior censorship had not been exercised in this country for many years.

This long-standing principle was challenged in the early 1970s, however, first in the celebrated Pentagon Papers case and later in a case involving a federal judge and reporters in Louisiana. The Pentagon Papers case developed in June 1971 after the *New York Times* and the *Washington Post* began publication of classified information contained in a 47-volume study entitled "History of the U.S. Decision-Making Process on Vietnam Policy." The study, prepared at the Pentagon, was essentially historical and nonmilitary in nature, but it included political and diplomatic information that could prove embarrassing to some.

Copies of the still-classified report were stolen and then leaked to several newspapers in the spring or early summer of 1971. First, the *Times* and later the *Post* began series based on the information received. The government asked that the publication be halted, and when it was not sought to restrain publication through court action. A federal district court in New York granted a temporary restraining order against the *Times,* but the court of appeals there reversed the ruling. Both the district court and the court of appeals in the District of Columbia ruled in favor of the *Post.* The cases were quickly appealed to the Supreme Court, which in a five-four decision agreed to restrain publication while considering the issues involved.

In a six-three *per curiam* decision,[15] the court decided that the government could not prevent publication of these papers because it had not proved that their publication threatened national security. It said that any system of prior restraints of expression bears a heavy burden of showing justification for the enforcement of such a restraint, and in this instance had not met the burden. The long-standing rule that prior restraints would be permitted only in exceptional cases was continued. Many newsmen expressed concern, however, that a prior restraint had been enforced for about two weeks while the courts were resolving the issues involved. The delay did not seem critical in this case, but a possible precedent for delays, which might prove critical in other situations, had been suggested. On the other hand, dissenting justices expressed concern at the haste with which the case was handled. "It is not disputed," said Chief Justice Burger, "that the *Times* has had unauthorized possession of the documents for three to four months. . . . During all of this time, the *Times,* presumably in its capacity as trustee of the public's 'right to know,' had held up publication. . . . After these months of deferral, the alleged right-to-know had somehow and suddenly become a right that must be vindicated instanter." Justice Harlan argued that "because of the time element the Government had not been given an adequate opportunity to present its case to the District Court."

This precedent for temporary prior restraints was strengthened by the Supreme Court in 1973 in a case involving two reporters for Baton Rouge, Louisiana newspapers.[16] The reporters were cited for contempt in United States District Court in New Orleans in November 1971 for publishing testimony given in open court in their newspapers in violation of a judge's order not to do so. The United States Court of Appeals for the Fifth District held that the judge's order was unconstitutional, as the newsmen asserted, but said that they should have obeyed the order until they had completed all legal appeals. When the Supreme Court, without giving a written opinion, declined to upset the contempt fines against the two reporters it upheld a form of prior restraint.

The government in its brief to the Supreme Court contended that the judge's restraining order was not frivolous and that it was not unreasonable to conclude that newspaper accounts of the hearing might cause irreversible prejudice to the rights of the accused and the right of the public to have an impartial trial at the place where the crime allegedly was committed. Attorneys for the newsmen argued that coverage of the hearing did not pose a threat to anyone's right to a fair trial. They said the heavy burden which must be borne by the government to justify any prior restraint could not be met merely by the assertion of the possibility of a theoretical conflict arising in the future between constitutional rights. They argued that reporters and newspapers should not be asked to undertake expensive litigation to review muzzle orders which are so patently in violation of the Supreme Court's repeated admonitions against prior restraints and its admonition that the judiciary has no power to prevent the media from reporting on events which occur in open court.[17]

Newsmen feared the effects that the decision might have on coverage of courts. *Editor & Publisher,* the newspaper trade publication, said the Supreme Court had "created a weapon whereby officers of any court can impose prior restraint on news coverage of open court proceedings, in spite of the unconstitutionality of such action, until a higher court grants permission to print. Congress is prohibited from abridging freedom of the press, but the Supreme Court has. It is difficult to understand under what legal logic the court can find that an order is unconstitutional but has to be obeyed until some higher court agrees that it is." [18] The court's decision concerning alleged discrimination in want ads, discussed on page 143, was attacked by some as a form of prior restraint.

ACCESS TO INFORMATION

Newspapers are hopeful that the Supreme Court will reverse its recent approach toward temporary prior restraints and further restrict the situations in which any prior restraints may be imposed. But even if all restraints on publication were removed, would that be sufficient to assure the free flow of information the people need to make the democratic system work effectively? Obviously, it would not; for the press cannot publish information that it cannot obtain. There is a need not met by the "right to publish." In 1945 Kent Cooper, executive director of Associated Press, defined this additional need as "the right to know." This description met with general approval, and the media and other groups have sought to establish "the right to know" along with "the right to publish" as fundamental guarantees of democratic government. Under this concept the people have sought legislation at both federal and state levels to assure them access to the records and meetings of public bodies. The argument was documented in 1953 by Harold L. Cross, an outstanding newspaper lawyer and lecturer at Columbia University, in a book entitled *The People's Right to Know*. The book was sponsored by the American Society of Newspaper Editors which, along with other media groups, sought to penetrate the secrecy and confusion inherent in the rapidly expanding bureaucracy. Cross defined the problem and discussed the need for action at state as well as federal levels.

Sigma Delta Chi, the national professional journalistic society, in 1957 began a concentrated campaign for adoption of model access legislation in states without such statutes. The campaign, joined by other media groups, individual newspapers, broadcast stations and others, has achieved some success and is being continued. In 1957 only 21 states had laws guaranteeing citizens the right to inspect the records of their government and only 11 states had laws requiring that meetings of governmental bodies be open to the people. Fifteen years later, 41 states had open-record laws, and 38 states had open-meeting laws; 30 of the states had both. These statutes are variants of the model law suggested by Sigma Delta Chi, however, and their effectiveness varies greatly among the states.[19]

Dr. John B. Adams, journalism dean at the University of North Carolina, reported wide variation in the comprehensiveness of state open meetings laws in the summer of 1974 after completing a nationwide survey. Adams suggested 11 criteria for an ideal law and rated the states on how many of these criteria were included in their laws. Only Tennessee, which adopted a new open meetings law in early 1974, earned a score of "11" for having all criteria included. Laws in Arizona, Kentucky, and Colorado received a "10," and those in Kansas, Maine, and Minnesota got a "9." Only two states were reported not to have any sort of open meetings law at the time of the survey, but several others had laws which met only one or a few of the criteria suggested. Several states adopted legislation in 1974 that could change their ratings upward. Within a short time after it was ranked as the nation's most effective open meetings law, the Tennessee statute, challenged earlier in the year, was upheld by the State Supreme Court. Adams suggested that an ideal open meetings law should include a statement of public policy in support of openess, provide for an open legislature, provide for open legislative committees, provide for open meetings of state agencies or bodies, provide for open meetings of agencies and bodies of political subdivisions of the state, provide for open county boards, provide for open city councils, forbid closed executive sessions, provide legal recourse to halt secrecy, declare actions taken in meetings which violate the law to be null and void, and provide penalties for those who violate the law.[20]

Some newsmen have been reluctant to support right-to-know campaigns because they fear that weak laws may be worse than no laws at all. Open record laws have been vitiated by lists of exemptions, and open meetings laws have been rendered ineffectual by authorization of executive meetings of public bodies. The effectiveness of the laws also has been hampered on occasion by the time and costs involved in obtaining enforcement against alleged violators.

Efforts to assert the public's "right to know" about their federal government also have been successful to some extent. After a decade of discussion the Congress in 1966 passed a Freedom of Information Act [21] designed to open up many records of the federal bureaucracy. The law, when it became effective in July, 1967, applied to all federal executive branch and administrative agencies, but specified a number of exemptions. These include such things as matters of national defense and foreign policy where the government requires secrecy, trade secrets and financial data given to the government as confidential, and personal and medical files.

These exemptions raised questions about the value of the new law, but its overall approach to the subject seemed promising. The law provided that the President would have to issue specific orders exempting any given item of intelligence in such affairs as national defense and foreign policy if it were to be excluded from public records; blanket orders and looping policies were prohibited. The law provided that any person could seek information; he need not demonstrate that he had proper direct concern. Further the law provided that anyone denied information could appeal to the courts for an order requiring that it be made available to him; the burden of responsibility was placed on the agency withholding information to show why it should be withheld rather than upon the individual to show why he should have the information.[22]

Efforts to use the law during the first few years after its adoption bore out both the optimism and reservations expressed by its proponents. The law did open records that otherwise would have been kept secret; the exemptions listed did make it easier for officials who did not want to cooperate to avoid doing so. Strong dissatisfaction with the bureaucracy's response to the law was expressed by the House Government Information subcommittee that had sponsored the legislation. This committee, which had been a strong advocate of the people's right to know under long-time chairman John E. Moss, indicated that it would continue this path under new chairman Willian S. Moorhead.

After holding 41 days of formal hearings in 1972 to determine what the law had accomplished during its first five years and what changes might be needed to improve its operation, the Moorhead committee reported that while some agencies had tried to implement the law, its efficient operation had been "hindered by five years of foot-dragging by the Federal bureaucracy." The committee cited major problem areas including bureaucratic delay in responding to individual's requests for information, abuses in fee schedules by some agencies for searching and copying of documents requested by individuals, and lack of priority given by top-level administrators to full implementation and proper enforcement. Major agencies took an average of 33 days to respond to an individual's request for information and longer if appeals were involved. The committee also cited as problems the cumbersome and costly legal remedy under the act by which persons denied information can invoke injunctive procedures to obtain access and the relative lack of utilization of the act by the news media. It indicated the media, which had been among the strongest backers of legislation, were discouraged from using it by the time involved and their need to meet deadlines. The committee charged that agencies had misused exemptions intended to safeguard vital defense and state secrets, personal privacy and trade secrets. Still it noted that, in general, the act had helped thousands of citizens gain access to information by overcoming government roadblocks.[23]

The Moorhead Report recommended that the Department of Justice review all agency regulations to bring them into line with the letter and spirit of the law, that all agencies consult their public information officers when they receive requests and require top-level officials to make decisions under the law. Moorhead also proposed legislation to require initial action on a request within ten days and require the government to pay court costs and reasonable attorney's fees when it is found that it improperly withheld records.[24]

The need for improving the Freedom of Information Act was evident in the first interpretation of it by the United States Supreme Court in early 1973. The high court in *Mink v. Environmental Protection Agency*[25] denied Representative Patsy Mink of Hawaii and 32 of her colleagues access to an executive interdepartmental report on an underground nuclear test set for Amchitka Island, Alaska. The executive's refusal of the information was based on exemptions (1) and (5) of the Freedom of Information Act. These deal, respectively, with matters of national defense or foreign policy and with inter-agency or intra-agency memorandums or letters which would not be available by law to a party other than an agency in litigation with the agency.

The District Court granted summary judgment in favor of the President on the basis of the two exemptions claimed. The Court of Appeals found this judgment in error and instructed the Court to determine which non-secret components could be separated from the document as a whole and released and which materials claimed exempt under exemption (5) were purely factual information that could be separated from policymaking processes and released. Regarding exemption (1) the Supreme Court majority held that it was not the intent of

Congress to permit judicial inspection of national security documents to sift out so-called non-secret components, that citizens could not use the Freedom of Information Act to gain access to unclassified sections of secret and top secret national security papers. Concerning exemption (5) the majority held that agencies could be compelled to produce memoranda in court unless they could establish in advance that such papers could not legally be subpoenaed in an ordinary court case. It said the agency should be given an opportunity by detailed affidavits or oral testimony to establish to the satisfaction of the District Court that the documents sought were beyond the range of material that would be available to a private party in litigation with the agency.[26]

While the decision appeared stifling, it did hold out hope for better access to information in the future because it represented an interpretation by the Court of the intent of Congress rather than a ruling on constitutional claims. The Moorhead committee, which already was working on amendments to the Freedom of Information Act, indicated that it would seek to nullify the Supreme Court's Amchitka ruling and establish the guidelines suggested by the appellate court instead.

Representative Moorhead also proposed that legislative guidelines be substituted for executive orders in classifying government documents. He suggested the establishment of a nine-member independent classification review commission that would oversee a highly accelerated system of downgrading most documents and making them available to the public. The commission would include three members appointed by the President, three chosen by the Speaker of the House, and three chosen by the President pro tem of the Senate. It was pointed out that the proposal, if enacted, would for the first time provide for government classification by statute. The executive branch system of classification has rested on executive assumption of implied powers. Moorhead cited a pressing need for an improved and accelerated system of classifying documents. He pointed out that expert testimony before his subcommittee estimated that 75% to 99% of the hundreds of millions of so-called classified documents should not be classified at all.[27]

President Nixon took some steps toward improving the classification system when he issued an Executive Order on Classification and Declassification of National Security Information and Material, effective June 1, 1972. This order, which superseded an Executive Order issued by President Eisenhower, November 3, 1953, reduced the number of agencies and officials that can classify information and provided for more data to be made available more quickly to public and press. It further provided that classification policies be reviewed and that individuals adjudged responsible for "flagrant" overclassification receive administrative reprimands. The new order was expected to help some, but not relieve the major problem. It did not relax the Doctrine of Executive Privilege, it did not eliminate the system of nonselective classifying under which material that does not need to be classified is classified by virtue of being included along with classified materials, and it did not end the document-by-document approach to classification and declassification that requires so much time and expense. Robert Goralski, a Washington correspondent for NBC, in analyzing the new order expressed hope that it would help; but he suggested that it might do less actual good than former Deputy Secretary David Packard's action in ordering the Pentagon to stop buying more safes in which to hoard its secret documents.[28]

Continuing concern over the improper classification of documents was heightened in 1973 with the introduction of proposed reforms in the Federal Criminal Code. Senator Edmund S. Muskie described the bill, S. 1400, as an attempt to stifle the flow of information to the public. He said sections of the bill would prohibit and penalize disclosure of classified information regardless of whether it damaged security. Officials who disclosed such information could not defend their action by proving that the information was improperly classified. Newsmen who published the information could be penalized even though it was improperly classified, related to abuses, dishonesty or waste in government, and its publication clearly served the national interest. Senator Muskie pointed out in criticizing the proposal that adequate criminal sanctions against disclosure of true defense secrets already existed.[29]

The public's right to know was advanced in late 1974 when the Congress overrode a Presidential veto and adopted 17 amendments designed to close loopholes in the Freedom of Information Act. While favoring the legislation in principle, President Ford objected to provisions that would 1) authorize a federal judge to examine agency records privately to determine if they were properly withheld and overturn the agency's classification if he found the plaintiff's position just as reasonable, 2) permit access to additional law enforcement files unless the government could prove on a line-by-line examination that such disclosure would be harmful, and 3) reduce the time given an agency to respond to requests for documents—10 days to decide whether to withhold a document and 20 days for determinations on appeal.[30]

PROTECTION OF SOURCES

Newsmen have asserted with some success that the right to publish without prior restraints and the right to obtain information about government are essential to the success of the democratic system. Both rights are asserted on behalf of the public at large. Anyone should be able to publish without prior restraint, provided he is responsible for what he publishes; anyone should have broad access to information about his government. Some newsmen also assert that protection of confidential sources of information is essential to the free flow of information. They contend that forced disclosure of information about these sources to grand juries or other government bodies would dry up the sources and deprive the public of useful information. In this instance the newsmen are asserting the need for a special dispensation that would not be shared by the public at large. They are seeking a relationship somewhat similar to that assigned lawyers in dealing with their clients. It is argued that the investigative reporting which exposes corruption and other questionable practices in government and in the private sector often depends on protecting sources; to insist on revelation of these sources would eliminate them and greatly reduce the potential of investigative reporting.

So far newsmen have failed to establish protection of sources as a constitutional right through court action; they are continuing efforts to obtain statutory immunities at both federal and state levels. The U.S. Supreme Court in a five-four decision in June 1972, held that requiring newsmen to appear and testify before state or federal grand juries is not an abridgement of the freedom of speech and press guarantees of the First Amendment.[31] Three cases were included in the decision. One involved Earl Caldwell, a black reporter for the *New York Times* who had written extensively about militants in the San Francisco area. He was convicted of contempt for refusing to testify about activities of the Black Panthers before a federal grand jury. The Ninth Circuit Court of Appeals ruled, however, that Caldwell could not be forced to testify or even appear before the jury because to do so would jeopardize his relationship with his sources and abridge the freedom of the press. The Circuit Court said he could not be forced to appear unless the Justice Department could show a "compelling need" for his testimony.

The second case involved Paul Pappas, a reporter-cameraman for a New Bedford, Massachusetts, television station, who was held in contempt for refusing to tell a grand jury about what he had seen in a visit to a Black Panthers headquarters. He had been invited to the headquarters to witness an expected raid, but it did not take place. He had agreed not to write a story if there were no raid and he did not. He also refused to tell a grand jury what he observed. The highest court in Massachusetts ruled against him. The court held that there is no constitutional newsmen's privilege, either qualified or absolute, to refuse to appear before a court or grand jury.

The third case involved Paul M. Branzburg, a reporter for the *Louisville Courier-Journal* who refused to give two Kentucky grand juries information beyond his published eye-witness accounts of the manufacture and sale of hashish and marijuana. Branzburg sought protection under a Kentucky law that grants newsmen immunity from disclosing confidential sources, but the Kentucky Court of Appeals held that the statute does not apply to newsmen who see their sources commit a crime.

In its five-four decision the high court reversed the Ninth Circuit Court of Appeals ruling for Caldwell and upheld the Massachusetts and Kentucky court rulings against Pappas and Branzburg, respectively. Dissenting justices argued that the decision is harmful to the public. Justice William O. Douglas wrote that a "reporter is no better than his source of information. Unless he has a privilege to withhold the identity of his source, he will be the victim of governmental intrigue or aggression. If he can be summoned to testify in secret before a grand jury, his sources will dry up and the attempted exposure, the effort to enlighten the public will be ended. . . ." Justice Potter Stewart, in a dissent joined by Justices William J. Brennan, Jr. and Thurgood Marshall, said the Court's "crabbed view of the First Amendment reflects a disturbing insensitivity to the critical role of an independent press in our society. . . ." He wrote the majority view "invites state and federal authorities to undermine the historic independence of the press by attempting to annex the journalistic profession as an investigative arm of the government."

The majority rejected these arguments in refusing to grant newsmen immunities not shared by other citizens against testifying before grand juries. Justice Byron White, who wrote the majority opinion, reaffirmed many constitutional protections of the press. But he noted that the cases under discussion involved "no intrusions upon speech or assembly, no prior restraint or restriction on what the press may publish, and no express or implied command that the press publish what it prefers to withhold. No exaction or tax for the privilege of publishing, and no penalty, civil or criminal, related to the content of published material is at issue here. The use of confidential sources by the press is not forbidden or restricted; reporters remain free to seek news from any source by means within the law. No attempt is made to require the press to publish its sources of information or indiscriminately to disclose them on request."

The sole issue in the majority's view was whether newsmen should be granted privileges not enjoyed by other citizens to protect confidential relationships with their informers. This they refused to do. Said Justice White, "On the records now before us, we perceive no basis for holding that the public interest in law enforcement and in ensuring effective grand jury proceedings is insufficient to override the consequential, but uncertain burden on newsgathering which is said to result from insisting that reporters, like other citizens, respond to relevant questions put to them in the course of a valid grand jury investigation or criminal trial."

The majority viewpoint rejected the "compelling need" concept suggested by the California court. Although it indicated that such a need existed in the instant cases to carry out legitimate grand jury functions, it questioned the wisdom of making that the standard. First, a conditional privilege probably would not satisfy the fears of those who wished to remain unmasked. Second, it would be very difficult to administer the rule. As Justice White pointed out, "Sooner or later, it would be necessary to define those categories of newsmen who qualified for the privilege, a questionable procedure in light of the traditional doctrine that liberty of the press is the right of the lonely pamphleteer who uses carbon paper or mimeograph just as much as of the large metropolitan publisher who utilizes the latest photocomposition methods." Moreover, in making decisions about which instances met the compelling need requirement, the courts could become embroiled in decisions about which laws to enforce, a legislative rather than judicial function.

Justice Lewis F. Powell, Jr. wrote a brief concurring opinion "to emphasize what seems to me to be the limited nature of the Court's holding. The Court does not hold that newsmen, subpoenaed to testify before a grand jury, are without constitutional rights with respect to the gathering of news or in safeguarding their sources. Certainly, we do not hold, as suggested in the dissenting opinion, that state and federal authorities are free to 'annex' the news media as 'an investigative arm of government.' The solicitude repeatedly shown by this Court for First Amendment freedoms should be sufficient assurance against any such effort, even if one seriously believed that the media—properly free and untrammeled in the fullest sense of these terms—were not able to protect themselves."

Although some of the points raised in the majority decision suggest that newsmen's privilege statutes could run into problems if not carefully constructed, the court left open the possibility of legislative remedies. Said Justice White, "At the federal level, Congress has freedom to determine whether a statutory newsmen's privilege is necessary and desirable and to fashion standards and rules as narrow or broad as deemed necessary to address the evil discerned and, equally important, to refashion those rules as experience from time to time may dictate. There is also merit in leaving state legislatures free, within First Amendment limits, to fashion their own standards in light of the conditions and problems with respect to the relations between law enforcement officials and press in their own areas."

Some newsmen and others responded to the high court's decision by renewed efforts to obtain passage of laws, sometimes called "shield laws" or "confidentiality laws," to protect newsmen from having to reveal their sources to government inquiries. At the time of the 1972 decision less than two-fifths of the states had such laws, and the decision raised questions about the usefulness of some of those. There was no federal law either, although several proposals had been offered in Congress.

Among the national proposals discussed in the wake of the 1972 decision was an absolute shield law sponsored by the American Newspaper Publishers Association entitled "The Free Flow of Information Act." It sought to protect newsmen from having to disclose "a source of information or disclose unpublished information" in "any proceeding or investigation before or by any federal or state judicial, legislative, executive or administrative body. . . ." The act was termed necessary "to insure the free flow of information and to implement the First and Fourteenth Amendments and Article I, Section 8 of the Constitution." The act would apply to those who gather, write or edit information for the media, which would include but not be limited to "any newspaper, magazine, other periodical, book, pamphlet, news service, wire service, news or feature syndicate, broadcast station or network, or cable television system. . . .[32]

This proposal and others which provided for limited shields were discussed at Congressional hearings in early 1973 and both inside and outside Congress in subsequent months. The newsmen themselves were divided on the issue. Some argued that an absolute shield was essential for the press to engage successfully in investigative reporting; they said that confidential sources would dry up without it. Others seemed willing to accept a partial shield; such a shield might protect reporters from revealing sources unless there was a compelling and overriding public need for the information and it could not be obtained in any other way. Many objected to any shield law at all; they argued that the Constitution was sufficient to protect the press and that any law might tend to diminish its effectiveness. Some persons argued that a shield was needed to prevent the press being made an investigative arm of the government; others argued that a shield would encourage irresponsible journalism.

Representatives of the Justice Department said that the Attorney General's "Guidelines for Subpoenas to the News Media," adopted in 1970, afforded sufficient protection to the legitimate interests of the press. These guidelines, clarified and amplified in late 1973, stated in part that the Justice Department will seek information desired from non-media sources before comtemplating a subpoena of a media person and that the Attorney General must authorize any subpoenas issued.[33] The guidelines evidently did help reduce the number of federal subpoenas issued in the early 1970s, but at the same time the number of subpoenas being used against newsmen at state and local levels was increasing.[34]

Many looked to additional court decisions to clarify the question of newsman's privilege, but such clarification had not come by the middle of 1974. Professor David Gordon of Northwestern University reported in a study published by the Freedom of Information Foundation that the privilege issue had been back in the court at least a dozen times, but that its status was not clear. "It appears that there is little First Amendment protection for confidentiality before properly functioning grand juries; only slightly more in criminal trial proceedings," he reported. "In civil proceedings, although the situation is quite unclear, the balance has perhaps weighted slightly in favor of journalistic privilege in the post-Branzburg cases." [35]

Gallup polls reported in late 1972 and late 1973 indicated strong and increasing public support for the protection of reporters from having to reveal their sources. Respondents in both polls were given this question: "Suppose a newspaper reporter obtains information for a news article he is writing from a person who asks that his name be withheld. Do you think that the reporter should or should not be required to reveal the name of this man if he is taken to court to testify about the information in the news article?" In the 1973 poll, 62% as compared with 57% in 1972, said he should not have to reveal the source, 27% as compared with 34% in 1972 said he should, and 11% as compared with 9% in 1972 offered no opinion.[36]

But Congress and the states still had to decide whether reporters should rely on an absolute shield, a partial shield, or the Constitution as interpreted by the courts for their protection. General agreement was reported in early 1974 between a House judiciary subcommittee and representatives of some major news media organizations on what appeared to be a partial shield. The bill provided that newsmen would not be required to reveal confidential information or its source to a state or federal grand jury or in any pretrial proceeding but would be required to disclose it in an actual trial if the information were deemed indispensable to the prosecution or defense case, it could not be obtained from any other source, and there was a compelling public interest.[37]

The prospects for favorable Congressional action were dimmed, however, when the House of Delegates of the American Bar Association voted 157 to 122 not to support such legislation. Proponents in the debate at the association's meeting in early 1974 argued that a shield law was necessary to enable journalists to expose government corruption at all levels. They said it would protect the general public's interest in freedom of information. Opponents argued such a law could encourage violations of grand jury secrecy. They said it could limit the ability of libel victims to protect themselves against irresponsible reporting, and predicted that such a law, if passed, might eventually lead to demands by the public for regulation of the press.[38]

Six states adopted shield laws during 1973 to bring the total number of states that had some sort of protection for newsmen to 25. The protection afforded under these laws varies greatly, however. Prior to 1973 newsmen relying on state statutes were successful in defending against compulsory disclosure in only three of 16 cases. It was not certain what deterrent value the shield laws had upon aggressive prosecutors.[39]

Any statute adopted by Congress or the states would, of course, be subject to constitutional challenges. Would an absolute shield law for reporters violate rights guaranteed all citizens under the Sixth Amendment? Would a qualified privilege, or even an absolute one, violate the First Amendment proviso that Congress shall make no law abridging freedom of speech or of the press? The need to keep information flowing was becoming more accepted in the middle 1970s, but the means to assure the flow were open to continued debate.

Access to the Media

Many persons today are agreed that individual freedom and democratic government are fostered by laws that assure to the public and press access to information about government and public affairs. Some maintain that furtherance of these goals also requires laws that would guarantee public access to the media. They contend that the cost of engaging in media operations has become so great and the number of media units so small that existing media must assume to some degree the role of common carriers. They must be open to divergent views if the individual's right to speak and the public's right to hear divergent views are to be realized.

Dean Jerome A. Barron of the Syracuse University College of Law has suggested that an informed public opinion and democracy itself will be endangered unless right of access to the mass news channels is extended to all points of view. He wrote that the First Amendment must be returned to its true proprietors—the readers, viewers and listeners—and that press freedom must be more than a guarantee of property rights for media owners. Barron wrote that the right of access should include the right of reply to an attack and the right to purchase advertising for expression of opinion. He argued that access laws would leave news columns to the judgment of the paper's staff and publisher but assure openness in areas such as editorial pages and advertising. He said that assuring the right of reply to an attack only implements that debate which presumably freedom of the press exists to assure.[40]

Newspaper officials argue that public access laws would violate their rights to control their products and invite further governmental interference in the press. They argue that such laws could discourage newspapers from speaking out on issues and reporting election campaigns and open up a flood of irrelevant material and harangue which could crowd important news out of the newspaper. They contend that newspapers voluntarily provide an adequate means of reply through their letters to the editor columns, news stories and advertising.

As the 1970s opened it appeared that the courts agreed with the newspapers' contention that they should not be forced to give access to their news or advertising columns. Courts had upheld a right of access to school newspapers in state-supported schools; but they had rejected the idea that private enterprise newspapers could be required to grant access. One of the key cases was *Chicago Joint Board v. Chicago Tribune Company* in 1969.[41] It involved a union which sought to place advertisements in four Chicago newspapers to explain its position in a dispute with a Chicago department store. When the newspapers refused to print the advertisement, the union sued. It asserted that it had a "right of access" under the First Amendment. The federal district court rejected the idea of state involvement advanced by the union, and the Seventh U.S. Circuit Court rejected an expanded argument of state involvement and public interest. The Circuit Court said that newspapers were not like company towns or shopping centers; the newspapers had not consented to unrestricted access to their advertising pages and these pages could not be pressed into service against the publishers' wills. The Supreme Court declined to review the case.[42]

Those urging a right of public access to newspapers got brief encouragement in 1973 when the Florida Supreme Court held that a 60-year-old access law in that state was constitutional.[43] The law says, in essence, that if a newspaper assails the personal character of a candidate or otherwise attacks his political record that the newspaper shall provide equal space for him to reply. The case arose when an unsuccessful candidate for the Florida legislature sued the *Miami Herald* for refusing to print verbatim his replies to two editorials it ran that were critical of him. The Dade County Circuit Court held that law unconstitutional. It said that if the state cannot prohibit what a newspaper may print it cannot assume the editorial function and direct the newspaper what to print. The State Supreme Court, in a six-one decision, reversed the circuit court. It said the law was designed to add to the flow of information and ideas and did not constitute an incursion upon First Amendment rights. The court suggested that a right of reply was needed to assure that citizens could obtain information about all sides of a controversy. The *Herald* appealed the decision to the U.S. Supreme Court. It argued that the statute imposes governmental controls on editorial decisions to publish critical stories about political candidates and places the government in the editor's chair. It said that censorship in the guise of promoting fairness is still censorship. The U.S. Supreme Court in June 1974 reversed the Florida Supreme Court's ruling by holding that the right of reply law violated the First Amendment and is unconstitutional. Chief Justice Warren Burger delivered the opinion for a unanimous court. Justice Byron White and Justice William J. Brennan, joined by Justice William H. Rehnquist, delivered separate concurring opinions. Justice Burger said that the government could not compel editors or publishers to publish that which reason tells them should not be published. He described the Florida statute as an intrusion into the function of editors. "A newspaper is more than a passive receptacle or conduit for news, comment, and advertising," he wrote. "The choice of material to go into a newspaper, and the decisions made as to limitations on the size of the paper, and content, and treatment of public issues and public officials— whether fair or unfair—constitutes the exercise of editorial control and judgment. It has yet to be demonstrated how governmental regulation of this crucial process can be exercised consistent with First Amendment guarantees of a free press as they have evolved to this time." [44]

FREE PRESS AND FAIR TRIALS

Important constitutional questions related to the First and Sixth Amendments have been raised in connection with the press-bar debate over coverage of the judicial system. At stake are the individual's rights under the Sixth Amendment to a fair trial and the public's rights under the First Amendment to receive information about crime and the administration of justice. Members of the press and bar generally agree that the rights were intended to be complementary, not contentious; the Supreme Court has refused to assert the primacy of one section of the Bill of Rights over any other and has consistently treated them as equal. But disagreements have arisen over the specific procedures to follow in administering the rights and the extent to which reports concerning crimes, persons accused of crimes, and judicial procedures can prejudice juries and make fair trials impossible.

The conflict is not new, but it has received increasing attention since 1959 when the Supreme Court ruled that a defendant had not received a fair trial because of prejudicial newspaper publicity despite statements of jurors that they would not be influenced by news articles. In five subsequent cases the courts reaffirmed the rule that prejudicial publicity may be grounds for setting aside convictions.[45] Additional attention was focused on the issue in 1964 by the Warren Commission report on the results of its investigation into the assassination of President John F. Kennedy and the launching of a massive study by the American Bar Association to explore the total criminal justice process. One committee was assigned to study questions related to fair trial and free press. It was headed by Justice Paul C. Reardon of the Supreme Judicial Court of Massachusetts, and its report and recommendations, released in October 1966, came to be known as the Reardon report. Included in the report are recommendations relating to the conduct of attorneys in criminal cases, the conduct of law enforcement officers, judges, and judicial employes in criminal cases, the conduct of judicial proceedings in criminal cases, and the exercise of the contempt power.[46] These standards were approved by the American Bar Association House of Delegates in February 1968.

Newsmen objected to some of the recommendations, and an effort was was made in 1969 to get representatives of the American Bar Association, the American Society of Newspaper Editors and other newspaper groups together to resolve their differences. Out of the meetings came a general agreement to work for the adoption of voluntary guidelines at the state level concerning procedures for covering the criminal process.[47] A number of states already had such guidelines, and by 1972 almost half of the states had adopted guidelines and several others were considering them. Although problems were reported in states with guidelines, the approach appeared to serve the interests of all concerned. A survey taken by the Freedom of Information Committee of the Associated Press Managing Editors Association reported in early 1973 was encouraging. Editors, lawyers and judges were surveyed, and a large majority of those replying in the 23 states with guidelines indicated that the codes had resulted in improved news coverage of trials and arrests while protecting freedom of the press and fair trial.[48]

Since half of the states did not have guidelines and violations had been reported in some that did, the future of the press-bar controversy was still uncertain in the middle 1970s. Many in the press were concerned that what they considered objectionable aspects of the Reardon Report might be adopted or other restrictive measures taken by judges and other officials. Press-bar disagreements concerning the Reardon Report have developed in the following areas: 1) Official release of prior criminal records of accused persons; official sources are asked not to release such information, but the press can obtain it on its own initiative. 2) Use of contempt power of the courts; the American Bar Association suggests that its recommendation is a narrow interpretation of the court's powers. It suggests that the contempt power may be exercised during the trial "against a person who disseminates an extrajudicial statement by any means of public communication that is 'willfully designed by that person' to affect the outcome of the trial, or who makes such a statement intending it to be so disseminated. Also against a person who knowingly violates a valid judicial order not to disseminate (until completion of the trial) specified information referred to in the course of a judicial hearing closed to the public." 3) Closure of pretrial hearings at the discretion of the courts when prejudicial information may be disclosed; the defendant can request that all or a part of the hearing be closed to the public, provided that a complete record of the proceedings is kept and made available to the public after the disposition of the case. 4) Pretrial release of "confessions," or the results of examinations or tests; information as to the performance of any examination or test, or the accused's refusal or failure to submit to an examination is not to be released; and 5) Photographing and interviewing of accused persons or their counsel; it is recommended that the deliberate posing of a person in custody for photographing or televising be prohibited and that interviews with such persons not be granted unless the accused requests an interview in writing or consents to one after being informed of his right to refuse an interview.[49]

Many newsmen reject efforts by the American Bar Association or others to restrict pretrial news; they contend that neither lawyers nor publishers have a right to bargain away the right of the people to know about crime and the operation of the judicial process. The special committee of the American Newspaper Publishers Association on Free Press and Fair Trial presented a lengthy argument against any restrictions in a report issued in 1967. The committee's report read in part: "Even granted that in rare and isolated cases pre-trial reporting may be a factor in creating an overriding prejudice in potential jurors, there are procedural remedies present to provide effective safeguards. Such procedural safeguards include change of venue, change of venire, continuance, severance, voir dire, blue ribbon juries, isolation of the jury, instructions, retrial, appeal, and habeas corpus. Our studies indicate that these remedies are fully adequate to protect the rights of a defendant." [50]

Members of the press must be careful in considering press-bar guidelines and in all their activities not to bargain away the people's rights. They must work with the courts and the lawyers in efforts to resolve differences; fair, accurate, unsensational reporting may be their most effective approach in convincing these interests that full coverage is beneficial, not detrimental to the judicial process. Finally, they must take their case to the people whose support can assure that the people's right to know and the individual's right to a fair trial are complementary, not exclusive interests.

LIBEL AND PRIVACY

Newspapers and citizens generally have a great deal of freedom today to provide information and commentary about public officials, public figures, and other persons involved in matters of public interest. Court decisions in the past decade have dramatically changed the status of libel laws in the United States and markedly changed the status of those concerning invasion of privacy. The newspaper that is doing a fair and conscientious job of reporting matters of public interest is not likely to have problems in either area unless present court trends are reversed.

Libel laws vary from state to state. But prior to 1964 any published statement about an identifiable person that held him up to public contempt, scorn, or ridicule or tended to injure him in his business or professional standing probably would have been considered libelous in most states. The primary defenses against libel suits were truth, fair comment and criticism of public persons acting in their public capacities, and the fair and accurate reporting of privileged materials such as court and legislative records. The burden was on the newspaper or other party accused of libel to prove the truth of its statements and demonstrate its fairness in reporting.

The Supreme Court's decision in 1964 in *New York Times Co. v. Sullivan*[51] redefined libel and transferred the burden from the defendant to the plaintiff. The Court held that First Amendment guarantees prohibit a public official from recovery for a defamatory falsehood relating to his official conduct unless he can prove that the statement was made with "'actual malice''—that is, with the knowledge that it was false or with reckless disregard of whether it was false or not. In a subsequent case in 1967, *St. Amant v. Thompson*,[52] the Court further clarified what it means by "reckless disregard." It suggested that "reckless disregard" is not determined by whether a reasonably prudent man would have published or would have investigated before publishing; rather it requires that the publisher have entertained serious doubts about the truth of the statement involved.

Subsequent cases provided additional clarification and expansion of the *Times-Sullivan* doctrine. The principle was extended to public figures as well as public officials in 1967 in *Associated Press v. Edwin A. Walker* and *Curtis Publishing Company v. Wallace Butts*.[53] Walker, a retired Army general, sued Associated Press for statements made about him in a report concerning the integration of the University of Mississippi. Butts, who had just resigned as athletic director of the University of Georgia, sued the *Saturday Evening Post* for statements accusing him of participating in a plot to fix a football game involving the university. The court held that both men were public figures; it reversed a judgment against the Associated Press but upheld one for Mr. Butts. It ruled against General Walker because no actual malice was shown in the spot news report of the Associated Press; it held, however, that the *Post* had shown "reckless disregard for the truth" in its magazine story about Mr. Butts.

The new approach to libel was extended in 1971 to include private persons involved in matters of public or general interest. In *Rosenbloom v. Metromedia Inc.*,[54] the Court ruled against a magazine distributor who sued radio station WIP in Philadelphia for publishing statements he said were tantamount to calling him a criminal. He was arrested on a criminal charge of selling obscene material, but later was acquitted. The Pennsylvania Court of Appeals overturned a verdict in his favor and the U.S. Supreme Court affirmed that ruling. In what has been described as a plurality decision, the court said, "We honor the commitment to robust debate on public issues, which is embodied in the First Amendment, by extending constitutional protection to all discussion and communication involving matters of public or general concern, without regard to whether persons involved are famous or anonymous. . . ." Three members of the court promulgated the rule of law; two concurred in the decision but did not fully endorse the rule; three dissented; one abstained. At least five members of the Court would support the following rules suggested by Justice White: "For public officers and public figures to recover for damage to their reputations for libelous falsehoods, they must prove either knowing or reckless disregard of the truth. All other plaintiffs must prove at least negligent falsehood, but if the publication about them was in an area of legitimate public interest, then they too must prove deliberate or reckless error. In all actions for libel or slander, actual damages must be proved, and awards of punitive damages will be strictly limited."[55]

The Supreme Court modified its position on libel in 1974 to draw a sharp distinction between public officials and public figures on the one hand and ordinary citizens on the other. In *Gertz v. Robert Welch, Inc.*, the court held that an ordinary citizen could recover actual damages in cases involving matters of public interest by showing that a false statement was published negligently; to collect punitive damages the ordinary citizen would have to show that the statement complained of was made in the knowledge that it was false or with reckless disregard for the truth. Justice Lewis F. Powell, writing for the majority in the 5–4 decision, said that the ordinary citizen as contrasted with the public official or public figure, "has relinquished no part of his interest in the protection of his own good name, and consequently he has a more compelling call on the courts for redress of injury inflicted by defamatory falsehoods." Powell said the state legislatures may decide what standards of carefulness and accuracy should be imposed on publishers and broadcasters. It appears that in the future the state courts will be called upon to define the boundaries of negligence and determine who is an ordinary citizen as opposed to a public figure.[56]

Court decisions in recent years also have reduced somewhat the number of situations in which an individual may successfully assert a right of privacy. In 1967 the Supreme Court extended the constitutional guarantees of freedom of the press to include right of privacy cases. The court held, in *Time, Inc. v. Hill*,[57] that "newsworthy" persons cannot collect damages for invasion of privacy unless they can prove that the defendant published the report with knowledge of its falsity or in reckless disregard of the truth. In addition, the decision pointed out that a person may become newsworthy involuntarily. This case involved a 1955 article in *Life*, "True Crime Inspires Tense Play," about the opening of a new play, "The Desperate Hours," in which a family is held hostage by escaped convicts. The author said the play had been inspired by a true-life incident involving the Hill family in 1952. The Hill family did not suffer violence; the family in the play did. *Life* posed actors in the house where the Hill family was held captive, and the article contained pictures allegedly showing Hill and members of his family being mistreated. Hill sued under a New York law that prohibits the use "for advertising purposes or for the purposes of trade the name, portrait or picture of any living person without first having obtained the written consent of such person." He charged that *Life* knew that the family's experience as mirrored in the play "was false and untrue." *Life* contended that the article was "basically truthful." [58] The court upheld *Life's* position, but there were four dissents to Justice Brennan's application of the *Times-Sullivan* falsity standards to this case, and the future of the rule in privacy cases remains uncertain.

It appears that the rule would apply to only one of four privacy torts as they were summarized by a Delaware court. It would apply to placing the plaintiff in a false position in the public eye, but would not apply to intrusion upon the plaintiff's physical solitude, publication of private matters violating the ordinary decencies, or appropriation of some element of the plaintiff's personality for commercial use.[59]

In the early 1970s 33 states and the District of Columbia recognized some kind of legal right of privacy. The status of all these laws was not certain, however. Newsworthiness is generally a good defense, but not always. For example, the identity of rape victims is protected in several states. Placing someone in a false light can also be cause for trouble. The *Saturday Evening Post* was sued successfully when it used a picture of a small child being run down by a car to illustrate an article about pedestrian carelessness. The child had been hit while crossing in a marked crosswalk and won the suit on the grounds that her role had been reversed and she had been put in a false light.[60]

New court guidelines on privacy may be forthcoming in 1975 as a result of cases heard by the U.S. Supreme Court in late 1974. One involved a woman in West Virginia who asserted that her privacy had been violated by what she said was a false article describing the effect on her family of her husband's death in the collapse of a bridge. The other case involved a challenge to a Georgia law which forbids broadcasters and newspapers to identify rape victims. In this case a television station identified the victim after her alleged attackers were indicted for murder.[61]

In summary, it appears that newspapers and other media have made considerable progress in their efforts to assert the "right to publish" and the "right to know." Some previously closed information sources have been opened; some efforts to thwart reporting and commentary have been resisted successfully. As James J. Kilpatrick suggested in October 1971, "Freedom of the press has not merely survived, it has flourished. Americans today have access to more information and opinion than they have ever had. This material is presented far more readably and attractively than it was in the days of the 'party press.' It is timely. Most of it is objective." [62] But the struggle continues. Loopholes in access laws, efforts to exercise prior restraints, possible misuse of subpoenas, and other problems remain. The press must continue the fight, and it must convince the people that the struggle for a free press is their struggle, too. Freedom of the press is embodied in the Constitution for the benefit of all the people; all must be concerned with upholding it for everyone. The concerns of newspapers noted here are equally the concerns of the people at large. All Americans must be made aware that it is their First Amendment, too, that it is their freedoms which are at stake.

7

Revolutions in
Newspaper Technology

THE CONTINUING SUCCESS of newspapers will depend to a great extent on their ability and willingness to develop and adopt new technology to carry out their information functions. Newspapers can provide services not available through any other medium, but they face increasing competition for the individual's time and money from other media and other activities. They also face spiraling costs for the personnel and equipment to do their work. The use of new methods and new technology is essential to their success if not their survival. Since print is indispensable to acquiring much of the information individuals need, it is essential to human progress and democratic government that efficient, economic ways be developed to use it effectively. Newspapers that change with the times can continue to be an important source of printed information and vital participants in the continuing human story.

Newspaper production developments have tended to reflect the expansion of knowledge and the need of individuals and groups to communicate with each other. Newspaper technology did not change greatly from Johann Gutenberg's breakthrough about 1450 until the latter half of the nineteenth century. But as knowledge increased rapidly in the century and the need to communicate grew, new methods of communication were developed. The major technological advances at the turn of the century seemed sufficient to meet early twentieth century needs; but when the knowledge explosion came in the middle of the century, a computer-oriented revolution came to the communications media. Newspapers and other media sought to meet the challenge.

Some publishers were hesitant to join the technology revolution of the 1960s, in part because changes were coming fast and equipment was expensive. But as an increasing number took the plunge into offset, photocomposi-

234

tion, letterpress adaptations and electronics, their experience made it easier and cheaper for others to follow. This chapter will outline existing newspaper production and printing systems, explore the electronic revolution that gained momentum in the early 1970s, and suggest some of the possible directions which newspaper technology may take in the next decade or so.

Most newspapers in the early 1970s were using either letterpress or offset systems to produce their basic products; some turned to gravure for the production of special sections such as Sunday magazines. Letterpress, or relief printing, involves the transfer of an impression from a raised, inked surface to newsprint or other material. Offset is a photochemical printing process based on the art of lithography. Both will be discussed at some length later in the chapter. The gravure printing image is formed in tiny dots below the surface of a printing cylinder rather than above. Ink is placed in the dots or wells and their depth determines the tone of the resultant image. Gravure sometimes produces a fuzzy effect on type characters, but is a very effective system for reproducing pictures. The comparatively long time involved in preparing printing cylinders and other factors have made it less practical for regular production than letterpress or offset, but it is effective for special sections.[1]

Letterpress Developments

Letterpress printing, which is still employed by most of the nation's large newspapers, had its origin in the 1450s and remained the primary system for printing most newspapers until the 1950s. Its introduction by Gutenberg and others provided one of the major breakthroughs in communication. Gutenberg developed the means to cast individual type letters that could be held together in sentences for printing and then separated and used again. The letters were raised above the surface of the type and created a printed image when they were inked and paper was pressed against them. Gutenberg used a press somewhat similar to the wine presses of the day. A wooden frame held the type in place on a flat bed of wood. Ink was placed on the type, then paper, and a wooden platen controlled by a lever screw pressed the paper down on the type.

Gutenberg set each letter of type into place by hand at the rate of about one line a minute, and so did everyone else until a second revolution in printing evolved in the late nineteenth century. One major aspect of this revolution was the development of the Linotype, or line of type, machine by Ottmar Mergenthaler in Baltimore in 1886. The Linotype, still in use in many shops, has a mechanical capacity for creating type letters and a keyboard similar to that of a typewriter. As each letter is typed by a Linotype operator a mold of that letter falls into place in the machine. When a line of molds and spaces is completed, molten lead is poured into them and a line of type is produced. These lines are arranged in columns as they are produced and then removed from the machine and taken to the tables where page makeup is done. Using Mergenthaler's machine, operators could set type at almost five lines a minute, a major advance.

Other major technological advances brought together in the production of newspapers in the late nineteenth century included the stereotype, the webfed rotary press, the half-tone engraving, wood pulp paper, and techniques for printing in colors. The press used by Gutenberg was not greatly modified until the early nineteenth century when printers adapted the steam engine to it and doubled the number of impressions that could be made from about 100 to about 200 an hour. This number was increased twelve-fold and mass circulation made feasible when Friedrich Koenig in England developed a rotary press. The rotary press with its continuous web of paper being printed on both sides as it passes through was made feasible by the development of the stereotype. The stereotype is a solid metal reproduction of a page of type. It is created by making an impression of the page in papier-mache rather than paper, then placing this mat in a form and pouring molten lead against it. This process can be used for creating flat plates for long press runs on flatbed presses. But the big advantage is that curved plates for rotary presses can be produced by placing the papier-mache in cylinders. The curved plates can be placed on the rotary press and the paper moved through them at accelerated speeds. The stereotype also facilitated the use of pictures, multicolumn headlines, and multicolumn advertisements because it was a solid piece that could not pi, or fall apart. In some of the early power presses, the page forms moved during printing and it was essential to use full column rules to help hold them tightly together.

Development of the half-tone engraving process enabled newspapers and other printed media to achieve attractive reproduction of pictures. The process involves taking a picture of a picture through a screen which cuts it into thousands of tiny dots. This image is projected onto a photosensitized metal plate which is treated with acid to lower the metal around the dots. These dots pick up the ink in printing just as the raised metal letters do. Dark areas in a picture have many ink-bearing dots, shaded areas some, and white areas none. These photo-engravings, or cuts, are placed into page forms along with the type set by Linotype or other machines. Mats and stereotypes can then be made, or the paper can be printed directly from the forms.

The development of a paper made from wood pulp rather than from cloth or other materials was a major breakthrough because it greatly reduced the cost of paper. A comparatively inexpensive paper, or newsprint, was essential to financing the mass circulations developed in the late nineteenth century. The development of color printing was important also, although its primary use in newspapers until recent years has been in special sections such as the comics. The typewriter and the telephone, developed in the late nineteenth century, also helped, at least indirectly, to improve newspaper production. The typewriter not only produced copy faster, but it made it easier for printers to read and helped reduce errors. The telephone accelerated the gathering of information and enabled newspapers to check quickly on reports and rumors.

Technological developments such as the stereotype and half-tone engraving were developed over a period of many years, but they were not applied in concert until Joseph Pulitzer, William Randolph Hearst and others produced the mass-circulation newspapers of the late nineteenth century. This breakthrough was so spectacular and so greatly improved the production of newspapers that most publishers were content just to modify what had been achieved until the middle of the twentieth century. Little else seemed necessary.

One modification in typesetting procedures was particularly far-reaching, however, and may be seen as the precursor of the current newspaper production revolution. A Teletypesetter device was invented in the 1930s that accelerated the production of Linotype machines. This device made it possible to operate the machines by use of a perforated paper tape rather than an operator continually typing on a keyboard. This increased the speed of typesetting and eliminated some of the pauses inherent in operation by human beings who may not be able to understand a sentence or who must rest their eyes a moment. Operators still had to feed the tapes into the machines, but the machines could operate at their optimum speed of between five and six lines a minute. The tapes were produced by typists who punched them on perforator machines from the edited copy. The potential speed of the perforators was reduced by the necessity of justifying lines, but the overall operation was a big step forward.

Wire services encouraged the development of the system in the 1950s by providing a perforated tape version of their stories for subscribers that ordered them. This step enabled many newspapers to accelerate type production, although it did tend to discourage the editing of wire service copy and pushed newspapers toward a uniform style sheet for editing. Many newspapers also purchased perforators to handle locally written copy, and their shops became increasingly automated. As might be expected, the elimination of some jobs evoked union opposition, but many papers sought to resolve it by attrition or by retraining programs.

What may be the full potential of the Linotype-Teletypesetter combination was reached in the 1960s when the computer was incorporated in the typesetting process. Computers were programmed to handle the hyphenation and justification of lines that had slowed the speed of perforator or tape-punch operators. These persons can now type a continuous tape as rapidly as possible without regard to division into lines. This tape is fed into a computer that is programmed to justify the lines using proper methods of hyphenation. By the 1960s the speed of setting type had risen to about 14 lines a minute, a significant advance. But it was soon overshadowed by developments in cold type production, and publishers of letterpress as well as offset newspapers looked to cold type as the type-setting method of the future.

Cold Type/Photocomposition

Cold type systems have been developed extensively in the past two decades in conjunction with the adaptation of offset printing to the publication of newspapers. Cold type copy preparation seems especially well suited to offset, which does not need hot metal at typesetting or printing stages. But methods have been developed to use it in conjunction with letterpress printing as well. The term refers to reproducing copy on paper as a typewriter might produce it rather than in hot metal as a Linotype produces it. The punched tape provided by wire services or produced by perforator machines installed in the newspaper's plant can be used to activate cold type equipment as well as hot type machines.

Cold type has been an integral part of the offset operation and has become increasingly important in letterpress operations because of its flexibility and speed. Type on paper can be manipulated much more readily in advertisements and other layouts than can type in metal. Type can also be produced much faster by cold type methods than in hot metal. The big breakthrough has been photocomposition, which uses optics and electronics to project images of letters on photosensitized paper. It can project these letters in many sizes and styles at various line lengths.[2] Phototypesetting machines can be activated by tapes and they can be tied into some of the sophisticated electronic systems described later in this chapter. The machines photographically reproduce type on sheets which can be cut and pasted on a makeup page for subsequent photographing and plate-making. In the middle 1960s phototypesetting machines were introduced that could produce type at the rate of 80 lines a minute; by the middle 1970s machines were developed that could produce type at 150 to 175 lines a minute.[3]

Many newspapers switched to phototypesetting in the late 1960s and early 1970s to take advantage of its quality, flexibility and speed, and others were expected to make the shift in the latter part of the decade. Photocomposition was not without problems, however, in areas such as mark-up, the correction cycle and proofing.When a single line was corrected, for example, it was sometimes troublesome to get the new line pasted down properly and keep it there until the page was photographed. The answer appeared to lie in electronic systems that would eliminate errors before the type was set. Systems were also being developed to enable an editor to give a simple instruction such as "Use Style 126" and let the computer handle the details.[4]

Peter P. Romano of the ANPA Research Institute predicted in early 1973 that photocomposition would be replaced within ten years by cathode ray tube composition systems. He said that he believed such machines would be designed and priced so that even the smallest newspapers could take advantage of them.[5] But during the 1960s and early 1970s photocomposition fostered a revolution in newspaper technology that greatly enhanced the production of both letterpress and offset newspapers.

Letterpress Changes

As the potential of cold type and photocomposition became known, publishers of letterpress newspapers sought ways in which they could help realize it. A first step for many was the use of cold type in setting advertisements, which could then be engraved and used in the regular hot metal/letterpress system. This approach provided greater flexibility in the design and layout of advertisements and appealed to advertisers as well as to newspaper publishers. The publishers also explored the possibility of developing plates and procedures that would enable them to use cold type for all of their copy. Various companies conducted research to help them, and by the middle 1970s some of the systems were in operation.

Many newspapers turned to the use of plastic relief plates in place of the traditional stereotype. These plates are produced by a photographic process somewhat similar to the one used in making offset plates. Entire pages are set in cold type and photographed on the plates. The most widely adopted plastic plates in the early 1970s were the Letterflex plate made by the W. R. Grace Company and the Dyna-Flex plate developed by Dyna-Flex Corporation. The Letterflex plates were being used by newspapers as large as the *Cincinnati Post* and *Washington Star-News* in 1973 and the Dyna-Flex plates were being used by a number of newspapers in the 100,000 circulation class and smaller. Several users of these plates reported in 1973 that their color capabilities were comparable to those of stereotype plates once the problems involved in their use were ironed out.[6] One of the early problems with the new direct printing plates involved mounting them on the presses. They are thinner than stereotypes, and adjustments had to be made to accommodate the difference. On the plus side, the plates are also lighter than stereotypes, which makes them easier to handle and may facilitate higher press speeds.[7]

Some newspapers looked to the development of shallow relief engravings of zinc and magnesium to make the conversion to photocomposition with letterpress. Still others, especially some with large circulations, explored other possibilities, including the use of pattern plates. These plates were used to transfer the image picked up from the cold type to the traditional stereotype. Their use enabled newspapers to take advantage of cold type without abandoning the use and benefits of their stereotype equipment. The Grace and Dyna-Flex companies were among several companies that worked with the ANPA Research Institute in the development of pattern plates.[8]

Still other newspapers explored the possibilities of Di-Litho printing to make fuller use of cold type. In this system, the presses are modified to accommodate lithographic or offset plates. Dampening units must be mounted on the presses to provide the water needed for the ink/water printing system. Although the lithographic plates are commonly called offset plates, the Di-Litho printing operation should not be confused with offset because the printing is done directly from the plates. The Dahlgren Company of Dallas and Inland Newspaper Machinery Corp. of Kansas City introduced the system in 1970, and by 1973 it was being used in eight newspapers in the United States and South America. The Cottell division of Harris Intertype also developed a Di-Litho process.[9]

Gannett Company, Inc., reported in the fall of 1973 that it had successfully field-tested a laser-plate system for combining cold type and letterpress. The tests were conducted during daily operating conditions at Gannett's *Elmira* (New York) *Star-Gazette* letterpress plant. The laser system transfers the image on the pasteup page directly to the plate. Gannett officials indicated that marketing and production studies would be continued to determine the system's commercial feasibility.[10]

It appeared as the middle 1970s approached that letterpress printing could be used successfully in conjunction with cold type/photocomposition and was still a healthy and viable system. Many newspapers, especially the very large and the very small, still preferred it for a variety of reasons, including lower paper and ink costs. Developments in plate-making and other areas indicated that letterpress owners need not succumb to the offset revolution.

Offset Revolution

An offset revolution in the printing of American newspapers evolved in the 1960s and early 1970s. It developed conjointly with the cold type revolution mentioned earlier, and until methods of combining cold type and letterpress were developed the two did appear to be one. Thousands of small and medium-sized newspapers switched to offset, and many of the larger ones were expected to follow. Figures help tell the story. In the late 1950s fewer than 200 newspapers in the United States were printed by offset methods; by early 1964 the number had risen to 1,400, and by 1968 it was more than 5,000. By early 1974 many weeklies and 55.4% of the dailies, representing 25.4% of the daily circulation, were being published by the offset process. New technology that enabled letterpress papers to use cold type could throw off an early 1970s prediction that 87% of the nation's dailies would be offset by 1978, but the number was still growing.[11]

Offset printing involves the production of columns of type on paper rather than in metal. The paper type is placed on a paste-up page the size of a newspaper page according to instructions from news and advertising departments. Space is blocked out for negatives of any pictures scheduled for the page, and a negative of the entire page is made. Picture negatives are stripped into the page negative and the completed page is placed on a highly sensitive metal plate. A powerful arc light is then shined through the openings in the negatives to burn the images onto the metal. The plate, which is flexible and can be bent to fit the curvature of a rotary press, is chemically treated so that ink will adhere only to the proper places. When the press is activated the plates pass first by moistening rollers that place a thin film of water on the non-image areas and then by ink rollers. The ink is rejected by the water-covered areas but accepted by the treated image areas. The image is transferred from the plate to a blanket roll and then to the web of paper as it passes by the cylinder. The process is referred to as offset because the image is first offset on the blanket roll and then printed rather than being printed directly from the plate. Offset printing can be combined with hot metal typesetting rather than cold type; proofs of type set on a Linotype can be used in the page paste-ups. But the process is generally used with cold type because the cold type processes are cheaper, quicker or both.

Many small newspapers turned to offset printing and cold type in the early 1960s to avoid buying or replacing expensive hot metal equipment and to produce a more attractive and competitive product. Those making the switch could purchase comparatively inexpensive electric typewriters, paste-up equipment and cameras to replace Linotypes, metal make-up procedures and stereotype operations. Machines for producing cold type were developed that could be activated by the punched tape produced by the wire services and locally installed perforators. Moreover, the end product was more attractive. Cold type encouraged flexibility in appearance, for it is easier to move paper and photographic negatives around on a paste-up page than to position lead type. The offset process of printing provided a better quality of reproduction for pictures and other illustrations. Advertisers as well as readers were impressed by this fact.

Conversion to offset printing and cold type soon appeared to be an advantageous move for weeklies and small dailies, but the larger papers remained dubious of its value for them. They expressed concern about production time, the durability of offset plates, the cost of offset plates and ink, newsprint waste, retraining of personnel and possible conflicts with unions, the fact that they had huge sums of money invested in letterpress equipment, and other possible problems. Research eliminated or reduced many of the problems, and the offset movement spread to larger newspapers. But research also developed means of combining cold type and letterpress and of improving the appearance of letterpress, which may slow the trend.

By the middle 1970s plate production time had been reduced, offset press speeds had been increased to 60,000 or more copies an hour, and plate life had been extended several times beyond the 30,000 impressions once considered maximum. Researchers were talking in terms of plates that could be produced at costs and speeds comparable to stereotype equipment and that would last from 200,000 to 500,000 impressions. Laser beams were being used in plate-making experiments.[12] By the middle 1970s, ink prices were also more competitive, especially for color inks, and paper wastes in the start-up and stop operations had been substantially reduced. The 10% waste figures associated with the early days had been in many instances reduced to a more acceptable

2% to 4%. This was still higher than letterpress, however, and the increased use of color tended to compound the problem.[13]

Personnel problems provided a challenge in converting from letterpress to offset operations. Unions and individuals are understandably concerned about changes that could eliminate jobs. But many newspapers have alleviated these fears and worked out satisfactory agreements by providing good retraining programs and generous severance allowances. Many have sought to handle any personnel reductions through attrition. Retraining is, of course, a key to successful conversions. Experienced representatives of manufacturers and suppliers often can help in developing retraining programs as well as in installing new equipment; area vocational schools can provide special training programs for workers needing new skills.[14] Those who work with equipment changeovers or retraining programs on a regular basis should be able to help with the psychology as well as the technology of conversion.

The huge investments that many newspapers had in letterpress equipment continued to be a deterrent to converting to offset. Large papers often had millions of dollars invested in equipment. These investments also encouraged letterpress papers to seek means by which they could use cold type with their existing printing operations, and the success of these efforts, mentioned earlier, made the conversion to offset less desirable to many. Equipment does depreciate in value and wear out, however, so even this deterrent was not sufficient to discourage some who saw great benefits in offset operations.

What the distant future holds for offset or letterpress printing is difficult to predict in a time of rapidly changing technology. Some contend that ink jet printing, discussed later in the chapter, or some other new technology could make both obsolete. But offset definitely appeared to be a viable system for many newspapers, including some large ones, in the middle 1970s. *The Sacramento Union,* a Copley newspaper with a circulation of 90,000, demonstrated as early as 1968 that cold type/offset production need not be limited to small newspapers. Even larger papers in St. Louis, St. Petersburg and San Diego confirmed it in the early 1970s, and the Portland *Oregonian* hoped to complete its conversion to offset by early 1975.[15]

The adaptation of offset printing techniques to the publication of newspapers, improvements in letterpress printing procedures, and the evolution of cold type production methods including photocomposition all contributed to a new revolution in newspaper technology in the 1960s and early 1970s. But the changes wrought in those years were only the beginning. Far more revolutionary developments were soon to follow.

AN ELECTRONIC REVOLUTION

By the middle 1970s an electronic revolution was well under way in the American newspaper industry. It was based on new technology made possible by the development and evolution of computers and their adaptation to newspaper functions such as typesetting. Increases in the capability and speed of computers coupled with reductions in their size and cost opened the way for exciting changes. Otis Booth, operations manager of the *Los Angeles Times* in the early 1960s, referred to the application of computers to newspapers as the fourth fundamental step in the development of written communication. The first breakthrough was the translation of a spoken language into symbols or letters. That was followed after a long period of time by the invention of movable type and after several more centuries by the development of the linecasting machine.[16] Then came the computer with its potential for changing virtually all newspaper operations.

John Diebold, president of the Diebold Group, Inc., described what the newspaper of the future could be like in a talk to the 1963 meeting of the American Society of Newspaper Editors. Diebold envisioned an electronic system in which all incoming copy would be fed into a computer whether it came from wire services, reporters or the newspaper's library. This copy would then be manipulated electronically for editing and processing. Stories would be displayed on screens similar to television screens for editors to read and edit. Light pencils, light erasers and an input keyboard would be used not only to edit individual stories but to make up entire pages. In time, he said, typesetting in the traditional sense would be eliminated entirely because the page image that finally was approved on the display screen would be transmitted directly to printing plates at one or several locations. Eventually, the printing would be electro-static and the plates, too, would be eliminated. This step would allow for continuous variations in the newspaper while the presses were running. Diebold said that in time some of the transmissions instead of going to printing plates might go directly into the home. He emphasized that the roots or technical essence of every development he described already existed and he said that newspapers could be using the system he described by 1973.[17]

Many believed that the proposed electronic system would come far in the future, if at all, but their timetables were soon altered by the rapid development of computer-driven photocomposition machines. Phototypesetters were developed in the 1960s whose output capability far outstripped input, and publishers and manufacturers sought electronic input systems to restore the balance. At the same time, they searched for ways to eliminate the necessity of using correction lines that had to be pasted on paste-up pages. The search led to systems that could both increase input and eliminate errors before the type was set. A vast array of keyboards and computers soon was on the market or in the trial stages. The era of the electronically produced newspaper was at hand.

The key word in the new electronic era was, and is, systems. Peter P. Romano of the ANPA Research Institute said in 1970 that the newspaper could no longer be considered merely a group of loosely connected but basically separate areas of operation. He said the newspaper of the 1970s must see itself as a total system, a closely woven chain of many interlinked departments whose traditional lines of separation would blur if not be obliterated altogether. Romano said the difficult and challenging questions of the decade concerned how the new electronic technology and existing newspaper organizations would interface and how one or the other would change in order to exist with the other effectively.[18]

Newspapers came to realize, too, that they must develop their own systems to fit their own particular situations. The size and location of the newspaper, the kind and value of existing equipment, union contracts and other factors all entered into the decision. They had common goals; they were seeking ways to improve their products and reduce their costs. They could benefit from the experience of others. But they must determine their own needs and design and equip systems to meet those needs.

OCRs, VDTs, and Hard Wire

Much attention was given during the early phases of the electronic revolution to meeting input needs created by high-speed photocomposition machines and eliminating correction line problems referred to as the Achilles Heel of photocomposition. One goal was to capture the original keystrokes of the reporter and input them quickly and cleanly into the typesetters. Re-keying was to be avoided, if possible; it takes time, opens the way to additional errors, and is costly. Another goal was to make all corrections before typesetting. Various machines have been developed to meet these goals and complete a link in a broader electronic system. They include a variety of optical character recognition (OCR) devices, video display terminals (VDT), and electric typewriters wired directly to computers. Each approach has its proponents, and some newspapers have combined approaches to develop input and editing systems.

Optical character recognition devices, or scanners, scan copy that is typed on an electric typewriter with a compatible typeface and transfer the information there to perforated tape or electronic signals. These are fed into a computer for formatting, hyphenation and justification and then into a typesetting machine. Programming instructions are typed along with the copy. Corrections can be made in one of several ways by the writer or by the editor. If the writer notices an error as he is typing his story, he can delete a character, word or line by typing the appropriate deletion symbol one or more times. If he or an editor wants to delete something after the story is completed, either can mark through it with an ink that is out of the scanner's optical range. Corrections, insertions or additions can be typed at the appropriate spot below the line on the copy or on a separate sheet of paper and keyed to the copy by use of symbols. Newspapers that use scanners for input and video screens for editing can call the copy out of the computer and make corrections on the screen.[19]

Scanners help meet the input challenges mentioned earlier by eliminating the necessity for re-keyboarding the reporter's copy and by making it possible for corrections to be made before type is set. Even allowing for the time that may be involved in typing in corrections, the scanners provide much faster copy preparation than perforators and they do not require special operators, only typists. OCRs were developed by early 1974 that could scan 1,800 words a minute,[20] and faster ones were being discussed. At the same time the costs were being reduced drastically, from about $250,000 before 1970 to $50,000 or less in 1973.[21]

While scanners were expected to become a dominant method of copy input in the middle 1970s, they were not universally praised. Some editors argue that the use of scanners slows the editing process and discourages editing. They say that editors and reporters may not make desirable but unessential changes because too many changes produce copy that is hard for scanners to read. They argue that it takes much longer to type changes in on the copy at just the right place, or key insertions and additions on separate sheets with the typewriter than it would to use pencil and paste.[22] Some of these problems can, of course, be reduced or eliminated by using video screens for editing.

Despite these challenges, the use of scanners was expanded rapidly after they were introduced in 1970. The *Worcester Telegram & Evening Gazette* installed a prototype of the ECRM Autoreader in late 1970, and units of the CompuScan and Datatype corporations were field-tested and introduced at the ANPA Research Institute production management conference in June 1971.[23] By early 1973, there were five companies offering OCRs and that many more were expected to enter the field in the near future. Newspapers of all sizes were converting to scanner operations.

Research also was conducted in the early 1970s to find ways in which syndicate copy and wire service copy could be adapted for scanner operations. Publishers-Hall Syndicate, ECRM, and the A. B. Dick Company worked out a system in 1972 for mass-producing the syndicate's copy, and more than 40 clients signed up for the service within the first few months.[24] Prospects for developing machines that could provide wire service copy for scanners were reported good in 1973.

Video display terminals can be used to generate and edit copy and lay out advertisements and whole pages. The terminal looks very much like a television screen with a typewriter keyboard attached to it. In a sense, it is, for the image appears on a cathode ray tube similar to the one used for television sets; the terminals are sometimes referred to as CRTs as well as VDTs. The person creating copy on a VDT types out his story on the keyboard as he would on an electric typewriter. As he types the story appears on the video screen as it would on a piece of copy paper in a typewriter. If the story is long enough, the lines typed first will disappear off the top of the screen into the system's storage; but they can be scrolled back just as a typist can roll back a long piece of copy paper that has fallen over the back of a typewriter. If the writer wishes to delete or insert something, he can do so easily by using his keyboard and cursor. The cursor is a blinking pulse on the screen that can be moved to indicate where the deletion or insertion is to be made. Once the story is finished to the writer's satisfaction, it is stored in the computer until called out for editing and typesetting. Portable video screen terminals were being developed in the middle 1970s that would enable reporters to file stories directly from any location that had telephone lines. ·

Some newspapers are now generating copy on video screens to eliminate a keyboard step and accelerate the input of copy to typesetters. Many newspapers are using them as editing devices to make corrections before type is set and thereby eliminate the correction line problem. Video screens can be used to edit copy created on video screens, produced by optical character recognition devices, or fed directly into computers by wire services and typewriters wired to the computers. Editors call the copy from the computers to their screens, manipulate it with keyboard and cursor, insert any needed typesetting commands, and return it to the computer, which sends it on to the typesetting machines. The computer output may be a tape to activate the typesetters, or it may be in the form of signals that directly drive the typesetters.[25]

Some questions have been raised about the desirability of creating and editing stories on video screens, but most seem to have been answered satisfactorily. Some persons argue, for example, that it takes more time to edit on a video screen than with a pencil; but any time lost there is more than offset by time gained in the rest of the operation. Some also raised questions about possible radiation dangers in using the machines, but extensive tests for such dangers were negative. Tests were conducted by the Occupational Safety and Health Administration of the U.S. Labor Department on equipment used by both major wire services.[26] Eyestrain could be a problem for some, but the devices have brightness controls similar to those on television sets.

Video screens, like optical character recognition devices, are largely a development of the 1970s. By 1973, they were being used extensively for creating copy and editing by the wire services, for creating copy by a few newspapers, and for editing copy by even more newspapers. Their potential for accelerating the makeup of advertisements and entire newspaper pages was also being explored, as indicated in a later section of this chapter. The Gannett Company's *Today* in Cocoa, Florida, the *Augusta* (Georgia) *Chronicle* and *Herald,* and the *Detroit News* were among those using video terminals for both generating and editing copy in the early 1970s. Harris-Intertype, Hendrix Electronics, Mergenthaler Linotype, Digital Equipment Corporation, Graphic Systems, Imlac, Mohr Enterprises, and Tal-Star were among companies selling one or more types of video terminals.

A third approach developed during the early 1970s to help meet the need for faster copy input involved the wiring of electric typewriters directly to computers. Xylogics Systems, Inc. explored this concept using a series of Facit-Odhner or IBM Selectric typewriters. The typewriters, or "Typeterminals," have a photoelectric read unit and light source that transfer the information into the mass memory. Wire service input can also be delivered into the system, and all copy can be called out for editing on video terminals. The *Daytona Beach* (Florida) *News Journal* and the *Farmington* (New Mexico) *Daily Times* worked with Xylogics in the development of the system. Star Graphics Systems, Inc. signed an agreement to market Xylogic's on-line, computerized editorial and typesetting system in 1973.[27]

By 1973 a number of newspapers were using electronic systems that provided a more expeditious way of getting copy from its creators to reproduction proofs ready for page makeup. Moreover, newspapers of all sizes were involved. Peter P. Romano of the ANPA reported in early 1973 that 96 ANPA newspapers plants were using a total of 478 video display terminals. The papers ranged in size from the metropolitan *Los Angeles Times* to the *Taylorsville* (Illinois) *Breeze-Courier,* with less than 10,000 circulation. Romano said that more than 60 newspapers, ranging in circulation from 8,000 to more than 900,000, were using a total of more than 100 optical character recognition systems. He said that 21 newspapers had combined or soon would combine OCRs and VDTs with a computer in their copy preparation systems.[28]

Leaders in Technology

Both major wire services pioneered in the use of video terminals in their effort to get more news out faster and with fewer errors. A United Press International official said in late 1973 that electronic editing enabled the service to file 20% to 30% more news, provided clearer and cleaner copy, and permitted faster filing of important stories. UPI began using video editing terminals in 1970 in New York. Later it installed terminals in Washington and Chicago, and in late 1973 announced plans to begin installing them in all of its 100 United States Bureaus. When this project is completed all UPI newsmen will be composing copy on video screens and dispatching it into a computer system. The copy will be called out for editing on video screens, assigned priorities and returned ready for distribution.[29]

UPI was also working on other plans to accelerate its distribution system. In the fall of 1973 it announced that testing was under way on an experimental high-speed newswire for newspapers with electronic editing systems. UPI DataNews would combine an abstract wire and a Dataspeed circuit to deliver general, sports and financial news to newspaper computers in a form that could be easily stored and retrieved. The initial test was to link UPI's Information Storage and Retrieval system in New York with a large daily in the metropolitan area and with Univac's King of Prussia, Pennsylvania development center. Officials described the experiment as a step toward the development of a Demand Service system that would enable subscribers to scan abstracts of stories on a teleprinter in their news rooms, select stories from UPI's entire news base and have them delivered over high-speed data transmission facilities. Under the proposed demand system, newspapers could take the news into their own computers for further editing or receive it on punched paper tape or magnetic tape to drive their composing equipment. Hard-copy monitors would also be available for those that desired a print-out of the story.[30]

At the same time, UPI sought to improve its distribution of pictures through the development of a Unifax II photo-facsimile receiver. The machine was an update of the Unifax I, developed by UPI about 1950. Unifax II delivered a high fidelity reproduction of a news photograph on dry paper that eliminated the variances in previous facsimile materials. It allowed for accurate reproduction of more than 30 shades of gray and also could be used in transmitting color transparencies. Initial installations were scheduled in the spring of 1974.[31]

Similarly exciting developments in technology were under way at Associated Press. The AP began to install video display units in its sub-regional bureaus for direct input of stories by reporters and for local editing in 1970. When the stories were completed, the text was transmitted on-line via telegraph speed lines directly to an AP regional computer center for processing and distribution.[32] The AP sought to build its system around regional headquarters in contrast to the UPI's plan for a central headquarters in New York. The two obtained basic equipment from difference sources, but their basic goals of improving and accelerating services were similar.

The Associated Press joined with the *Detroit News, Baltimore Sun* and *Washington Star-News* in late 1973 in an experiment involving high-speed transmission of news. During the experiment the AP's A Wire, or primary transcontinental wire, its regional B circuit and its business news and sports news were to be transmitted at the rate of 1,050 words a minute to the participating newspapers. The AP had been transmitting sports news, financial news and text data at that speed for several years, but the general news circuits in the early 1970s were operating at only 66 words a minute. The plan called for the AP's computers in New York to transmit to computers at the *News* and *Star-News* and to a special high-speed teleprinter at the *Sun*. An AP official indicated that studies already under way indicated that high-speed transmission could provide many editorial benefits for many AP members. It also appeared that the system would become more economically feasible as the telephone company changed to digital transmission in many big city areas in 1974.[33]

The Associated Press announced in 1973 the development of a new system of photo transmission by wire. The new system, called Laserphoto, harnesses a laser beam to deliver dry glossy prints of photographic reproduction quality. The laser beam exposes dry silver paper which is processed by heat exposure; no chemicals are used and there is no reported drift in quality. The AP expected to begin installation of Laserphoto equipment in 1974 and to have every one of its photo receivers and transmitters replaced in approximately two years. The AP also announced plans in 1973 for electronic darkrooms where pictures would be stored in computers, edited on video screens and transmitted at high speeds.[34]

New Makeup Procedures

Research was under way in the 1970s to extend the electronic systems to include improved methods of handling classified advertising, the schedule and makeup of display advertising, and the makeup of entire pages, whatever the content. The Economist Newspapers, publishers of suburban weeklies in the Chicago Area, and Compugraphic Corporation developed a computerized page formating system for classified advertisements. The system not only classifies, sorts and alphabetizes ads, but also makes up the page inside the computer and turns out tapes for photocomposition in page order. Each tape produces one complete justified column, which the paste-up operator can paste on the page in proper order. The system leaves space for any display ads scheduled for the classified pages and inserts a message telling the paste-up personnel to get a particular ad and place it in the indicated position.[35]

The *Marion* (Indiana) *Chronicle-Tribune* went on line in February 1972, with an ad layout computer program to accelerate the preparation of page dummies. The IBM computer prints out a list of all ads for a given day—including pickup ads, color ads and ads in a series—and using programmed advertising-editorial space guidelines, schedules all standard editorial features.[36] Such systems can provide a rapid means of preparing ad dummies without placing like ads together; and they can provide quickly such information as the number of pages needed to meet a prescribed news-to-advertising ratio and the size of news holes.[37]

By early 1973 there were three companies producing video terminals for use in making up advertisements and pages. At that time the mark up/page-layout terminals had two principal newspaper applications. First, they enabled the user to apply various typographical instructions to raw copy and immediately see the results of his instructions on a video screen. Second, they enabled an editor to make up an entire page without pictures. In both applications, the user can enter raw text, format and correct it, add typographical instructions, change these as desired, and proofread and correct errors before sending it to final photocomposition. Harris-Intertype, Hendrix Electronics, and Tal-Star Computer Systems, Inc. were among the first to develop models in this field.[38]

Researchers in the early 1970s also were predicting that automated page makeup involving news stories, advertising and pictures could be achieved in the decade if publishers were willing to finance the costs involved. It appeared that the system might well resemble the one envisioned by Diebold in the early 1960s. The make up editor would operate at a computer-connected display console that would include an 18 by 24 inch video display terminal and one or more smaller display units. The console would have a typewriter keyboard, light pen, various function buttons, and the levers required for picture-cropping and page-formating. The makeup editor would call up news, ads and pictures according to a slug and page dummy shown on one of the auxiliary display sets, preview them and position them on the page. Photos would be called up on an auxiliary display set, and the editor would crop and electronically screen them as he placed them into position on the page. Once assembled the page would be returned to temporary storage until called for. At edition time it would be transmitted to a photocomposition unit that could create it in less than two minutes.[39]

Several barriers must still be overcome before the system becomes operational. One is the cost of the mass memory needed to store the large number of bits contained in photographs. Fortunately, the cost of such storage has been dropping each year. Another problem has been reading the graphics into the system. Harris, Mergenthaler, RCA and other firms appear to have this fairly well resolved. The most serious problem has been the lack of software development. Researchers said in late 1971 that this problem could be overcome in five years if enough money were made available.[40] Eight metropolitan newspapers were working with IBM in 1973 in a project to develop a video page layout system that would enable the newspapers to put out whole pages at a time. It was projected that such a system could be operational by the end of 1977.[41]

New Press Systems

Development of electronic page makeup could accelerate a revolution in press systems during the next decade. The first steps likely will involve improved plate-making techniques. The second could involve elimination of plates and printing directly on paper. As indicated earlier in the chapter, important advances in plate-making have been made in recent years to enable letterpress as well as offset newspapers to take advantage of the cold type revolution. Many of the existing systems photograph a paste-up page onto a plate that can be used for direct printing or one that can serve as a pattern for a stereotyping operation; lasers also are being used to transfer the image. Future processes may transfer a page image created on a video screen directly to the printing plate. Diebold suggested this possibility in his discussion of tomorrow's newspaper back in 1963.[42]

Printing plates may be eliminated in the 1980s by the development of electrostatic or direct image electronic newspaper press systems. In such a system the computer would transmit the page images directly onto the moving printing cylinder via laser beam projectors or through the actuation of some microdroplet ink jet devices. Such a system could eliminate the need for color separations, press make-ready and similar steps, and open the way for the daily use of high-quality color printing.[43]

Members of the Scientific Advisory Committee of the American Newspaper Publishers Association reported in late 1972 that printing without plates through the application of ink jet technologies already being utilized in nonnewspaper areas could be developed for newspaper production including color within ten years. Dr. Eugene Fubini of E. G. Fubini Consultant, Ltd., said the concept involves a battery of ink jets each controlled by an electronic memory unit which would form characters and pictures by controlled application of almost microscopic ink dots. Because the input is electronic, the news copy, classified ads or any other part of the paper could be changed during the press run. Elimination of plates and pressures would permit the use of simplified press structures and help eliminate paper breaks. The system should also make it possible to decentralize newspaper printing and customize both editorial matter and advertising for various circulation zones. Dr. Fubini said he believed ink jets looked more promising than electrostatic printing and noted that at least 10 ink jet technologies were under study.[44]

Press improvements were expected prior to the development of plateless printing through the development of computer control systems. It was suggested that a process control computer using a closed-loop instrumentation package could monitor and correct page and color registration, ink control, web tension, speed, length of run and other operations while the press was running. Presses capable of producing more than 100,000 newspapers an hour were predicted for 1975. They were expected to continue the four-plate-wide, two-around configuration and be available for both offset and shallow relief letterpress printing. Research also was under way to develop presses large enough to accommodate 4 plates around and 6 plates across. In 1974 the *New York Daily News* contracted for a 6-page-wide, 2-plate-around press of two units and one folder from each of two manufacturers. The change could reduce newsprint waste and effect economies.[45]

Systems already in operation and research under way indicate that some newspapers by the middle 1980s will be electronically oriented from the time editorial and advertising personnel input copy until the finished product comes off the presses in one or more locations. Systems for handling and distributing those newspapers also are being automated, although studies in the early 1970s indicated that electronic delivery of complete newspapers into the home by facsimile or some other system is unlikely in the immediate future. Systems have been developed to facilitate the folding, counting, stacking and wrapping of newspapers as they come off the presses. A new infeed to stuff newspapers was reported in late 1972 that made it possible to convey, insert, address, stack, tie and wrap newspapers in one in-line operation. This system offered by Hans Mueller Corp. operated at speeds up to 60,000 papers an hour and delivered compensated stacks of standard or programmed count.[46] The home consumers undoubtedly appreciated efforts to develop plastic wraps to protect newspaper bundles and individual papers in bad weather.

Facsimile and Satellite Plants

It did not appear in the early 1970s that newspapers would soon abandon their existing distribution approaches for a facsimile home delivery system but would employ facsimile in other ways.[47] Basically, a facsimile system involves a transmitter, a transmission line and a receiver. The transmitter scans copy with a light which is reflected through a lens to a photoelectric sensing device. This device converts the image into electrical impulses that are sent along the transmission line to the receiver where they are recorded graphically. A beam of light at the receiver inscribes the image onto a sensitized material such as paper or film.[48]

It was demonstrated as early as the 1940s that newspaper pages could be transmitted by facsimile, but the system still seemed an impractical method of home delivery in the early 1970s. First, it seemed unlikely that consumers would pay for receiving sets to get a facsimile of a product they already got in a convenient fashion. Second, the size of the modern newspaper presented a problem. In the early 1970s newspapers averaged 53 pages on weekdays and 178 pages on Sundays. Third, the distribution of materials such as paper and ink for the receivers presented a problem. Even assuming the newspaper provided this service, would the consumer want to bother with storing and replacing these materials? Barring a major breakthrough in technology, it appeared that newspapers would be more likely to serve as suppliers of information for a home communications system print-out service than as producers of a total home facsimile product. It should be noted, however, that the Japanese newspaper *Asahi Shimbun* had developed plans to experiment with home-delivered newspapers by 1976.[49]

Newspapers in the early 1970s were making use of facsimile, however, to transmit pictures and copy from other sites to their offices for processing and to transmit completed pages to satellite printing plants. Portable facsimile machines can be set up anywhere a telephone is available to send in copy and pictures on news, sports or other events. The *Honolulu Advertiser* used facsimile in its coverage of the University of Hawaii's participation in a New York basketball tournament in 1971. In 1973, the *St. Louis Post-Dispatch* developed a facsimile system to send pages from its main plant downtown to its new offset printing facility 20 miles away, and the *Christian Science Monitor* designed a facsimile system to send page proofs from its home office in Boston to offset facilities in California, Illinois and New Jersey.[50]

An expansion of satellite plants and offices using facsimile or some other transmission system seems likely in the future. Such systems could not only help solve distribution problems, but could also help newspapers tailor their products to fit particular geographic areas. For example, satellite offices could feed news and advertising into central plant processing and get back completed pages for printing. The completed product could include state, national and international news and advertising generated at the central plant for all newspapers in the system and information generated at the satellite offices for that particular area.

Two electronic character generation systems that could replace facsimile in satellite operations before the decade is over were described by Jules Tewlow, former director of special projects for ANPA, in early 1973. One would involve the transmission of computer-paginated news and ad text information via a telecommunications link. The data would be captured on magnetic tape or disks and utilized to drive electronic character generators at the satellite plant. The other would be an electronically driven character generator that could produce its output directly on offset or plastic letterpress plates. It would use laser scanning and recording techniques.[51]

Techniques such as this might also be used by several independent newspapers in a metropolitan area or by small city dailies in close proximity to each other. In these instances the central plant would function only as a computer-composition facility. Each newspaper would maintain its own offices for news, advertising and other operations. Each would feed its material into the center for processing and receive back pages ready for printing. Such developments might enable smaller newspapers to save on expensive equipment costs and invest their money in producing high-quality editorial products.

The central system approach is already being used for some phases of copy processing and printing by some newspapers. All six dailies in the Westchester-Rockland Newspapers group, a division of Gannett Company located in a heavily populated area 25 miles north of New York, are printed in the same plant. The composing room makes use of modern equipment, including video display terminals, optical character readers, TTS perforators, and typesetters to meet its schedule. Local copy is received both through facsimile and through keyboarding from outlying offices.[52]

Booth newspapers, with headquarters in Ann Arbor, Michigan, has operated a central computer system since 1967 to service its eight newspapers. Copy from the wire services and Booth bureaus is stored in the central computer for use by the group's papers as they see fit.[53] Lee Enterprises, with headquarters in Davenport, Iowa, has a time-sharing system including five computers in four locations to serve 14 Lee newspapers in six states. The Lee system involves IBM 1130 computers and Bell System Data Speed senders. Newspapers that do not have a computer system in their own plants can send their raw paper tape over the Data Speed system to one that does for processing. The new tape including all proper instructions regarding hyphenation, justification, point size, line lengths, and formats necessary to driving the phototypesetting machines is returned by the same system.[54]

Everything Changes

The computer revolution is making possible many useful changes in the newspaper production system; it also is accelerating and improving techniques utilized in circulation, advertising and general business accounting operations. Computers can be used for a wide variety of accounting functions such as payroll, general ledger, accounts payable, accounts receivable, paper distribution and subscriber billing processing. Circulation stops, starts, and delivery complaints can be processed more quickly in this way. The *Florida Times-Union* and *Jacksonville Journal* developed plans to use an IBM computer to establish work standards, determine exact costs of producing advertising, project peak work loads and create accounting transactions associated with advertising production.[55] The *Indianapolis Star* and *News* worked out a plan using video display terminals to provide automatic routing to the proper carriers of all starts, stops, and complaints and provide better information for management about complaints and carrier incentive programs. Officials there say the automatic generation of notices and reports has resulted in savings in manpower, forms and equipment. They reported a reduction of 50% in poor service stops, a reduction of approximately 50% in repeat complaints, new lows for the average number of complaints received daily and virtual elimination of misrouted starts, stops, and complaints and duplicate starts and stops.[56]

Punchcards and paper tape have been used for some time to input data on business operations for computer processing. In the future optical character recognition devices and incremental magnetic tape typewriters will accelerate the operation. Incoming invoices and other documents can be read directly into the OCR devices and the information stored on high density magnetic tapes. Data on payrolls and production statistics can be captured directly from timeclocks, and other data can be generated on incremental magnetic tape typewriters. Computers also will be used to generate all sorts of management information such as the status of credit risks, inventory of work-in-process, daily reports of newsprint inventory, and reader and market survey statistics. Publishers will be able to ascertain the effects of a wage increase on corporate profits if there are no commensurate increases in advertising rates or determine the effect of a postal rate increase on a certain group of newspaper subscribers.[57] Editors can use computers to automate their futures books and analyze data compiled by reporters concerning economics, legislative action, crime or other matters. The *New York Times* used a computer to analyze murder cases in New York, and the *Philadelphia Inquirer* did a computer analysis of that city's criminal justice system.[58]

Computers can also be used to automate newspaper libraries and make the information contained in them easily accessible to staff members and the public. The *New York Times* began feasibility studies into a computerized information retrieval system in 1966, and further committed itself to the development of such a system in 1969. The *Times* had its system ready for testing beginning in November 1972, and it announced the start of full commercial operations in the spring of 1973. The Times Information Bank stores articles published in the *Times* and more than 60 other newspapers and magazines. Abstracts of articles are made available on a video terminal and full text of articles is made available on microfiche or microfilm. The bank is used by *Times* staffers and is available to other organizations through subscription.[59]

The many beneficial changes wrought by new technology do not come without challenges, and sometimes problems. Publishers seek assurance that they will not invest large sums in systems that are ineffective or soon outdated. Editors want assurance that automation will work for them and not them for it. Unions want assurance that their members will have as much job security as possible. The union challenge is particularly great, for new technology does eliminate many types of jobs while creating others. Some optimism about improving labor-management relations was expressed in early 1973 after a local board of arbitration settled a dispute over the introduction of new composing room equipment at the *San Francisco Chronicle* and *San Francisco Examiner*. The decision permitting newspapers there to install automated equipment including scanners, computers and CRT terminals was termed unusual because all of the participants on the panel agreed without dissent. An editorial in *Editor & Publisher* suggested that it indicated an awareness on the part of the ITU, in that area at least, that such efficiencies in newspaper production are necessary. The editorial expressed the hope that the language and spirit of that agreement would have beneficial influence in other areas, particularly New York. Under the San Francisco agreement, jobs to be eliminated were to disappear by attrition, which was to be hastened by an early retirement plan and by lump-sum severance payments.[60]

New processes can also bring new challenges in health and safety fields. Newspapers must be concerned about conditions that might affect their employes. Their actions in this field have been guided to some extent by research conducted by the Research Institute of the American Newspaper Publishers Association and by the provisions of the federal Occupational Safety and Health Act. In 1972, Cleve Rumble, then director of employe relations for the *Louisville Courier-Journal* and *Louisville Times,* noted that the OSHA should be beneficial. He said, "it leads industry in the right direction to do some of the things we should have already done," and "will make our places of business safer for the individual." [61] Newspapers must take steps to assure that their operations do not adversely affect the public health or safety. The *New York Daily News,* for example, installed an air recycling system in the gravure printing and inserting facility it constructed at Newspoint, Long Island City, in 1972 to help control air pollution.[62]

By the early 1970s it was evident that new technology would affect all phases of newspaper operation. Reporters, editors, advertising salesmen and carriers would be affected along with those in the production department. The changes would present many challenges as they opened new potential for service and economic gain. But only through making the changes to new technology could most papers hope to compete with other media and other activities for the individual's time and money. Newspapers that ignore the new technology may not survive. Those that employ it to do their jobs quicker, better and more economically should continue to serve and prosper.

Some Leaders and Seekers

INDIVIDUAL NEWSPAPERS can be judged and, with some reservations, compared on the basis of how well they meet their responsibilities to seek out truth, foster the operation of the democratic system, help individuals and communities improve themselves, improve their own performance, and retain their solvency and independence. Assessments can be made by studying the breadth, depth, accuracy and fairness of their coverage, the courage and argument of their editorial viewpoints, the emphasis and attractiveness of their presentations, and the clarity and style of their writing.

Readers should continuously assess their newspapers and encourage and support efforts by editors and publishers to improve the quality of their performance and service. Editors and publishers should assess each other's efforts and join in recognizing excellence and decrying mediocrity. Overall coverage and service and individual stories, editorials, pictures and advertisements can all be considered in reaching judgments. If proper allowance is made for the great diversity in purpose and audience of American newspapers, models of excellence can be suggested for other newspapers to study and perhaps emulate.

Contests such as the Pulitzer prizes, Sigma Delta Chi awards, National Newspaper Association awards, and state press association competitions have recognized individual excellence over the years. Several surveys and studies also have been conducted in an effort to recognize the ten best daily newspapers in the country and thereby perhaps suggest them as models. While the great diversity of newspapers and newspaper audiences makes exact numerical rankings unsatisfactory, if not impossible, such rankings can be suggestive if those making them are knowledgeable of the total field and the individual newspapers being judged. Several such studies will be mentioned here.

Edward L. Bernays, nationally prominent public relations counsel, has on several occasions asked American newspaper publishers to list the ten daily newspapers in the United States that best meet the ideals of Thomas Gibson, Adolph S. Ochs and Joseph Pulitzer.[1] Bernays included with the request the credos of the three men as follows:

* THOMAS GIBSON, *Rocky Mountain News* (Denver) May 1, 1860

A newspaper untrammeled by sinister influence from any quarter—the advocate of the right and the denouncer of the wrong—an independent vehicle for the free expression of all candid, honest and intelligent minds—a medium of free discussion, moral, religious, social and scientific.

* ADOLPH S. OCHS, *The New York Times,* August 18, 1896

It will be my earnest aim that *The New York Times* give the news, all the news, in concise and accurate form, in language that is permissible in good society, and give it early, if not earlier, than it can be learned through any other medium. To give the news impartially, without fear or favor, regardless of party, sect or interest involved; to make the columns of *The New York Times* a forum for the consideration of all public questions of public importance, and to that end, to invite intelligent discussions from all shades of opinion.

* JOSEPH PULITZER, *New York World,* May 10, 1883

An institution that should always fight for progress and reform, never tolerate injustice and corruption, always fight demagogues of all parties, never belong to any party, always oppose privileged classes and public plunderers, never lack sympathy with the poor, always remain devoted to the public welfare, never be satisfied with merely printing news, always be drastically independent, never be afraid to attack wrong, whether by predatory plutocracy or predatory poverty.

The top ten daily newspapers in 1961, listed according to the frequency of their mention by publishers in the Bernays survey, were as follows: *The New York Times, St. Louis Post-Dispatch, The Christian Science Monitor, Milwaukee Journal, Louisville Courier-Journal, New York Herald Tribune, The Washington Post, Los Angeles Times, Chicago Tribune,* and *Kansas City Star.* Eight of these ten newspapers also were cited in the top ten selected by a *Saturday Review* survey of journalism teachers that same year; the teachers ranked *The Wall Street Journal* third and the *Chicago Daily News* tenth and included the *Kansas City Star* and *Los Angeles Times* in a second ten, tied for fourteenth.

Eight of the same ten newspapers were included in response to a similar survey of publishers by Bernays in 1970, although not in the same order or with the same degree of support. This listing omitted the *New York Herald Tribune,* which had ceased publication in the 1960s, and the *Kansas City Star,* and added the *Miami Herald* and *The Wall Street Journal.* The ten, in order of percentage of responding publishers listing them, were as follows: *The New York Times,* 61%; *Los Angeles Times,* 51%; *Louisville Courier-Journal,* 42%;

St. Louis Post-Dispatch and *Washington Post,* 38%; *Christian Science Monitor* and *Miami Herald,* 30%; *Milwaukee Journal,* 29%; *Chicago Tribune* 23%; and *The Wall Street Journal,* 20%.

Bernays noted that the *Los Angeles Times,* which jumped from eighth to second, and *The Washington Post,* which jumped from seventh to a tie for fourth, received a higher percentage of votes in 1970 than in 1961; the *Louisville Courier-Journal,* which jumped from fifth to third, got the same percentage of votes; and the other five mentioned in both polls all got a smaller percentage in 1970 than in 1961. He noted too, that overall the percentages of the top ten in 1970 were lower than those of the winning ten in three previous surveys conducted by him. The votes in 1970 were less concentrated than in any of the other surveys. Thirty-nine newspapers got more than 3% of the vote in 1970 as compared with 29 in 1961 when more than twice as many publishers responded; 101 newspapers got one vote each in 1970.

The same 10 newspapers and the *Boston Globe* were included in response to a Bernays survey in 1974. *The New York Times* got 82% of the publishers' votes as compared with 61% in 1970 to retain its first-place ranking. The *Washington Post* got 76% of the votes, twice its 1970 total, and moved up to second place. The *Los Angeles Times,* with a 73% ranking, was a close third. The others in order were the *Miami Herald,* 59%; *Louisville Courier-Journal,* 52%; *Chicago Tribune,* 40%; *Milwaukee Journal,* 39%; *The Wall Street Journal,* 37%; *St. Louis Post-Dispatch,* 36%; and *Christian Science Monitor* and *Boston Globe,* each with 33%.

The *Saturday Review* survey mentioned earlier was conducted for the magazine by Benson & Benson, Inc. a professional polling organization in Princeton, New Jersey. It was directed to deans, full professors and associate professors in 46 journalism programs that were accredited by the American Council on Education for Journalism. They mentioned many criteria as valid in rating a daily newspaper as "best" or "outstanding." Those criteria cited most frequently as basis for judgment included: complete news, comprehensive treatment, 66% of the respondents; unbiased, objective treatment of news, 47%; judgment in selection of news, 28%; layout, typography, 28%; good writing style, 26%; and accuracy, 25%.

According to the *Saturday Review* poll, the 15 leading dailies, with the percentage of respondents voting for them were as follows: *The New York Times,* 71%; *Christian Science Monitor,* 46%; *The Wall Street Journal,* 42%; *St. Louis Post-Dispatch,* 39%; *Milwaukee Journal,* 35%; *Washington Post,* 34%; *New York Herald Tribune,* 25%; *Louisville Courier-Journal,* 22%; *Chicago Tribune,* 16%; *Chicago Daily News,* 12%; *Baltimore Sun,* 11%; *Atlanta Constitution* and *Minneapolis Tribune,* 10%; and *Kansas City Star* and *Los Angeles Times,* 9%. In order after them were the *Des Moines Register, Denver Post, Washington Star, Minneapolis Star, San Francisco Chronicle, Toledo Blade, Miami Herald, Chicago Sun-Times, St. Louis Globe-Democrat,*

Detroit Free Press, and *Buffalo News.* Thirty-nine other newspapers on a list of 119 received three or fewer mentions.[2]

John Merrill includes many of the same newspapers in his study of *The Elite Press: Great Newspapers of the World,* published in 1968. Merrill bases his listing of 100 newspapers in an "Elite Press Pyramid" on his study of surveys by others and his own endeavors to determine the world's leading dailies. He summarizes the marks of the elite in five broad categories as follows:

(1) Independence; financial stability; integrity; social concern; good writing and editing.

(2) Strong opinion and interpretive emphasis; world consciousness; nonsensationalism in articles and makeup.

(3) Emphasis on politics, international relations, economics, social welfare, cultural endeavors, education, and science.

(4) Concern with getting, developing, and keeping a large, intelligent, well-educated, articulate, and technically proficient staff.

(5) Determination to serve and help expand a well-educated, intellectual readership at home and abroad; desire to appeal to, and influence, opinion leaders everywhere.

Merrill includes 22 United States newspapers in his elite pyramid as follows: *The New York Times,* among ten primary elite; *Christian Science Monitor, St. Louis Post-Dispatch,* and *Washington Post* among 20 secondary elite; Baltimore *Sun, Los Angeles Times, Louisville Courier-Journal, Miami Herald,* and *The Wall Street Journal* among 30 tertiary elite; and *Atlanta Constitution, Chicago Tribune, Cleveland Plain Dealer, Dallas Morning News, Denver Post,* St. Louis *Globe-Democrat, Houston Post, Kansas City Star, Milwaukee Journal, Minneapolis Tribune, Philadelphia Inquirer,* Portland *Oregonian,* and *New Orleans Times-Picayune,* among 40 near-elite.[3]

Time Magazine included some of the same newspapers cited by publishers and teachers in its selections of the ten best United States newspapers in 1964 and again in 1974; on both occasions it mentioned two or three not ranked so prominently elsewhere. *Time*'s correspondents and editors based the magazine's selections on factors such as these: the top ten newspapers make a conscientious effort to cover national and international news as well as monitor their own communities; they can be brash and entertaining as well as informative; they are willing to risk money, time and manpower on extended investigations; they offer a range of disparate opinion through their opposite editorial pages and dissenting columns. The magazine said its judgments were based on editorial excellence rather than commercial success but noted that economically the 1974 winners ranged from the sound to the very prosperous.

Time's 1964 selections, listed alphabetically by the magazine, included the Baltimore *Sun, Cleveland Press, Los Angeles Times, Louisville Courier-Journal, Milwaukee Journal, Minneapolis* morning *Tribune, New York Daily News, New York Times, St. Louis Post-Dispatch,* and *Washington Post. Time*'s 1974 rankings retained the *Los Angeles Times, Louisville Courier-Journal, Milwaukee Journal, The New York Times,* and *Washington Post,* but replaced the other five with the *Boston Globe, Chicago Tribune, Miami Herald, Newsday,* and *The Wall Street Journal.*[4] All but the *Globe* and *Newsday* had received high rankings in earlier ratings by publishers and teachers.

While the surveys of publishers and editors and the studies cited cannot be considered conclusive evidence for ranking the best newspapers in numerical order, they are suggestive of what newspapers should be included among the top 10 to 25 newspapers. Others not as well known nationally may be equally deserving of praise for the manner in which they serve their particular audiences. National studies along the lines of The New England Daily Newspaper Survey of 109 newspapers conducted in 1973 might prove helpful in making further comparisons and determining more exact ratings. The study critically examines that area's dailies in 2,500 to 5,000 word essays based primarily on a review of six weeks' issues and interviews with publishers and editors. It was funded by a grant from the John and Mary R. Markle Foundation to the University of Massachusetts.[5]

The remainder of this chapter will provide brief sketches of many of the newspapers regarded as the best by publishers, teachers and others cited. Rather than suggest another numerical listing, the author will discuss the dailies in several groups suggested by geography. The first group deals with six newspapers that have a strong national orientation; the next four review some of the better daily newspapers in the East, South, Midwest, and West. The final section in the chapter touches briefly on a number of weeklies that have scored well in National Newspaper Association competition during the 1970s and may be studied as possible models for others in the weekly field.

A NATIONAL ORIENTATION

Strictly speaking, the United States does not have a group of national newspapers in the same sense that Great Britain and some other countries do. The absence of such papers is one of the reasons often cited for opposing the development of a national press council in this country similar to the one that has operated with some success in Great Britain. Nevertheless, there are several newspapers with substantial national circulations and others that strongly emphasize news of the national government. Included for discussion here are the *Christian Science Monitor,* which emphasizes in-depth coverage of national and international affairs; *The Wall Street Journal,* which includes some general news but specializes in coverage of business; *The National Observer,* a weekly which looks in depth at the national government and American life generally; *The New York Times,* which endeavors to cover the world without neglecting its own immediate geographical area; and the *Washington Post* and *Washington*

Star-News, which seek to cover the national government thoroughly without neglecting other Washington area news.

Christian Science Monitor

The *Christian Science Monitor* is an international daily newspaper published by The Christian Science Publishing Society in Boston, Massachusetts. Since its founding in November 1908, it has sought to provide a constructive, solution-oriented journalism for the nation and its people. In a sense the *Monitor* was founded as a protest against the sensationalism of some early twentieth century American newspapers and the emphasis which many gave to news of crimes, accidents and disasters. But it has been much more than a protest. It has provided extensive coverage and explanation of important issues and offered insight into many of the nation's needs and problems. The *Monitor* has not overlooked crime and disaster; it has won awards for its crime reporting and its coverage of war and disaster. But it has been more concerned with the unfoldment of good and progress in human experience.

Through the years the *Monitor* has sought to adhere to the statement of purpose offered by its founder, Mary Baker Eddy, in the lead editorial of the newspaper's first edition, November 25, 1908: "The object of the *Monitor* is to injure no man, but to bless all mankind." Its mission, according to Erwin D. Canham, who served as editor from 1945 to 1964 and has served as editor-in-chief since then, is "to help give humankind the tools with which to work out its salvation." [6] Canham said these tools include information, explanation of that information, and the arousing of dormant thinking. He said the *Monitor* strives to expose whatever needs to be uncovered in order to be removed or remedied and that it seeks to place the news in perspective. It tries to give greatest emphasis to what is important and reduce the merely sensational to its place in an accurate system of values. The *Monitor's* philosophy was aptly characterized by Eric Sevareid, the noted CBS news correspondent and analyst, when he said: "The *Monitor* takes note of the world's ugliness, sin and danger but only briefly, as if to say, 'all this shall pass' and order, sanity and goodness shall prevail. . . ." [7]

The *Monitor* has pioneered in interpretive reporting and analysis of national and world affairs. Recognizing that newspapers cannot compete with the "instant news" of television, it has added to the traditional "who, what, when, where, and how" of journalism, the constructive "why" and "what-to-do-about-it." The *Monitor* has chosen to eschew the endorsement of political candidates, but its editorial writers have sought to bring their considered judgment to bear on various issues and suggest conclusions. In 1972, for example, the newspaper did not endorse either Richard Nixon or George McGovern but did try to tell its readers where these men stood on vital issues such as government spending, taxation, consumer protection and foreign relations. [8] The *Monitor* has offered thoughtful studies of urban needs, racial problems, education and other aspects of public affairs, and it has fostered the development and understanding of the arts through stories and essays, particularly on its Home Forum page.

Numerous recognitions and awards document the success of the *Monitor* in carrying out its mission. More than ten national polls have selected the *Monitor* as one of the top two or three newspapers in the United States and one of the top four or five newspapers in the world. It has won hundreds of journalistic awards,[9] including several Pulitzer prizes, and a wide variety of others. It has been cited for stories about the criminal justice system, slum clearance, gambling, race relations, business and financial coverage, education, art criticism, typography, and many other accomplishments. Surveys indicate the *Monitor* is read by most of the nation's Congressmen, many government officials, foreign diplomats, editors, school teachers, students, and many others in the United States and overseas. Information is provided for them by an award-winning staff that includes correspondents in all the states and many foreign countries and columnists such as Editor-in-Chief Canham, Joseph C. Harsch, and Roscoe Drummond.

Some questions have been raised as to whether the *Monitor* serves as a proselytizing instrument of the church which owns it and whether its relationship with the church affects policy adversely. Certainly it appears that the tenets of the church have affected the policy and approach of the newspaper in the past, and it seems likely that they will to some extent in the future. But in the early 1970s it did not appear that the newspaper was suffering from any strictures on coverage caused by its religious ownership. The *Monitor* joined with other leading newspapers in printing excerpts from the Pentagon Papers before the Supreme Court decision sanctioned the publication, and in 1971 its editor John Hughes was quoted as saying, "There is nothing we can't touch now." [10] Aside from one daily article, sometimes translated into a foreign language, on the Home Forum page, the newspaper was not engaged in proselytizing for the Christian Science faith. The newspaper's positive image and excellence performance may of course, reflect favorably on the church.

The *Monitor* made a number of significant changes in the late 1960s and early 1970s to keep step with the times and broaden its audience. Typographical changes including a six-column format on most pages and conversion to offset printing improved the newspaper's appearance. Development of a facsimile system to transmit page proofs from the home office in Boston to offset printing facilities in other parts of the country promised to accelerate distribution. Changes in the editorial operation promised to get more news out to more people. Overall coverage was expanded, a number of aggressive young reporters were hired and assigned to youth-oriented topics, and a new immediacy was encouraged in covering news. John Hughes, a prize-winning veteran of the paper's overseas staff, was named editor in 1970 with a reported mandate "to uncloister" the newspaper's goals and reach out to more persons, including "the poor, the blacks, and all the others who were not included before." [11]

In early 1972 the *Monitor* and the Register and Tribune Syndicate began operation of a Christian Science Monitor News Service. Its purpose was "to make available the *Monitor*'s news and feature file to newspapers which are themselves unable to maintain costly national and overseas staffs." The Register and Tribune Syndicate was to serve as sales agent for the service, which included information on sports, business, books, travel, music, science, art, gardening, household budgeting, antiques, theater, education, motion pictures, and fashions in addition to editorial page columns, reports on problems and issues, and other features. By 1974 the service was being used by 171 newspapers with a total circulation of 21.5 million. [12]

The Monitor was expected to continue its emphasis on "problem solving journalism." Under this approach the newspaper seeks to define major shortcomings and problems that affect large numbers of individuals, organizations or communities. It then assigns teams of reporters to collect case histories of how individuals and communities have tackled these problems and report on which techniques have worked and which have not. The paper seeks to assure readers that problems can be attacked systematically and intelligently by citizens with proper information.

Dow Jones Newspapers

The Wall Street Journal is a national daily newspaper that specializes in the coverage of business but also includes summaries of important national and international news and other features. It is published by Dow Jones & Co., which also publishes the *National Observer* and *Barron's National Business and Financial Weekly* and operates the Dow Jones News Service. Charles H. Dow and Edward T. Jones founded the company as a financial news service for private clients in 1882. The service originally consisted of handwritten news bulletins that were delivered to clients in New York's financial district at intervals throughout the day. In time the bulletins were summarized in a two-page printed sheet called Customers' Afternoon Letter, and in 1889 this was enlarged, improved and turned into a newspaper. [13] Clarence W. Barron, who already was publisher of financial newspapers in Boston and Philadelphia, acquired Dow Jones & Co. in 1902. His heirs and trusts created by them continued to own a majority of the shares when the company marked its seventy-fifth anniversary in 1964, although a substantial number of shares by then were publicly held. During the years that Mr. Barron was publisher, the newspaper operated both morning and afternoon editions. The morning edition had been started in 1898; the afternoon edition was eliminated in 1934. [14]

The *Journal* was essentially a financial newspaper until about 1940 when it broadened its concept of business news, or what constitutes news of importance to its readers. The new concept defined business news to embrace everything that somehow relates to making a living.[15] Under the astute guidance of Bernard Kilgore, the *Journal* was transformed from a financial news organ of 50,000 circulation into a national newspaper of more than a million copies. Lucid summaries of major news were included, and in-depth trend stories about business and related matters were emphasized. Kilgore, who retired from active management in 1966 and died in 1967, was also cited for encouraging the further development of *Barron's,* the expansion of the Dow Jones News Service, the founding of the *National Observer,* and the creation of the Newspaper Fund to help develop journalism talent.[16]

Editors William H. Grimes and later Vermont Royster also played key roles in the *Journal's* rise to national prominence during the 1950s and 1960s. Both won Pulitzer prizes for editorial writing. In commenting editorially on the *Journal's* philosophy, Grimes indicated that the newspaper's function was to report, analyze, and explain business news, both the good and the bad. He suggested that since the *Journal* regarded business as a national community, each of the four regional editions was essentially the same newspaper. He emphasized that the newspaper's editorial page comments and interpretations were made from a definite point of view: "We believe in the individual, in his wisdom and his decency. We oppose all infringements on individual rights, whether they stem from attempts at private monopoly, labor union monopoly or from an overgrowing government. People will say we are conservative or even reactionary. We are not much interested in labels but if we were to choose one, we would say we are radical. Just as radical as the Christian doctrine. We have friends but they have not been made by silence or pussyfooting. If we have enemies we do not placate them." [17]

Almost 40% of the journalism teachers responding to the 1961 *Saturday Review* poll cited earlier indicated that the *Journal* was the newspaper showing the greatest improvement in the previous ten years. They ranked it third in their list of 15 leading dailies behind the *New York Times* and *Christian Science Monitor.* Publishers responding to the Bernays poll in 1970 included the *Journal* among their list of ten best newspapers, and *Time* included it among its top ten in 1974. *Time* said that the *Journal* had emerged as one of the most distinctive voices in U.S. daily journalism and that the *Journal's* editorial page was the country's most widely quoted source of conservative opinion.[18]

As the middle 1970s began, the *Journal* ranked second only to the *New York News* in circulation among U.S. dailies. It had approximately 1.3 million readers in the United States and more than 90 foreign countries. Its four editions—East, Midwest, Southwest, and Pacific Coast—were printed in nine different plants, and a tenth was scheduled for opening in Florida in 1975. The multiple plants were part of the *Journal's* efforts to provide rapid delivery of its product to a widely dispersed audience. It helped develop new technology such as the use of perforated tapes and facsimile to transmit information across the country. In early 1974, the *Journal* launched its own private delivery system to cut down on mail postage costs and reduced the width of its paper to that of the *New York Times* to cut newsprint costs.[19] The *Journal's* format remained gray in the early 1970s; line drawings were used instead of photographs. But its coverage and writing were considered excellent and its impact considerable.

The *National Observer,* started by Dow Jones & Company in February 1962, seeks to provide a compact weekly presentation of world-wide events and cultural developments. An editorial in the first issue, February 4, suggested that the *Observer* would provide background for the news of the week so that its readers who are interested in the world around them could see it as a whole and understand it better. In addition, the newspaper would seek to entertain its readers and offer some things that would be "just plain 'good reading' to either stimulate or relax the mind." News selection was to be guided by standards "which we think will best serve our readers, whom we take to be all those with a ceaseless curiosity about the world around them." [20]

The *Observer* did not catch on immediately, but by 1970 it had a circulation of more than a half million and was recognized as a leader in interpretive reporting. John Merrill included it in his discussion of elite weeklies,[21] and others spoke favorably of its achievement. It would appear that the *Observer* can provide a valuable source of background and in-depth coverage of national and international events for persons in small towns whose local newspapers are locally oriented and an additional source for others. In addition to national and world affairs, the *Observer* provides information and commentary on the arts and sciences, social trends, fashions, sports, home and family problems, and other matters of general interest. It includes features for all members of the family, including school-age children. The *Observer* seemed particularly adept at relating its stories and the issues they discussed to its readers and their needs and interests.

Editor William E. Giles and Managing Editor Don Carter helped to guide the *Observer* during its formative years. Edmund Arnold, the noted typographer, helped to design the format and select the type faces, including the nameplate, which Arnold's teen-age daughter said had a nice Jeffersonian flavor. Officials reportedly liked the Jeffersonian impression not because of any political implication but rather because it recalled an era when Americans were first flexing the national muscles and were proud of being Americans.[22] Henry Gemmill, an associate editor of *The Wall Street Journal,* was named editor in late 1970 when Giles was promoted to be an assistant general manager of Dow Jones & Co.[23] Carter meanwhile had moved on to be executive editor of another paper.

The *Observer* abandoned the traditional institutional editorial in March 1971, when it announced that it was throwing the "Observations" column open to members of the *Observer* staff.[24] The results left readers wondering at times where the *Observer* stood on major issues, although the move may have prompted readers to write letters about issues discussed as the *Observer* anticipated. The editorial page continued to serve as a forum for the exchange of opinion and the newspaper generally continued to run in-depth reports on issues and interesting features as the middle 1970s began.

The New York Times

The New York Times is a highly regarded newspaper that seeks to provide complete and thorough coverage of national and international affairs without neglecting its responsibilities to its city and state of publication. It was ranked first among United States dailies in *Saturday Review* and Bernays polls cited earlier and has been included among national and world leaders in other rankings. Because of its thorough coverage, often including complete texts of important speeches and Congressional reports, the *Times* has been regarded as a principal "newspaper of record" in the United States. A periodical index of information reported in the *Times* is compiled to assist persons seeking information about past events.

The *Times* tradition of thoroughness has been developed by a series of responsible owners and publishers. The pattern was set by Henry J. Raymond, the founding editor, and continued by Adolph Ochs, who acquired the newspaper in 1896, and his successors. When Ochs died in 1935, his son-in-law Arthur Hays Sulzberger was named publisher. He remained in the post until 1961 when he was succeeded by his son-in-law Orvil E. Dryfoos. When Dryfoos died unexpectedly of a heart attack in 1963, he was succeeded as publisher by Sulzberger's only son, Arthur Ochs (Punch) Sulzberger, 37. The younger Sulzberger assumed full command after his father's death in 1968, and was serving as president and publisher as the middle 1970s approached.

The management struggle which Gay Talese describes in his book *The Kingdom and the Power* [25] contributed to a number of changes in major staff positions during the 1960s. In key changes announced by Sulzberger in late 1969 James Reston, executive editor, was named vice-president with primary responsibility in the areas of news coverage; Clifton Daniel, managing editor, was named associate editor with various duties including supervision of the New York Times News Service; Abe Rosenthal, associate managing editor and former foreign correspondent, was named managing editor; and Seymour Topping, foreign news editor, was named assistant managing editor. Reston planned to return to Washington where he had previously headed the *Times* bureau and continue his column from there.[26]

Rosenthal, in a memorandum to the staff after he took over as managing editor, said the *Times* would adjust to changes in society but would maintain its personality and its purpose. He said personality and purpose go together and are based on a plain, uncomplicated set of beliefs including the following: (1) The people who buy the *Times* expect and demand more information from it about what is important, significant, and revealing than they do from any other journal; (2) "The *Times* is a newspaper of continuity." It cannot record everything that happens, but when something important does happen, it stays with it to let the people know the outcome; (3) "The *Times* is a newspaper of relativity." It grades the importance of the news; (4) "The *Times* maintains a decent level of discourse." It tries to write and edit without shriek or invective, for if everyone screams, nobody hears a thing; and (5) "The *Times* is a newspaper of objectivity." Rosenthal said this was the most important of all, the bedrock principle. Staff members should be as objective as humanly possible.[27]

Not everyone agreed that the *Times* was always as objective as possible or as effective in its coverage as it could be. Critics suggested that biases were reflected in news columns,[28] that coverage of local affairs was uneven, that national coverage lacked proper depth. Criticism by Vice-President Spiro Agnew and others concerning a liberal Eastern press may have caused publishers and others to question the *Times'* objectivity and reporting. But it was still ranked first among United States dailies by publishers in the 1974 Bernays poll as it had been by publishers and teachers in the 1961 Bernays and *Saturday Review* polls cited earlier.

Time magazine in ranking the *Times* among the nation's ten best newspapers in 1974 said its total news staff, about 650, was by far the largest of any U.S. daily, its coverage the most exhaustive, and its influence on national and world leaders "daunting— as its publication of the Pentagon papers demonstrated." *Time* cited various aspects of the *Times,* including its improved appearance, its opposite editorial page, its women's coverage, and its cultural coverage.[29]

The inauguration of an Opposite Editorial Page in September 1970, promised to further the *Times'* efforts to stimulate thought and provoke discussion of public problems. The object of the new page, as explained in a *Times* editorial, is "to afford greater opportunity for exploration of issues and presentation of new insights and new ideas by writers and thinkers who have no institutional connection with the *Times* and whose views will very frequently be completely divergent from our own." [30] The Op. Ed. page is, of course, not a new idea; many newspapers have had such pages for years. But the *Times* approach is different. Instead of relying on syndicated columnists to help fill its two pages, the *Times* has run guest articles by government officials, scholars and others. The extra page has also made it possible for the newspaper to double the amount of space devoted to letters to the editor. Harrison E. Salisbury edited the Op. Ed. page from its inception until his retirement in December 1973; Charlotte Curtis, who had been cited for her efforts in developing the *Times'* women's news pages, was named to succeed him.[31] John B. Oakes, who was appointed editorial page editor in the early 1960s, continued to serve in that post in the early 1970s.

The guest columns and additional letters were expected to provide an improved forum for the exchange of opinions on important issues. Another step to provide balance in commentary on the editorial pages was taken in 1973 when William Safire, a presidential speechwriter, left the president's staff to write a column for the *Times*. Safire was expected to provide a conservative viewpoint in contrast to those of the *Times* regular domestic-affairs commentators James Reston, Tom Wicker and Anthony Lewis.[32] Many other newspapers have sought to provide this balance through the use of syndicated columnists.

Times staff members continued to provide extensive coverage of cultural affairs in the early 1970s through the regular pages and The New York Times Book Review. Theater critic Clive Barnes and architectural commentator Ada Louise Huxtable were among the newspaper's influential writers in the field. Cultural coverage was also expanded to include regular reports of rock music and other outgrowths of the counterculture that flourished in the late 1960s and early 1970s. The Book Review section continued its efforts to evaluate works and place them into perspective in the contemporary scene. Francis Brown retired as editor of the Book Review in 1970 after having served for some two decades; he was succeeded by John Leonard, a daily book reviewer for the *Times* and author of three books.[33]

The New York Times Company expanded considerably in the early 1970s with acquisitions in the communications and educational fields and development of services that spin off byproducts from material gathered by the *Times'* staff around the world. In a major development in 1971 the *Times* acquired *Family Circle* magazine, several Florida newspapers, and other interests from Cowles Communications, Inc. for Times stock. Subsidiary activities in 1972 included such operations as the New York Times Index, the Information Bank, the New York Times News Service, Large Type Weekly, School Weekly, several book publishing houses, a one-third interest in the *International Herald Tribune* in Paris, and Canadian newsprint companies.[34]

The Herald Tribune

The *International Herald Tribune* in Paris continues the name and perhaps some of the traditions of the highly respected *New York Herald Tribune*. It was jointly owned in the early 1970s by John Hay Whitney, owner of the *New York Herald Tribune* when it succumbed to high costs and other problems in 1966; the *New York Times;* and the *Washington Post*. Robert T. MacDonald was serving as publisher. MacDonald said that the paper was edited to reflect a European viewpoint and read by persons who are concerned with the political and financial affairs of all of Europe. He said the paper's editorial policies represented the views of the American community abroad as well, for by the nature of the circumstances persons in that community adopt a European viewpoint. In late 1973 the paper had about 360 employes, half of whom were in the mechanical department; enjoyed full use of the Washington Post–Los Angeles Times wire service, AP, UPI, Reuters and other services; and produced a comparatively small product, 16-page limit, for distribution throughout Europe, North Africa and the Middle East. The paper had plans to develop a facsimile printing operation in Uxbridge, near London, to increase British circulation in 1974. The projected press run at Uxbridge was 55,000 copies; the paper's circulation in late 1973 was approximately 140,000.[35]

The *New York Herald Tribune* was ranked among the nation's top dailies in both the Bernays and *Saturday Review* polls of 1961. It was noted for its Washington and foreign correspondence and its coverage of cultural news. Over the years its syndicated columnists had included Mark Sullivan, Walter Lippmann, Joseph Alsop, Roscoe Drummond and others. The paper was created in 1924 when Ogden and Helen Rogers Reid, owners of the *Tribune,* purchased the *Herald* from Frank Munsey. It remained in the Reid family until 1958, when it was acquired by Whitney. He and his staff continued the excellence developed by the Reids until the middle 1960s when money problems, aggravated by a long strike, led to its demise. Efforts to save the *Tribune* together with Scripps-Howard and Hearst papers in New York that also were having financial difficulties through merger failed. The *Herald Tribune* was to become the morning edition of a World Journal Tribune Company, but arrangements could not be worked out with the unions and the paper's death was announced in August. A *World Journal Tribune* was begun in September 1966, but it ceased publication in May 1967.[36]

Washington's Dailies

The *Washington Post* has improved rapidly in recent decades to become one of the nation's most highly regarded daily newspapers. It should be considered a newspaper of national orientation and influence because of its extensive and impressive coverage of the national government. Yet it must also be considered a newspaper of local and regional impact because of its services to the city of Washington and adjacent areas in Virginia and Maryland where it has extensive circulation. Publishers responding to Bernays' polls ranked the *Post* seventh in 1961 and tied for fourth in 1970. It was one of only two newspapers that drew more support in 1970 than in 1960; the *Los Angeles Times* was the other. The *Post* ranked second in the Bernays poll of 1974.

The *Post* was founded in 1877 by Stilson Hutchins, who gave it a momentum that continued for nearly half a century. In the early years the paper was lively, combative, and crowded with news and features, but in the late 1920s and early 1930s it languished. When it was unable to pay its bills, it was put in a receivership and then in June 1933 put up for auction. Eugene Meyer, a civic-minded banker, purchased it and gave it new life. Under Meyer's direction for the next 15 years, the newspaper was improved editorially; but it did not become an economic success. In 1948 Meyer and his wife transferred the voting stock to their son-in-law and daughter, Philip and Katharine Graham, and Graham set out to expand the economic base.[37]

In the late 1940s and early 1950s the Post Company acquired radio and television interests, and in 1954 purchased its only remaining morning competitor, the *Washington Times-Herald*. In 1961 the Post Company acquired *Newsweek* magazine; in 1963 it joined in the creation of the Los Angeles Times/Washington Post News Service and purchased stock in a newsprint company; in 1966 it formed a partnership in the publication of the *International Herald Tribune,* and in subsequent years acquired other interests.[38]

Katharine Graham has provided the impetus for the *Post's* surge toward excellence in the past decade. After her husband's death in 1963, she took control of both the newspaper and the corporation. Within a short time she set out to hire the personnel necessary to make her newspaper great. A key move was the appointment of Benjamin Bradlee, *Newsweek's* Washington bureau chief, as managing editor in 1965. He was named executive editor in 1968, and subsequently other top newsmen were brought in to help carry the load. Among them was Philip Geyelin, long-time State Department correspondent for *The Wall Street Journal,* who was named editor of the editorial pages.[39]

The *Post* has been especially noted in recent years for its editorials and investigative reporting. Under Geyelin the editorials have been long and stimulating, but rarely pontifical. They seek to support viewpoints with evidence and often contain fresh reporting. Geyelin said that since readers more or less know how an editorial will conclude, they have no reason to read it unless they will learn something. He won a Pulitzer prize for his efforts in 1970.[40] Herbert Block (Herblock) also contributed substantially to the *Post's* editorial page with his award-winning cartoons. The *Post's* achievements in investigative reporting are perhaps best typified by its exposure of the Watergate scandal in 1972. Reporters Bob Woodward and Carl Bernstein won numerous awards for their efforts in uncovering the Watergate story, and the newspaper received the 1973 Pulitzer Prize for distinguished public service.

Time magazine suggested in ranking the *Post* among the nation's top ten newspapers in 1974 that it was challenging *The New York Times* for national pre-eminence. *Time* particularly cited the "wise, reasoned, dispassionate commentary" of the *Post's* editorial writers and the achievements of its political staff under the direction of David Broder, who won a Pulitzer Prize in 1973.[41]

A new "Style" section was created at the *Post* in early 1969 to provide a new format for women's news, cultural coverage including reviews, and entertainment. The section was designed to include more sociology and less gossip; but rumors spread at parties sometimes make big news in Washington, and gossip was not eliminated. The Style section's most controversial feature has been a regular column, or commentary, by Nicholas Von Hoffman, a literate, witty writer who views life from the far left. Columns by Art Buchwald and Ann Landers also have run in the section along with women's news, reviews and other features.

Various criticisms have been leveled at the *Post*. Some say its reporters are permitted to advocate causes in their news stories; some say it does not exercise good news judgment; still others contend that its foreign coverage is spotty and that it lacks long-term planning.[42] While the *Post*'s staff may not agree with these or other criticisms, it has taken them seriously. As noted in Chapter 1, it assigned its own "resident critic" to review performance and recommend changes.

The *Post*'s continued editorial improvement not only resulted in awards but also brought in circulation and advertising. By the beginning of the middle 1970s, its daily circulation had passed the half-million mark, and its Sunday circulation was at 700,000 copies. In metropolitan Washington three out of every five adults were reading the *Post* daily and two of every three were reading it on Sunday. Moreover, it was getting more than 60% of the daily newspaper advertising in the metropolitan area and ranked fifth among all U.S. dailies in the amount of advertising lines carried.[43] A new plant completed in 1972 helped to facilitate production.

By the early 1970s, the *Post* had assumed the strong economic position that the *Star* had enjoyed in the middle 1950s when it dominated the Washington scene and was the fifth largest U.S. daily in ad linage. The *Post* was doing very well, while both the *Star* and the *Daily News,* a Scripps-Howard tabloid, were losing money. But the competition was expected to grow more intense again after the *Star* purchased the *Daily News* in July 1972. *Star* editor Newbold Noyes promised that once the paper got into the black a major effort would be made to expand its national and foreign coverage and then beef up its business and arts sections.[44]

The *Washington Star* was founded in 1852 and developed by members of the Noyes, Kauffmann, and Adams families from the late 1860s into the early 1970s. Until the *Post*'s recent drive to prominence, it was considered the best paper in town, and many still prefer it. The *Star* was cited in 1967 for its good judgment in selecting and displaying news, its ability to keep its biases out of its news columns, its use of hard news in an afternoon paper, and its editing.[45] The *Star* has not kept pace with change in Washington and the nation as well as the *Post* has, however, and it has fallen well behind the *Post* in circulation and advertising revenue. Elimination of afternoon competition brought the *Star,* now *Star-News,* an additional 100,000 circulation but did not bring a commensurate increase in advertising revenue. In the summer of 1974 the *Star-News* had 420,000 weekday circulation and 345,000 Sunday circulation as compared with the *Post's* 535,000 on weekdays and 700,000 on Sunday. The *Star-News* could become increasingly competitive in the middle and late 1970s, however, as a result of changes in ownership and management. Agreements were approved in September 1974 for Joe L. Allbritton, a millionaire banker from Houston, to acquire for $25 million a 38% interest in Washington Star Communications, Inc., which owns the *Star-News,* the Washington Star Syndicate, and radio and TV stations in Washington, D.C., Charleston, S.C., and Lynchburg, Va. Allbritton was expected to exercise control over the company and bring new management ideas as well as new money into its operations.[46]

All the nationally oriented newspapers mentioned in the previous section are located in the East, and several have strong local as well as national commitments. Others cited as leaders in the East in recent years have included the *Boston Globe, Hartford Courant,* and *Providence Journal-Bulletin* in New England; *Newsday* in New York; and the Baltimore *Sun* in Maryland.

New England Leaders

The *Boston Globe* was included by *Time* magazine in its list of the ten best daily newspapers in the United States in 1974. *Time* said the *Globe* was one of the nation's most improved newspapers over the previous decade; it credited Tom Winship, who became editor in 1965, with providing the impetus for excellence. The *Globe* won Pulitzer Prizes for its investigative efforts in 1966 and 1971, and it was the third newspaper to publish excerpts from the Pentagon Papers.[47] Charles H. Taylor served as publisher of the paper from the late 1870s until his death in 1921. Members of his family and descendents of Eben D. Jordan, a founder, have been the chief operating officers. When the newspaper went public in August 1973, almost half of its 2,200 employes purchased stock. The prospectus prepared at that time showed a steady growth in total revenues during recent years.[48] Combined morning and evening circulation was close to 480,000 in early 1974 and Sunday circulation was 625,000. The *Globe*'s first 100 years are described in a book written by Louis M. Lyons, former member of the staff and former curator of the Nieman Foundation at Harvard, and published by the Belknap Press of Harvard University Press.

The *Hartford Courant* continued to provide distinguished journalism for the people of Connecticut in the 1970s as it had for many decades. The weekly *Connecticut Courant* was founded at Hartford in 1764, a dozen years before the United States declared its independence. Its owners started a daily edition in 1837 under the name *Hartford Courant,* but continued the weekly edition under the old name until 1914. While the daily could not be called a continuation of the weekly, it was a branch of the original *Courant* under the same ownership. The paper, which celebrated its 200th birthday in 1964, appeared to have strong support for its assertion that it is the nation's oldest newspaper of continuous publication. Frank Luther Mott, distinguished journalism historian, said he adhered to the following statement by *Courant* editor Herbert Brucker in the early 1960s: "Everything considered, it looks to me as though the *Hartford Courant* has the best claim to priority at the present time." [49]

Editor Brucker, who has been a leader in efforts to develop a better and more responsible American journalism, and Publisher John R. Reitemeyer provided strong leadership at the *Courant* for a number of years. Reitemeyer said much about the newspaper's philosophy when he told stockholders at a meeting: "A newspaper's greatest asset is not its building, its equipment, or the money in the bank or the bonds in its vault. A newspaper's greatest asset is public confidence, public belief in its fairness, in its honesty, in its integrity. Without this confidence, no newspaper can long survive." [50] The traditions established early and advanced by Brucker and Reitemeyer were continued in the late 1960s and 1970s by Editor and Publisher Bob Eddy. He said in 1973 that while the paper had perhaps won more than its share of prizes, he believed its major achievement in recent years has been covering Connecticut thoroughly day in and day out. In 1973, the *Courant* had nearly 100 correspondents in addition to 15 state bureaus staffed by full-time persons and a live and active city desk. It had five full-time editorial writers and a part-time secretary for its editorial page. Eddy described the paper as liberal Republican but noted that it does not hesitate to criticize Republican office-holders when a need arises.[51]

The *Providence Journal* and *Bulletin* also continued to provide distinguished service in New England. They earned recognition both for their news presentation and their editorial page leadership. Edwin Emery, distinguished journalism historian, said that under the executive leadership of Sevellon Brown from 1921 to 1957 the Providence papers became "the conscience of Rhode Island." [52] Their excellence was continued in the 1970s under the direction of Editor Michael J. Ogden.

New York's Other Dailies

Newsday, the *New York Daily News,* and the *New York Post* all provided local competition for the *New York Times* in the early 1970s. *Newsday,* discussed as perhaps the nation's best-known suburban newspaper in Chapter 3, was ranked among the nation's ten best newspapers by *Time* magazine in 1974. *Time* suggested that *Newsday* combines solid local coverage with ambitious national and international undertakings; it said that *Newsday* is heavy on interpretive reporting and features and light on spot or breaking news that commuters already have seen in the Manhattan press or heard on their car radios. The magazine also reported that *Newsday* was carrying more advertising linage than any of New York City's three dailies.[53] Two recent examples of *Newsday*'s investigative reporting emphasis concerned a six-month look at heroin, which reporters traced from the poppy fields of Turkey to the streets of Long Island, and a year-long sociological study of Long Islanders and their life-styles called "The Real Suburbia." By late 1973 *Newsday* was the fifth largest evening newspaper in the country with a net paid daily circulation of more than 450,000. It was read by three of five families in Nassau and Suffolk Counties, Long Island, the nation's ninth largest metropolitan market area.[54] *Newsday*'s Sunday edition, started in 1972, was reported to be doing well in 1973.

The *New York Daily News,* discussed in Chapter 3 as the nation's most successful tabloid, continued to lead the nation in circulation in the early 1970s with more than 2 million readers daily and almost 3 million on Sunday. It also announced plans in early 1974 to increase its coverage and thereby its circulation and advertising in New Jersey. The plan called for the number of pages devoted to local New Jersey news in the papers delivered there to be increased from two to ten pages. The *News* already had approximately 300,000 daily readers and 540,000 Sunday readers in New Jersey.[55]

The *New York Post* completed its 170th year of service in American journalism in 1971 and looked to the future with continued enthusiasm and confidence. The *Post* has a long and intriguing history; it was founded by Alexander Hamilton in 1801, and its spokesmen in the nineteenth century included William Cullen Bryant and Edwin Lawrence Godkin. The paper experienced financial difficulties during the depression before being purchased in 1939 by Dorothy Schiff. Under her ownership and leadership the paper was transformed into a streamlined tabloid that not only survived but prospered. Mrs. Schiff said she favors strong local news coverage and wants to have a good general newspaper. She described the *Post* politically as an independent liberal newspaper which covers all bases. The *Post* obtained a new home, the old *Journal-American* plant, as the 1970s began which was expected to facilitate both production and distribution of the newspaper. Executive editor Paul Sann spoke enthusiastically about the new facility and how it could help the *Post* put out a new brighter afternoon tabloid full of news.[56] The *Post's* afternoon monopoly could be challenged by development of a new paper, the *New York Press,* by oilman John Shaheen. Officials said it would start in 1975, be New York rather than nationally oriented, and carry substantial business news.[57]

Baltimore Sun

Farther to the south, the *Baltimore Sun* continued to provide distinguished coverage of national and international affairs in the 1970s. Since it was founded in 1837, the *Sun* has been a leader in the coverage of nearby Washington; it has maintained one of the larger bureaus there and its Washington reporters, many of whom also have served in overseas bureaus, provide in-depth reports on national and international affairs. Paul Kumpa, who previously headed the *Sun's* Moscow bureau, directed a staff of 14 in Washington in 1972. The *Sun* took some steps in the early 1970s to brighten the drab gray appearance that had characterized it for many years, and in 1974 completed arrangements for installation of the largest front-end electronic news room system on the Eastern seaboard.[58]

Many other notable newspapers are published in the East, some of which may challenge for wider recognition in the 1970s. One that could be headed for greater eminence is the *Philadelphia Inquirer,* which was obtained by Knight Newspapers, Inc. from Triangle Publications in 1970. The *Buffalo News* was listed among the top 26 newspapers cited by educators in the *Saturday Review* poll of 1961.

THE MIDWEST

The Midwest with its massive business and industrial development and its many metropolitan areas has produced numerous good newspapers and a number of excellent ones. The *St. Louis Post-Dispatch, Milwaukee Journal,* and *Chicago Tribune* have ranked highest in the recent polls cited in this chapter; several others are highly regarded.

St. Louis Papers

The *Post-Dispatch* ranked second in the Bernays poll and fourth in the *Saturday Review* polls of 1961, and it was tied for fourth in the Bernays poll of 1970. It was also one of only four United States newspapers included among the 20 leading dailies in the world selected by a panel of 26 journalism educators in 1964; the other three were *The New York Times, Christian Science Monitor* and *Washington Post*.[59]

The *Post-Dispatch* has achieved continued recognition through consistent application of the sound principles laid down by its founder Joseph Pulitzer in 1878 and summarized by him in 1907. At that time Pulitzer presented the *Post-Dispatch* Platform as follows:

> I know that my retirement will make no difference in its cardinal principles, that it will always fight for progress and reform, never tolerate injustice or corruption, always fight demagogues of all parties, never belong to any party, always oppose privileged classes and public plunderers, never lack sympathy with the poor, always remain devoted to the public welfare, never be satisfied with merely printing news, always be drastically independent, never be afraid to attack wrong, whether by predatory plutocracy or predatory poverty.[60]

The traditions developed by Joseph Pulitzer, the founder, were continued by his son, also named Joseph Pulitzer, and his grandson, Joseph Pulitzer, Jr. The second Pulitzer directed the paper from his father's death in 1911 until his own death in 1955; the third of the Pulitzers took over at that time and continued to serve as editor in the 1970s. Joseph Pulitzer, Jr. discussed the *Post-Dispatch* Platform in terms of its application to contemporary problems in a speech to the National Conference of Editorial Writers in St. Louis in 1961. He suggested that the paper could be considered conservative "in its jealous protection of Constitutional liberties deriving from the Bill of Rights and might be called progressive for endorsing "the compensatory role of government in economic affairs." He said the paper was more concerned with the "values of human dignity and liberty than with the values of inert property" and that it supported the people's aspirations for "better housing, for sound medical assistance, for brighter opportunities in education." Pulitzer said that in the debate over procedures, the paper encouraged bold remedies and "when the need is demonstrated, national rather than local solutions." [61]

Many outstanding journalists have joined with the Pulitzers to make the *Post-Dispatch* a great newspaper. Among them were Oliver K. Bovard, who was managing editor for 30 years until 1938, and Daniel R. Fitzpatrick, editorial cartoonist for 45 years until his retirement in 1958. In recent years, Arthur R. Bertelson has served as managing editor and executive editor; Evarts A. Graham, Jr. as managing editor; Robert Lasch as editor of the editorial page; and Tom Engelhardt as cartoonist. *Post-Dispatch* journalists have won numerous awards, including 15 Pulitzer Prizes. Lasch was cited for distinguished editorial writing in 1965 and Marquis W. Childs, nationally known columnist, won for commentary in 1969.

Post-Dispatch officials have made changes in the content, appearance and production of the newspaper in recent years to keep pace with the twentieth century. Zone sections have been added to present local news for many suburban areas, and the society section has been converted into a women's section with broadened news of women's participation in civic, cultural and other activities. The paper has conducted a program to improve color printing and in 1965 began publication of a daily page of photographs in color. Edmund C. Arnold, an authority on typography, was called in as consultant, and the paper was given a face-lifting in 1968 that included more legible headlines and more horizontal makeup. In the early 1970s the paper developed plans for conversion to cold type and offset printing both in its downtown plant and a new satellite plant, linked to the downtown operation by facsimile transmission. These plants print both the *Post-Dispatch* and its rival the *St. Louis Globe-Democrat*.

The *Globe-Democrat* was formed in 1875 through merger of the *Missouri Democrat*, founded in 1852, and the newly begun *Morning Globe*. It gained stature through the efforts of Joseph B. McCullagh in the late nineteenth century and Casper S. Yost and others in the twentieth century. The *Globe-Democrat* was a strong advocate of the Republican party before it absorbed the *Republic*, a strongly Democratic rival, in 1919. At that time it developed an independent platform, pledging to print the news impartially, "supporting what it believes to be right, and opposing what it believes to be wrong, without regard to party politics." [62] E. Lansing Ray guided the fortunes of the paper for several decades until 1955 when it was sold to Samuel I. Newhouse. The *Globe-Democrat*, which has been especially noted over the years for its efforts to build a better St. Louis, was listed among the nation's top 25 newspapers in the *Saturday Review* poll of 1961.

Milwaukee Journal

Under the guidance of Lucius Nieman and his successors, the *Milwaukee Journal* has been established as one of the leading newspapers in the Midwest and the nation. It was ranked fourth in the Bernays poll and fifth in the *Satur-*

day Review poll in 1961, seventh in the Bernays poll of 1974, and included among *Time*'s top ten in 1974. Nieman bought a half interest in the *Journal* shortly after it was founded in 1882 and soon established it as an independent, aggressive newspaper dedicated to serving the people of Milwaukee. The *Journal* has fought negligence and corruption in government and elsewhere and campaigned for community progress in various fields. For these efforts it has earned numerous awards and recognitions, including four Pulitzer Prizes. The first Pulitzer came in the public service category in 1919 for the *Journal*'s courageous fight against anti-Americanism by German-Americans in Wisconsin during World War I. Cartoonist Ross Lewis was cited in 1935; Austin C. Wehrwein won for international reporting in 1953, and the newspaper won another public service citation in 1967 for its campaign to foster conservation.[63] Among the other recent awards was the Inland Daily Press award for community service in 1973 for a year-long campaign to improve the business climate of Wisconsin. The campaign resulted in tax law changes which were credited with making Wisconsin more attractive as a site for industrial expansion.[64] The paper has been praised both for its thorough and fair-minded news coverage and its editorial page.

When the Niemans died, Lucius in 1935 and his wife Agnes Wahl Nieman in 1936, they left two substantial legacies to American journalism: the *Journal* and the Nieman Foundation at Harvard. His will left 55% of the stock in the newspaper to his widow with the proviso that it be sold within five years to persons who would maintain the *Journal* as an independent newspaper devoted to the community. Trustees were authorized to sell to other than the highest bidder to attain this end. Harry J. Grant, the *Journal*'s business manager, and a stockholder himself, worked out an employe-ownership plan similar to one in Kansas City whereby employes of the newspaper could buy the stock, but the plan was stalled briefly by Mrs. Nieman's unexpected death. She left her share of the stock to Harvard University to promote and elevate the standard of journalism in the United States. After involved negotiations, an arrangement was worked out whereby Harvard sold its stock to the *Journal* for resale to employes. At the same time the Nieman Foundation was established to enable selected newspapermen to study for a year at Harvard. Other stockholders also agreed to sell stock to the employes and the amount of employe-owned stock climbed steadily.[65] In late 1973 the company's more than 1,300 employe-stockholders owned 82.5% of the stock, and plans were being developed for them to acquire an additional 7.5% over the next few years.[66]

During the early 1970s the *Journal* made increasing use of team reporting to handle investigative projects and cover urban affairs generally. It began to run more consumer type stories on its women's pages, which gradually have evolved away from the traditional society format; and it moved aggressively into consumer related treatment of foods, groceries and nutrition in its weekly food section. The paper has inaugurated an opposite editorial page, which permits an expanded use of letters from readers and in a gradual manner it has moved toward more horizontal makeup.[67] The *Milwaukee Sentinel,* acquired by the *Journal* in 1962, has also emphasized investigative reporting and public service programs in recent years.

Chicago's Dailies

The *Chicago Tribune* was engaged in a revitalization program during the early 1970s that could enhance its national ranking as well as enable it to compete more effectively with newspapers in the area. The *Tribune* was ranked ninth in Bernays and *Saturday Review* polls in 1961 and sixth in the Bernays poll of 1974. It was also included in *Time* magazine's top ten rankings for 1974. The *Tribune* is owned by the Chicago Tribune Company, which also owns the *New York Daily News* and other interests. The Tribune Company operated *Chicago Today,* a compact or tabloid newspaper, in Chicago from 1969 until late 1974. When the company decided to stop publication of *Chicago Today,* it concurrently announced that the *Tribune* would become a 24-hour newspaper. Its chief competitors in Chicago are Marshall Field's morning *Sun-Times* and afternoon *Daily News.*[68]

Under the direction of Colonel Robert R. McCormick from the 'teens until his death in 1955 the *Tribune* became noted as a spokesman for a nationalist-isolationist point of view and ultraconservatism in politics. Critics argued that its prejudices were reflected in its news columns. Sometimes overlooked outside Chicago, however, was the fact that the *Tribune* provided extensive coverage of local and area news and highly readable sections on sports, women's news and other interests. It was one of the best-written newspapers in the country, its circulation was large and its advertising revenues substantial.

McCormick's successors generally sought to continue his policies and approach. But by the last third of the century it was apparent that some of the old formulas were not going to work so well in solving new challenges. The *Sun-Times* was gaining in the struggle for circulation and advertising. Many persons evidently wanted something they were not finding in the *Tribune.* A "Feminique" section on fashion and home decor was added in the Monday *Tribune* beginning in 1965 and an Action Express column, featuring a mobile "city desk" that went into the city and suburbs to interview persons about their problems, was initiated in 1968. But the major shift in approach came with the appointment of Clayton Kirkpatrick as editor in early 1969.

Kirkpatrick, a *Tribune* veteran, has instituted a wide range of changes to improve the content, appearance and overall image of the newspaper. A "Perspective" section including in-depth articles on local, national and international subjects and a remodeled editorial page was introduced in the Sunday paper in 1970, and a daily Perspective section, usually two pages, was begun the next year. This section has featured *Tribune* writers, syndicated columnists ranging from Nicholas von Hoffman to William Safire, a column by a blue-collar worker, and a "Speak Out" section to give readers an opportunity to write about subjects of special interest to them. The political cartoon was shifted from page one to the editorial page in 1971, and a second full-time editorial cartoonist was added in 1973. Editorials generally appeared less strident than some had been in the past.

A "Lifestyle" feminine-oriented section addressing itself to problems of today's society such as ecology, child care, family relations and women's liberation was introduced in 1971; the financial section was expanded in 1972; and the Sunday *Tribune*'s news section was expanded in 1973 with increased coverage of metropolitan area news. Typographical improvements included introduction of caps and lower case banner headlines, the use of six-column formats on a number of pages in the Sunday edition, and the development of modular makeup wherein stories are made up in blocks rather than "legs" or "turns." Many energetic young staff members were added to help implement all the changes.

Of particular significance was the creation of a Task Force or investigative reporting team in 1971. Under the direction of George Bliss, a 1962 Pulitzer Prize winner, this team uncovered evidence of voting frauds that led to 79 indictments.[69] Investigative reporting was, of course, not new for the *Tribune,* but the task force approach involving several persons on a regular basis and others as needed appeared to have great potential.

It was not certain as the middle 1970s began whether the changes in the *Tribune* would enable it to dominate Chicago journalism again, but they seemed certain to make it a better newspaper. "I want this paper to be intensely professional." Editor Kirkpatrick said in 1973. "It's not possible to practice personal journalism in a metropolitan paper any more. But it is possible to have character, and that will come from high professional competence and responsibility." [70]

The *Tribune* must produce good newspapers to compete successfully with Field's *Sun-Times* and *Daily News.* The *Sun-Times* was formed in 1948 through merger of the *Sun,* founded by Marshall Field III in 1941, and the *Chicago Times.* Within a little more than a decade it grew to become one of the nation's ten largest newspapers. D. J. R. Brucker, a national columnist for the *Los Angeles Times,* wrote in a *Columbia Journalism Review* article in early 1972 that the *Sun-Times* probably produced the best national news package in the Midwest. "It has the best Washington bureau of the Chicago papers and it is used well," Brucker wrote. "It makes maximum use of its wires. . . . ; its Sunday paper is as complete as any but a few in the country." [71]

The *Chicago Daily News* was ranked tenth among United States daily newspapers in the *Saturday Review* poll of 1961 mentioned earlier. Founded in 1876, the *News* was developed as a solid newspaper by Melville E. Stone, Victor Lawson and others. Subsequent owners, including Field, who acquired it in 1959, sought to continue its tradition of excellence. Over the years the paper has been noted for its news coverage—especially its foreign coverage, its independence and its aggressive editorial policies. The Daily News Foreign Service, started in 1898, has been recognized by Sigma Delta Chi, national journalism society, as the oldest continuing foreign service operated by an American newspaper.[72] The foreign service had accounted for seven of the 14 Pulitzer Prizes that the newspaper had won through 1972, although recent winners have been in other areas. Lois Wille won a Pulitzer for public service in 1963, John Fischetti for editorial cartooning in 1969, William J. Eaton for National affairs reporting in 1970, and Mike Royko for commentary in 1972. Daryle Feldmeir was named editor of the Daily News in 1971 to succeed Roy Fischer, who resigned to become dean of the School of Journalism at the University of Missouri.

The Daily News has continued to emphasize investigative reporting, business coverage and cultural reporting in recent years, and it has broadened its concept of women's news. The paper's weekend edition has a special magazine called "Panorama" devoted to culture and the arts. Service news about homemaking is included in a special section called "Everyday," which is designed to interest all family members and includes information about education, medicine, travel, consumer news, and other topics besides fashions and foods.

Kansas City Star

The Kansas City Star in the early 1970s continued to pursue the program of excellence developed by its founder William Rockhill Nelson in the 1880s. The program emphasized local and area coverage, community service campaigns and good writing. Some feared the Star's brilliance might dim after Nelson died, and it may have dimmed somewhat during the trusteeship period that followed his death in 1915. But in 1926 employes of the Star and Times, its morning edition, worked out an arrangement with Nelson's heir to buy the newspaper for $11 million. They got together $2.5 million in support of their bid, and, despite predictions of failure from outside, paid off the remaining amount by 1939, two years ahead of schedule. Continued employe ownership was assured when all stockholders agreed to give options on their stock to other stockholders or the company at death or should they leave the Star.[73]

With ownership questions resolved, the Star moved ahead strongly again under the leadership of Roy A. Roberts, Henry J. Haskell and others. Roberts retired as chairman of the board of the Star in January 1965 after 56 years of service to the organization. He began his career as a reporter, and later during his executive years remarked that he would always be a reporter looking for a story. He covered the Missouri state legislature for a number of years, and worked in the Star's Washington bureau from 1915 to 1928 when he became managing editor. He was elected president and general manager in 1947. Haskell joined the Star as editor of the editorial page in 1910 and served as editor from 1928 to 1952. These two men provided the impetus for the Star's continued efforts to put out a quality newspaper for the people of Kansas City and surrounding areas; but they had considerable help, and their successors have stressed similar goals. William W. Baker was named editor in 1967 and continued to serve in that post into the middle 1970s.

During recent years the *Star* has significantly expanded its suburban coverage with the establishment of a Metro Desk, headed by a Metro Editor; started its own locally edited Sunday magazine, *Star;* and reorganized its entire Sunday package. The old society and women's section has been replaced by a new section called "People"; business, real estate and agriculture news have been combined in a new section called "Business"; the arts and entertainment section has been renamed "The Arts"; and a new four-page section without advertising has been created for editorials and commentary—it's called "Forum." The *Star* also began running its "Public Mind," or letters column, six days a week, including eight full columns on Sunday, to accommodate a doubling in the number of letters received. The paper has expanded its space for coverage of sports and business news, and it has adopted a new corrections policy that provides for immediate publication of any corrections under a standing head, "Corrections," that always runs on page two. In addition, with help from Ed Arnold, the typography specialist from Syracuse University, the *Star* has redone its typography; multi-deck heads have been abolished, and horizontal makeup has come to be emphasized.[74]

Cowles Newspapers

The Cowles family newspapers in Des Moines and Minneapolis also continued to be leaders among Midwestern newspapers in the 1970s. Gardner Cowles acquired and developed the *Des Moines Register* and *Tribune* during the early decades of the twentieth century; his son Gardner Jr. continued that operation while another son John developed the *Minneapolis Star* and *Tribune,* acquired during the late 1930s. The *Minneapolis Tribune* was ranked in a tie for twelfth, the *Des Moines Register* was ranked sixteenth, and the *Minneapolis Star* nineteenth among United States dailies in the *Saturday Review* survey of journalism educators in 1961. Moreover, the educators ranked the *Star* and *Tribune* second and *Register* and *Tribune* third behind the *Louisville Courier Journal* and *Times* among the best combinations of morning and evening newspapers published by the same organization. These three were well ahead of the other 15 combinations mentioned in the poll.[75]

The Des Moines papers have won numerous awards over the years, including three Pulitzer Prizes for editorial writing and four for national reporting. More importantly their news coverage and editorial comment have contributed toward solving problems in their region. About half the people in Iowa read the daily *Register* and some three-fifths of them read the *Register* on Sunday. The *Tribune* concentrates on a 38-county area in central Iowa. Both papers stress service to their readers and their communities.

In recent years, under the direction of Editor Kenneth MacDonald, both newspapers have been expanding their news operations, adding additional news bureaus in the state, and adding reporters to facilitate more team coverage and more specialization. The papers, already noted for sports coverage, have increased emphasis on sports such as sailing, camping, cycling and hiking; and they have phased out the old society approach to women's news in favor of an emphasis on family news and features. The papers have increased the amount of locally produced materials on the editorial pages and in the opinion sections, and broadened their coverage of cultural activities. A graphics consultant who came to the paper in 1973 to help develop a new format for the Sunday *Register* joined the staff as art director.[76]

The Minneapolis newspapers also have won numerous awards in recent years, including several Pulitzers, Raymond Clapper awards for Washington reporting, and national awards for coverage of agriculture, religion, education and medicine. Minneapolis was one of only four cities to have two newspapers cited among the top 20 dailies in the *Saturday Review* poll of 1961; the other three were New York, Chicago and Washington. By the 1970s the papers also had won national recognition for their independent editorial endorsements and their opposition to right-wing movements.[77] John Cowles, Jr. assumed control of the news and editorial pages after 1960.

Cowles newspapers shared a Washington bureau from the time that John Cowles started the Minneapolis operation until separate bureaus were created for the two cities in 1968. Several newsmen including Dick Wilson, Clark Mollenhoff and Fletcher Knebel achieved national prominence while working in the joint bureau.[78]

Many other highly regarded newspapers are published in the Midwest. The *Toledo Blade* and the *Detroit Free-Press* both were included among the top 26 newspapers cited by educators in the *Saturday Review* poll of 1961; the *Cleveland Plain Dealer* was included in Merrill's list of near elite newspapers, and the *Cleveland Press* was cited by *Time* magazine as one of the nation's ten best in 1964. The *Free-Press*, one of the Knight newspapers, announced an agreement in early 1974 to buy land in downtown Detroit for future construction of a complete newspaper publishing facility. Its rival, the *Detroit News*, relocated its production facilities in a new suburban plant in 1973 and became one of the pioneers in using video screens for originating as well as editing stories. The *Cleveland Press* has placed more emphasis on investigative reporting and expanded its business coverage in recent years.

THE SOUTH

Fewer nationally recognized newspapers developed in the South than in the East and Midwest during the first century and a half of the nation's life because the region itself developed more slowly and produced fewer large cities. But economic and cultural changes in the middle twentieth century gave rise to an energetic, dynamic New South and the number of good newspapers being published had risen substantially by the early 1970s. A few such as the *Louisville Courier-Journal* and *Miami Herald* have achieved excellence and have been recognized among the nation's best.

Louisville Courier-Journal

The *Courier-Journal* has long been established as both a regional and national leader. It achieved national recognition under the long and distinguished leadership of Henry Watterson from 1868 when the paper was created through merger until the time of World War I, when he earned a Pulitzer Prize for editorial writing. It was purchased at that time by Judge Robert Worth Bingham, and he and his descendants have continued and enhanced its many traditions. Judge Bingham stated the family's policy toward the newspaper when he said, "I have always regarded the newspapers owned by me as a public trust, and have endeavored so to conduct them as to render the greatest public service." [79] His son, Barry Bingham; grandson, Barry Bingham, Jr.; and other noted journalists such as Mark Ethridge, James S. Pope, and Norman Isaacs, have continued the emphasis on public service.

The *Courier-Journal* has been cited for its ability to cover national and international affairs without neglecting Louisville and surrounding areas, its vigorous editorial page, its efforts to assure fairness and accuracy in its presentation, and its many public service activities. The paper was a leader in developing an ombudsman plan to monitor its efforts and handle complaints, and it has stressed the use of letters to the editor on its editorial pages; it began using an opposite editorial page to provide a broader forum for discussion of issues in 1940. The *Courier-Journal* was also among the first to adopt the six-column front page to improve appearance and foster readability, and it has been a leader in the development of the Newspaper-in-the-Classroom program. It has won numerous awards, including several Pulitzer Prizes.

Publishers responding to the Bernays polls ranked the *Courier-Journal* fifth in 1961 and fifth in 1974 among the nation's ten best dailies. Journalism teachers responding to the *Saturday Review* poll of 1961 ranked the *Courier-Journal* as the eighth best daily and rated the *Courier-Journal* and *Times,* established in 1884, as the best combination of morning and evening newspapers published by the same organization. [80] *Time* magazine included it as one of its top ten in both 1964 and 1974. In 1974 *Time* credited Robert Bingham and his son with playing a major role in getting Kentuckians to accept peaceful integration and noted that grandson Barry, Jr., had maintained the newspaper's public-spirited tradition. [81] The grandson succeeded his father as publisher in 1971.

Miami Herald

The *Miami Herald* developed rapidly in the early 1970s to challenge the *Courier-Journal*'s preeminence among Southern newspapers and join the list of the nation's best newspapers. The *Herald* began publication under that name in 1910 when Frank Shutts bought the *News-Record* and changed its name. It achieved considerable prominence during the Florida boom of 1925 and 1926 when it did a huge volume of business and printed editions averaging 96 pages a day. The boom did not last, however, and a hurricane on September 18, 1926, also hurt the community. The paper dropped back to between 20 and 28 pages a day. Shutts refinanced the paper in 1927, and it weathered the depression that soon followed; but he decided to sell and retire from the newspaper business in 1937. Frank B. Stoneman, who had helped establish the *Evening Record* in 1903, remained with the *Herald* until his death in 1941.[82]

John S. Knight, owner of the *Akron Beacon-Journal,* bought the *Herald* from Shutts and became its editor and publisher. He also acquired the morning *Tribune,* abolished it, and brought some of its outstanding staffers to the *Herald*. The purchase signaled the beginning of a new era both for the *Herald* and its owner. The *Herald* went on to become one of the nation's outstanding newspapers; Knight went on to develop one of its most successful newspaper groups with papers in Detroit and Philadelphia as well as Charlotte, N.C.; Macon and Columbus, Georgia; Lexington, Kentucky; and Boca Raton, Bradenton, and Tallahassee, Florida by 1974.

James L. Knight, brother of the publisher, and Lee Hills, Alvah H. Chapman, Jr., John McMullan, Don Shoemaker, George Beebe and Larry Jinks are among the many who have helped the *Herald* achieve excellence. Jinks was serving as editor in 1974. The *Herald* won a Pulitzer Prize for its efforts to combat organized crime in Miami in 1950; *Herald* investigative reporter Gene Miller earned a Pulitzer in 1967 for his efforts to free two persons innocently jailed on murder charges, and John S. Knight earned a Pulitzer for editorial writing in 1968. Various *Herald* staffers have won numerous awards.

The *Herald* has been a national leader in recent years in both news coverage and advertising linage. In 1970, for example, it led the entire nation in news linage and was second to the *Los Angeles Times* in total advertising linage carried. The *Herald* was ranked twenty-second in the *Saturday Review* poll of 1961 and fourth in the Bernays poll of 1974; *Time* included it among its top ten in 1974. The *Herald* has been cited for its coverage of the diverse Miami area, its Latin American editions, its attractive format, its use of color and various other achievements.

Despite its group affiliation, the *Herald* regarded itself as an independent newspaper in the early 1970s. It was not obligated to any political party or special interest; its purpose was to serve as a constant auditor of government and public affairs. In recent years the paper has added specialist reporters in the areas of consumerism, the environment and urban affairs, and expanded its use of team reporting. Women's news coverage has evolved into more of a lifestyle approach.[83] In early 1974 circulation for the morning edition was slightly more than 400,000 and for the Sunday edition slightly more than a half-million.

Atlanta's Dailies

The *Atlanta Constitution* and its afternoon partner, the *Atlanta Journal,* moved into a new $4.5 million office building in 1972 that should facilitate their efforts to serve Georgia and the Southeast. The office structure completed a three-phase building program begun in 1968 that also includes a $26 million mechanical plant completed in late 1970 and a garage and warehouse three blocks long completed in 1969. The facilities are located on the edge of the downtown business district but are only a few blocks from a major highway interchange involving Interstates 75, 85 and 20. They provide the sixth home for the *Constitution* since it was founded in 1868 and the fifth for the *Journal,* which was begun in 1883. The two newspapers, now owned by the Cox newspaper group, have prospered in a city where more than 100 papers have failed in the past 120 years. Their combined Sunday circulation reached 573,726 and their combined weekday circulation 467,690 in 1972.[84]

Henry W. Grady brought national recognition and stature to the *Constitution* in the 1880s when he called for the development of a New South based on industrial development and implemented many techniques of the new journalism at the newspaper. His successors, especially Ralph McGill and Eugene Patterson, continued the search for a new and better South and the development of a great newspaper. McGill joined the *Constitution* in 1929 as an assistant sports editor and advanced through the ranks to become editor; he was publisher for nine years before his death in 1969. Patterson joined the *Constitution* and *Journal* as executive editor in 1956 after having served as chief of the London Bureau of the United Press. He was named editor of the *Constitution* in 1960 when McGill was named publisher, and remained in that post until 1968 when he resigned and became managing editor of the *Washington Post.* More recently he has been serving as president and editor of the *St. Petersburg Times.* McGill and Patterson provided courageous leadership for the *Constitution* and the South during the early troublesome years of integration. Their writing was clear, reasoned and persuasive, whatever the subject.

Constitution writers have won numerous awards over the years, including four Pulitzers. McGill in 1959 and Patterson in 1966 were honored for commentary. Herman Hancock was recognized in 1931 for local reporting, and Jack Nelson, now with the *Los Angeles Times,* was cited in 1960 for a series that led to improvements in the state's mental health program. Cartoonist Cliff (Baldy) Baldowski has been cited by Sigma Delta Chi and others for his forceful drawings. The *Constitution* was tied for twelfth among the top United States dailies selected in the *Saturday Review* poll of 1961.

The *Journal* has received less national recognition than its morning partner, but it has about 45,000 more readers; its staff also has earned a number of awards, including a Pulitzer for George Goodwin's efforts in exposing a vote fraud in 1948. Jack Spalding has been editor of the *Journal* since 1957; Reg

Murphy succeeded Patterson as editor of the *Constitution*. In recent years both papers have continued to emphasize local and state coverage, and both have expanded their sports coverage to accommodate the advent of major league teams in the city. With strong traditions and new and expanded facilities, both appeared to have great potential for development in the 1970s.

Elsewhere in the Southeast

Several impressive newspapers have been developed in North Carolina, including the *Charlotte News* and *Observer,* the *Raleigh News* and *Observer,* the *Winston Salem Journal* and *Twin City Sentinel,* and the *Greensboro News* and *Record.* The Charlotte *Observer* and *News,* acquired by the Knight group in 1954 and 1959, respectively, have provided good service in recent years under the direction of publisher James L. Knight and editors C. A. Pete McKnight, *Observer,* and Stewart Spencer, *News.* The Raleigh newspapers, developed by Josephus and Jonathan Daniels, continued to provide vigilant coverage of state government and community affairs under the leadership of publisher Frank A. Daniels, Jr. The Winston-Salem papers developed rapidly in the late 1960s and earned a Pulitzer Prize for public service in 1971 for blocking a strip mining operation that threatened the areas's ecology. Editor Wallace Carroll and Executive News Editor J. Pat Kelly have provided strong leadership. The Greensboro traditions have been continued in the 1970s under the direction of publisher C. O. Jeffress, Editor William D. Snider and Executive News Editor Porter L. Crisp.

The *St. Petersburg Times,* owned by the Poynter family since 1912, has established itself as a leader in Florida journalism and appears headed for higher recognition under the direction of Nelson Poynter and Eugene Patterson, who became editor in 1972. The paper has won a number of awards, including a Pulitzer for public service in 1953, and it has been a national leader in the development of new technology. Poynter was chairman of the board, Patterson president and editor, and John B. Lake publisher in the early 1970s.

The *Nashville Tennessean* and the *Chattanooga Times* have been cited for their continued progress in recent years, and the *Memphis Commercial Appeal* has been recognized as one of the best representatives of the Scripps-Howard group. The *Richmond Times-Dispatch* and *Richmond News-Leader,* which gained national recognition under editors Virginius Dabney and Douglas Southall Freeman in earlier years, were leaders in the move toward new technology in the early 1970s. D. Tennant Bryan was publisher and John E. Leard executive editor in the early 1970s.

THE SOUTHWEST

The *Arkansas Gazette* gained national recognition, including two Pulitzer Prizes, for its editorial leadership during the school desegregation crisis in Little Rock in 1957. The newspaper was cited for public service, and Harry S.

Ashmore, executive editor, was honored for his editorials. The *Gazette* was established at the Post of Arkansas in 1819 and moved to Little Rock two years later when that settlement was named capital of the territory; it has proclaimed on its masthead that it is the oldest newspaper west of the Mississippi River. The *Gazette* was guided during much of the twentieth century by J. N. Heiskell, who was editor and president during the 1950s and subsequently chairman of the board until his death in late 1972. Serving in key roles in the early 1970s were Hugh B. Patterson, Jr., president, treasurer and publisher, and A. R. Nelson, executive editor.

During recent years the *Gazette* has formed an investigative reporting team, established regional bureaus in northwest and southeast sections of Arkansas, and added a full-time Washington correspondent. The efforts of the investigative team in 1972 led to the indictment of three persons by a federal grand jury for alleged mishandling of poverty fund programs. The *Gazette* also has expanded its stock market coverage and replaced its "For and About Women" section with one on "People and Events." Leland Duvall, business and farm editor, has won two awards and has been cited by two secretaries of agriculture for his writing on farm problems.[85]

Competition continued to thrive in a number of Texas cities in the 1960s and early 1970s. In Dallas, the *Dallas News* was matched against the *Dallas Times Herald,* acquired by the Los Angeles Times-Mirror Company in 1970. In Houston, the *Post,* developed by William P. Hobby and his wife Oveta Culp Hobby, was squared off against the *Chronicle.* Both newspapers completed new facilities about 1970. In San Antonio, Hearst's *Light* was in competition with the jointly owned *News* and *Express,* purchased from Harte-Hanks Newspapers in 1973 by Keith Rupert Murdoch, owner of newspapers in Great Britain and Australia. In Fort Worth, the *Star-Telegram* established by Amon G. Carter, was paired against the Scripps-Howard *Fort Worth Press.* The *Dallas News* and the *Houston Post* were included among John Merrill's near elite newspapers in the middle 1960s.

THE WEST

Generally speaking, newspapers developed later and more slowly in the Western United States than along the East Coast, where the population was heavily concentrated even in Colonial times. But as the settlers migrated to the West and business and industry developed, many newspapers were begun. San Francisco was a major spawning ground of newspapers in the nineteenth century, and the San Francisco-Oakland and Los Angeles areas have major concentrations of newspapers today. A number of good newspapers have been published in the West; a few such as the *Los Angeles Times, San Francisco Chronicle* and *Portland Oregonian* on the coast and the *Denver Post* in the Rocky Mountains have achieved national recognition.

Los Angeles Times

The *Los Angeles Times* has improved dramatically in the past 15 years to rank high among the nation's leading newspapers. It jumped from a laudable eighth place in 1961 to a solid second place in 1970 in the Bernays polls of the nation's publishers. Educators ranked it fifteenth in the *Saturday Review* poll of 1961; *Time* magazine included it among its top ten in 1964 and again in 1974. The newspaper has established itself as a leader in circulation, advertising linage, the amount of space devoted to news, and the type of coverage and commentary provided in that space. Its image has been remade from ultra-conservative and often unfair to independent and responsible.

The *Times* has been a successful paper for a good many years under the guidance of the Otis and Chandler families. Harrison Gray Otis joined the *Times* shortly after it was started in 1881 and, with another man that he later bought out, acquired the paper in 1883. Otis served as publisher until his death in 1917 when he was succeeded by his son-in-law Harry Chandler, who served until 1944. Chandler was succeeded by his son, Norman Chandler, who served as publisher until 1960 when he passed the job along to his son Otis Chandler, who continued to serve in the early 1970s.

Under Otis and the first two Chandlers the paper developed a strong tradition of conservatism. It strongly favored Republicans, who at times got more news coverage as well as editorial support. The paper also tended to be anti-labor, especially after 1910 when its plant was dynamited by union radicals. Washington correspondents voted the *Times* the third "least fair and reliable" paper in 1937, and some critics referred to it as an unofficial house organ of the Republican party. On the other hand, the paper engaged in numerous public service activities and earned Pulitzer Prizes in 1942 and again in 1960. Mrs. Norman Chandler, also an executive of the *Times,* was instrumental in raising millions of dollars for construction of the Los Angeles Music Center.[86]

The *Times* started a tabloid called the *Mirror* in 1948 to help compete with Hearst's morning *Examiner* and afternoon *Herald-Express* and Manchester Boddy's *Daily News*. The five-way struggle continued until 1954 when the *Daily News* dropped out. Then in 1962 the *Times* stopped publication of the *Mirror* and the Hearst organization dropped the *Examiner* and renamed its evening paper the *Herald-Examiner*. The *Herald-Examiner* continued to provide opposition for the *Times* in the 1960s and 1970s, although its effectiveness was substantially reduced by a strike that began in 1967 and continued into 1973. Circulation dropped from more than 700,000 to around 500,000, advertising revenues fell, and the staff had to be reduced considerably. The newspaper continued to publish however, and in 1973 announced plans for expansion of coverage and greater emphasis on background articles and features.[87]

The *Times'* rise to prominence was occasioned by changes in its own organization, however, and not by any reduction in outside competition. The paper improved in virtually every phase of its operation in the 1960s and early 1970s to earn recognition as one of the nation's very best newspapers. In the early 1960s the *Times* had one foreign correspondent and three reporters in its Washington bureau; by the early 1970s it had 18 bureaus overseas, seven bureaus in the United States, and more than 20 reporters in Washington. At the local level it developed a strong metropolitan staff of almost 100 persons, added a special edition for Orange County, and made other improvements. By the early 1970s the *Times* had greatly increased its interpretive and background reporting, and its editorial pages provided a good balance of columnists as well as thought-provoking institutional editorials and cartoons. In addition, the *Times* developed a Sunday tabloid magazine called "Calendar" to expand coverage of drama, the arts and literature, and added a new rotogravure magazine called "West" to serve the area. It improved its appearance through typographical changes that included the six-column format, and it adopted many aspects of the new technology, including cold type. As might be expected with all these improvements, it continued to be a leader in advertising linage. As the middle 1970s began the paper had a circulation of slightly more than a million and was averaging more than a hundred pages a day.

Key figure in the drive for excellence has been Otis Chandler, who succeeded his father as publisher in 1960 at the age of 33. He has had much help from Nick Williams, who served as editor until 1971; William F. Thomas, who served as metropolitan editor until he succeeded Williams as editor; Robert J. Donovan, distinguished Washington correspondent; Paul Conrad, prize-winning cartoonist who joined the paper in the early 1960s; James Bassett, James G. Bellows, Anthony Day, Frank P. Haven and many others. Norman Chandler also continued to play an important role in supervising the growth of the Times-Mirror Company until his death in 1973. The *Times* joined with the *Washington Post* in creating a major news service in 1962; and it has added various properties in recent years, including two major newspapers, the *Dallas Times Herald* and *Newsday*.

Portland Oregonian

Under the direction of Harvey W. Scott, Henry L. Pittock, Palmer Hoyt, Robert C. Notson and others, the Portland *Oregonian* has been a leader in West Coast journalism for more than a hundred years. Scott served the paper, founded in 1850, as editor from 1865 until his death in 1910. He and Pittock bought the *Oregonian* in 1877 and their heirs continued it until 1950 when it was sold to Samuel I. Newhouse. Hoyt provided strong leadership in the 1930s and 1940s before leaving to become publisher of the *Denver Post*.

The *Oregonian* experienced some difficulties in 1959 and the early 1960s as the result of a prolonged strike, but appeared to be moving strongly again in the early 1970s. It was partially redesigned in the early 1970s, and further revisions were planned after a changeover to offset production was completed.

The *Oregonian* has used the team reporting concept to handle complex issues, and it developed a Sunday "Forum" section to provide extensive coverage of major issues such as the energy crisis. It was cited by the Atomic Industrial Forum in 1970 for excellence in covering the atomic energy field.[88] William Arthur Hilliard, who was named city editor in 1971, was the first black to rise that high in the editorial organization of a major United States daily newspaper. Notson was serving as publisher of the *Oregonian* in the early 1970s. He was also an officer in the Oregonian Publishing Company, which published the *Oregonian* and the *Oregon Journal,* acquired by Newhouse in 1961.

Denver Post

After providing new impetus for the Portland *Oregonian* in the 1930s and 1940s, Palmer Hoyt moved on to revitalize the *Denver Post* and help it become one of the top newspapers in the Western part of the United States. The *Post* had gained national recognition in the late 1890s and early twentieth century under the ownership of Harry H. Tammen and Frederick G. Bonfils. Although it engaged in some crusades that undoubtedly helped the area and its people, it was primarily known in that era for its sensationalism; its brand of deep yellow journalism included banner headlines in red ink.

Tammen died in 1924 and Bonfils in 1933, but their general approach was continued until Hoyt arrived on the scene in 1946. Under his leadership the *Post* developed a strong, independent editorial page, emphasized background and interpretation in reporting, and increased local and regional news coverage. *Post* cartoonists Paul Conrad in the 1950s and early 1960s and Patrick Oliphant in subsequent years earned national recognition for their efforts.

Control of the *Post* was expected ultimately to lodge in its employes under provisions of an ownership plan developed by Helen Bonfils, daughter of Frederick Bonfils, in the 1960s. Samuel I. Newhouse, who bought a minority interest in the *Post* in 1960, contested the validity of the employe plan in his efforts to gain a controlling interest; but when an appeals court ruled against him in 1973, he sold his interests to the Frederick G. Bonfils Foundation, established after Bonfils' death in 1933. This acquisition increased the amount of stock held by that foundation to 46.9%. Other shareholders were the Helen G. Bonfils Foundation, created before her death in 1972, 44.7%, and the Denver Post Employes Stock Trust, 8.3%. Miss Bonfils bequeathed most of her estate to the Helen G. Bonfils Foundation for purchase by the employes' trust at a formula price. Hoyt retired as editor and publisher of the *Post* in 1970 and was succeeded by Charles R. Buxton.[89]

Elsewhere in the West

The *San Francisco Chronicle,* started in 1865, established a strong reputation for public service under co-founder Michel H. de Young, who served as publisher until his death in 1925. It was noted for its extensive national and international reporting in the 1930s and 1940s, but in more recent years it has turned increasingly to highly readable stories and features that produce more circulation. Students of Bay Area journalism suggested that Paul Smith, who became executive editor in 1935, offered San Franciscans a chance to support a quality newspaper, but most of them declined.[90] The *Chronicle* succeeded in passing its rival, the *Examiner,* in circulation but fell behind it in the production of solid news. Columnists such as Herb Caen, Art Hoppe, Ralph Gleason, William Hogan, Terrence O'Flaherty and Art Rosenbaum contributed substantially to the *Chronicle*'s general appeal.

Elsewhere in California, the *Sacramento Bee,* the *Santa Barbara News-Press,* and other smaller newspapers were making big strides forward. The *Sacramento Bee,* one of several *Bees* developed by the McClatchy family, was especially noted for its coverage of state government news in California. The *News-Press* gained national recognition in the early 1960s when its publisher Thomas M. Storke received the Pulitzer Prize for editorials. In recent years it has expanded its coverage in almost all areas, including the environment, business and culture. The *Redwood City Tribune* was cited in the late 1960s for its ability to report on teen-age life in its community, and the *Riverside Press* and *Enterprise* were praised for their reporting of local government.[91]

The *Arizona Daily Star* and the *Tucson Daily Citizen* received national attention in the late 1960s and early 1970s when a court test of their joint operating agreement led to adoption of the Newspaper Preservation Act, discussed in Chapter 4. The *Citizen* was required to divest itself of the *Star,* in 1971, but joint operating agreements were sanctioned for Tucson and other cities. In 1973, when the two newspapers moved into a new $11 million home, they were separately owned and independent; but their business operations and production were handled through a joint agency, Tucson Newspapers, Inc. The *Citizen* was owned by William A. Strong, who also served as publisher; Paul A. McKalip was editor and executive vice president. The *Star* was owned by Pulitzer Publishing Company, which acquired it in 1971. Michael E. Pulitzer was serving as editor and publisher and David F. Brinegar as executive editor.

The *Citizen* received the Gavel Award of the American Bar Association and the Award of Merit of the trial Lawyers of America in 1973 for investigative stories and editorials that led to the revamping of Pima County's probate court system. It had won the statewide community service award given by the Arizona Newspapers Association 15 times in the previous 20 years. Under its new ownership, the *Star* expanded its staff and coverage, and added a new Sunday analysis section called comment. Both papers looked to the future with optimism.[92]

SOME OUTSTANDING WEEKLIES

Attempting to rank the nation's weekly newspapers is even more difficult than attempting to rank its dailies. There are approximately 9,000 of them, they come in varying circulation groups, they serve diverse audiences, and they are not so likely to be well known outside their immediate environs. Many are doing an excellent job, however, and it seems appropriate to call attention at least to those that have done well in the early 1970s in competition sponsored by the National Newspaper Association.

Several newspapers received one of the top three rankings or honorable mention in general excellence in their circulation groups two or three times in the first four years of the 1970s. Those placing high three times include the *Williamston* (Michigan) *Enterprise, Burlington* (Colorado) *Record, Denville* (New Jersey) *Citizen* of Morris County, and the *Birmingham* (Michigan) *Eccentric.* Those placing twice include the *Folsum* (California) *Telegraph,* Lewisburg (Pennsylvania) *Union County Journal,* Swainsboro (Georgia) *Forest-Blade,* Bainbridge (Georgia) *Post-Searchlight, Walden* (New York) *Citizen-Herald,* Libertyville (Illinois) *Independent-Register, Princeton* (New Jersey) *Packet,* Lancaster (South Carolina) *News,* Chicago Heights (Illinois) *Star, Brighton-Pittsboro* (New York) *Post, Manassas* (Virginia) *Journal-Messenger, Skokie* (Indiana) *Life,* and Zelienople (Pennsylvania) *Butler County News-Record.* [93]

The *Eccentric,* the *East Lansing* (Michigan) *Towne Courier,* and the Pacific Palisades (California) *Palisadian Post* each received almost 20 other awards, and more than a dozen papers got between five and ten awards during the four years. The *Palisadian Post* had the best women's page three of the four years in its circulation group; the *Eccentric* had the best newspaper promotion three of the four years in its group. The *Cresco* (Iowa) *Times Plain Dealer* scored first in service to agriculture three times and first in use of photographs twice in its group, and the *Hillsboro* (Oregon) *Argus* earned two firsts in service to agriculture in its group. The Jesup (Georgia) *Wayne County Press* had the best editorial page two years in a row, and the Plaquemine (Louisiana) *Greater Plaquemine Post* had three firsts among its nine awards.

General excellence winners in the Under 3,000, 3,000–6,000, 6,000–10,000, and over 10,000 categories in recent years have included the following: 1970) *Hartwell* (Georgia) *Sun,* Zelienople (Pennsylvania) *Butler County News-Record, Union* (New Jersey) *Leader,* and the *Chicago Heights* (Illinois) *Star;* 1971) *Folsom* (California) *Telegraph,* Swainsboro (Georgia) *Forest-Blade,* Kennebunk (Maine) *York County Coast Star,* and the Zelienople (Pennsylvania) *Butler County News-Record;* 1972) *Clinton* (New York) *Courier,* Swainsboro (Georgia) *Forest-Blade, Denville,* (New Jersey) *Citizen* of Morris County, and the *Downer's Grove* (Illinois) *Graphic Herald;* 1973) *Galva* (Illinois) *News, Hood River* (Oregon) *News, Walden* (New York) *Citizen Herald,* and the *Oak Forest* (Illinois) *Star Tribune.*

The good weeklies, like the good dailies, appear to have some things in common despite their diversity. They place major emphasis on news and community service; they speak their minds on issues; they are aware of new technology, and they are trying to improve. The *Swainsboro* (Georgia) *Forest-*

Blade, which earned first in general excellence two years in a row, averages 100 local news stories a week and runs two editorial pages featuring mostly local commentary. It has shifted to a six-column format and provides spot color for advertisers on a regular basis. The *Hood River* (Oregon) *News,* another general excellence winner, has built its successful newspapers on a strong news emphasis and local editorial comment. It runs several columns of locally written editorials each week and has its own local cartoonist. The paper strives hard to maintain reader credibility.[94]

Weeklies such as the *Forest-Blade,* the *News,* the *Jensen Beach* (Florida) *Mirror,* the *Greater Plaquemine* (Louisianna) *Post* and the *Eunice* (Louisiana) *News* have demonstrated that their newspapers can make a difference in their communities. The *Mirror* received a special citation for community service from the National Newspaper Association in 1972 for its investigative reporting on health law violations in its state. The *Post* earned a top community service award for its efforts to save the historic downtown area of Plaquemine. The *News,* which recently won a national award for its special "Eunice Showcase" edition, has been cited for its efforts to bring desirable industry to its community.[95]

The achievements of these and other newspapers mentioned in this chapter provide strong evidence for the contention that newspapers not only can live up to the ideals suggested earlier in this book but are doing it. Only a few of the nation's many newspapers are even approaching greatness, and even the best of them can be greatly improved; but the potential for excellence and the benefits that communities as well as newspapers can derive from such excellence have been demonstrated. Business success and public service are not mutually exclusive for newspapers; they can expect to receive a reasonable financial return on their investments while providing the services that the public needs to function in today's increasingly complex world. Newspaper owners, employes and readers should work together in efforts to assure these needed newspaper services for their communities.

Notes

NOTES TO CHAPTER I

1. "Congressional Quiz," *The Gallup Opinion Index,* No. 64 (October 1970), 10; Curtis D. Mac-Dougall, *Understanding Public Opinion: A Guide for Newspapermen and Newspaper Readers* (Dubuque, Iowa, 1966), 8; William P. Steven, "The Social Responsibility of the Press," *Nieman Reports* (June, 1967), 15–16.

2. For a discussion of newspapers as part of an information processing system, see comments by Dr. Herbert Simon, associate dean of the Graduate School of Industrial Administration at Carnegie Mellon University and professor of computer science and psychology, "Are Newspapers With It?: A Panel Discussion," *Problems of Journalism* (New York, 1969), 193–200.

3. "Crime and disaster news," *Editor & Publisher* (May 5, 1973), 4.

4. The editorial influence of newspapers and other media is widely debated. Some recent studies include Maxwell McCombs, "Editorial Endorsements: A Study of Influence," *Journalism Quarterly* (Autumn, 1967), 545–548; Del Brinkman, "Do Editorial Cartoons and Editorials Change Opinions?" *Journalism Quarterly* (Winter, 1968), 724–726; N. J. Spector, "The Impact of the Editorial Page on a Municipal Referendum," *Journalism Quarterly* (Winter, 1970), 762–766; and "Interpersonal Communication and the Editorial Writer," News Research Bulletin, American Newspaper Publishers Association, No. 22 (December 2, 1970), 79–80.

5. "Our Basic News Medium," *Saturday Review* (August 9, 1969), 41–42; Robert U. Brown, "What is 'primary'?" *Editor & Publisher* (April 12, 1969), 60; "Roper survey: TV is public's top news source," *Editor & Publisher* (April 7, 1973), p. 7.

6. "Research professor rejects Roper data on credibility," *Editor & Publisher* (November 4, 1972), 32.

7. "Newspapers are still dominant news source, publishers told," *Editor & Publisher* (February 10, 1973), 9; "That myth about TV news dominance," *Editor & Publisher* (August 4, 1973), 6; Robert U. Brown, "100 million read a newspaper every day, BOA study finds," *Editor & Publisher* (November 18, 1972), 13.

8. See the 20-page printed report *News about the news media from a nationwide opinion research study conducted in March–April, 1971,* published by the Bureau of Advertising, American Newspaper Publishers Association, New York; "Study shows preference for papers," *Editor & Publisher* (August 31, 1971), 32.

9. "CBS-TV claims newspaper ad reading time is under 6 seconds," *Editor & Publisher* (September 5, 1970), 9–10; "Bureau's research expert pokes holes in CBS study," *Editor & Publisher* (September 12, 1970), 11, 16; "Adman says print must prove it has 'supermotivat-ability,' " *Editor & Publisher* (October 26, 1968), 17.

10. See the 20-page printed report *News about the news media from a nationwide opinion research study conducted in March–April, 1971,* published by the Bureau of Advertising, American Newspaper Publishers Association, New York; "New Study Refutes Television Claims," *Editor & Publisher* (April 29, 1967), 102.

11. Susan Pilchik, "Media buyers flay tv bargain hunting," *Editor & Publisher* (May 3, 1969), 17.

12. Permission to use the verse was given by Mr. Phelps. It was quoted by Jerry Walker, Jr., "Ad-ventures," in *Editor & Publisher* (September 12, 1970), 16.

13. "Newspapers outsell tv," *Editor & Publisher* (January 23, 1971), 4.

14. Special edition of *St. Louis Globe-Democrat,* June 1, 1962.

15. "Dominant source of news," *Editor & Publisher* (December 11, 1971), 6.

16. "Survey exposes some ideas for closing the youth gap," *Editor & Publisher* (November 13, 1971), 14, 78.

17. "News and the Functional Illiterate," *Saturday Review* (June 13, 1970), 51–52.

18. Fred S. Siebert, Theodore B. Peterson, and Wilbur Schramm, *Four Theories of the Press* (Urbana, Illinois, 1956); John Calhoun Merrill, *The Imperative of Freedom* (New York, 1974).

19. Commission on Freedom of the Press, *A Free and Responsible Press* (Chicago, 1947), 20–29.

20. *Ibid.*

21. John H. Colburn, "What Makes a Good Newspaper?" *Saturday Review* (June 9, 1962), 50, 52.

22. "Newsday ends its endorsement of candidates," *Editor & Publisher* (September 9, 1972), 11; "Endorsement of candidates," *Editor & Publisher* (September 9, 1972), 6.

23. James Russell Wiggins, "The Press in an age of controversy," *The Quill* (April, 1969), 8–14. See discussion by Dr. Warren Bennis, vice-president for academic development at the State University of New York at Buffalo, "Are Newspapers With It?: A Panel Discussion," *Problems of Journalism* (New York, 1969), 179–192.

24. John Hohenberg, *The News Media: A Journalist Looks at His Profession* (New York, 1968), 290–291; "Newspapers Get ACTION For Readers," *Editor & Publisher* (December 31, 1966), 9–10.

25. Candace Hollar, "Action Line: editors act like detectives for readers," *Editor & Publisher* (September 15, 1973), 13.

26. James D. Hartshorne, "Action Lines," a letter to the editor in *Editor & Publisher* (November 17, 1973), 7. Hartshorne is deputy executive director of the Ohio Turnpike Commission.

27. "109 participate in Action Line Clearinghouse," *Editor & Publisher* (December 9, 1972), 50–51.

28. "National 'action line' names firms and brands," *Editor & Publisher* (October 13, 1973), 28.

29. "3 reader help projects in Chicago Today cited," *Editor & Publisher* (October 24, 1970), 28; Nancy Lewis, "Role of consumer reporter examined in SNPA seminar," *Editor & Publisher* (May 22, 1971), 9–10.

30. "Newspaper class gains sharply in reading score," *Editor & Publisher* (August 28, 1971), 26.

31. "Elementary school uses newspapers for textbook," *Editor & Publisher* (June 2, 1973), 38; "Newspaper Best School Textbook?", an Associated Press story in *The Atlanta Journal* (December 8, 1973), 4-A.

32. News release prepared by the American Newspaper Publishers Association Foundation, December 8, 1971.

33. Robert U. Brown, "Newspaper in adult classrooms," *Editor & Publisher* (March 10, 1973), 52.

34. "Copley Service offers plan for home education," *Editor & Publisher* (June 17, 1972), 46; "College-Level Courses Due Via Papers," an Associated Press story in the *Athens* (Ga.) *Banner-Herald* (September 27, 1973), 24; "Newspaper U. idea goes into phase 2 with 'Dream' series," *Editor & Publisher* (August 24, 1974), 26.

35. "National journalist's group adopts standard of conduct," *Editor & Publisher* (December 8, 1973), 13.

36. Ben H. Bagdikian, "Fat newspapers and slim coverage," *Columbia Journalism Review* (September/October, 1973), 15–20.

37. Ralph Z. Hallow, "Pittsburgh's ephemeral 'riot,' " *Columbia Journalism Review* (January/February, 1972), 34–40.

38. "How newspapers hold themselves accountable," *Editor & Publisher* (December 1, 1973), 7, 16, 28; the full study is published in *ANPA Research Bulletin* (November 30, 1973).

39. "Coping with readers' gripes becomes task for specialists," *Editor & Publisher* (January 30, 1971), 7.

40. *Ibid.,* 7–8.

41. Joe Smyth, "Newspapers do err but are willing to admit it," *The Quill* (October, 1970), 13–15.

42. See editorial page of the *Miami Daily News,* March 17, 1970; Robert U. Brown, "Tell the public about it," *Editor & Publisher* (April 11, 1970), 52.

43. "Coping with readers' gripes becomes task for specialists," *Editor & Publisher* (January 30, 1971), 7.

44. Ben H. Bagdikian, "Bagdikian's post-mortem: keep up criticism," *The Bulletin of the American Society of Newspaper Editors* (October, 1972), 1, 12–13.

45. "Reader surveys are being made by 60 papers," *Editor & Publisher* (February 5, 1972), 10.

46. George N. Gill, "It's Your Move, Publishers," *The Quill* (August, 1973), 21–22.

47. "National journalist's group adopts standard of conduct," *Editor & Publisher* (December 8, 1973), 13.

48. M. L. Stein, "The Press Under Assault; 1. View from the U.S.," *Saturday Review* (October 12, 1968), 75–77; Newton H. Fullbright, "Gallup: Public is fed up with journalistic excesses," *Editor & Publisher* (September 28, 1968), 11.

49. "Press is the victim of its achievements," *Editor & Publisher* (July 25, 1970), 32.

50. "What America Thinks of Itself," *Newsweek* (December 10, 1973), 45.

51. Robert Davis, "Harris urges: reflect reader changes," *Editor & Publisher* (April 29, 1972), 9, 12; "Crisis in confidence," *Editor & Publisher* (May 20, 1972), 6.

52. See especially the April, May and June, 1972 issues of *[MORE]: A Journalism Review*.

53. "Media review paper started for St. Louis," *Editor & Publisher* (October 3, 1970), 34.

54. "A review of reviews," *Columbia Journalism Review* (March/April, 1972), 4–7; "Journalism's In-House Critics," *Time* (December 6, 1971), 74.

55. Donald E. Brown, "British journalists change their attitudes toward reorganized Press Council," *Editor & Publisher* (April 17, 1971), 22, 58.

56. *Ibid.,* 58.

57. *Ibid.,* 58, 60.

58. Donald E. Brown, "Press Council rulings serve as guidelines for journalists," *Editor & Publisher* (April 24, 1971), 17, 30.

59. *Ibid.*, 34.

60. Richard L. Tobin, "Does the U.S. Need a National Press Council?" *Saturday Review* (October 14, 1967), 115–116; Warren Agee, "Is the Public Commission Idea Still Relevant Today?" *The Bulletin of The American Society of Newspaper Editors* (October, 1968), 10; Norman E. Isaacs, "Why we lack a national press council," *Columbia Journalism Review* (Fall, 1970), 22.

61. *Ibid.*

62. Houstoun Waring, "A First Report of the National Press Council?" *Grassroots Editor* (May–June, 1969), 4; Houstoun, Waring, "Control of Media Is Major Concern," *Grassroots Editor* (March–April, 1973), 22–24.

63. Norman E. Isaacs, "Why we lack a national press council," *Columbia Journalism Review* (Fall, 1970), 23–26; Herbert Brucker, "A Conscience for the Press," *Saturday Review* (May 9, 1970), 59; "ASNE unit studies complaint procedure," *Editor & Publisher* (July 4, 1970), 28; "New Look at ethics plan urged in ASNE," *Editor & Publisher* (January 23, 1971), 36; "Quest for ethics mechanism renewed by editors' groups," *Editor & Publisher* (June 3, 1972), 9–10.

64. Norman E. Isaacs, "Why we lack a national press council," *Columbia Journalism Review* (Fall, 1970), 25–26; Herbert Brucker, "A Conscience for the Press," *Saturday Review* (May 9, 1970), 60.

65. Alfred Balk, *A Free and Responsive Press* (New York, 1973).

66. "National News Council," *The Quill* (June, 1973), 10.

67. Mark Mehler, "National News Council launches its operation," *Editor and Publisher* (July 21, 1973), 12.

68. "News council to study Fla. reply law case," *Editor & Publisher* (October 27, 1973), 20; "Press council upholds conflict of interest charge against Lasky," *Editor & Publisher* (June 29, 1974), 11.

69. Barry Bingham, Sr., "The Case for a National Press Council," *Nieman Reports* (June, 1973), 19–22.

70. Alfred Balk, "Minnesota launches a press council," *Columbia Journalism Review* (November/December, 1971), 22–27; J. Edward Gerald, "The New Minnesota Press Council," *Grassroots Editor* (November/December, 1971), 13–15.

71. "Five cases settled by press council," *Editor & Publisher* (June 16, 1973), 28.

72. Nancy Baggett, "Press councils: a summing up," *The Bulletin of the American Society of Newspaper Editors* (September/October, 1972), 17–19.

73. "Local Press Councils: A Panel Discussion," in *Problems of Journalism* (New York, 1969), 77–93; Norman E. Isaacs, "Why we lack a national press council," *Columbia Journalism Review* (Fall, 1970), 19–20; "News media council active in Honolulu," *Editor & Publisher* (November 28, 1970), 30.

74. "Poll shows most editors can live with watchdogs," *Editor & Publisher* (August 31, 1974), 38.

75. "Press council helps small-city newspaper," *Editor & Publisher* (January 17, 1970), 10.

NOTES TO CHAPTER 2

1. "The Sedition Act," *U.S. Statutes at Large* (Boston, 1848), I, 596.

2. Letter from Jefferson to President Washington, September 9, 1792, in Henry S. Randall, *The Life of Thomas Jefferson* (New York, 1858), II, 82.

3. Letter from Jefferson to Edward Carrington of Virginia, January 16, 1787, in Randall, *The Life of Thomas Jefferson,* I, 463–64.

4. *The* (New York) *Herald,* May 6, 1835.

5. For additional information on Pulitzer's philosophy, see the section on the *Post-Dispatch* in Chapter 8.

6. Delos F. Wilcox, "The American Newspaper: A Study in Social Psychology," *Annals of the American Academy of Political and Social Science* (July, 1900), 78.

7. Included in a booklet titled *The World in Focus: The Story of the Christian Science Monitor,* published by The Christian Science Publishing Society in 1965.

8. Walter Lippmann, "The Candidacy of Franklin D. Roosevelt," *New York Herald Tribune* (January 8, 1932), 19.

9. *Near v. Minnesota* ex rel Olson, County Attorney, 283 *United States Reports* 697 (1931).

10. Grosjean, Supervisor of Public Accounts of Louisiana v. American Press Co., Inc., 297 *United States Reports* 233 (1936).

11. Lee G. Miller, *The Story of Ernie Pyle* (New York, 1950), 427.

12. John Hohenberg, *The News Media: A Journalist Looks at His Profession* (New York, 1968), 51.

13. *Ibid.,* 47, quoting *Editor & Publisher,* April 16, 1966.

14. "Guild raises wage goal to $400 a week," *Editor & Publisher* (July 4, 1970), 12.

15. Raymond B. Nixon, "Half of nation's dailies now in group ownerships," *Editor & Publisher* (July 17, 1971), 7.

16. "Newspaper Preservation Act of 1970," *United States Statutes at Large* (Washington, 1971), LXXXIV (Part 1 of 2 Parts), 466.

17. "Freedom of Information Act of 1966," *United States Statutes at Large* (Washington, 1967), LXXX (Part 1 of 2 Parts), 250.

NOTES TO CHAPTER 3

1. John C. Merrill, *The Elite Press: Great Newspapers of the World* (New York, 1968), 7 27.

2. *Ibid.,* 23–24.

3. Kenneth R. Byerly, "Dailies on Skids? No!" *The Quill* (August, 1969), 13–15.

4. Robert U. Brown, "A 50-year record," *Editor & Publisher* (November 1, 1969), 52; "N.Y. News breaks ground for new $29 million production facility," *Editor & Publisher* (December 19, 1970), 28, 30; "New York News home delivery gains hailed," *Editor & Publisher* (December 11, 1971), 20.

5. "Chicago's War of the Losers," *Time* (August 9, 1971), 52–53; "A New Newspaper for Chicago!" *The Little Trib* (May, 1969), 6–12; "Chicago's American in 'compact' format," *Editor & Publisher* (March 22, 1969), 10; Dan Rottenberg, "An old new paper bows in Chicago," *Columbia Journalism Review* (Summer, 1969), 50–51; Wesley Hartzell, "Chicago Today . . . how a new compact newspaper was created," *The Quill* (August, 1970), 28–30; Gerald B. Healey, "Chicago Today—name of the game is change," *Editor & Publisher* (April 19, 1969), 134, 138.

6. "Chicago Today to fold; Tribune to go 'all-day,' " *Editor & Publisher* (August 31, 1974), 10, 43; "Chicago's War of the Losers," *Time* (August 9, 1971), 52–53.

7. Kenneth R. Byerly, "Dailies on Skids? No!" *The Quill* (August, 1969), 13–15.

8. Robert G. Marbut, "Newspapers' future bright . . . with some 'ifs' in picture," *Editor & Publisher* (November 13, 1971), 56.

9. "Suburban papers need much more market research," *Editor & Publisher* (July 21, 1973), 20.

10. Gene Balliett, "Newsday's First Two Decades," *The Quill* (January, 1961), 12–14.

11. "Times-Mirror will buy rest of Newsday stock," *Editor & Publisher* (October 31, 1970), 14; "Harry F. Guggenheim, Newsday founder, dies," *Editor & Publisher* (January 30, 1971), 34.

12. "Attwood leaves Cowles; named Newsday publisher," *Editor & Publisher* (September 5, 1970), 11; "Newsday has plans only for Long Island," *Editor & Publisher* (October 17, 1970), 11; "Attwood sets goals as Newsday publisher," *Editor & Publisher* (November 7, 1970), 12; William Sexton, "Sunday Newsday, $1.3 million project, fires up competition," *Editor & Publisher* (April 15, 1972), 7–8; Daniel L. Lionel, "Newsday's Sunday on Solid Ground," *Editor & Publisher* (October 13, 1973), 24.

13. Newton H. Fulbright, "Suffolk Sun ends three-year struggle on Long Island," *Editor & Publisher* (October 25, 1969), 9, 14.

14. *Ibid.*

15. Clarence O. Schlaver, "Suburban Journalism Battleground," *The Quill* (July, 1969), 8–11; "Four new a.m. dailies for Chicago suburbs," *Editor & Publisher* (March 1, 1969), 13; "Field ends suburban venture with sale to Paddock group," *Editor & Publisher* (June 27, 1970), 11.

16. "Fields ends suburban venture with sale to Paddock group," *Editor & Publisher* (June 27, 1970), 11.

17. Joseph N. Bell, "New Power in Publishing," *Saturday Review* (January 14, 1967), 118, 120, 131; Campbell Watson, "New concept in expansion brings gains," *Editor & Publisher* (March 1, 1969), 17–18.

18. William L. Rivers and David M. Rubin, *A Region's Press: Anatomy of Newspapers in the San Francisco Bay Area* (Berkeley, 1971), 149–153.

19. Jeffrey A. Tannenbaum, "Suburban Newspapers Find News and Profits on Cities' Outskirts," *The Wall Street Journal* (November 14, 1972), 1, 34.

20. "225 publishers are enrolled in new suburban press group," *Editor & Publisher* (January 6, 1973), 18.

21. "Three Suburban Press Groups Merge, Form Suburban Newspapers of America," *The Quill* (April, 1971), 23; "Suburbans get panel of 10 as market advisors," *Editor & Publisher* (February 5, 1972), 15; "Suburbans plan study of their reader impact," *Editor & Publisher* (May 27, 1972), 16; Andrew Radolf, "Survey findings shed light on suburban paper readers," *Editor & Publisher* (April 21, 1973), 70.

22. John Cameron Sim, *The Grass Roots Press: America's Community Newspapers* (Ames, Iowa, 1969), xii–xiii.

23. *Ibid.*, xv.

24. Ibid., 90–92; Ben H. Bagdikian, "Behold the Grass-Roots Press, Alas!" *Harper's* (December, 1964), 102–105, 110.

25. Richard McCann, "Leadership in Suburbia," *Grassroots Editor* (July–August, 1968), 18, 35.

26. Newton H. Fulbright, "Sex on shelf, National Enquirer goes after supermarket shoppers," *Editor & Publisher* (August 23, 1969), 15, 40; "The Common Touch," *Newsweek* (February 18, 1974), 87–88.

27. Roland E. Wolseley, *The Black Press, U.S.A.* (Ames, Iowa, 1971), 7.

28. L. F. Palmer, Jr., "The black press in transition," *Columbia Journalism Review* (Spring, 1970), 31.

29. *Ibid.*; Wolseley, *The Black Press*, 11, 12, 87.

30. "Report lists 208 papers for blacks," *Editor & Publisher* (March 10, 1973), 12.

31. Wolseley, *The Black Press*, 35–40, 70.

32. *Ibid.*, 31, 70–71, 74–75.

33. *Ibid.*, 73–74; "Black daily started in Columbus, Ga.," *Editor & Publisher* (November 21, 1970), 52.

34. "Black-Owned Papers Decline as Circulation Falls Off," a Los Angeles Times Service article in *The Atlanta Journal* (July 30, 1973), p. 7-A.

35. Wolseley, *The Black Press,* 246, 293–314; L. F. Palmer, Jr., "The black press in transition," *Columbia Journalism Review* (Spring, 1970), 33.

36. Harmon Perry, "Black Press Elects Officers, Sets Goals," in *The Atlanta Journal* (June 20, 1971), 6-A.

37. Herman A. Estrin and Arthur M. Sanderson, eds., *Freedom and Censorship of the College Press* (Dubuque, Iowa, 1966), vii; Linda A. McKillop, "College daily thrives with income from ads," *Editor & Publisher* (December 27, 1969), 13; Spyridon Granitsas, "Newspapers on campus are popular," *Editor & Publisher* (December 5, 1970), 12.

38. Melvin Mencher, "Student journalists have constitutional rights, too," *The Quill* (October, 1972), 9–13. *Dickey v. Alabama State Board of Education* et al. 273 F. Supp. 613 (M.D. Ala., 1967); *Antonelli v. Hammond,* 308 F. Supp. 1329 (D. Mass. 1970).

39. Linda A. McKillop, "College daily thrives with income from ads," *Editor & Publisher* (December 27, 1969), 13, 37.

40. Melvin Mencher, "Independence (by fiat) for the campus press," *The Quill* (March, 1973), 14–16.

41. *The Student Newspaper: Report of the Special Commission on the Student Press to the President of the University of California* (Washington, 1970), 47–56.

42. Julius Duscha and Thomas G. Fischer, *The Campus Press: Freedom and Responsibility* (Washington, 1973); "AASCU Sponsors Study of Collegiate Press," *Higher Education and National Affairs* (July 14, 1972), 5; Guy T. Ryan, "Campus Independence," *The Quill* (October, 1973), 11–12; Louis E. Ingelhart, *The College and University Campus Student Press: An Examination of Its Status and Aspirations and Some of the Myths Surrounding It* (Terre Haute, Indiana, 1974).

43. Melvin Mencher, "The Curse of Gutenberg? The College Press," *The Quill* (May, 1971), 11–14.

44. Douglas E. Kneeland, "The Campus Press, 1972—It's Changing Again," *The Quill* (March, 1972), 8–12.

45. *Ibid.*

46. Spyridon Granitsas, "Ethnic press alive and well; 440 published in the U.S.," *Editor & Publisher* (November 28, 1970), 12, 23.

47. Frank del Olmo, "Voices for the Chicano Movimiento," *The Quill* (October, 1971), 8–11.

48. *The Wall Street Journal* is published by Dow Jones & Company, which also publishes *Barron's National Business and Financial Weekly* and operates the Dow Jones News Service.

49. Daniel L. Lionel, "400 regional business papers tap sophisticated news field," *Editor & Publisher* (April 8, 1972), 22.

50. Gareth D. Hiebert, "Reformation is order of day for 'new' Army newspapers," *Editor & Publisher* (September 25, 1971), 33.

51. " 'Stars and Stripes' Going Strong on 30th Birthday," *The Atlanta Constitution* (November 2, 1972), 16-B; Robert Hodierne, "How the G.I.'s in Vietnam Don't Learn About the War," *The New York Times Magazine* (April 12, 1970), 28, 29, 133–135, 140.

52. George Brandsberg, *The Free Papers* (Ames, Iowa, 1969), 2, 150.

53. *Ibid.,* 5, 140–142.

54. *Ibid.,* 148–150.

55. Mark Mehler, "CM's show little enthusiasm for saturation shoppers," *Editor & Publisher* (November 3, 1973), 14, 27; "Shoppers return publishers large profits in most cases," *Editor & Publisher* (November 3, 1973), p. 14.

56. Russell N. Baird, *The Penal Press* (Evanston, Illinois, 1967), 10–16; Philly Murtha, "Penal press prods prison reform, and understanding," *Editor & Publisher* (June 8, 1974), 42, 65.

57. Robert J. Glessing, *The Underground Press in America* (Bloomington, Indiana, 1970), 3, 11.

58. Ross K. Baker, "ZAP! No More Underground Press," *The Washington Post* (April 8, 1973), C5; "The Odd Couple," *Time* (June 17, 1974), 42.

59. Glessing, *The Underground Press in America*, 17–18; Donna Lloyd Ellis, "The Underground Press in America: 1955–1970," *Journal of Popular Culture* (Summer, 1971), 107; John Burks, "The Underground Press: A Special Report," *Rolling Stone* (October 4, 1969), 18; Jim Scott, "L.A. Free Press sheds underground image," *Editor & Publisher* (April 20, 1974), 92, 94.

60. Glessing, *The Underground Press in America*, 20–24; Peter A. Janssen, "Rolling Stone's quest for respectability," *Columbia Journalism Review* (January/February, 1974), 59–65.

61. Ellis, "The Underground Press in America: 1955–1970," *Journal of Popular Culture* (Summer, 1971), 105.

62. Glessing, *The Underground Press in America*, 69–70; Ellis, "The Underground Press in America: 1955–1970," *Journal of Popular Culture* (Summer, 1971), 110–113; "Underground Papers Calm Down," *The Atlanta Journal* (August 18, 1972), 1-C.

63. Glessing, *The Underground Press in America*, 143–149.

64. *Ibid.*, 168–174; Ellis, "The Underground Press in America: 1955–1970," *Journal of Popular Culture* (Summer, 1971), 102; Baker, "ZAP! No More Underground Press," *The Washington Post* (April 8, 1973), C5.

65. "Underground Papers Calm Down," *The Atlanta Journal* (August 18, 1972), 1-C.

66. Ellis, "The Underground Press in America: 1955–1970," *Journal of Popular Culture* (Summer, 1971), 110, 123; Douglas E. Kneeland, "The Campus Press, 1972—It's Changing Again," *The Quill* (March, 1972), 9.

NOTES TO CHAPTER 4

1. Jon G. Udell, *Economic Trends in the Daily Newspaper Business, 1946 to 1970* (Madison: The Bureau of Business Research Service, Graduate School of Business, Wisconsin Project Reports, Vol. IV, No. 6, 1970), 4–19.

2. "Commerce Dept. sees papers' growth 'modest but steady,' " *Editor & Publisher* (March 27, 1971), 11, 15.

3. "Dailies hit high with '72 plant expansion costs," *Editor & Publisher* (April 14, 1973), 35.

4. Ben H. Bagdikian, "The myth of newspaper poverty," *Columbia Journalism Review* (March/April, 1973), 21.

5. "Newspaper economics: the analyst's point of view," *Newspaper Production* (April, 1973), 46.

6. Bagdikian, "The myth of newspaper poverty," *Columbia Journalism Review* (March/April, 1973), 21; "Newspaper quiz," *Columbia Journalism Review* (July/August, 1973), 6–7.

7. "Book review," *Editor & Publisher* (January 12, 1974), 22. The report was published by Knowledge Industry Publications Inc., White Plains, N.Y.

8. Jerry Walker Jr., "Merrill Lynch hails bullish newspaper industry trends," *Editor & Publisher* (November 4, 1972), 15.

9. Edward M. Swietnicki, "Tour of modern news plants impresses Wall St. analysts," *Editor & Publisher* (December 8, 1973), 9, 51.

10. "Newspaper economics: the analyst's point of view," *Newspaper Production* (April, 1973), 47.

11. "Book review," *Editor & Publisher* (January 12, 1974), 22.

12. "ANPA forecasts tight newsprint supply by 1974," *Editor & Publisher* (December 23, 1972), 17; Mark Mehler, "Effects of tight newsprint being felt by some papers," *Editor & Publisher* (August 11, 1973), 12; Stanford Smith, "Newsprint supplies are adequate, retailers told," *Editor & Publisher* (September 29, 1973), 40; Gerald B. Healey, "86% of IDPA papers have cut news hole," *Editor & Publisher* (October 20, 1973), 7, 13; "11 million tons of newsprint needed by newspapers in '74," *Editor & Publisher* (January 12, 1974), 9; "Price Firm Will Hike Newsprint," an Associated Press report in The *Atlanta Constitution* (September 24, 1974), 8-D.

13. Stan Darden, "Kenaf May Be a Solution To Shortage of Newsprint," a United Press International story in *The Atlanta Journal and Constitution* (November 22, 1973), 28-F.

14. "Why newspapers are making money again," *Business Week* (August 29, 1970), 40, 46.

15. Maxwell E. McCombs, *Mass Media in the Marketplace* (Journalism Monographs, No. 24, August, 1972), 1–104. McCombs is associate professor of journalism at the University of North Carolina.

16. Robert L. Bishop, "The rush to chain ownership," *Columbia Journalism Review* (November/December, 1972), 10; Raymond B. Nixon, "Half of nation's dailies now in group ownerships," *Editor & Publisher* (July 17, 1971), 7.

17. Paul Block, Jr., "Facing up to the 'Monopoly' Charge," *Neiman Reports* (July, 1955), 3–7.

18. *Citizen Publishing Co. et al. v. United States,* 89 S.Ct. 927 (1969).

19. *Newspaper Preservation Act of 1970 in United States Statutes at Large* (Washington: U.S. Government Printing Office, 1971), LXXXIV (Part 1 of 2 Parts), 466; Luther A. Huston, "President signs antitrust exemption for newspapers," *Editor & Publisher* (August 1, 1970), 9; Patrick Young, "Newspapers Win Their Long Fight To Pool Some Operating Facilities," *National Observer* (July 13, 1970), 4.

20. "Newspaper Preservation Act upheld in first court test," *Editor & Publisher* (July 8, 1972), 13, 30; "A Progress Report: The Guardian v. The Chronicle," an article from *The San Francisco Bay Guardian* reprinted in *Grassroots Editor* (November/December, 1973), 14–15.

21. Raymond B. Nixon, "Half of nation's dailies now in group ownerships," *Editor and Publisher* (July 17, 1971), 7, 32.

22. *Ibid.,* 32; Raymond B. Nixon, compiler, "Groups of Daily Newspapers Under Common Ownership Published in the United States," *Editor & Publisher Year Book—1971* (New York, 1971), 346–349.

23. "Number of dailies in groups increased by 11% in 3 years," *Editor & Publisher* (February 23, 1974), 9; "Knight and Ridder to merge; to divest broadcast holdings," *Editor & Publisher* (July 13, 1974), 9; "Knight and Ridder complete merger," *Editor & Publisher* (September 21, 1974), 32.

24. Ben H. Bagdikian, "The myth of newspaper poverty," *Columbia Journalism Review* (March/April, 1973), 23.

25. Nixon, "Half of nation's dailies now in group ownerships," *Editor & Publisher* (July 17, 1971), 32.

26. John C. Quinn, "The Big Myth," *Nieman Reports* (September, 1972), 11.

27. Robert L. Bishop, "The rush to chain ownership," *Columbia Journalism Review* (November/December, 1972), 10.

28. "256 stations have newspaper ties," *Editor & Publisher* (April 4, 1970), 11.

29. "Paper-Owned Stations Hailed," an Associated Press report in the *Atlanta Constitution* (July 6, 1971), 10A.

30. Armando M. Lago, "The Price Effects of Joint Mass Communication Media Ownership," *The Antitrust Bulletin* (Winter, 1971), 789–813.

31. Stephen R. Barnett, "The FCC's nonbattle against media monopoly," *Columbia Journalism Review* (January/February, 1973), 44–45; "Publishers attack FCC rule requiring sale of stations," *Editor & Publisher* (June 12, 1971), 42; Robert U. Brown, "Cross ownership," *Editor & Publisher* (January 19, 1974), 58.

32. "Publishers attack FCC rule requiring sale of stations," *Editor & Publisher* (June 12, 1971), 42; Robert U. Brown, "Cross ownership," *Editor & Publisher* (January 19, 1974), 58.

33. Luther A. Huston, "FCC weighs arguments on cross-ownership rights," *Editor & Publisher* (August 3, 1974), 9, 28; "Senate bill lets FCC deny cross-ownership licenses," *Editor & Publisher* (September 21, 1974), 9, 30.

34. "Report approves publisher-owned cable tv system," *Editor & Publisher* (January 19, 1974), 50.

35. "Publishers form group to fight cable tv ban," *Editor & Publisher* (May 31, 1969), 45.

36. "Giants' media control called national menace," *Editor & Publisher* (June 12, 1971), 22.

37. Robert U. Brown, "14% of dailies, 24% of circ. in 19 'publicly-held' groups," *Editor & Publisher* (April 21, 1973), 14, 46. The others included American Financial Corp., Booth, Capital Cities Broadcasting, Harte-Hanks, Jefferson Pilot, Lee Newspapers, Media General, Multimedia, Panax Corp, Post Corp, and Speidel Newspapers.

38. Bishop, "The rush to chain ownership," 16; Ben H. Bagdikian, "The myth of newspaper poverty," *Columbia Journalism Review* (March/April, 1973), 23.

39. James Stanford, "Advertising Makes the Free Press Possible," in *The Newspaper in The Classroom: A report of the 1963 workshop at the University of Georgia* (Athens, 1963), 21–23; Ben H. Bagdikian, *The Information Machines* (New York, 1971), 208.

40. "Promoting Self-Policing," *Time* (June 14, 1971), 81–82; Robert U. Brown, "Subtle attacks," *Editor & Publisher* (November 13, 1971), 84; "Hows and whys of the Ad Review Board," *Editor & Publisher* (October 2, 1971), 40, 42.

41. "Admen want consumer protection," *Editor & Publisher* (April 22, 1972), 50; "Survey shows newspapers receive few ad complaints," *Editor & Publisher* (March 30, 1974), 10–11.

42. "The Right to Turn Down Advertising," *Saturday Review* (June 12, 1971), 55–56; "Court Upholds Papers' Right To Reject Ads," a United Press International story reprinted in the *Atlanta Journal* (May 18, 1971), 9-A.

43. "12 new ad taxes proposed," *Editor & Publisher* (April 3, 1971), 40.

44. "Tax on advertising," *Editor & Publisher* (March 15, 1969), 64.

45. Stephen M. Krist, Jr., "Ad managers face problems with 'cold type' process," *Editor & Publisher* (March 18, 1972), 18.

46. "Prevention of ad piracy," *Editor & Publisher* (January 22, 1972), 34, 44; *ANPA General Bulletin,* No. 3, January 13, 1972.

47. Robert U. Brown, "Color is a way of life," *Editor & Publisher* (March 27, 1971), 84; Stuart Tolley, "Color in newspaper ads: Is it worth the Money?" *Editor & Publisher* (March 27, 1971), 16, 18; "Color linage up 6%," *Editor & Publisher* (March 25, 1972), 6; George Wilt, "Leaders score gains in ROP color ads," *Editor & Publisher* (March 25, 1972), 15.

48. George Wilt, "Color linage leaders show 12% gains," *Editor & Publisher* (March 31, 1973), 10.

49. "High court upholds sexless ad headings," *Editor & Publisher* (June 23, 1973), 9, 12; Robert U. Brown, "That classified ad decision," *Editor & Publisher* (July 14, 1973), 58; "Discrimination in ads," *Editor & Publisher* (August 5, 1972), 6; "Ban on sex in job ads taken to Supreme Court," *Editor & Publisher* (August 5, 1972), 9.

50. "Ad revenue will hit $12 billion in next decade," *Editor & Publisher* (January 29, 1972), 10.

51. Gerald B. Healey, "Sluggish circulation growth linked to 'Little Merchant,' " *Editor & Publisher* (June 23, 1973), 9; "Future of the 'little merchants,' *Editor & Publisher* (June 23, 1973), 6.

52. "Marketing exec defends Little Merchant system," *Editor & Publisher* (September 1, 1973), 13.

53. "Courts' decisions leave dealer criteria beclouded," *Editor & Publisher* (September 23, 1972), 11; Gerald B. Healey, "Carrier system pitfalls defined for circulators," *Editor & Publisher* (April 1, 1972), 9–10.

54. John D. Hopkins, "Heavy response greets pre-payment program," *Editor & Publisher* (January 12, 1974), 16.

55. "Survey finds circulation problem in black community is escalating," *Editor & Publisher*

(August 30, 1969), 17–18; Virgil Fassio, "Circulation practices change to keep vitality in ad medium," *Editor & Publisher* (January 16, 1971), 17.

56. Robert U. Brown, "Public service and the P.O.," *Editor & Publisher* (July 28, 1973), 36.

57. "Smith says postal rate hike will hit small paper hardest," *Editor & Publisher* (June 24, 1972), 13; "Public service of the mails," *Editor & Publisher* (July 29, 1972), 6.

58. "Postal rate bill defeated," *Editor & Publisher* (August 4, 1973), 6; Edward M. Swietnicki, "Publishers push for postal hike phase-in period," *Editor & Publisher* (September 29, 1973), 13.

59. "U.S. daily circulation is at new high—62.5 million," *Editor & Publisher* (March 10, 1973), 9.

60. "90% in survey receptive to 15¢ a copy, Gallup says," *Editor & Publisher* (April 24, 1971), 11; "Almost as many dailies at 15¢ as at 10¢ now," *Editor & Publisher* (March 18, 1972), 10; Jerome H. Walker, Jr., "Neuharth says 25-cent daily needs newsroom excellence," *Editor & Publisher* (November 24, 1973), 9; "More dailies charge 15¢ per copy, according to ANPA survey," *Newspaper Production* (April, 1973), 34. "The 20-cent newspaper," *Editor & Publisher* (January 12, 1974), 6.

61. Udell, *Economic Trends in the Daily Newspaper Business, 1946 to 1970*, 5.

62. Stanford Smith, "The Challenge of Newspaper Management," *Nieman Reports* (September, 1966), 16.

63. Thomas E. Engleman, "The Job Picture: how it looks right now," *The Quill* (November, 1972), 22–23.

64. Guido H. Stempel III and Paul H. Wagner, "An Analysis of Newspaper Editorial Pay, 1954–66," *Journalism Quarterly* (Summer, 1969), 281–286.

65. Robert U. Brown, "Newspaper starting salaries," *Editor & Publisher* (April 10, 1971), 54.

66. Lenora Williamson, "Guild to continue push for higher wage pacts," *Editor & Publisher* (June 24, 1972), 14.

67. Joann S. Lublin, "Women in the newsroom," *The Quill* (November, 1972), 45–47; Robert U. Brown, "Women in journalism," *Editor & Publisher* (November 2, 1974), 36.

68. Clayton Kirkpatrick and Judith W. Brown, "Women at the top?" *The Bulletin of the American Society of Newspaper Editors* (March, 1973), 3–4.

69. "ASNE survey shows minimal gain in black reporters," *Editor & Publisher* (April 13, 1974), 10, 40.

70. James Aronson, "Black Journalists: why the dearth?" *The Bulletin of the American Society of Newspaper Editors* (March, 1972), 10.

71. "Hiring of minorities seen as massive job of decade," *Editor & Publisher* (April 22, 1972), 11.

72. "Black hiring demands face Washington Post," *Editor & Publisher* (April 1, 1972), 34.

73. John H. Jack Francis, Jr., "Why aren't more students entering journalism?" *The Quill* (January, 1968), 16–17; "Career attitudes shown in SNPA personnel poll," *Editor & Publisher* (November 14, 1970), 9, 72.

74. "Staff control of newspaper policy? Symposium finds idea off-base," *Editor & Publisher* (January 17, 1970), 12–15.

75. William Serrin, "The ultimate shutdown: the Detroit strike of 1967–1968," *Columbia Journalism Review* (Summer, 1969), 36–44; "Schmick calls for revision of labor-management laws," *Editor & Publisher* (April 25, 1970), 11–12.

76. David K. Stern, ed., *Newspaper Promotion Handbook* (Providence, R.I., 1966), 1.

77. *Ibid.*, 10.

78. George Wilt, "Spezzano identifies service with IMAGE," *Editor & Publisher* (April 24, 1971), 48a.

79. "Advises no cover-up by newspaper PR," *Editor & Publisher* (May 22, 1971), 32.

80. George Wilt, "Promotion's come a long way: Taubkin," *Editor & Publisher* (May 15, 1971), 44.

81. George Wilt, "56 best promotion campaigns cited," *Editor & Publisher* (May 19, 1973), 10–13; George Wilt, "Total—Sum of All The Parts," *Editor & Publisher* (December 1, 1973), 24.

Notes to Chapter 5

1. "Investigative writing fund has aided successful probes," *Editor & Publisher* (November 17, 1973), 15.

2. Robert A. Juran, "The decline and fall? of objectivity," *The Quill* (August, 1968), 24.

3. *Ibid.*

4. Luther A. Huston, "Proponents of objectivity win barbed ASNE debate," *Editor & Publisher* (April 24, 1971), 54.

5. John DeMott, "Opinion in 'Spot' News Stories," *Editor & Publisher* (August 22, 1970), 7.

6. "Poynter gift seeks to stem erosion of public confidence," *Editor & Publisher* (September 9, 1972), 9.

7. Stanford Sesser, "Journalists: Objectivity and Activism," *The Quill* (December, 1969), 7. (The "guest opinion" was reprinted by *The Quill* from *The Wall Street Journal,* October 21, 1969.).

8. Everette Dennis, *The Magic Writing Machine: Student Probes of the New Journalism* (Eugene, Oregon, 1971).

9. Tom Wolfe, "The New Journalism," *The Bulletin of the American Society of Newspaper Editors,* (September, 1970), 22.

10. Sharon Fell, "The Latest 'New' Journalism" (Unpublished Honors Thesis at the University of Georgia, Athens, Ga., 1972), 43–47.

11. Dwight MacDonald, "Parajournalism II," *New York Review of Books* (February 3, 1966), 18.

12. Alex S. Edelstein and William E. Ames, "Humanistic Newswriting," *The Quill* (June, 1970), 28.

13. "Wire service study views 'news control,' *Editor & Publisher* (June 13, 1970), 15.

14. "Gallagher: AP geared for 'news explosion.' " *Editor & Publisher* (March 21, 1970), 11; "UPI awards contract for automated editing," *Editor & Publisher* (April 18, 1970), 112.

15. " 'New Establishment' corps added by AP," *Editor & Publisher* (April 18, 1970), 102; Lenora Williamson, "Variety is the spice of 'Living Today,' " *Editor & Publisher* (July 25, 1970), 36; "UPI team delves into young radicals," *Editor & Publisher* (August 29, 1970), 11–12.

16. Thomas B. Littlewood, "Supplemental News Services Growing— . . . what will it mean for the American Newspaper?" *The Quill* (April, 1971), 9–11.

17. Boyd Lewis, "The Syndicates and How They Grew," *Saturday Review* (December 11, 1971), 68.

18. Lenora Williamson and Mark Mehler, "Syndicates and ads feel paper pinch," *Editor & Publisher* (September 8, 1973), 10.

19. "File Drawer Comes to Clerk in Library," *Editor & Publisher* (August 5, 1967), 15, 43.

20. "Where the past is prologue: library has 'tomorrow look.' " *Editor & Publisher* (October 25, 1969), 17.

21. More on automated libraries and the new *Times* system is included in the chapter on new technology. See also "The Automated Library," *R. I. Bulletin 1062* (ANPA Research Institute, September 17, 1971), 243–245.

22. Woody Klein, "The Racial Crisis in America: the news media respond to the new challenge," *The Quill* (January, 1969), 8–12; William F. Noall, "Editors ahead of Kerner: Report on rioting

doesn't change newspapers' policy,'' *Editor & Publisher* (August 17, 1968), 18, 40; Jake Highton, ''Black Is News—At Last,'' *The Quill* (February, 1970), 20–21.

23. Comments on press coverage of the Watergate scandal are included in the discussion of relationships between the President and the press in Chapter 6.

24. Bob Chick, ''Military-Press Relations: Like It is in Vietnam,'' *The Quill* (November, 1969), 20–22.

25. ''Government, not press confused Viet issues,'' *Editor & Publisher* (November 21, 1970), 41.

26. Edwin Emery, *The Press and America* (Englewood Cliffs, N.J.: Prentice-Hall, 1972), 327.

27. Bill Surface, ''The shame of the sports beat,'' *Columbia Journalism Review* (January/February, 1972), 48–55.

28. *Ibid.,* 49.

29. ''Survey finds many men read women's pages,'' *Editor & Publisher* (April 21, 1973), 95.

30. Frank Luther Mott, *American Journalism,* (New York: The Macmillan Company, 1962), 233, 599; Emery, *The Press and America,* 328.

31. ''The Bridal Desk,'' *Editor & Publisher* (June 30, 1973), 30.

32. ''Flight from Fluff,'' *Time* (March 20, 1972), 48, 53.

33. Gene Corea, ''How papers can conduct serious coverage of women,'' *Editor & Publisher* (April 28, 1973), 28, 30.

34. Sandra Kelly, ''Editors: Don't drop women from paper's women's pages,'' *Editor & Publisher* (July 15, 1972), 34.

35. ''How they would liberate the women's pages from drab content,'' *Editor & Publisher* (May 1, 1971), 9–10.

36. Sandra Kelly, ''Editors: Don't drop women from paper's women's pages,'' *Editor & Publisher* (July 15, 1972), 30, 32, 34.

37. June Anderson Almquist, ''Women's Sections: Are they opening windows?'' *Editor & Publisher* (May 12, 1973), 28.

38. Lenore Brown, ''Women's Page Editors Talk Over Problems,'' *Editor & Publisher* (March 30, 1968), 15, 115; Gloria Biggs, ''The topflight women's department,'' *The Gannetteer* (October, 1970), 43.

39. ''Favorite reading matter for women covers wide area,'' *Editor & Publisher* (October 17, 1970), 13.

40. Jack B. Haskins, ''Women Readers and Women's Editors,'' *Editor & Publisher* (January 27, 1968), 34.

41. Sandra Kelly, ''Editors: Don't drop women from paper's women's pages'' *Editor & Publisher* (July 15, 1972), 30.

42. Chris Welles, ''The bleak wasteland of financial journalism,'' *Columbia Journalism Review* (July/August, 1973), 41.

43. *Ibid.*

44. Jerome K. Full, ''Reporting on business,'' *Editor & Publisher* (September 6, 1969), 20.

45. Mark Mehler, ''Making It Readable,'' *Editor & Publisher* (February 10, 1973), 18.

46. Welles, ''The Bleak wasteland of financial journalism,'' 44–45.

47. Blaine K. McKee, ''Rules code urged as curb to profiting business writer,'' *Editor & Publisher* (September 23, 1972), 28, 35; ''Business writer's code pinpoints conflict areas,'' *Editor & Publisher* (May 25, 1974), 24.

48. Paul Cracoft, ''Arts editors are underdogs in space match with sports,'' *Editor & Publisher* (May 13, 1972), 15, 56, 57.

49. Mott, *American Journalism,* 53.

50. *Ibid.,* pp. 206, 321–22, 373, 395, 584.

51. "Better religion news needed, AP writer says," *Editor & Publisher* (April 7, 1973), 20.

52. Louis Cassels, "Covering Religion News" *The Bulletin of the American Society of Newspaper Editors* (September–October, 1969), 7–9.

53. "America's Largest Children's Syndicate: MINI PAGE," in the 48th Annual Directory of Syndicated Services in *Editor & Publisher* (July 28, 1973), 18-A. Other examples of what newspapers are doing or can do to reach young readers may be found in "Catching the Small Fry," *The Gannetteer* (January, 1973), 20–21; "Teen Readers Wooed in Variety of Ways," *Editor & Publisher* (December 31, 1966), 18, 30; "Survey exposes some ideas for closing the youth gap," *Editor & Publisher* (November 13, 1971), 14, 78, and "Color teen sections advised for papers," *Editor & Publisher* (October 25, 1969), 32, 34.

54. George Gerbner, "Newsmen and Schoolmen: the State and Problems of Education Reporting," *Journalism Quarterly* (Summer, 1967), 213, 223–224.

55. Harvey K. Jacobson, "Needed Improvements in Education News Coverage as Perceived by Media and Education Gatekeepers," *The Journal of Educational Research* (February, 1973), 274–278.

56. Alden Whitman, "So You Want to Be an Obit Writer," *Saturday Review* (December 11, 1971), 70–71; Newton H. Fulbright, " 'They know why I'm here'; Interview for obituary," *Editor & Publisher* (August 17, 1968), 17, 32.

57. Laurence T. Herman, "Advertising salesmen's roundtable: What sales pointers does your staff make in selling Sunday comic advertising space?" *Editor & Publisher* (May 1, 1971), 17.

58. "Comics hold audiences of all ages," *Editor & Publisher* (June 19, 1971), 36; Lenora Williamson, "Prayers and promotion needed to save the comics," *Editor & Publisher* (October 19, 1974), 33.

59. Herman, "Advertising salesmen's roundtable . . . ," *Editor & Publisher* (May, 1971), 17.

60. Arthur Berger, "Comics and Culture," *Journal of Popular Culture* (Summer, 1971), 176.

61. Emery, *The Press and America,* 356–7, 359, 499.

62. "New Look on the Funny Pages," *Newsweek* (March 5, 1973), 76–77.

63. *Ibid.* 77.

64. Gerald B. Healey, "Makeup of comic pages discussed in symposium," *Editor & Publisher* (November 11, 1972), 89.

65. James Carrier, " 'Relevance' Fad Growing in the Comics, but Dagwood, Nancy, Popeye Hang On," as Associated Press story in *The Atlanta Journal and Constitution* (Sunday, January 7, 1973), 12-C.

66. Susan Rosenbaum, " 'It shouldn't have failed.' The rise and fall of This Week," *Editor & Publisher* (August 30, 1969), 16, 34.

67. "Ad agency issues optimistic report on Sunday supplements," *Editor & Publisher* (August 25, 1973), 22, 24.

68. Jerome H. Walker, "Business sun shines in Parade's 30th year," *Editor & Publisher* (July 17, 1971), 13, 30; Robert C. Davis, "Gorkin, Parade's editor, marks 25 years at helm," *Editor & Publisher* (July 1, 1972), 15.

69. Davis, "Gorkin, Parade's editor," 15; Craig Tomkinson, "The leader of the parade sees bright Sunday magazine future," *Editor & Publisher* (October 25, 1969), 12, 47.

70. "Close to 8 million copies: Family Weekly's list grows to 240 papers," *Editor & Publisher* (December 6, 1969), 16; "Family Weekly shares its profit for sixth year," *Editor & Publisher* (January 22, 1972), 14; "Family Weekly reports '73 revenues up 9.65%," *Editor & Publisher* (April 20, 1974), 9.

71. *Ibid.*

72. Emery, *The Press and America*, 641.

73. Bill Jerome, "Magazine supplement editors agree on space, staff needs," *Editor & Publisher* (July 22, 1972), 13, 28.

74. "The vanishing copy editor," *The Bulletin of The American Society of Newspaper Editors* (September, 1970), 14–17. Mort Stern, assistant to the publisher of the *Denver Post*, directed the survey for the *Bulletin* on which this story was based.

75. "Remarks by Paul Swensson," *Problems of Journalism, 1968* (Washington, D.C.: American Society of Newspaper Editors, 1968), 160–165.

76. Phillip Ritzenberg, "The designer as journalist, *The Bulletin of the American Society of Newspaper Editors*, (March, 1972) 18. (Article reprinted with permission from *Print*, September/October, 1971).

77. Edmund C. Arnold, "Talking Typographically," *Editor & Publisher* (April 1, 1972), 28; "Traditional vs modern format tested by ANPA," *Editor & Publisher* (June 15, 1974), 78, 82.

78. Contemporary design shifts lead to left," *Editor & Publisher* (April 17, 1971), 68.

79. Edmund C. Arnold, "Typographically speaking," *Editor & Publisher* (March 3, 1973), 18.

80. "The Color Multi-Millionaires," *Editor & Publisher* (March 31, 1973), 72–76; "1973 ROP Color Total Advertising, Top 25 Media Records Newspapers," *Editor & Publisher* (March 30, 1974), 72.

81. William C. Sexton, "Style, The Newspaper in the 1970s: A Revolution?" *The Quill* (July, 1968), 7–18.

82. Jim Scott, "Frank Ariss on newspaper make-up," *Editor & Publisher* (May 11, 1974), 10–11.

83. Ritzenberg, "The designer as journalist," *The Bulletin of the American Society of Newspaper Editors* (March, 1972), 20.

84. "Future Front Page? New Look for Tomorrow's Newspapers," *The Quill* (May, 1971), 20–21; John Tebbel, "What Tomorrow's Front Page Will Look Like," *Saturday Review* (May 8, 1971), 50–52; "Front Page. . . . produced by ad agency artists," *Editor & Publisher* (March 20, 1971), 12–13.

85. Jack B. Haskins, "Journalism Research: More study needed on picture editing," *Editor & Publisher* (November 2, 1968), 22; Haskins is reporting on thesis at Indiana University by Don Hall, who conducted the study while serving as picture editor of *Waukegan* (Ill.) *News-Sun.*; Jerry Rife, "Let's Upgrade Newspaper Photography," *The Quill* (March, 1971), 12.

86. Hillier Krieghbaum, "Cluttering Up the News Picture," *The Quill*, (February, 1972), 9.

87. Curtis D. MacDougall, *News Pictures Fit to Print—Or Are They?* (Stillwater, Okla., 1971).

88. Niel Plummer, "The Publication of Ghastly Photographs: Recipe for Judicial Restraints Possible," *Grassroots Editor* (March/April, 1972), 38–40.

89. Edmund C. Arnold, "Talking Typographically," *Editor & Publisher* (January 22, 1972), 36.

90. Lawrence A. Pryor, "Notes on the art, Retouching: making pictures lie?" *Columbia Journalism Review* (Fall, 1969), 54–56.

91. "Editorial writers see need to curb partisan activities," *Editor & Publisher* (August 7, 1971), 7.

92. James M. Perry, "Here's Herblock, Carrying On In His Ivory Tower," *The National Observer* (June 1, 1970), 11.

93. Charles Long, "The Cartoonist Conrad," *The Quill* (July, 1971), 12.

94. Donald W. Carson, "What Editorial Writers Think of the Columnist," *The Masthead* (Spring, 1971), 4–5.

95. Daniel St. Albin Greene, "Dear Mr. Editor, You Fink: Masses of Letters Deluge Nation's Newspapers as Readers Speak Out," *The National Observer* (May 4, 1970), 22.

NOTES TO CHAPTER 6

1. "Cracks in the First Amendment," *Editor & Publisher* (June 30, 1973), 4; "White house 'enemies list' contains scores of newsmen," *Editor & Publisher* (June 30, 1973), 12.

2. Lenora Williamson, "Nixon and the Press: a feeling of distrust," *Editor & Publisher* (April 24, 1971), 14.

3. "Nixon admits press reports on Watergate are factual," *Editor & Publisher* (May 5, 1973), 7; "Press and the administration," *Editor & Publisher* (May 12, 1973), 6.

4. "Nixon aides' remarks reopen media battles," *Editor & Publisher* (November 3, 1973), 7, 29; "The President's Complaint," *Newsweek* (November 5, 1973), 71; Jeff Mill, "News Council's first case results in a "no decision," *Editor & Publisher* (February 2, 1974), 12.

5. Jane Levere, "President Ford pledges 'openness and candor,' " *Editor & Publisher* (August 17, 1974), 7; "President Ford appoints terHorst press secretary," *Editor & Publisher* (August 17, 1974), 10; "Ter Horst felt Ford's aides used him to lie," *Editor & Publisher* (September 14, 1974), 18; "Lost Confidence," *Time* (September 23, 1974), 86.

6. Comments by 10 persons involved in the practice or study of journalism are included in "Has the Press Done a Job on Nixon?" *Columbia Journalism Review* (January/February, 1974), 50–58.

7. Edward Jay Epstein, "How press handled Watergate scandal," *Editor & Publisher* (October 20, 1973), 38; The story was reprinted with permission from the *Los Angeles Times,* September 14, 1973, 1,18,19.

8. Finlay Lewis, "Some errors and puzzles in Watergate coverage," *Columbia Journalism Review* (November/December, 1973), 26–32.

9. "Harris poll on Watergate," *Editor & Publisher* (July 7, 1973), 6; "Public Contends the Media Guilty of Excess Coverage," a Gallup Poll report in The *Athens Banner-Herald and the Daily News* (July 7, 1974).

10. Daniel P. Moynihan, "The President & the Press," *The National Observer* (March 29, 1971), 22; The story originally appeared in *Commentary,* March, 1971, 41–52.

11. Jules Witcover, "How well does the White House press perform?" *Columbia Journalism Review* (November/December, 1973), 39–43.

12. Delbert McGuire, "Democracy's Confrontation: The Presidential Press Conference, II," *Journalism Quarterly* (Spring, 1968), 37–40; Jules Witcover, "Salvaging the presidential press conference," *Columbia Journalism Review* (Fall, 1970), 27–34; Winston H. Taylor, "The White House Press Conference," *Neiman Reports* (December, 1971), 9–14.

13. For a further discussion of this idea, see Jules Witcover, "Washington's uncovered power centers," *Columbia Journalism Review* (March/April, 1972), 14–19.

14. *Near v. Minnesota ex rel Olson,* 283 U.S. 697 (1931).

15. *New York Times Company v. United States* and *United States v. The Washington Post Company,* 403 U.S. 713 (1971).

16. 42 *U.S. Law Week* 3247, Case No. 72-1511 (October 23, 1973).

17. "Justice Dept. wants judges to have right of censorship," *Editor & Publisher* (October 13, 1973), 10; "Prior restraint upheld," *Editor & Publisher* (October 27, 1973), 6; Martin Arnold, "Attacks on the Press Quietly Increasing," a New York Times service article in *The Atlanta Journal and Constitution* (November 22, 1973), 22-D.

18. "Prior restraint upheld," *Editor & Publisher* (October 27, 1973), 6.

19. Charles B. Kopp, "The People's Right To Know Their Business," *The Athens Banner-Herald and The Daily News* (August 23, 1972), 4–5.

20. John B. Adams, *State Open Meeting Laws: An Overview* (Columbia, Missouri, 1974). The study was published by the Freedom of Information Foundation through a grant from the American

Newspaper Publishers Association Foundation. See also, Philly Murtha, "Most 'open meeting' laws found to be ineffective," *Editor & Publisher* (August 24, 1974), 11–12; Patrick Riordan, "Tennessee high court upholds Sunshine Bill; called 'nation's best," *Editor & Publisher* (August 10, 1974), 8.

21. 5 U.S.C. 552.

22. *Ibid.* For further discussion, see Kopp, "The People's Right To Know Their Business," *The Athens Banner-Herald and The Daily News* (August 23, 1972), 4–5; John R. Reynolds, "Four years of FOI law: is secrecy gap widened?", *Editor & Publisher* (May 16, 1970), 14, 36; Peter G. Miller, "Freedom of Information Act: Boon or bust for the press?", *Editor & Publisher* (July 8, 1972), 20, 22, 24.

23. The Moorhead Report, H Rept. 92-1419, September 20, 1972.

24. *Ibid.* For further discussion, see Samuel J. Archibald, "The Freedom of Information Law Today," *Report of the 1972 Sigma Delta Chi Advancement of Freedom of Information Committee* (Sigma Delta Chi Professional Journalism Society, Fall, 1972), 10–11; "Agencies Stall Information Access," an Associated Press report in *The Atlanta Constitution* (September 22, 1972), 16A.

25. *Mink et al. v. Environmental Protection Agency et al.* 71 S.Ct. 909.

26. Herbert A. Terry, "What's left of the FOI Act," *Columbia Journalism Review* (July/August, 1973), 58–59; "USSC Amchitka Rule Upholds Secrecy; May Be Nullified by Future Legislation," *FOI Digest* (January–February, 1973), 1.

27. "USSC Amchitka Rule Upholds Secrecy . . . , *FOI Digest* (January–February, 1973), 1.

28. Robert Goralski, "How Much Secrecy Can A Democracy Stand?", *Lithopinion* (Fall, 1972), 78–81; "Nixon order limits 'Top Secret' label," *Editor & Publisher* (March 11, 1972), 12.

29. "S.1400—A National Security Act?", *Editor & Publisher* (April 21, 1973), 7, 72; Robert U. Brown, "Analyzing S.1400," *Editor & Publisher* (April 21, 1973), 104; "New Criminal Code Threatens Reporters, Sources," *The Quill* (May, 1973), 34.

30. Paul A. Miltich, "Reasonable FoI bill needed," *Editor & Publisher* (November 2, 1974), 7.

31. *Branzburg v. Hayes et al.,* Judges, 408 U.S. 665 (June 29, 1972).

32. "ANPA's Full Privilege Bill," *Editor & Publisher* (January 6, 1973), 9.

33. "Justice Dept. issues amended subpoena guides," *Editor & Publisher* (November 10, 1973), 32; "Department of Justice Guidelines for Subpoenas to the News Media," *Editor & Publisher* (August 15, 1970), 9.

34. Mark R. Arnold, "Pressure on the Press Alarms Newsmen," *The National Observer* (December 30, 1973), 20.

35. David Gordon, *Newsman's Privilege and the Law* (Columbia, Missouri, 1974); "Court rulings fail to end news privilege quandary," *Editor & Publisher* (October 12, 1974), 13.

36. George Gallup, "News Source Confidentiality Gains Support," *The Athens Banner-Herald* (November 8, 1973), 5; George Gallup, "Majority Favor 'Shield Law' for Newsmen," *The Athens Banner-Herald* and *The Daily News* (December 3, 1972), 32.

37. "Shield Law Gains Ground," *The Quill* (February, 1974), 8.

38. "Shield Law Proposal rejected by lawyers," *Editor & Publisher* (February 9, 1974), 11.

39. "Shield laws passed by 6 states, in '73," *Editor & Publisher* (December 29, 1973), 16.

40. Jerome A. Barron, *Freedom of the Press for Whom?* (Bloomington, Indiana: 1973).

41. *Chicago Joint Board v. Chicago Tribune Company,* 435 F 2d 470 (1970).

42. Gene Wiggins, "Access Is Limited: Publishers Still Control," *Grassroots Editor* (March–April, 1972), 25–28.

43. *Tornillo v. Miami Herald Publishing Co.,* (Fla. Supt. C) 42 U.S. Law Week 2073 (Sept. 7, 1973).

44. U.S. Court to review Fla. 'right to reply' statute," *Editor & Publisher* (January 19, 1974), 9; Warren Weaver Jr., "Justices Void Florida Law on Right to Reply in Press," *New York Times* (June 26, 1974), 1, 18; " 'Right of Reply' law in Florida declared void," *Editor & Publisher* (June 29, 1974), 9, 37; "Excerpts from ruling on 'Right of Reply,' " *Editor & Publisher* (June 29, 1974), 10–11.

45. The American Bar Association Legal Advisory Committee on Fair Trial and Free Press, *The Rights of Fair Trial and Free Press* (Chicago, 1969), 3–4.

46. *Ibid.,* Appendix A.

47. "Lengthy press, bar feud ends in broad agreement," *Editor & Publisher* (November 1, 1969), 11.

48. "Voluntary bench-bar press guides found to be working," *Editor & Publisher* (January 20, 1973), 11.

49. The American Bar Association Legal Advisory Committee on Fair Trial and Free Press, *The Rights of Fair Trial and Free Press* (Chicago, 1969), 15–19.

50. American Newspaper Publishers Association, *Free Press and Fair Trial* (New York, 1967), 8.

51. *New York Times Co. v. Sullivan,* 376 U.S. 265 (1964).

52. *St. Amant v. Thompson,* 390 U.S. 727.

53. *Associated Press v. Edwin A. Walker; Curtis Publishing Co. v. Butts,* 388 U.S. 130 (1967).

54. *Rosenbloom v. Metromedia, Inc.,* 403 U.S. 29 (1971).

55. *Ibid.* For further discussion, see Clifton O. Lawhorne, "Truth May be Bygone Standard in Libel Suits," *Grassroots Editor* (March–April, 1972), 11–12.

56. Gertz v. Robert Welch, Inc.; "Ordinary Citizen Given Right to a Libel Suit Over False Report," *New York Times* (June 26, 1974), 1; D. Charles Whitney, "LIBEL: New Ground Rules for an Old Ball Game," *The Quill* (August, 1974), 22–25.

57. *Time, Inc. V. Hill,* 87 S.Ct. 534 (1967).

58. Luther A. Huston, "Top Court Broadens Defense for Libel" *Editor & Publisher* (January 14, 1967), 11.

59. Don R. Pember, "Privacy and the Press: The Defense of Newsworthiness," *Journalism Quarterly* (Spring, 1968). 15; William Prosser, "Privacy," *California Law Review,* 48 (August, 1960), 389; *Barbieri v. News Journal Co.,* 189 A 2d 773 (1963, Delaware.).

60. Pember, "Privacy and the Press . . . ," *Journalism Quarterly* (Spring, 1968), 14–24; Pember, "Newspapers and Privacy: Some Guidelines," *Grassroots Editor* (March–April, 1972), 3–7.

61. "High Court Ponders Privacy Conflict," an Associated Press report in *The Atlanta Journal* (November 14, 1974), 5-A.

62. James J. Kilpatrick, "Free Press is Alive and Well," column syndicated by the Washington Star Syndicate in *The Atlanta Constitution* (October 9, 1971), 4.

NOTES TO CHAPTER 7

1. Frank W. Rucker and Herbert Lee Williams, *Newspaper Organization and Management* (Ames, Iowa: The Iowa State University Press, 1969), 44–48.

2. Ben H. Bagdikian, *The Information Machines* (New York, 1971), 94–95.

3. "Photon unveils new equipment; laser prototype," *Editor & Publisher* (June 17, 1972), 42; Eldon Phillips, "Cincinnati Post joins ranks of metros using all cold-type," *Editor & Publisher* (November 11, 1972), 65.

4. Edward R. Padilla, "Problems in 100 per cent Photocomposition," *R.I. Bulletin* 1095 (Easton, Pa.: ANPA Research Institute, September 12, 1972), pp. 205–210.

5. Peter P. Romano, "The Electronic Newspaper of Today," a speech delivered to the Georgia Press Association in Athens, Ga., February 23, 1973, 6–7.

6. "Progress reported with plastic plates," *Editor & Publisher* (September 13, 1969), 62; Phillips, "Cincinnati Post joins ranks of metros using all cold-type," 65; "Papers report satisfaction with plastic plate color," *Editor & Publisher* (March 31, 1973), 13.

7. Walter A. Strong, "Letterpress: The muscle stays hard," *Newspaper Production* (February, 1973), 37.

8. *Ibid.*, 199.

9. Craig Tomkinson, "Litho on letterpress system stirs interest," *Editor & Publisher* (April 25, 1970), 80; "Litho-letterpress system is called 'a forward step,' " *Editor & Publisher* (March 13, 1971), 9; Margaret Cronin Fisk, "More U.S. dailies using direct lithography process," *Editor & Publisher* (April 21, 1973), 64.

10. "Gannett reports its Laser-plate passed tests," *Editor & Publisher* (September 15, 1973), 10.

11. Norman E. Issacs, "The Future of the American Newspaper," *Problems of Journalism,* 1964 (Washington: American Society of Newspaper Editors, 1964), 112; "New American Press Survey Points Out Growth of Offset," *Offset Seminary News* (October 6, 1968), 1; Peter P. Romano, "The Electronic Newspaper of Today," 3–5; George Wilt, "Growth of new production processes are detailed," *Editor & Publisher* (March 17, 1973), 14; "Offset dailies now 55.4% of total," *Editor & Publisher* (March 30, 1974), 11.

12. "Publisher shatters some offset myths," *Editor & Publisher* (June 12, 1971), 48; S. Eugene Buttrill, "Offset Plates," *R.I. Bulletin No. 1093,* (Easton, Pa.: ANPA Research Institute, August 24, 1972), 184–185.

13. "Benefits of OCR depend on all-out managerial plan," *Editor & Publisher* (January 15, 1972), 39; "Publisher shatters some offset myths," 48; "Key to offset efficiency?—Personnel," *Editor & Publisher* (August 14, 1971), 37; Gerald B. Healey, "Offset publisher expresses concern over paper wastes," *Editor & Publisher* (January 27, 1973), 9; "Successful offset study leads St. Louis P-D to conversion," *Editor & Publisher* (April 10, 1971), 29, 37.

14. Richard H. Bell, "Offset conversion requires systems approach and training" *Editor & Publisher* (July 10, 1971), 48, 50.

15. Lyle Erb, The Sacramento Project," *The Quill* (August, 1968). 16–19; "Offset success hinges on page flow, makeovers," *Editor & Publisher* (July 14, 1973), 38, 40; "Copley's San Diego dailies move to $24 M offset plant," *Editor & Publisher* (December 8, 1973), 12.

16. Sky Dunlap, "Reporter-Computer System 'Feasible' for Many Dailies," *Editor & Publisher* (January 5, 1963), 9–10.

17. John Diebold, "Automation and the Editor: A Preview of Newsroom Procedures in 1973," *Problems of Journalism,* 1963 (Washington: American Society of Newspaper Editors, 1963), 140–150.

18. "42nd ANPA/RI Conference in New Orleans June 7–11," *Editor & Publisher* (March 14, 1970), 12.

19. For a good discussion of OCR operation, see I. Gregg Van Wert, "OCR Optical Character Recogniton: Using Technology To Clear Input Bottlenecks," *Printing Magazine* (June, 1973), 48–56; Frank J. Romano, "OCR: A Forms Approach to Photocomposition Input," *Inland Printer/American Lithographer* (March, 1973), 46–48.

20. "New Products," *Editor & Publisher* (January 12, 1974), 34.

21. Frank J. Romano, "OCR: A Forms Approach To Photocomposition Input," *Inland Printer/American Lithographer* (March, 1973), 46–47.

22. Glenn Waggoner, "New Technology? Bah! Give Me Back My Old Royal," *The Quill* (November, 1973), 29–30.

23. Robert C. Achorn, "Get Ready for the Newsroom Revolution," *The Quill* (November, 1973), 17.

24. "Another Electronic EXTRA—OCR Scanner-Ready Copy," *R.I. Bulletin 1095* (ANPA Research Institute, September 12, 1972), 218–219; "Syndicate sends scanner-ready copy to clients," *Editor & Publisher* (June 10, 1972), 78.

25. Jules Tewlow, "Video Terminals, Oral Input, Home Fax; Satellite Plant Communications," *Printing Impressions* (February, 1973), 26P; "Reporter in the field to go 'on/line' via terminal," *Editor & Publisher* (May 18, 1974), 13.

26. "No radiation danger detected in CRT devices," *Editor & Publisher* (October 6, 1973), 34.

27. John Gallant, "News System at Daytona Beach," *R.I. Bulletin 1092* (ANPA Research Institute, August 24, 1972), 169–173; "Farmington, New Mexico: On-Line with Xylogic System," *R.I. Bulletin 1104* (ANPA Research Institute, October 4, 1972), 283–288; "Xylogic system for calling up copy is shown," *Editor & Publisher* (June 10, 1972), 74; "Star Graphic will market Xylogic no-tape typesetting," *Editor & Publisher* (February 10, 1973), 52.

28. Romano, "The Electronic Newspaper of Today," 8, 11.

29. "Electronic Editing Planned for 100 UPI News Bureaus," *Printing Impressions* (November, 1973), 53.

30. *Ibid.;* Margaret Cronin Fisk, "UPI predicts system will enable on-demand news," *Editor & Publisher* (July 21, 1973), 11; "UPI tests experimental fast-speed wire," *Editor & Publisher* (September 29, 1973), 60.

31. "300 on waiting list for UPI's photo receiver," *Editor & Publisher* (October 13, 1973), 10.

32. Jules Tewlow, "Video Terminals, Oral Input, Home Fax; Satellite Plant Communications," *Printing Impressions* (February, 1973), 26P.

33. "Three dailies in high speed test with AP," *Editor & Publisher* (October 6, 1973), 18.

34. "Laserphoto delivers 'pure pictures,' " *Newspaper Production* (June, 1973), 56–57.

35. "Economist group formating classified pages in computer," *Editor & Publisher* (August 12, 1972), 16, 40.

36. Lawrence Newman, "Tomorrow is now, now, now!" *The Bulletin of the American Society of Newspaper Editors* (April, 1972), 4.

37. Craig Tomkinson, "Editors getting to know technology they'll be using," in *Editor & Publisher* (January 22, 1973), 13.

38. Tewlow, "Video Terminals, Oral Input, Home Fax; Satellite Plant Communications," *Printing Impressions* (February, 1973), pp. 26P–26Q.

39. Jules Tewlow, "The Newspaper of Tomorrow—Revisited," *R.I. Bulletin 1062* (ANPA Research Institute, September 17, 1971), 242–243.

40. *Ibid.,* 243.

41. "8 publishers contract for IBM's makeup system," *Editor & Publisher* (November 10, 1973), 74. The eight included the *Dallas Morning News, Atlanta Journal and Constitution, Norfolk* (Va.) *Pilot-Ledger, Washington Post, Miami Herald, Minneapolis Star-Tribune, Toronto Star* and Scripps-Howard newspaper group.

42. Tewlow, "The Newspaper of Tomorrow—Revisited," (R.I. Bulletin 1062), 250; Diebold, "Automation and the Editor," 147.

43. Tewlow, "The Newspaper of Tomorrow—Revisited," (R.I. Bulletin 1062), 250.

44. Robert U. Brown, "Publishers-scientists, eye plateless ink-jet printing," *Editor & Publisher* (October 7, 1972), 9.

45. Tewlow, "The Newspaper of Tomorrow-Revisited," (R.I. Bulletin 1062), 250; Earl W. Wilken, "The Total Systems Approach," *Editor & Publisher* (August 10, 1974), 31.

46. "New stuffing machine runs at press speed," *Editor & Publisher* (September 2, 1972), 11.

47. Craig Tomkinson, "Seers nix home fax papers, see widespread computer use," *Editor & Publisher* (March 20, 1971), 9.

48. Frances I. Flynn, "facsimile transmission: Technological Art of Spanning Time Barriers," *Printing Magazine* (June, 1973), 34, 36.

49. Several facsimile scanning and recording techniques are described in "How Facsimile Operates," *R.I. Bulletin 1102* (ANPA Research Institute, September 19, 1969), 256–257; Derek Lyons, "Asahi Shimbun lays cables for facsimile transmission," *Editor & Publisher* (March 2, 1974), 9, 26.

50. "St. Louis firm installs facsimile transmission system; satellite, downtown plants to print newspapers jointly," *Newspaper Production* (February, 1973), 11; "Monitor newspaper facsimile transmission system set for coast to coast operation by end of year," *Newspaper Production* (August, 1973), 9.

51. Tewlow, "Video Terminals, Oral Input, Home Fax; Satellite Plant Communications," *Printing Impressions* (February, 1973), 26S.

52. Edward H. Owen, "Gannett's latest—a plant that prints six dailies," *Newspaper Production* (June, 1973), 63–65.

53. Gerald B. Healey, "Inland papers are showcase of modern printing methods," *Editor & Publisher* (October 14, 1972), 30.

54. "Lee supports 14 newspapers with 4 computer locations," *Editor & Publisher* (July 8, 1972), 38.

55. "Florida papers use computer to control ad production," *Editor & Publisher* (September 18, 1971), 18.

56. "CRT's valuable in circulation data processing," *Editor & Publisher* (September 16, 1972), 24.

57. Tewlow, "The Newspaper of Tomorrow—Revisited," 238, 253–254.

58. "Computer aids reporter in his crime survey," *Editor & Publisher* (August 18, 1973), 16.

59. "Times markets information bank retrieval system," *Editor & Publisher* (May 26, 1973), 44.

60. "Pact on automation," *Editor & Publisher* (February 3, 1973), 4; "San Francisco papers and union reach agreement on automation," *Editor & Publisher* (January 27, 1973), 7.

61. "ANPA conducts newspaper plant safety studies," *Editor & Publisher* (June 10, 1973), 68.

62. "Charcoal filters will purify air from print plant," *Editor & Publisher* (March 11, 1972), 34.

NOTES TO CHAPTER 8

1. Letter and mimeographed release from Edward L. Bernays, 7 Lowell Street, Cambridge, Mass.; "Times Heads List In Publisher Poll," an Associated Press report in *The New York Times* (May 7, 1974), 42.

2. Richard L. Tobin, "Rating the American Newspaper," *Saturday Review* (May 13, 1961), 59; John Tebbel, "Rating the American Newspaper—Part I," *Saturday Review* (May 13, 1961), 60–62.

3. John C. Merrill, *The Elite Press: Great Newspapers of the World* (New York, 1968), 30–31, 42–45.

4. "The Ten Best American Dailies," *Time* (January 21, 1974), 58–61.

5. "Survey evaluates daily newspapers in New England," *Editor & Publisher* (January 26, 1974), 9.

6. Included in a printed statement titled "What is The Christian Science Monitor?" provided by the newspaper. The quote is from Canham's *Commitment to Freedom: The Story of the Christian Science Monitor* (Boston, 1968).

7. Included in a brochure titled *The World in Focus: The Story of The Christian Science Monitor,* published by The Christian Science Publishing Society in 1965.

8. "On voting," an editorial in *The Christian Science Monitor* (November 3, 1972), 16.

9. Included in *The World in Focus* brochure mentioned earlier.

10. "Out of the Cloister," *Newsweek* (August 23, 1971), 51.

11. *Ibid.*

12. "Monitor News Service starts in January," *Editor & Publisher* (December 4, 1971), 16; Information supplied by the newspaper in response to a request by the author in late 1973.

13. *From Wall Street to Main Street: A Story of Publishing Progress,* a sixty-four page booklet published by Dow Jones & Co. to mark the company's seventy-fifth anniversary in 1964, 5, 6, 9. A detailed account of Dow Jones Co. development can be found in Winthrop and Frances Neilson, *What's News–Dow Jones: Story of The Wall Street Journal* (Radnor, Pa., 1973).

14. *Ibid.*, 17–18.

15. *Ibid.*, 33–34.

16. "Bernard Kilgore Dies; Sparked WSJ Growth," *Editor & Publisher* (November 18, 1967), 14.

17. The Grimes editorial was reprinted in the anniversary booklet, *From Wall Street to Main Street,* 61–63.

18. Tebbel, "Rating the American Newspaper," *Saturday Review,* 60; "The Ten Best American Dailies," *Time,* 60.

19. Edward M. Swietnicki, "WSJ size may be trimmed; office delivery is studied," *Editor & Publisher* (December 8, 1973), 15.

20. A Word About Ourselves," *National Observer* (February 4, 1962), 14.

21. Merrill, *The Elite Press* . . . , 53.

22. Edmund C. Arnold, "Typographic swaddling clothes of a newborn newspaper," *The Quill* (February, 1962), 17.

23. "Giles, Observer Editor, Is Named To a New Post," *The National Observer* (December 28, 1970), 9.

24. Henry Gemmill, "Note from the Editor," in *National Observer* (March 8, 1971), 12.

25. Gay Talese, *The Kingdom and the Power* (New York, 1969).

26. "Change of the Guard At the Times," *Time* (August 8, 1969), 45.

27. A. M. Rosenthal, *If everybody screams, nobody hears,* a printed brochure adapted from a memorandum by Rosenthal to the staff when he became managing editor in September, 1969.

28. For a sampling of criticism and comments about the *Times,* see Herman H. Dinsmore, *All The News That Fits: A Critical Analysis of The News and Editorial Content of the New York Times* (New Rochelle, New York, 1969); Nat Hentoff, "The Times as a story; is it all there?" *Columbia Journalism Review* (Fall, 1969), 45–50; John C. Ottinger & Patrick D. Maines, "Is It True What They Say about the New York Times? *National Review* (September 15, 1972), 999–1006.

29. "The Ten Best American Dailies," *Time* (January 21, 1974), 60.

30. "Op. Ed. Page," an editorial in *The New York Times* (September 21, 1970), 40M.

31. Lee Rosebaum, "Charlotte Curtis—Opting for Op-Ed," *The Quill* (January, 1974), 22–24.

32. "The Times's Right Hand," *Newsweek* (February 12, 1973), 46.

33. "Leonard named as next editor of book section," *Editor & Publisher* (October 24, 1970), 29; "Buckley, Berkeley and Back," *Time* (November 2, 1970), 62.

34. "Changes proposed in directorate of New York Times," *Editor & Publisher* (April 7, 1973), 10.

35. Andrew Radolf, "International Herald Tribune to print in Great Britain," *Editor & Publisher* (December 15, 1973), 11, 34.

36. Edwin Emery, *The Press and America*. . . . (Englewood Cliffs, New Jersey, 1972), 656.

37. Edward T. Folliard, "A Brief History of The Post," *The Washington Post: Behind the Front Page,* an undated tabloid published by the *Post* in the early 1970s.

38. *Facts About the Washington Post Company,* a brochure published by the Washington Post Company in 1973.

39. Stanford N. Sesser, "It Irks Administration, But Washington Post Becomes a Top Paper," *The Wall Street Journal* (August 18, 1970), 1.

40. *Ibid.*

41. "The Ten Best American Dailies," *Time* (January 21, 1974), 61.

42. Sesser, "It Irks Administration, But Washington Post Becomes a Top Paper," *The Wall Street Journal* (August 18, 1970), 1.

43. *Facts About The Washington Post Company,* a brochure published by the company in 1973.

44. "A New Star Is Born," *Newsweek* (July 31, 1972), 36–37; "Capital's Star Buys Tabloid," a United Press International story in *The Atlanta Constitution* (July 13, 1972), 10B.

45. Ben H. Bagdikian, "What makes a newspaper nearly great?" *Columbia Journalism Review* (Fall, 1967), 31.

46. Warren Weaver Jr., "A Texas Banker Buys Into Washington Star-News," *The New York Times* (July 18, 1974), 25; "Allbritton takes over control of Washington S–N," *Editor & Publisher* (September 28, 1974), 9.

47. "The Ten Best American Dailies," *Time* (January 21, 1974), 58.

48. "About half of Boston Globe's employes buy into company," *Editor & Publisher* (August 18, 1973), 9.

49. Frank Luther Mott, "What Is the Oldest U.S. Newspaper?" *Journalism Quarterly* (Winter, 1963), 95–96. Mott quotes Brucker's statement from an editorial in the *Hartford Courant,* September 18, 1962.

50. Included in information supplied by the newspaper in response to a request by the author in late 1973.

51. *Ibid.*

52. Emery, *The Press and America* . . . , 667.

53. "The Ten Best American Dailies," *Time* (January 21, 1974), 58.

54. Included in information supplied by the newspaper in response to a request by the author in late 1973.

55. Carla M. Rupp, "Larger New Jersey section in the works at N.Y. News," *Editor & Publisher* (March 2, 1974), 28.

56. Tony Brenna, "N.Y. City Looks Fine From Post Penthouse," *Editor & Publisher* (January 27, 1968), 10; Newton H. Fullbright, "Improved New York Post promised in modern plant," *Editor & Publisher* (March 7, 1970), 10.

57. Carla Marie Rupp, "New York Press publisher 'confident' of success," *Editor & Publisher* (October 19, 1974), 22.

58. Luther A. Huston, "The Baltimore Sunpapers," *Editor & Publisher* (November 25, 1972), 20; Earl Wilken, "All-electronic newsroom will become a reality in Balitmore," *Editor & Publisher* (June 1, 1974), 10–11.

59. Information about the poll is given in *The Story of the St. Louis Post-Disptach,* 10th edition, revised by Harry Wilensky, 1970, and published by The Pulitzer Publishing Company, 55.

60. *Ibid.,* 1.

61. *Ibid.*, 58.

62. *The Globe-Democrat Story: "Fighting for St. Louis Since 1852,"* a pamphlet published by the newspaper in 1966, 10.

63. Dwight E. Sargent, "The Legacies of Lucius Nieman," *Nieman Reports* (June, 1972), 24–25.

64. Information supplied by the newspaper in response to a request by the author in late 1973.

65. Paul Ringler, "Employee Ownership Plan of the Milwaukee Journal," *Nieman Reports* (June, 1969), 20–21.

66. Information supplied by the newspaper in response to a request by the author in late 1973.

67. *Ibid.*

68. "Chicago Today to fold; Tribune to go 'all-day,' " *Editor & Publisher* (August 31, 1974), 10, 43.

69. "How voting frauds were uncovered by Chi Tribune," *Editor & Publisher* (May 26, 1973), 55.

70. "The 'Liberal' Trib," *Newsweek* (July 2, 1973), 50.

71. D. J. R. Brucker, " 'High Noon' in Chicago," *Columbia Journalism Review* (January/February, 1972), 30.

72. Donald Zochert, "Around the world for 73 years," *Chicago Daily News* (Saturday–Sunday, May 8–9, 1971), 5.

73. Frank Luther Mott, *American Journalism* (New York, 1962), 652.

74. Included in information supplied by the newspaper in response to a request by the author in late 1973.

75. Tebbel, "Rating the American Newspaper," *Saturday Review* (May 13, 1961), 62.

76. Included in information supplied by the newspaper in response to a request by the author in late 1973.

77. Emery, *The Press and America*, 669.

78. Luther Huston, "Minneapolis Tribune," *Editor & Publisher* (December 22, 1973), 18.

79. Included in a brief mimeographed history of the *Courier-Journal* and *Louisville Times* provided by the paper.

80. Tebbel, "Rating the American Newspaper," *Saturday Review* (May 13, 1961), 62.

81. "The Ten Best American Dailies," *Time* (January 21, 1974), 59.

82. Included in a brief mimeographed "History of The Miami Herald" provided by the newspaper.

83. Included in information provided by the newspaper in response to a request by the author in late 1973.

84. "Atlanta papers installed in new downtown building," *Editor & Publisher* (July 15, 1972), 18.

85. Included in information supplied by the newspaper in response to a request by the author in late 1973.

86. "L.A. Times Ex-Publisher Chandler Dies," an Associated Press story in The *Atlanta Journal* (October 21, 1973), 28-A.

87. "Strike against Los Angeles H-E enters 6th year," *Editor & Publisher* (January 20, 1973), 22; "Assistant M.E. traces changes in LA Her-Ex," *Editor & Publisher* (July 14, 1973), 8.

88. Included in information supplied by the newspaper in response to a request by the author in late 1973.

89. "Helen G. Bonfils leaves her stock subject to debts," *Editor & Publisher* (June 24, 1972), 42; "Denver Post buys Newhouse's interest for $4,785,306.96," *Editor & Publisher* (September 1, 1973), 9.

90. David M. Rubin and William L. Rivers, "The Chronicle: schizophrenia by the Bay," *Columbia Journalism Review* (Fall, 1969), 39.

91. William L. Rivers, "New Winds in the South, New Splash in the North," *Saturday Review* (September 23, 1967), 107.

92. Included in information supplied by the newspaper in response to a request by the author in late 1973.

93. "1970 Winners, National Better Newspaper Contest," *Publishers' Auxiliary* (June 27, 1970), 11; "156 newspapers are winners in annual contest," *Publishers' Auxiliary* (June 26, 1971), 8; "Tallahassee Democrat wins 4 first place honors," *Publishers' Auxiliary* (July 25, 1972), 11; "1973 Winners, National Better Newspaper Contest," undated tabloid provided by National Newspaper Association.

94. Included in information supplied by the newspapers in response to a request by the author in early 1974.

95. *Ibid.*

Selected Bibliography

THOUSANDS OF daily and non-daily publications provide an ever-changing bibliography for the study of contemporary American newspapers. The newspapers themselves provide a multitude of primary sources that grows with every edition of every paper. National and local reviews, numerous magazines, and a substantial number of books, monographs and other studies concern themselves with newspapers and their performance. Many national and state laws and court decisions affect newspapers in some way. To list all of the sources used in preparing the account presented here would be impracticable, so the author has selected a number of articles, speeches, monographs, pamphlets and books that are suggestive of the materials used and can provide much additional information for those who wish to pursue the study further. Laws, court decisions, newspaper responses to specific requests by the author for information and the newspapers referred to themselves are not included in the bibliography. But specific information from these and other sources, whether included in the bibliography or not, is attributed in the chapter notes at appropriate places.

PERIODICALS AND SPEECHES

Achorn, Robert C., "Get Ready for The Newsroom Revolution," *The Quill* (November, 1973), 14–18.

Arnold, Mark R., "Pressure on the Press Alarms Newsmen," *The National Observer* (December 30, 1972), 20.

Aronson, James, "Black journalists: why the dearth?", *The Bulletin of the American Society of Newspaper Editors* (March, 1972), 1, 6–10.

Bagdikian, Ben H., "Bagdikian's post-mortem: keep up criticism," *The Bulletin of the American Society of Newspaper Editors* (October, 1972), 1, 12–13.

————, "Fat newspapers and slim coverage," *Columbia Journalism Review* (September/October, 1973), 15–20.

————, "The myth of newspaper poverty," *Columbia Journalism Review* (March/April, 1973), 19–25.

————, "What makes a newspaper nearly great?", *Columbia Journalism Review* (Fall, 1967), 30–36.

Baggett, Nancy, "Press councils: a summing up," *The Bulletin of the American Society of Newspaper Editors* (October, 1972), 17–19.

Baker, Ross K., "ZAP! No More Underground Press," *The Washington Post* (April 8, 1973), C5.

Balk, Alfred, "Minnesota launches a press council," *Columbia Journalism Review* (November/December, 1971), 22–27.

Balk, Alfred, et al., "Personal involvement: a newsman's dilemma," *The Quill* (June, 1972), 24–32.

Balliett, Gene, "Newsday's First Two Decades," *The Quill* (January 1961), 12–14.

Balz, Daniel, "Want to see new journalism in newspapers? Well, don't hold your breath." *The Quill* (September, 1972), 18–21.

Barnett, Stephen R., "The FCC's nonbattle against media monopoly," *Columbia Journalism Review* (January/February, 1973), 43–50.

Bell, Joseph N., "The Suburban Daily: New Power in Publishing," *Saturday Review* (January 14, 1967), 118, 120, 131.

Berry, James P., "The Newspaper of Tomorrow . . . Today," *Richmond Times-Dispatch* (November 7, 1971), F-1.

Bingham, Barry, Sr., "The Case for a National Press Council," *Nieman Reports* (June, 1973), 19–22.

Bishop, Robert L., "The rush to chain ownership," *Columbia Journalism Review* (November/December, 1972), 10–19.

Brown, Donald E., "British journalists change their attitudes toward reorganized Press Council," *Editor & Publisher* (April 17, 1971), 22, 58, 60, 62.

————, "Press Council rulings serve as guidelines for journalists," *Editor & Publisher* (April 24, 1971), 17, 22, 24, 30, 34.

Brown, Robert U., "Publishers-scientists eye plateless ink-jet printing," *Editor & Publisher* (October 7, 1972), 9.

Brucker, Herbert, "A Conscience for the Press," *Saturday Review* (May 9, 1970), 59–61.

————, "What's Wrong With Objectivity?", *Saturday Review* (October 11, 1969), 77–79.

Bruckner, D. J. R., " 'High Noon' in Chicago," *Columbia Journalism Review* (January/February, 1972), 23–33.

Byerly, Kenneth R., "Dailies on Skids? No!", *The Quill* (August, 1969), 13–15.

Carson, Donald W., "What Editorial Writers Think of the Columnists," *The Masthead* (Spring, 1971), 1–5.

Carter, Hodding III, "The Deteriorating First Amendment," *Grassroots Editor* (January–February, 1973), 16–17.

Cassels, Louis, "Covering Religion News," *The Bulletin of The American Society of Newspaper Editors* (September–October, 1969), 7–9.

Chick, Bob, "Military-Press Relations: Like It Is in Vietnam," *The Quill* (November, 1969), 20–22.

Colburn, John H., "What Makes a Good Newspaper?", *Saturday Review* (June 9, 1962), 50–52.

Coonradt, Frederick C., "The Law of Libel has been all but repealed," *The Quill* (February, 1972), 16–19.

Corea, Gene, "How papers can conduct serious coverage of women," *Editor & Publisher* (April 28, 1973), 28, 30.

Coren, Marty, "The perils of publishing journalism reviews," *Columbia Journalism Review* (November/December, 1972), 25–28, 41–43.

Cracroft, Paul, "Arts editors are underdogs in space match with sports," *Editor & Publisher* (May 13, 1972), 15, 56–57.

Dedmon, Emmett, "How to live with journalism reviews," *The Bulletin of the American Society of Newspaper Editors* (March, 1973), 1, 9–11.

Del Olmo, Frank, "Voices for the Chicano Movimiento," *The Quill* (October, 1971), 8–11.

DeMott, John, " 'Interpretative' News Stories Compared with 'Spot' News," *Journalism Quarterly* (Spring, 1973), 102–108.

Diebold, John, "Automation and the Editor: A Preview of Newsroom Procedures in 1973," *Problems in Journalism, 1963* (Washington: American Society of Newspaper Editors, 1963), 140–150.

Edelstein, Alex S., and William E. Ames, "Humanistic Newswriting," *The Quill* (June, 1970), 28–31.

Ellis, Donna Lloyd, "The Underground Press in America: 1955–1970," *Journal of Popular Culture* (Summer, 1971), 102–124.

Epstein, Edward Jay, "An Analysis: How Press Handled Watergate Scandal," *Los Angeles Times* (September 14, 1973), 1, 16, 19.

Erb, Lyle, "The Sacramento Project," *The Quill* (August, 1968), 16–19.

Evans, Harold, "Is the press too powerful?", *Columbia Journalism Review* (January–February, 1972), 8–16.

Falk, Gene, "Command chief to all stations, ready for press?", *Newspaper Production* (August, 1973), 34–37.

Fisher, Paul, "The Experience with State Access Legislation: An Overview of the Battle for Open Records," *Grassroots Editor* (March–April, 1972), 14–18, 37.

Gerald, Edward J., "The New Minnesota Press Council," *Grassroots Editor* (November/December, 1971), 13–15.

Gibson, Martin L., "The public thinks we slant the news," *The Bulletin of the American Society of Newspaper Editors* (September, 1972), 1, 16–19.

Gilliam, Dorothy, "What do black journalists want?", *Columbia Journalism Review* (May/June, 1972), 47–52.

Goralski, Robert, "How Much Secrecy Can a Democracy Stand?", *Lithopinion* (Fall, 1972), 78–81.

Graham, Fred P., and Jack C. Landau, "The federal shield law we need," *Columbia Journalism Review* (March/April, 1973), 26–35.

Granitsas, Spyridon, "Ethnic press alive and well; 440 published in the U.S.," *Editor & Publisher* (November 28, 1970), 12, 23.

Grant, Gerald, "The 'new journalism' we need," *Columbia Journalism Review* (Spring, 1970), 12–16.

Greene, Daniel St. Albin, "Dear Mr. Editor, You Fink: Masses of Letters Deluge Nation's Newspapers as Readers Speak Out," *The National Observer* (May 4, 1970), 22.

Hallow, Ralph Z., "Pittsburgh's ephemeral 'riot,' " *Columbia Journalism Review* (January/February, 1972), 34–40.

Hartzell, Wesley, "Chicago Today . . . how a new compact newspaper was created," *The Quill* (August, 1970), 28–30.

Harwood, Richard L., "Press criticism: who needs it?", *The Bulletin of the American Society of Newspaper Editors* (February, 1972), 1, 10–11.

"Has the Press Done a Job on Nixon?", *Columbia Journalism Review* (January/February, 1974), 50–58.

"How newspapers hold themselves accountable," *Editor & Publisher* (December 1, 1973), 7, 16, 28.

Hvistendahl, J. K., "The Reporter as Activist: A Fourth Revolution in Journalism," *The Quill* (February, 1970), 8–11.

Issacs, Norman E., " 'There may be worse to come from this Court,' " *Columbia Journalism Review* (September/October, 1972), 18–24.

———, "Why we lack a national press council," *Columbia Journalism Review* (Fall, 1970), 16–26.

Jacobson, Harvey K., "Needed Improvements in Education News Coverage as Perceived by Media and Education Gatekeepers," *The Journal of Educational Research* (February, 1973), 274–278.

"Journalism's In-House Critics," *Time* (December 6, 1971), 74.

Kelly, Sandra, "Editors: Don't drop women from paper's women's pages," *Editor & Publisher* (July 15, 1972), 30, 32, 34.

Kirkpatrick, Clayton and Judith W. Brown, "Women: room at the top?", *The Bulletin of the American Society of Newspaper Editors* (March, 1973), 3–5.

Klein, Woody, "The Racial Crisis in America: the news media respond to the new challenge," *The Quill* (January, 1969), 8–12.

Kneeland, Douglas E., "The Campus Press, 1972—It's Changing Again," *The Quill* (March, 1972), 8–11.

Krieghbaum, Hillier, "Cluttering Up the News Picture," *The Quill* (February, 1972), 8–15.

Lawhorne, Clifton O., "Truth May be Bygone Standard in Libel Suits," *Grassroots Editor* (March–April, 1972), 11–13.

Lewis, Finlay, "Some errors and puzzles in Watergate coverage," *Columbia Journalism Review* (November/December, 1973), 26–32.

"The 'Liberal' Trib," *Newsweek* (July 2, 1973), 50, 53.

Lionel, Daniel L., "400 regional business papers tap sophisticated news field," *Editor & Publisher* (April 8, 1972), 22.

Littlewood, Thomas B., "Supplemental News Services Growing— . . . what will it mean for the American newspaper?", *The Quill* (April, 1971), 9–11.

Long, Charles, "Are news sources drying up?", *The Quill* (March, 1973), 10–13.

———, "The Cartoonist Conrad," *The Quill* (July, 1971), 9–12.

Lublin, Joann S., "Women in the Newsroom; 'the road has been rough before, but it's going to get smoother,' " *The Quill* (November, 1972), 45–47.

Lyons, Louis M., "The Role of the Editorial Page," *Nieman Reports* (December, 1970), 2, 21–24.

Macdonald, Stewart R., "Tomorrow's Newspaper and the Enduring Nature of Print," a speech delivered to the Newspaper in the Classroom Workshop at the University of California at Los Angeles, July 1, 1968.

Marbut, Robert G., "Newspapers' future bright . . . with some 'ifs' in picture," *Editor & Publisher* (November 13, 1971), 56, 58, 60.

McCombs, Maxwell, "Editorial Endorsements: A Study of Influence," *Journalism Quarterly* (Autumn, 1967), 545–548.

McGuire, Delbert, "Democracy's Confrontation: The Presidential Press Conference, II," *Journalism Quarterly* (Spring, 1968), 31–41.

Mencher, Melvin, "Independence (by fiat) for the campus press," *The Quill* (March, 1973), 14–16.

————, "Student journalists have constitutional rights, too," *The Quill* (October, 1972), 9–13.

Miller, Peter G., "Freedom of Information Act: Boon or bust for the press," *Editor & Publisher* (July 8, 1972), 20, 22, 24.

Monroe, Jr., James O., "Press coverage of the courts; a judge asks: Why, when it can be so good, is it now and then so bad?", *The Quill* (March, 1973), 20–24.

"The New press Critics," Supplement to *Columbia Journalism Review* (September/October, 1973), 29–40.

Newman, Lawrence, "Tomorrow is now, now, now!", *The Bulletin of The American Society of Newspaper Editors* (April, 1972), 3–7.

"Newspapers in the Classroom," a Special Issue of the *Ganetteer* (March, 1970).

"Nixon and the Media," *Newsweek* (January 15, 1973), 42–44, 47–48.

Nixon, Raymond B., compiler, "Groups of Daily Newspapers Under Common Ownership Published in the United States," *Editor & Publisher Yearbook, 1971,* 346–349.

————, "Half of the nation's dailies now in group ownerships," *Editor & Publisher* (July 17, 1971), 7, 32.

————, and Jean Ward, "Trends in Newspaper Ownership and Inter-Media Competition," *Journalism Quarterly* (Winter, 1961), 3–14.

Oakes, John B., "The Editorial Page," *Nieman Reports* (September, 1968), 2, 8.

"Out of the Cloister," *Newsweek* (August 23, 1971), 51.

Padilla, Edward R., "Problems in 100 per cent Photocomposition," *R. I. Bulletin 1095* (ANPA Research Institute, September 12, 1972), 205–210.

Palmer, L. F., Jr., "The black press in transition," *Columbia Journalism Review* (Spring, 1970), 31–36.

Paul, Noel S., "Why the British Press Council works," *Columbia Journalism Review* (March/April, 1972), 20–26.

Pember, Don R., "Privacy and the Press: The Defense of Newsworthiness," *Journalism Quarterly* (Spring, 1968), 14–24.

Perry, James M., "Here's Herblock, Carrying On In His Ivory Tower," *The National Observer* (June 1, 1970), 1, 11.

Petrick, Michael, "When You've Got a Law, Use It," *The Quill* (March, 1972), 16–17.

Plummer, Niel, "The Publication of Ghastly Photographs: Recipe for Judicial Restraints Possible," *Grassroots Editor* (March/April, 1972), 38–40.

Price, Tom and Katie Sowle, "How broad the shield?", *The Quill* (February, 1973), 18–19.

Quinn, John C., "The Big Myth," *Nieman Reports* (September, 1972), 9–11.

Rife, Jerry, "Let's Upgrade Newspaper Photography," *The Quill* (March, 1971), 12–15.

Ringler, Paul, "Employee Ownership Plan of the Milwaukee Journal," *Nieman Reports* (June, 1969), 20–21.

"A review of reviews," *Columbia Journalism Review* (March/April, 1972), 4–7.

Roesgen, Joan, "How much relevance can a woman take?", *The Bulletin of the American Society of Newspaper Editors* (February, 1972), 4–5.

Romano, Frank J., "OCR: A Forms Approach To Photocomposition Input," *Inland Printer/American Lithographer* (March, 1973), 46–48.

Romano, Peter P., "The Electronic Newspaper of Today," a speech delivered to the Georgia Press Association at Athens, Ga., February 20, 1973.

Rubin, David M., and William L. Rivers, "The Chronicle: schizophrenia by the Bay," *Columbia Journalism Review* (Fall, 1969), 37–44.

Sargent, Dwight E., "The Legacies of Lucius Nieman," *Nieman Reports* (June, 1972), 2, 24–28.

Schlaver, Clarence O., "Suburban Journalism Battleground Northwest of Chicago," *The Quill* (July, 1969), 8–11.

Schmidt, Benno C., Jr., " 'The decision is tentative,' " *Columbia Journalism Review* (September/October, 1972), 25–30.

Serrin, William, "The ultimate shutdown: the Detroit strike of 1967–1968," *Columbia Journalism Review* (Summer, 1969), 36–44.

Sesser, Stanford N., "It Irks Administration, But Washington Post Becomes a Top Paper," *The Wall Street Journal* (August 18, 1970), 1, 18, 19.

Sexton, William C., "Style, The Newspaper in the 1970s: A Revolution?", *The Quill* (July, 1968), 7–19.

Smyth, Joe, "Newspapers Do Err but are willing to admit it," *The Quill* (October, 1970), 13–15.

Stammer, W. F., "Facsimile and Satellite Printing Planned for the St. Louis (Mo.) Post-Dispatch," *R. I. Bulletin 1077* (ANPA Research Institute, March 21, 1972), 22–24.

Stanczak, Frank, "Printing and Pattern Plates," *R. I. Bulletin 1094* (ANPA Research Institute, August 25, 1972), 199–203.

Starck, Kenneth, "Press Councils Revisited," *Grassroots Editor* (September–October, 1971), 10–13, 30.

Stein, M. L., "The Press Under Assault: 1 View from the U.S.," *Saturday Review* (October 12, 1968), 75–77.

Stein, Robert, "The excesses of checkbook journalism," *Columbia Journalism Review* (September/October, 1972), 42–48.

Steven, William P., "The Social Responsibility of the Press," *Nieman Reports* (June, 1967), 12–18.

Strong, Walter A., "Letterpress: The muscle stays hard," *Newspaper Production* (February, 1973), 36–41.

Surface, Bill, "The shame of the sports beat," *Columbia Journalism Review* (January/February, 1972), 48–55.

Tannenbaum, Jeffrey A., "Suburban Newspapers Find News and Profits on Cities' Outskirts," *The Wall Street Journal* (November 14, 1972), 1, 34.

Taylor, Jean S., "Hell hath . . . just ain't good enough," *The Bulletin of the American Society of Newspaper Editors* (October, 1971), 3–7.

Taylor, Winston H., "The White House Press Conference," *Nieman Reports* (December, 1971), 9–14.

Tebbel, John, "Rating the American Newspaper—Part I," *Saturday Review* (May 13, 1961), 60–62.

———, "What Tomorrow's Front Page Will Look Like," *Saturday Review* (May 8, 1971), 50–52.

"The Ten Best American Dailies," *Time* (January 21, 1974), 58–61.

Tewlow, Jules S., "The Newspaper of Tomorrow—Revisited," *R. I. Bulletin 1062* (ANPA Research Institute, September 17, 1971), 237–255.

———, "Video Terminals, Oral Input, Home Fax: Satellite Plant Communications," *Printing Impressions* (February, 1973), 26P, 26Q, 26S.

Tobin, Richard L., "Monopoly Newspapers and the Credibility Gap," *Saturday Review* (May 9, 1970), 57–58.

———, "Rating the American Newspaper," *Saturday Review* (May 13, 1961), 59.

———, "The Right to Turn Down Advertising," *Saturday Review* (June 12, 1971), 55–56.

———, "What's Wrong With the Woman's Page?", *Saturday Review* (September 11, 1971), 57–58.

Tomkinson, Craig, "Experts see technically changing but safe future for newspapers," *Editor & Publisher* (March 13, 1971), 9, 41–42.

———, "Experts' views differ concerning newspapers' future competition," *Editor & Publisher* (March 27, 1971), 12, 15.

———, "Seers nix home fax papers, see widespread computer use," *Editor & Publisher* (March 20, 1971), 9, 36.

"The vanishing copy editor," *The Bulletin of The American Society of Newspaper Editors* (September, 1970), 14–17.

Van Wert, I. Gregg, "OCR Optical Character Recognition: Using Technology To Clear Input Bottlenecks," *Printing Magazine* (June, 1973), 48, 51, 54, 56.

"Victory for the Press," *Newsweek* (July 12, 1971), 16–19.

Waggoner, Glenn, "New Technology? Bah! Give Me Back My Old Royal," *The Quill* (November, 1973), 29–30.

Walker, Jerome H., "19 'public' companies own 216 U.S. daily newspapers," *Editor & Publisher* (April 22, 1972), 20, 62, 64.

Waring, Houstoun, "Control of Media Is Major Concern," *Grassroots Editor* (March/April, 1973), 22–24.

———, "A First Report of the National Press Council?", *Grassroots Editor* (May/June, 1969), 3, 4, 26.

Welles, Chris, "The bleak wasteland of financial journalism," *Columbia Journalism Review* (July/August, 1973), 40–48.

"What America Thinks of Itself," *Newsweek* (December 10, 1973), 40, 45, 48.

Whitman, Alden, "So You Want to Be an Obit Writer," *Saturday Review* (December 11, 1971), 70–71.

Wiggins, Gene, "Access Is Limited: Publishers Still Control," *Grassroots Editor* (March–April, 1972), 25–28.

Williams, Roger M., "Newspapers of the South," *Columbia Journalism Review* (Summer, 1967), 26–35.

Williamson, Lenora, "Nixon and the Press: a feeling of distrust," *Editor & Publisher* (April 24, 1971), 14.

Witcover, Jules, "How well does the White House press perform?", *Columbia Journalism Review* (November/December, 1973), 39–43.

———, "Salvaging the presidential press conference," *Columbia Journalism Review* (Fall, 1970), 27–34.

———, "Washington's uncovered power centers," *Columbia Journalism Review* (March/April, 1972), 14–19.

Wolfe, Tom, "The New Journalism," *The Bulletin of the American Society of Newspaper Editors* (September, 1970), 18–22.

BOOKS, PAMPHLETS, MONOGRAPHS

Adler, Ruth, *A Day in the Life of The New York Times,* Philadelphia and New York: J. B. Lippincott, 1971.

Agee, Warren K., ed., *Mass Media in a Free Society.* Lawrence: University Press of Kansas, 1969.

Arnold, Edmund C., *Ink on Paper Two: A Handbook of the Graphic Arts.* New York: Harper & Row, 1972.

Bagdikian, Ben H., *The Effete Conspiracy: And Other Crimes by the Press.* New York: Harper & Row, 1972.

———, *The Information Machines: Their Impact on Men and the Media.* New York: Harper & Row, 1971.

Baird, Russell N., *The Penal Press.* Evanston, Illinois: Northwestern University Press, 1967.

Balk, Alfred, *A Free and Responsive Press.* New York: Twentieth Century Fund, 1973.

Barron, Jerome A., *Freedom of the Press for Whom? The Right of Access to Mass Media.* Bloomington: Indiana University Press, 1973.

Becker, Stephen, *Marshall Field III: A Biography.* New York: Simon & Schuster, 1964.

Bernays, Edward L., *Crystallizing Public Opinion.* New York: Liveright Publishing Corp., 1961.

Blanchard, Robert O. *Congress and the News Media.* New York: Hastings House, Publishers, 1974.

Block, Herbert, *Herblock's State of the Union.* New York: Simon & Schuster, 1972.

Brandsberg, George, *The Free Papers: A Comprehensive Study of America's Shopping Guide and Free Circulation Newspaper Industry.* Ames, Iowa: Wordsmith Books, 1969.

Breckenridge, Adam Carlyle, *The Right of Privacy.* Lincoln: University of Nebraska Press, 1970.

Brucker, Herbert, *Communication Is Power: Unchanging Values in a Changing Journalism*. New York: Oxford University Press, 1973.

Bush, Chilton R., *Newswriting and Reporting Public Affairs*. 2d ed. Philadelphia: Chilton Book Co., 1970.

Byerly, Kenneth H., *Metropolitan Daily Newspapers: A Comparison of Their Numbers, Circulation and Trends for 1950, 1960, and 1968 in the Nation's 21 Most Populous Metropolitan Areas*. Chapel Hill: University of North Carolina School of Journalism, 1968.

Canham, Erwin D., *Commitment to Freedom: The Story of the Christian Science Monitor*. Boston: Houghton Mifflin, 1958.

Cater, Douglass, *The Fourth Branch of Government*. Boston: Houghton Mifflin, 1959.

Catledge, Turner, *My Life and The Times*. New York: Harper & Row, 1971.

Commission on Freedom of the Press, *A Free and Responsible Press*. Chicago: University of Chicago Press, 1947.

Conrad, Will C., Kathleen F. Wilson, and Dale Wilson, *The Milwaukee Journal: The First Eighty Years*. Madison: University of Wisconsin Press, 1964.

Copple, Neale, *Depth Reporting: An Approach to Journalism*. Englewood Cliffs, N.J.: Prentice-Hall, Inc., 1964.

Cross, Harold L., *The People's Right to Know*. New York: Columbia University Press, 1953.

Croswell, Alfred A., *Creative News Editing*. Dubuque, Iowa: Wm. C. Brown Company Publishers, 1969.

Dennis, Everette, *The Magic Writing Machine: Student Probes of the New Journalism*. Eugene, Oregon: University of Oregon Press, 1971.

Devol, Kenneth S., *Mass Media and the Supreme Court: The Legacy of the Warren Years*. New York: Hastings House, Publishers, 1971.

Dinsmore, Herman H., *All the News That Fits: A Critical Analysis of the News and Editorial Content of The New York Times*. New Rochelle, N.Y.: Arlington House, 1969.

Dunn, S. Watson, *Advertising: Its Role in Modern Marketing*. 2d ed. New York: Holt, Rinehart and Winston, Inc., 1969.

Duscha, Julius, and Thomas G. Fischer, *The Campus Press: Freedom and Responsibility*. Washington: American Association of State Colleges and Universities, 1973.

Edwards, Verne E., Jr., *Journalism in a Free Society*. Dubuque, Iowa: Wm. C. Brown Company Publishers, 1970.

Emery, Edwin, *The Press and America: An Interpretative History of the Mass Media*. 3d ed. Englewood Cliffs, N.J.: Prentice-Hall, Inc., 1972.

Emery, Edwin, Philip H. Ault, and Warren K. Agee, *Introduction to Mass Communications*. 4th ed. New York: Dodd, Mead & Company, 1973.

Estrin, Herman A., and Arthur M. Sanderson, eds., *Freedom and Censorship of the College Press*. Dubuque, Iowa: William C. Brown Company Publishers, 1966.

Facts About the Washington Post Company. Washington: The Washington Post Company, 1973.

Free Press and Fair Trial. New York: American Newspaper Publishers Association, 1967.

Gelfand, Louis I., and Harry E. Heath, Jr., *Modern Sportswriting*. 2d ed. Ames, Iowa: Iowa State University Press, 1969.

Gerald, J. Edward, *The Social Responsibility of the Press*. Minneapolis: University of Minnesota Press, 1963.

Gilmor, Donald M., *Free Press and Fair Trial*. Washington: Public Affairs Press, 1966.

Glessing, Robert J., *The Underground Press in America*. Bloomington: Indiana University Press, 1970.

The Globe-Democrat Story: Fighting for St. Louis Since 1852. St. Louis: St. Louis Globe-Democrat, 1966.

Hart, Jim Allee, *A History of the St. Louis Globe-Democrat*. Columbia: University of Missouri Press, 1961.

Haskins, Jack B., and Barry M. Feinberg, *Newspaper Publishers Look at Research: Its Role in Future Changes, Opportunities and Problems*. Syracuse, N.Y.: Syracuse University, Newhouse Communications Center, 1968.

Hess, Stephen, and Milton Kaplan, *The Ungentlemanly Art: A History of American Political Cartoons*. New York: Macmillan, 1968.

Hiebert, Ray Eldon, ed., *The Press in Washington*. New York: Dodd, Mead, 1966.

Hohenberg, John, *The News Media: A Journalist Looks at His Profession*. New York: Holt, Rinehart and Winston, Inc., 1968.

―――, *The Professional Journalist*. 3d ed. New York: Holt, Rinehart and Winston, Inc., 1973.

Hurley, Gerald D., and Angus McDougall, *Visual Impact in Print*. Chicago: American Publishers Press, 1971.

Johnson, Michael L., *The New Journalism*. Lawrence: University of Kansas Press, 1971.

Keogh, James, *President Nixon and the Press*. New York: Funk & Wagnalls, 1972.

Kobre, Sidney, *Development of American Journalism*. Dubuque, Iowa: Wm. C. Brown Company Publishers, 1969.

Krieghbaum, Hillier, *Facts in Perspective*. Englewood Cliffs, N.J.: Prentice-Hall, Inc., 1956.

―――, *Pressures on the Press*. New York: Thomas Y. Crowell Co., 1972.

―――, *Science and the Mass Media*. New York: New York University Press, 1967.

La Brie, Henry G., III, *The Black Press in America: A Guide*. Iowa City: Institute for Communications Studies, University of Iowa, 1970.

Levy, Herman Phillip, *The Press Council: History, Procedure and Cases*. London: Macmillan, 1967.

Liebling, A. J., *The Press*. New York: Ballantine Books, 1961.

Lindstrom, Carl E., *The Fading American Newspaper*. New York: Doubleday, 1960.

Logue, Calvin McLeod, *Ralph McGill, Editor and Publisher*. Durham, N.C.: Moore Publishing Company, 1969.

Lyle, Jack, *The News in Megalopolis*. San Francisco: Chandler Publishing Company, 1967.

Lyons, Louis M., *Newspaper Story: One Hundred Years of The Boston Globe*. Cambridge, Mass. Harvard University Press, 1971.

Marbut, F. B., *News from the Capitol: The Story of Washington Reporting*. Carbondale and Edwardsville: Southern Illinois University Press, 1971.

Martin, Harold H., *Ralph McGill, Reporter*. Boston: Little, Brown and Co., 1973.

MacDougall, A. Kent., ed., *The Press: A Critical Look from the Inside*. Princeton, N.J.: Dow Jones Books, 1972.

MacDougall, Curtis D., *Interpretative Reporting*. 6th ed. New York: Macmillan Company, 1972.

———, *News Pictures Fit to Print—Or Are They?* Stillwater, Okla.: Jounalistic Services, Inc., 1971.

———, *Principles of Editorial Writing*. Dubuque, Iowa: Wm. C. Brown Company Publishers, 1973.

———, Understanding Public Opinion: *A Guide for Newspapermen and Newspaper Readers*. Dubuque, Iowa: Wm. C. Brown Company Publishers, 1966.

McCombs, Maxwell E., *Mass Media in the Marketplace*. Lexington, Ky.: Association for Education in Journalism with the support of the American Association of Schools and Departments of Journalism, 1972. (No. 24 in Journalism Monographs series.)

McGivena, Leo E., et al., *The News: The First Fifty Years of New York's Picture Newspaper*. New York: News Syndicate Co., 1969.

McNaughton, Harry H., *Proofreading & Copyediting*. New York: Hastings House, Publishers, 1973.

Merrill, John C., *The Elite Press: Great Newspapers of the World*. New York: Pitman Publishing Corporation, 1968.

———, *The Imperative of Freedom: A Philosophy of Journalistic Autonomy*. New York: Hastings House, Publishers, 1974.

Meyer, Philip, *Precision Journalism: A Reporter's Introduction to Social Science Methods*. Bloomington: Indiana University Press, 1973.

Miller, Lee G., *The Story of Ernie Pyle*. New York: Viking Press, 1950.

Mott, Frank Luther, *American Journalism, A History: 1690–1960*. 3d ed. New York: The Macmillan Company, 1962.

Neilson, Winthrop and Frances, *What's News—Dow Jones: Story of The Wall Street Journal*. Radnor, Pa.: Chilton Book Co., 1973.

News about the news media from a nationwide opinion research study conducted in March–April, 1971. New York: Bureau of Advertising, American Newspaper Publishers Association, 1971.

Pember, Don R., *Privacy and the Press: The Law, the Mass Media, and the First Amendment*. Seattle: University of Washington Press, 1973.

The Pentagon Papers. New York: Bantam, 1971.

Pollard, James E., *The Presidents and the Press*. New York: Macmillan, 1947.

———, *The Presidents and the Press: Truman to Johnson*. Washington: Public Affairs Press, 1964.

Pride, Armistead, *The Black Press: A Bibliography*. Jefferson City, Mo.: Lincoln University Department of Journalism, 1968.

Problems of Journalism. Published annually by the American Society of Newspaper Editors. (Contains convention speeches, etc.)

Promoting the Total Newspaper. Washington: The International Newspaper Promotion Association, 1973.

Randall, Henry S., *The Life of Thomas Jefferson*. 3 vols. New York: Derby & Jackson, 1858.

Report of the National Advisory Commission on Civil Disorders. New York: Bantam Books, 1968.

Report of the 1972 Sigma Delta Chi Advancement of Freedom of Information Committee. Chicago: Sigma Delta Chi, 1972.

Reston, James B., *The Artillery of the Press.* New York: Harper & Row, 1967.

————, *Sketches in the Sand.* New York: Knopf, 1967.

Riblet, Carl, Jr., *The Solid Gold Copy Editor.* Tucson: Falcon Press, 1972.

The Rights of Fair Trial and Free Press. Chicago: The American Bar Association Legal Advisory Committee on Fair Trial and Free Press, 1969.

Rivers, William L., and William B. Blankenburg, Kenneth Starck, and Earl Reeves, *Backtalk: Press Councils in America.* San Francisco: Canfield Press, 1971.

Rivers, William L., Theodore Peterson, and Jay Jensen, *The Mass Media and Modern Society.* San Francisco: Rinehart Press, 1971.

Rivers, William L., and David M. Rubin, *A Region's Press: Anatomy of Newspapers in the San Francisco Bay Area.* Berkeley: Institute of Governmental Studies, University of California, 1971.

Rivers, William L., and Wilbur Schramm, *Responsibility in Mass Communication.* New York: Harper & Row, 1969.

Rosenthal, A. M., *If everybody screams, nobody hears.* New York: New York Times Company, 1969.

Rucker, Frank W., and Herbert Lee Williams, *Newspaper Organization and Management.* 3d ed. Ames, Iowa: The Iowa State University Press, 1969.

Sage, Joseph, *Three to Zero: The Story of the Birth and Death of the World Journal Tribune.* New York: American Newspaper Publishers Association, 1967.

Sandage, Charles, and Vernon Fryburger, *Advertising Theory and Practice.* 8th ed. Homewood, Illinois: Richard D. Irwin, 1971.

Siebert, Fred S., Theodore Peterson, and Wilbur Schramm, *Four Theories of the Press.* Urbana: University of Illinois Press, 1956.

Seigel, Kalman, ed., *Talking Back to the New York Times, Letters to the Editor, 1851–1971.* New York: Quadrangle Books, 1972.

Sim, John Cameron, *The Grass Roots Press: America's Community Newspapers.* Ames: Iowa State University Press, 1969.

Stein, M. L., *Blacks in Communication.* New York: Julian Messner, 1972.

Stern, Daniel K., ed., *Newspaper Promotion Handbook.* Providence, R.I.: National Newspaper Promotion Association, 1966.

Stewart, Kenneth, and John Tebbel, *Makers of Modern Journalism.* Englewood Cliffs, N.J.: Prentice-Hall, 1952.

The Story of the St. Louis Post-Dispatch. 10th ed. St. Louis: The Pulitzer Publishing Company, 1970.

Talese, Gay, *The Kingdom and the Power.* New York: The World Publishing Company, 1969.

Tebbel, John, *The Compact History of the American Newspaper.* New York: Hawthorn Books, Inc., 1969.

————, *Open Letter to Newspaper Readers.* New York: James H. Heineman, Inc., 1968.

Turnbull, Arthur T., and Russell N. Baird, *The Graphics of Communication.* New York: Holt, Rinehart and Winston, 1968.

Udell, Jon G., *Economic Trends in the Daily Newspaper Business, 1946 to 1970.*

Madison: University of Wisconsin, Graduate School of Business, Bureau of Business Research and Service, 1972 (Wisconsin Project Reporters, Vol. IV, No. 6).

Von Hoffman, Nicholas, *Left at the Post*. Chicago: Quadrangle Books, 1970.

Waldrop, A. Gayle, *Editor and Editorial Writer*. Dubuque, Iowa: Wm. C. Brown Company Publishers, 1967.

The Wall Street Journal: The First Seventy-Five Years. New York: Dow Jones & Company, Inc., 1964.

Weber, Roland, *The Reporter as Artist: A Look at the New Journalism Controversy*. New York: Hastings House Publishers, 1974.

Wiggins, James Russell, *Freedom or Secrecy*. New York: Oxford University Press, 1964.

Wolfe, Tom, *The New Journalism,* with an anthology edited by Wolfe and E. W. Johnson. New York: Harper & Row, 1973.

Wolseley, Roland E., *The Black Press, U.S.A.* Ames: Iowa State University Press, 1971.

The World in Focus: The Story of the Christian Science Monitor, Boston: The Christian Science Monitor Publishing Company, 1965.

Index